AF673229

Sarasvatichandra Part III

Ratnanagari's Statecraft

Govardhanram Madhavram Tripathi was born on 20 October 1855 at Nadiad. He published the first part of *Sarasvatichandra* in 1887, the second part in 1892, the third in 1898 and the fourth in 1901. He is also the author of *Snehmudra* (1889), *Navalram Nu Kavijivan* (1891), *The Classical Poets of Gujarat and Their Influence on Society and Morals* (1894), *Lilavati Jivankala* (1905), and *Dayaram No Aksherdeha* (1908). He presided over the first session of the Gujarati Sahitya Parishad in 1905. He died on 4 January 1907 in Mumbai.

Tridip Suhrud is Professor and Director of Archives, CEPT University, Ahmedabad.

To the first part he gave all his art. The novel is imbued with aesthetic delight; the characterisation is matchless. The second part depicts Hindu society, his art went deeper in the third part, and he gave all that he wished to give to the world in the fourth part.

M. K. Gandhi

No other work has left such an indelible mark on the life of Gujarat as *Sarasvatichandra* has. In fact ... Govardhanram is the only one before the arrival of Gandhiji who had the greatest success in shaping the cultural life of Gujarat.

Umashankar Joshi

In the great celebration that is India, Gujarat has two gifts to offer: Mahatma Gandhi, and the jewel among books *Sarasvatichandra*.

Manubhai Pancholi 'Darshak'

Sarasvatichandra Part III

Ratnanagari's Statecraft

Govardhanram Madhavram Tripathi

Translated from the original Gujarati
by Tridip Suhrud

Orient BlackSwan

SARASVATICHANDRA PART III: RATNANAGARI'S STATECRAFT

ORIENT BLACKSWAN PRIVATE LIMITED

Registered Office
3-6-752 Himayatnagar, Hyderabad 500 029, Telangana, India
e-mail: centraloffice@orientblackswan.com

Other Offices
Bengaluru, Bhopal, Chennai, Guwahati, Hyderabad,
Jaipur, Kolkata, Lucknow, Mumbai, New Delhi,
Noida, Patna, Vijayawada

Originally published in Gujarati as
Ratnanagarinu Rajyatantra (Bombay: N. M. Tripathi and Co., 1898).

© This volume, Orient Blackswan Private Limited 2016
© Translation, Tridip Suhrud 2016
© Introduction, Tridip Suhrud 2016
First published by Orient Blackswan Private Limited 2016
Reprinted 2018

ISBN 978 81 250 6346 9

026798

Typeset by
Le Studio Graphique, Gurgaon 122 001
in Adobe Jenson Pro 11/13

Printed at
Yash Printographics
Noida

Published by
Orient Blackswan Private Limited
3-6-752 Himayatnagar, Hyderabad 500 029, Telangana, India
e-mail: info@orientblackswan.com

For Binita Desai,

'With something of angelic light.'

—William Wordsworth

Contents

Translator's Acknowledgements

I remain indebted to Arindam Chakrabarti, Hank Heifetz, Gangeya Mukherji and Dr. Murli Manohar Dwivedi for their extraordinary generosity and help with the Sanskrit sources, and to Harmony Siganporia with the verses.

Conversations with Ela Bhatt, Rita Kothari, Howard Spodek, Salil Tripathi, Sitanshu Yashaschandra, Supriya Chaudhuri, Kavita Punjabi and Amiya Dev regarding the first two parts of the translation have benefitted the third part. Sudhir Chandra remains the first reader of the translation. Moyna Mazumdar's care is evident in making the translation what it is. Thank You all.

Megha, Katyayani and Suhrud, I thank you for being yourselves.

Tridip Suhrud

Translator's Introduction[*]

I

> I wish to produce, or see produced, not this or that event—but a people who shall be higher and stronger than they are, who shall be better able to look and manage for themselves than is the present *helpless* generation of my educated and uneducated countrymen. What kind of a nation that should be and how that spark should be kindled for the organic flame: these were, and are, the problems before my mind. I lay down this as, for the present, the only one fixed objective before me ...[1]

* Earlier versions of this text have been published by the translator as part of an essay titled 'Govardhanram Tripathi and "the Philosophy of Consumption": A Reading of *Sarasvatichandra*', in *Early Novels in India*, edited by Meenakshi Mukherji (New Delhi: Sahitya Akademi, 2002); in Tridip Suhrud, 'Consumption as Dharma', *Writing Life: Three Gujarati Thinkers* (New Delhi: Orient BlackSwan, 2009); and reproduced from Govardhanram Madhavram Tripathi, *Sarasvatichandra*, Part II: *Gunasundari's Household*, trans. Tridip Suhrud (New Delhi: Orient BlackSwan, 2016) xi–lviii, with a revised Section V.

1 K. C. Pandya, R. P. Bakshi and S. J. Pandya (eds), *Govardhanram Madhavram Tripathi's Scrap Book* (Bombay: N. M. Tripathi and Co., 1959), 29–30; emphasis in the original. This first scrap book covers the years 1884–1894 of the author's life. The scrap book for the period 1894–1904, compiled and edited by the same editors, was also published in 1959. The scrap book for the period 1904–06, edited by K. C. Pandya was published earlier in 1957, both volumes by N. M. Tripathi and Co., in Bombay. These volumes are, herein, referred to as *Scrap Book* I, II and III respectively. Although the chronology of publication goes against this arrangement, this has been done for the convenience of citation as well as to maintain the chronology in which they were

With these words, Govardhanram Madhavram Tripathi (1855–1907) articulated his *swadharma*. Govardhanram was born on 20 October 1855, in a Vadnagara Nagar brahmin vaishnav family at Nadiad.[2] The family had no remarkable tradition of learning. For at least three generations, this family had practised money lending. Govardhanram spent his formative years in Bombay and Nadiad. He acquired primary education in the Buddhivardhak Gujarati Shala in Bombay and Government English School at Nadiad. In 1871, he passed his matriculation examination as a student of Elphinstone School, and joined Elphinstone College for his graduation. Between 1871 and 1875, he studied history, economics, nyaya and nitishastra. He passed his B.A. examination at the second attempt at the age of twenty.

After passing his B.A., Govardhanram made three resolutions which he hoped would govern his entire life. He resolved to acquire a law degree, to start an independent legal practice, and to give up legal practice at the age of forty and, thereafter, dedicate his life to the service of the people through literature.

In 1876, he passed his first LL.B. examination. He was forced by circumstances to accept the post of a personal secretary to Samaldas Parmananddas, the *Dewan* of Bhavnagar state. This gave him the opportunity to observe and participate, in close proximity, the functioning of a native state. He had hoped that his stay at Bhavnagar would be short and only a minor aberration in his plan. He was repeatedly frustrated in his attempts to pass the remaining LL.B. examinations. He failed thrice and eventually passed it in 1883 on his fourth attempt. He immediately left Bhavnagar for Bombay, where at the age of twenty-nine he started independent legal practice.

originally written. Govardhanram Tripathi began writing the scrap books in January 1885 after he had achieved some stability in his profession as a lawyer in Bombay, and stopped maintaining them in November 1906. During this period, he filled seven notebooks, all of which were written in English. He had no intention of publishing them. They were published as a part of the celebrations to mark his birth centenary.

[2] This biographical section is largely based on K. C. Pandya, *Sriyut Govardhanram* (Bombay: N. M. Tripathi and Co., 1910, 1965).

His practice at the Bombay High Court flourished. At the height of his legal career, Govardhanram fulfilled his long cherished dream. At the age of forty-two, he retired from the practice to contemplate the state of his people and society in the quiet solitude of his ancestral house in Nadiad.

II

For Govardhanram Tripathi, the original cause of the universe lies in what he describes as the 'Great Will' or the 'Great Force'. Individual beings are a mere point, a manifestation of the Great Will. 'Our will is a manifestation, at a point, of his will. His will is universal, ours is a point of it.'[3] The vocation of human beings, according to him, is to understand the Great Will and function in harmony with it. 'We are unable to enter into the actual motives of the Great Will, but we can understand and join its music and poetry ... Our final cause—like all final causes—is to understand our proper function in this symphony and join it properly.'[4]

A perfect conscience, according to Govardhanram, recognises that 'I is a fiction',[5] and it is at this moment of recognition of self-identity that the individual being is in perfect harmony and union with the Great Will. In this union and realisation of identity lies salvation. But how is this salvation to be attained? The central question for Govardhanram is: How can an individual reconcile his vocation of final union with the Great Force, and his obligation towards his family, the society and the country? For Govardhanram, this reconciliation can be achieved only through what he describes as a Philosophy of Consumption.[6] 'Total sacrifice of the individual for the good of

[3] Pandya, Bakshi and Pandya, *Scrap Book* I, 45.

[4] Ibid., 123.

[5] Ibid., 46.

[6] The term 'Philosophy of Consumption' is Govardhanram's coinage. In Gujarati he uses the term *uttsargsiddhi*, or the attainment of higher ideals through sacrifice.

the whole is consumption ... Complete dissolution and sacrifice of the self for others is consumption. It is through consumption that individual existence and life achieve completion.'[7] 'Consumption' for Govardhanram is an all-encompassing philosophy and praxis. It is by leading a life of consumption that an individual offers his body and soul to the *yajna* [ritual sacrifice] of the Great Force. 'We must consume, both body and soul, ... in the Great and Patent *Yajna* that is blazing around us, we throw as *Havis* (oblation) the patent *Yajna* of body and soul ...'[8]

The philosophy of consumption becomes the sole mediator between the individual and the Great Will and also the individual and society. Through the philosophy of consumption, Govardhanram attempts to offer a critique of the philosophy of Vedanta, which was one of the earliest and most powerful influences on him. Vedanta, Govardhanram believes, leads to asceticism as the mode of attaining salvation. 'Patent is a thing to be avoided, and latent to be sought ... as to the censures passed against the Patent, as to the exclusive acceptance of the Latent as Transcendental Idea.'[9]

In 1877, aged twenty-two, Govardhanram offered a critique of the practice of renunciation as a mode of attaining salvation in an essay entitled 'Practical Asceticism in My Sense of the Word'. Care for the 'self' is at the heart of the practice of renunciation, he observed. Salvation cannot be attained through a self-centred mode. 'The great Bacon has said,' he wrote, 'it is a poor centre of man's action, himself, and it is true. But I go some steps beyond him. I say it is a poisonous centre of man's action—himself.'[10] Asceticism for Govardhanram is an act of rebellion against the Great Will. It is as unjustified as suicide. A real ascetic hands over the care of the 'self' to the Great Will and 'consumes' it for society. 'Asceticism, in its usual sense, is a mistake and a substitution of miscarriage for consumption. Asceticism, in

7 Ramprasad P. Bakshi, *Govardhanram Nu Manorajya*, 2nd ed. (Bombay: N. M. Tripathi and Co., 1992), 14–15.

8 Pandya, Bakshi and Pandya, *Scrap Book* I, 148.

9 Ibid., 100.

10 Pandya, *Sriyut Govardhanram*, 63.

its real sense, is most beautiful consumption.'[11] Consumption of an individual is conditioned by the capacities of the person. 'Consumption ... is not a promiscuous or unlimited duty. It is actually limited, and potentially unlimited, that it may be enlarged according to capacity.'[12] Notions of morality, ethics and justice are also contingent upon the idea of consumption. Defining vice and virtue, Govardhanram wrote:

> Whatever makes a man feed on the flesh of the world is ordinarily vice. Whatever is his consumption in order to feed the world is a virtue. Whatever is inconsistent with such consumption and the means of attaining it is vice. Whatever is consistent with it is innocent. Whatever furthers it is virtue. Whenever feeding oneself is instrumental to such consumption, it is virtue.[13]

For Govardhanram, poetry and philosophy, ethics and religion must converge in any philosophical system. He is aware that in his philosophy of consumption, he has created an all-encompassing world-view, a mode of life, his swadharma. 'To my mind ... Poetry and Philosophy, Ethics and Religion must eventually converge, and in Ethics, I include the world in all its aspects. Need I say that my vision of Philosophy of Consumption, with all its imperfections, reaches this very point?'[14]

A person who recognises virtue and vice, adopts the former and shuns the latter has a sense of duty. Thus for Govardhanram consumption is not only a virtue but it is *dharma*. This conception of dharma informed his vocation and defined his understanding of personal duty towards the country. While clarifying for himself 'Duties in regard to the country', Govardhanram set before himself the goal of moulding a generation of people who shall be 'higher and stronger' and 'better able to manage for themselves'.

In this articulation of swadharma, Govardhanram denies the relevance and the efficacy of *events*. Events are for him acts uninformed

11 Pandya, Bakshi and Pandya, *Scrap Book* I, 146.

12 Ibid., 125.

13 Ibid., 52.

14 Pandya, Bakshi and Pandya, *Scrap Book* II, 87.

by deep industry and knowledge. It was also not his aspiration to produce an event, which for him was a mere reflection of deeper societal processes. 'To produce a particular event—be it a political constitutional agitation or a social reform effervescence—this is too little for my mind and aspiration.'[15] He also eschewed commenting upon events. 'So obsessive was this concern for clarity that, unlike most of his contemporary creative writers in different Indian languages, Govardhanram tended to avoid journalism.'[16]

Aware as he was of 'the evil consequences which we may inflict on our country by our well-meaning follies', he decided to 'attempt or wish to assist nothing' before proper study; because, 'without study there is no sight and without sight no efficacy of action.'[17] In order to attain the requisite clarity to play out his conflicting, contradictory emotions, desires and ideas, Govardhanram regularly maintained his personal diaries. Readers of his *Scrap Books* cannot but be affected by his constant struggle and deep agony to attain the state of *aptavachana*—in which a person has a certain vision of life and society, and wishes to conduct his life accordingly.

This sense of duty was also conditioned by awareness of his capabilities as 'there is no duty beyond capacities'. He was aware that it was not given to him to be a 'public' person—which he would be forced to be if he wanted to produce an event—he wanted to cultivate the *sakshibhav* [bearing witness to] of a *sthitapragna* [one whose intellect is secure]. 'Glory, Public applause, Eminence, Moneys, Public Leadership, etc., are *Things I do not want at all*.'[18]

His desire to achieve the state of sthitapragna and his disinclination to produce an event should not lead us to conclude that Govardhanram is advocating either *nivritti* [detachment] or a form of

[15] Ibid., 34.

[16] Sudhir Chandra, 'A Nineteenth Century View of the Hindu Joint Family: Notes from Govardhanram Tripathi's *Scrap Book*', Occasional paper, 2, Centre for Social Studies, Surat.

[17] Pandya, Bakshi and Pandya, *Scrap Book* I, 29–30.

[18] Pandya, Bakshi and Pandya, *Scrap Book* II, 176; emphasis in the original.

asceticism. Asceticism for him is an act of rebellion against the Great Will. The state of sthitapragna does not entail a denial of duties. A sthitapragna is not one who is dislocated from the world; on the contrary, he is someone who experiences deeply the world around him, but who does not submit to the rule of the senses. Govardhanram would say that all acts of a sthitapragna are acts of consumption. He describes this state of being as a state of 'Practical Asceticism'.

He was aware that his goal of shaping a generation of people who shall be 'higher and stronger' and who shall be 'able to manage for themselves' and the act of 'kindling the spark of the organic flame'—which will bring about long lasting mediation in the forces shaping the destiny of his nation—was not a task given to mere mortals. At times he is plagued by deep doubts of self-worth: 'I am a pigmy and the pigmiest of pigmies ... I may never be able to attempt so much as a beginning in the right direction for the simple reason that abilities may be extinct ashes ....'[19] He was aware that the life of a country is much longer than that of an individual. Neither the magnitude of the task nor such daunting realisations could deviate him from his chosen path. 'I must fancy', he says, 'that I am an *Ajaramar*, when planning my duty to my country'.[20]

III

It was as a part of his duty towards the country that Govardhanram embarked upon a project which was to consume him for nearly fifteen years. At the age of thirty, in 1885, he started writing his novel *Sarasvatichandra*. When the fourth and final part was published in 1901, fourteen years had elapsed since the publication of the first part. He did not wish to write the novel at all. His initial plan was to write philosophical essays on the human condition; but he found the essay form limiting. This limitation arose from the form, its restricted

[19] Pandya, Bakshi and Pandya, *Scrap Book* I, 151.

[20] Ibid., 27.

reach, and the inability of the general reading classes to appreciate and comprehend discursive prose. Given the limiting circumstances, he came to the conclusion that illustrations of actual and ideal life were the most appropriate mode of communication.

> The conviction has also grown upon him [the author] that reality in flesh and blood under the guise of fiction can supply the ordinary reader with subtler moulds and finer casts for the formation of his inner self than abstract discussions, and that this is especially so with *a people who must be made, and not simply left, to read.*[21]

Govardhanram selected the novel form not for its aesthetic possibilities but for its potential as a medium of 'moulding inner selves' of people. 'Both women and the novel desire to be beautiful', he says, 'but fulfilment of this desire must be a means to achieve higher goals. Striving for mere aesthetic pleasure is not only undesirable, it is futile—indeed it could be harmful—to attain that step and not rise upwards.'[22] He is keenly aware of the functions and possibilities of the novel, which he calls a 'universal luxury', and says this form of literature is unrivalled in its popularity and reach amongst the educated middle classes.

He felt disappointed that the true potential of the novel form was not being utilised by authors, and that instead they used it as a medium to gratify the instincts of the reading classes. Functions of the novel, he says, are 'much higher and sacred'. An author who desires to use it as a means of education must be aware of his audience. Govardhanram takes a critical look at his readership and classifies them into three

[21] Govardhanram Madhavram Tripathi, 'English Preface' in *Sarasvatichandra*, Part I, 18th ed. (Bombay: N. M. Tripathi and Co., 1887, 1977), 8; emphases added. There are two prefaces to Part I, one in Gujarati and the other in English, with substantial variations between the two. See also Tripathi, 'Preface I' in *Sarasvatichandra*, Part I: *Buddhidhan's Administration*, trans. Tridip Suhrud (New Delhi: Orient BlackSwan, 2015), liii–liv.

[22] Tripathi, 'Prastavana' [Gujarati Preface] in *Sarasvatichandra*, Part I, 9. See also Tripathi, 'Preface II' in *Sarasvatichandra*, Part I, trans. Tridip Suhrud, lv–lx.

categories. In the first category are the scholars who read novels to acquire a deeper understanding of the human condition. The second class comprises discerning readers who read the novel to enrich their inner lives. And the third class is the general readership. This class reads novels either because it entertains them or gratifies some of their instincts. This is the class that for Govardhanram 'must be made, and not simply left, to read'. Most novels address themselves to this class and therein lies the reason for their popularity. According to him, the element of fiction or magic does not constitute the central concern of the novel—its function is to 'educate' and 'raise' the reading classes. The novel must show them the path of virtue. The characters and situations depicted in the novel thus assume centrality. Depiction of ideal types cannot inspire readers to aspire for a higher life. Nor can the depiction of evil alienate masses from it. Therefore, Govardhanram says that his novel will depict humane characters who constantly strive to raise their condition.

With the progress of his enterprise, we sense a certain satisfaction of accomplishment. 'The purpose of the writer is to enable the reader to rise to a stage higher than where he was ... *Sarasvatichandra*, thus undertaken at this point, *works* without doubt, and people *feel* the book. This is a mere literary work and will work on society.'[23] Eleven years after the publication of the first volume, Govardhanram notes with satisfaction that 'the progress of the reading classes is equal to the aspirations of the writer to interest them in the principal problems of the day.'[24]

The sense of achievement also brought with it a sense of greater responsibility for Govardhanram, who was plagued by the fear of illness and untimely death. 'I think I owe it as a duty to the world that I should finish before dying.'[25] India, he felt, was undergoing a strange transition in all spheres of community and personal life, and that

23 Pandya, Bakshi and Pandya, *Scrap Book* I, 31; emphases in the original.

24 Tripathi, 'English Preface' in *Sarasvatichandra*, Part III (Bombay: N. M. Tripathi and Co., 1898), 3. See also 'Preface I', p. lxiii of this volume.

25 Pandya, Bakshi and Pandya, *Scrap Book* II, 172.

certain 'forces have cast a gloomy shadow over our eyes'. Henceforth, his objective was not only to 'raise' readers but also 'to help his countrymen in groping their way out of the darkness into some kind of light'.[26]

Govardhanram captures the predicament of his society: both the advocates of change and those who wish to give 'eternal rigidity to the present' are uncertain as to how this transition will be harmonised. Will the process, which is heterogenous in its inception, result in an inward homogeneity? In this time of transition, only one certainty exists: 'Indian society must yield to the irresistible process of reciprocal assimilation'.[27] Can this society find repose? For Govardhanram, the realm of creative imagination can provide repose in such turbulent times—for the 'only place where we can safely look for a peaceful picture in spite of transient facts is in art and poetry'.[28] Henceforth, he resolved that the purpose of the novel would be to work towards a vision of a harmonised future. The narrative which had hitherto been a blend of the actual and the ideal, enters a different phase as 'the latter acquires a distinct predominance over the former'.

While dealing with the causes of the transition experienced by Indian society, Govardhanram refutes the widespread belief that India was witnessing a fusion of two different civilisations—the modern West and the East. Indian civilisation has passed through many phases in its evolution and what we are witnessing today, he says, is a fusion of three civilisations—the modern West, the modern East and the resurgent traditions of the ancient Indian civilisation. He is confident that this will one day result in 'reciprocal assimilation and harmony'. It is the possible visions of that day which are the source of anxiety for Indian people. His endeavour would henceforth be to provide one possible path to this assimilation and a vision of the future. In this 'drama of transition', the intellectuals, or those whom he calls the educated Indians, have a crucial function as they are

[26] Tripathi, 'English Preface' in *Sarasvatichandra*, Part IV (Bombay: N. M. Tripathi and Co., 1901), 6.

[27] Tripathi, *Sarasvatichandra*, Part III, 4.

[28] Ibid.

'directly involved by the actual contact and growing reactions of these civilisations.'[29] Their role is one of mediation between these civilisational forces and the masses so as to bring about the inevitable transition. 'It has fallen to the lot of the educated classes to serve as organic sheaths and conductors between multiform sets or organisms forming a repository of these energies.'[30] Although living through ambivalent times, Govardhanram is able to identify the problematic and its possible resolution with a rare sensibility and awareness.

Writing the novel for Govardhanram is a conscious act of tempering the souls of his countrymen. It is through this act that he wishes to fulfill his historical role of an 'organic sheath' between the great civilisational forces and the Indian masses.

IV

Sarasvatichandra is not 'one' unitary text. The novel was not only published in four parts but was also written in four parts over a period of fifteen years. Each part has a distinct thematic content, its own cast of characters and independent beginnings and ends. This is not to deny either the aesthetic or thematic unity of the novel. But readings which privilege one story—the story of Kumud, Sarasvatichandra and Kusum—as the principal theme and consider all others as unnecessary diversions do not allow an appreciation of the complete text.

The increasing influence of the East India Company in the affairs of the 'native states' provides the backdrop for the first part, *Buddhidhan's Administration* (1887). It deals with one individual's sustained efforts to assume complete control of the administration of a native state, Suvarnapur, and to rise above his circumstances. Govardhanram describes Buddhidhan's impoverished beginnings, his constant victimisation by Shathrai, the prime minister of the state, and Buddhidhan's opportunistic alliance and friendship with

[29] Tripathi, *Sarasvatichandra*, Part IV (Bombay: N. M. Tripathi and Co., 1901), 8.

[30] Ibid., 9.

Bhupsinh—a cousin of the ruling king and a claimant to the throne. Together they seek support of the British Resident officer of a neighbouring area, and with his intervention, Bhupsinh is declared the legitimate ruler. With patience, wisdom and foresight, Buddhidhan is gradually able to secure the complete trust of the new ruler, and to rid the state's administration of the influence of Shathrai. He also regains the post of prime minister which his family had traditionally held.

Part II of the novel, *Gunasundari's Household* (1892), deals with the state of a Hindu joint family in the latter half of the nineteenth century. Gunasundari and Vidya Chatura were married as children. Vidya Chatura was educated in Bombay and appointed as a teacher in an English school at Ratnanagari, another native state. He also obtained the post of tutor to the young prince, Maniraj of Ratnanagari. Gunasundari had acquired functional literacy, but as her name suggests, she was endowed with virtues 'natural' to women. Vidya Chatura trained and educated his young wife, enabling them to indulge in the pleasures of the mind and thereby avoiding the fate of many couples married in childhood. But just as they begin to experience a 'conjugality' driven by circumstances, Vidya Chatura's relatives come to live with them as dependents. From being a young, joyous wife, Gunasundari has to perforce become a *grihini* and manage a household of thirteen to fourteen people, all with different needs and personalities.

In this second part, Govardhanram achieves the height of his descriptive powers as a novelist. His minute descriptions of the dynamics of a joint family, his observation of human nature and its strengths and fragilities, his unencumbered prose and his characterisation have made this part most endearing to generations of readers. Govardhanram describes with a touch of humour—otherwise, entirely lacking in his prose—the interpersonal conflicts in the joint family, and pregnant Gunasundari's constant struggle to keep the family united and each member contented. She and her father-in-law, Manchatura, together succeed in both reforming and rehabilitating all constituent units of the joint family, without breaking the 'jointness' of the joint family.

The narrative thus far is a blend of actual and ideal aspects of life. From the third part on, the ideal acquires a distinctive predominance over the actual—a contrast which is immediately recognisable with the first part. Part III, *Ratnanagari's Statecraft* (1898), deals with the attempts of an enlightened ruler, along with his feudal chiefs and advisors, to create a responsible polity in times of general decay. Ratnanagari had survived the onslaught of British expansion because of the strength and vision of its rulers. It was governed by the concern for the welfare of all sections of society.

From state and society, Govardhanram moves on to dharma. The fourth part, *The Dream-Land of Sarasvatichandra and the Culmination* (1901), presents the ideal community of Sundargiri. This community of ascetics leads their life in perfect harmony with nature and her Creator, in accordance with the principles of dharma, under the benevolent gaze of Vishnudas. Their strivings are those of souls wishing to achieve complete non-duality with the Creator.

The love story—the story of Kumud, Sarasvatichandra and Kusum—links Govardhanram's reflections on state, society and dharma. Kumud, the naturally virtuous daughter of Gunasundari and Vidya Chatura, was engaged at an early age to Sarasvatichandra. Born into great wealth, Sarasvatichandra, as his name suggests, was a scholar and a luminary amongst the intellectuals of Bombay. Ascetic by nature and given to deep reflection on the state of his country, he was greatly enamoured by the natural charm and virtues of Kumud, and they fall in love with each other before marriage. But his insecure, jealous stepmother engineers a misunderstanding between the devoted son and the loving but short-sighted father, which results in Sarasvatichandra leaving home, renouncing not only his family and wealth but also Kumud. Kumud is disconsolate. He decides to live a life of an 'intellectual vagabond', travelling to remote parts of the country to experience the living reality of his countrymen.

As an unknown, rootless traveller with an assumed identity, in desperate search for purpose and peace, Sarasvatichandra reaches Suvarnapur. There he is invited to be the guest of Buddhidhan. Kumud's parents have by then married their uncomplaining daughter to Pramaddhan, the unworthy and debauch son of Buddhidhan. Sarasvatichandra, carrying the burden of his guilt, once again leaves Kumud to her fate, but not before Pramaddhan suspects the tenderness of their relationship. Before he can cause greater misery to Kumud, Sarasvatichandra disappears, and is given up as dead. Through a series of accidents he reaches Sundargiri, where he is celebrated as the heir to Sadhu Vishnudas. Kumud, believed to be drowned in a river, also reaches Sundargiri and lives in the care of *sadhvis* as an ascetic. Widowed Kumud—though she remains unaware of Pramaddhan's death for a long time—and Sarasvatichandra suffer greatly because of their mutual love. Vishnudas asks them to spend five nights together in a cave to contemplate their fate. Under divine intervention, they travel to the 'Land of the Enlightened' in their dreams where they experience a union of souls and emerge from the cave enlightened and pure. The novel ends with the inauguration of Sarasvatichandra's project for the regeneration of the country, and a new phase in the lives of Kumud, Kusum and Sarasvatichandra.

V

For those who came of age in late-nineteenth century India and felt concerned about the state of their society and nation, colonial rule was a fundamental reality. Awareness of subjection coupled with a profound uncertainty about the present and future shaped their response to the British presence in India. Given this ultimate objective—'one which never ought to be lost sight of'—of moulding his people into a great people who would be able to take care of themselves, Govardhanram grappled with the meaning of British rule. In an entry in *Scrap Book* I, dated 13 April 1891, he wrote:

> India is invaded and subdued already. There is no question of Offensive or Defensive here, and Elasticity would be a nice helpmate in Constitutional Warfare. The rulers are a clever set of people—an admixture of selfish aggressors and disinterested, benevolent helpmates. India is worked by "push and pull" among

> these, and naturally the Home Interest generally carries the day. Yet even here we win morsel by morsel, though often it is snatched away—sometimes even from near the lips.[31]

The only unambiguous, unqualified statement here is the fact of India's subjection. Accepting the British presence as given, Govardhanram advises his people to cultivate 'elasticity'. 'Coming after offense and defense have been ruled out, "elasticity" becomes the very epitome of ambiguity. The term here seems to suggest pragmatism.'[32] Relations between the rulers and the ruled are mediated by the idea of warfare. But this is neither an offensive nor a confrontation. The concept of 'constitutional'—given by the colonial rulers—and the need to cultivate elasticity, introduces an element of caution, of pragmatic moderation. Moving on to a depiction of the rulers, Govardhanram again displays ambivalence and a mixed assessment of British presence. Yet he is aware that in the ultimate analysis, 'the home interest carries the day' and that whatever ground is gained by Indians through their elasticity is snatched away.

Govardhanram may have been ambivalent towards British rule, but he displays remarkable consistency in his analysis of the 'native states', and the capacity of his people to effectively counter the colonial aggressor—he has no faith in their ability to take premeditated action and believes they can only indulge in 'well-meaning follies'. He has some faith in the Congress, owing to its 'well-chosen leadership' of A. O. Hume and Sir William Wedderburn.

> But in other matters our leaders are unfit. In view of these things, I would like to leave many things to our rulers rather than to our native leaders, for the former are at least most sensible people. If natives act, I shall not hinder them. If Europeans act I shall have some confidence.[33]

[31] Pandya, Bakshi and Pandya, *Scrap Book* I, 51.

[32] Sudhir Chandra, *The Oppressive Present: Literature and Social Consciousness in Colonial India* (New Delhi: Oxford University Press, 1992), 23.

[33] Pandya, Bakshi and Pandya, *Scrap Book* I, 58.

The high standards he had set himself in private and public conduct may have made him sceptical of the abilities of his own people. This severe denouncement and total lack of confidence in the abilities of Indians informed his vocation of creating a generation which shall be 'better able to look and manage for themselves'. This negative assessment of his countrymen to manage the political and social implications of the colonial encounter pervades all his reflections—whether in the *Scrap Books* or the novel. On the question of British presence, he did not allow any wishful thinking to colour his assessment. In a lengthy entry titled 'India and the foreigner', he wrote:

> India is under foreign control and the foreigner is the kindliest of all foreigners available. To get rid of the foreigner by force or fraud is an idea associated with all incidents that remind us of the rule being foreign. The idea naturally haunts our uneducated instincts; to educated instincts the idea is both foolish and fallacious. It is foolish because it is not practicable, and because any experiment founded upon it would send the country from the frying pan into the fire. It is a fallacious idea, because the distinction between a native and a foreigner is only transient, and the distinction is not a guarantee of a native being a better ruler than the foreigner in such a mass of heterogenous people as my country is.[34]

Govardhanram is not only emphasising his lack of faith in the strategies employed by Indians to get rid of the British but is also questioning the basic premise of 'foreign' and 'native' interests being mutually exclusive. Moreover, his absence of trust in the abilities of natives to manage a heterogenous people with differing aspirations and needs also colours his assessment of the problem. He goes on to articulate the real problem: '[the] problem is not the absolute eviction of the foreigner, but *his accommodation to the native element* ... where India and England *become one on Indian Soil* ...'[35] One can assume that while cautioning against attempts to evict the foreigner completely

[34] Ibid., 149.

[35] Ibid., 150; emphases in the original.

from Indian soil, he is referring not just to the physical presence, but to a civilisational encounter, and his stand is informed by the awareness that Indian culture and society will be transformed by this 'drama of transition'. The source of his anxiety lies in the uncertainty about the future and how these opposing tendencies will be harmonised and what kind of a resolution will emerge. To bring about a resolution where 'India and England become one on Indian Soil', he required to 'create a homogeneous nuclear class'.

This also was the central concern of *Sarasvatichandra*. At the same time, he was not unaware of the opposition between foreign and native interests. He elaborates in the same entry:

> In India the sovereign is enlightened and yet has an interest foreign to the country. Two things have to be done. This interest has to be made to cease to be foreign; and while it is foreign, we want the natives that shall guard against the civic temptations to which the foreigner is exposed by his position, that shall enable the native interests to grow and develop during their minority without any hindrance from the adverse interests of the rulers, that shall in fact watch over the real interests and develop the future welfare of the country. And it is possible to do these both loyally and patriotically.[36]

In the four volumes of *Sarasvatichandra*, Govardhanram attempted to demonstrate this wisdom. The first part of the novel—which is the depiction of reality according to him—portrays the expanding British influence over the native states. It is one of the most severe indictments of native states in the literature of that period. Govardhanram depicts a polity based on personal interests, plagued by widespread erosion of morals and values. The efforts of Buddhidhan and Bhupsinh to overthrow Shathrai's corrupt administration were in the final analysis motivated by personal animosity and gain. 'Buddhidhan had meanwhile turned Bhupsinh and his administration into mere instruments for his

[36] Ibid.

festering rage.'[37] The only thing that differentiates Buddhidhan from Shathrai is the former's high sense of personal morality.

A more condemning attitude towards the native states is perhaps reflected in the *Scrap Books*, where Govardhanram feels no compulsion for moderation. While he was contemplating retirement from legal practice, he had many tempting offers from the native states in Gujarat to join the administration as dewan. Given his financial insecurities, a few years of dewanship would have put many fears at rest. This position would have also provided him an opportunity to work for the good of society. Giving his reasons for refusing these offers, he writes: 'Baroda, Junagadh, Kutch, Bhavnagar, and what not?—all native states in fact stand before my eyes, with their whole nudity of weaknesses, complications and difficulties—from subjects, officers, the princes themselves and even from Agencies ....' The mere thought of being in that environment filled him with a 'vision of pettiest jealousies, meanest natures, foolishest ambitions, ridiculous follies and vanities, and adamantine obstructions.'[38] Perhaps this assessment of the native states has much to do with his unhappy three-year-long stay at Bhavnagar in the service of the Dewan. He also felt that efforts made in the native states for the betterment of society were unlikely to bear fruit. This would amount to narrowing his vision. He adds in the same entry:

> Besides, the greatest result available in this field can only be local influence—while the kind of influence that is wanted is one that could permeate and stimulate the whole constitution of India. This larger effect must be begun and produced in British India where the plant, if sown, can have a freer, larger growth along what Telang called the line of least resistance.[39]

During this period, he returned to this theme with regularity. Perturbed by his thoughts of retirement from active legal practice, his family and friends tried to persuade him to take up tempting

37 Tripathi, *Sarasvatichandra*, Part I, trans. Tridip Suhrud, 68.

38 Pandya, Bakshi and Pandya, *Scrap Book* II, 43.

39 Ibid.

offers. A few days after the entry quoted above, he elaborated upon the 'thorns of inferior society in Political life in Native States.'[40] His chief objection to working in a native state was that he would have to deal with people of inferior intellectual abilities. 'No Prince can be equal to your education, and no fellow servant disposed to have your conscience in the present state of things.' This situation he says is 'not much dissimilar to the marriage of a man of my education and age with an illiterate girl of twelve, whom you must try to please and educate with all the arts of one attempting to make love with such an odd match.'[41]

Govardhanram's other concern is about moral life in the native states. One may be forced to work with people who may not have any sense of duty, and even if they do, it is likely to be 'in a disfigured, mutilated, and even perverted form'. And therefore, 'I shall have to guard warily against the Fallacious Persuasions of the Serpentine Tempter, if ever he takes me near the Tree of Service.'[42] Govardhanram's assessment of the native states is without doubt largely negative and he does not see in them much potential for 'kindling the spark of organic flame'. Nevertheless, large parts of the country were under the administration of native states; he thus felt the imperative to turn his attention to them in the novel. Part III of *Sarasvatichandra*—subtitled *Ratnanagari's Statecraft*—deals with the creation of an 'ideal' native state. From here onwards, the narrative enters a different phase, and normative considerations are given primacy over the depiction of reality.

The third part of the novel deals with the efforts of the state to maintain autonomy and introduce elements of oligarchic democracy in times of greater British domination. In a courageous portrayal of the events of 1857, he showed how the British presence was oppressive and, at the same time, how it created the space for fundamental changes in the Indian polity.

[40] Ibid., 51.

[41] Ibid.

[42] Pandya, Bakshi and Pandya, *Scrap Book* I, 51.

When Part III was published in 1898, there was 'a strong rumour' in Ahmedabad that Govardhanram was arrested in Bombay 'for writing sedition in this part of the novel'. His wife, mother and sister spent two agonising days in Nadiad, until his telegram and letter reached them, quashing the speculation. This incident sparked off a reaction in him.

> Was it a mistake to have written a book which has so disturbed the peace and happiness of my family? What is my duty? To boldly write such a book for my people or secure the peace of my family against such contingency? I find it impossible to solve the question ...[43]

At that moment, he might have been uncertain about the desirability of his enterprise, but such doubts did not plague him for long. 'My book is not only loyal, but my innermost soul feels that it is written for and must tend to the welfare of both the rulers and the ruled.'[44] The inclusion of the rulers is not surprising as, for Govardhanram, the term 'my people' included Englishmen, 'so far as the lot of my country is joined with or rests upon them'.[45]

The third part also deals with the efforts of Maniraj—an embodiment of *kshtratej* or kshatriyahood and trained in Western learning under the wise counsel of his former teacher and present dewan, Vidya Chatura—to create a polity based on the principles of consumption.

Vidya Chatura, after a careful study of British administration and the native states, had formulated a guiding principle for the polity:

> If the administrators of the native states have the wisdom, intelligence, conscience and will, they can work for the welfare of the people and uplift the state to a level which subjects under English rulers cannot even dream of; for the British, however well-meaning, are ultimately guided by self-interest alone.[46]

43 *Scrap Book* II, 158.

44 Ibid., 159.

45 Ibid., 174.

46 Tripathi, *Sarasvatichandra*, Part II, trans. Tridip Suhrud, 27.

The efforts of the entire administration were geared towards the realisation of this vision. Vidya Chatura's private and public conduct was also reminiscent of Govardhanram's reflections in his *Scrap Books* on the role of an ideal minister. While discussing what, to his mind, were the shortcomings of the Dewan of Baroda, Govardhanram elaborated the role of a minister. The Dewan's chief shortcoming according to him was that, 'he lost sight of the fact that his master was his master, and not his child or subordinate'.[47] Going on to describe right conduct, he says,

> I think the ministers are bound to lead Princes by sweet arts and obedient power, to manage them as clever wives manage husbands and nurses manage patients, and to work upon their souls by inspiration of love, awe, reverence, spirit of friendship, regard for ability and experience, and shrewdness and sagacity, and confidence in motives.[48]

Govardhanram felt that most ministers, given their superior intelligence and ability, tend to consider themselves the fountainhead of all power and welfare and 'ignore, or even forget, that the well-being of the state *does* consist in allowing the last energy of power to retain its vested seat in the brain that wears the crown ...'[49] Such patient and ever watchful caution was embodied in Samaldas Parmananddas, the Dewan of Bhavnagar, on whose personality the character of Vidya Chatura is believed to be based.

Despite having created an ideal native state, Govardhanram remained suspicious of the desirability and efficacy of action taken in the native states. He gave release to his conflicting emotions through a dialogue between the residents of British India and the administrators of Ratnanagari in Part IV of the novel. Vir Rao, a touring intellectual from Bombay, takes an arrogant abolitionist stand. According to him, 'all is rotten to the core' in the native states and their corrupting influence has spread to other areas, obstructing their growth, destroying their

[47] *Scrap Book* II, 84.

[48] Ibid.

[49] Ibid.

morals and polity; 'damn your states and politics for preventing all dictates of truth'.[50] No remedial measures, observes Vir Rao, will be able to save these states from certain doom and they should be allowed to destroy themselves as, 'They are doomed and shall cease, and the sooner the better'.[51]

Against this, Chandrakant takes a more cautious stance. He firmly believes that change is inevitable. The native states have already been reduced to 'Local Governing Agencies' and their authority will ultimately be completely subordinate to the British administration. Echoing Govardhanram's desire for a homogenised group to mediate the relationship between the rulers and the ruled, Chandrakant says that the rulers and administrators of the native states should form such an enlightened aristocracy.

Shankar Sharma, an official in the administration of Ratnanagari, provides an impassioned defence of the native state. Like others he, too, lapses into English at times. 'The maturity of our own moral and intellectual attitude, whenever we reach it in the distant future, will not fail to command respect and love in the brightest circles among Englishmen, if English instincts will have survived that period.'[52] After this optimistic vision, he articulates the impulse which defines the administration of Ratnanagari:

> The Princes that will have then led their subjects to a climax of genuine prosperity, a vision of which a foreign Government will have tried in vain to conjure up before their own Indian subjects, will present a divine spectacle which will make your English Rulers blush with an awakened consciousness of their own inner frailties![53]

Trying to bring to a close this endless debate, Vidya Chatura feels that in these ambiguous times, only one thing is certain. We are witnessing a strange transition, he says, where the only certainty is change. The

[50] Tripathi, *Sarasvatichandra*, Part IV, 46.

[51] Ibid., 51.

[52] Ibid., 76.

[53] Ibid.

society will not be able to go back entirely to what it was, and those oblivious to these changes will be left behind in the dark legions. From these conversations and Govardhanram's own reflections, it is not difficult to discern the voice of Govardhanram.

Govardhanram was willing to accept British domination as a fact. His real concern was not the subjection, but the ability of the Indian people, their leaders and the rulers of the native states to reflect on their actions and work towards a harmonious, if uncertain future; his utter lack of faith in such ability is striking. Despite his total condemnation of the native states, he accepted them as a given reality in his attempts to create an ideal polity. But throughout his life, Govardhanram remained sceptical of both their desirability and normative superiority over British rule.

VI

Given his ambition of creating a generation of people 'higher and stronger than they are' through the philosophy of consumption, Govardhanram had to engage himself with the institutional structures of social organisation. Despite his self-perceived crucifixion within the family, his *Scrap Books* and the novel reflect a remarkable engagement with the institution of joint family.

Oppressed by the existential realities of living in a joint family, young Govardhanram while studying for his B.A. at Elphinstone College, in an essay entitled 'The State of the Hindu Society in the Bombay Presidency', offered to his countrymen the following advice: 'The moment you get married, start living separately from your parents ...'[54] This unambiguous pronouncement gives a misleading impression of finality. He was to return with embarrassing regularity to the issue of joint family in the *Scrap Books* despite his repeated resolves not to discuss the family.

[54] Pandya, *Sriyut Govardhanram*, 49.

The joint family was not only an oppressive existential reality for him—with an average of fourteen people living in the house throughout—it was also an important social and cultural institution. As Sudhir Chandra has pointed out, 'both the existential and the normative aspects of the joint family feature in Govardhanram's dialogues with himself'.[55] His *Scrap Books* open with a statement on his wife Lalita's angelic goodness and a severe denouncement of other family members, including his parents. So harsh was his criticism that he felt emotionally 'frozen' while referring to these notes.[56] Tired of playing the role of an impartial judge and arbitrator, Govardhanram decided to formulate a 'maxim in domestic management' and vowed to follow it: 'While everybody is to have his or her liberties in my family, the liberties of no one are to go to the extent of clipping the necessary liberties and moral rights of other members, including even minors'.[57]

His search for equanimity by formulating guiding principles does not provide any respite from the 'conjugal jar'. He is forced once again to examine the relative merits and peculiarities of individual members of his family. Mother, he says, 'is visited with short-sighted littleness of mind'[58] while father Madhavram's 'patriarchal cares' only result 'in hampering me and the whole family'.[59] Their partiality towards 'Mrs. Brother' (wife of Govardhanram's brother Narhariram) disturbs his wife Lalitagauri, although she has—largely due to Govardhanram's training—'conquered her overwhelmingly uncontrolled temper'.[60]

Govardhanram gives details of familial frictions and the ways in which he tries to resolve them. In an entry titled, 'Family Misunderstandings and the Way to Remove Them', he records his attempts to be an impartial judge between his wife and mother, Shivkashi. He feels an ideal situation would be one where they can

[55] Chandra, 'A Nineteenth Century View of the Hindu Joint Family', 11.

[56] Pandya, Bakshi and Pandya, *Scrap Book* I, 35.

[57] Ibid., 37.

[58] Ibid., 75.

[59] Ibid., 115.

[60] Ibid., 110.

resolve their conflicts without his mediation. This would require them both to be 'patient, enduring and forgiving'. But given their lack of literacy, Govardhanram has no faith in their abilities to resolve their conflicts 'intellectually'. 'Swallowing [their anger and pride] and explaining would both be impracticable between such illiterate people'.[61] Instead, he allows both his mother and wife to complain to him in each other's absence. Despite his maxim of allowing each family member their liberty and space, he feels compelled to mediate in their interpersonal relationships as 'illiterate people are sure to tyrannise over each other if left to themselves'.[62]

For Govardhanram, the only way to secure peace and harmony and to steer the joint family away from becoming a joint nuisance lies in the philosophy of consumption and in 'ungrudging and all sided sacrifices'.[63] Accordingly, during discussions on partitioning the family property, he proposed that he shall retain no part of the property; but this was not accepted. Govardhanram was aware that to an observer, his attitude may come across as 'Idiocy and spoilation', but this deliberate sacrifice fills him with supreme happiness: 'I have begun my consumption *at home*—charity must begin at home. It fulfills my aspiration ... to find myself so consumed into the atmosphere that surrounds me'.[64] With the arrangement of partitioning the family property that was finally arrived at—although they continued to live in a joint family—Govardhanram came much closer to his idea of a nuclear family.

In such an event, the possibility of his sudden death and inability to provide for his wife and children fills his heart with gloom. 'I am a houseless man, and my wife and children are houseless, and my parents think this is good.'[65] Though he is able to overcome such moments of gloom by his faith in the Great Will and his philosophy

[61] Ibid., 114.

[62] Ibid., 128.

[63] Ibid., 120.

[64] Ibid., 119; emphasis in the original.

[65] Ibid., 137.

of consumption, Lalita's subsequent illness and the possibility of her death make him resolve once again not to sit in judgement on family matters. Govardhanram decides to henceforth 'form judgement but be silent' and give full play to the old principle: 'I allow you your liberty and I shall have mine', and to allow his relations to settle their differences themselves and face the consequences of their follies. Henceforth, 'my only objects of care are now my children, neither wife, nor parents, nor brother ...'[66] Lalita's exclusion here from Govardhanram's 'objects of care' is quite puzzling and unexplained. For quite some time before this note was made, he was writing with some pride about her many virtues, and he goes on to write hereafter with great sensitivity about her pain and suffering.

With Lalita's illness, Govardhanram's identification with his nuclear family became more crystallised. He absolves his conscience from any guilt for having passed a judgement against his parents and others in the family: 'My conscience decides in favour of myself'.[67] For the first time in the *Scrap Books* he is willing to commit himself against the joint family: 'My lessons from all this, as a student of sociology, is confirmation of my views against a joint family system ...'[68] He feels that if the joint family system cannot be done away with completely, an attempt should be made to minimise the jointness of joint families. 'When one son serves in Bombay, the other in Karachi, and the father's home is at Surat. This preserves the nature of the family as a joint insurance and minimises the jointness in other respects.'[69] Lalita's suffering, her illness and his family's insensitivity towards her makes Govardhanram bitter about the nature of patriarchal society. Writing about the status of a daughter-in-law in a joint family, he says, 'It is not the daughter-in-law's maturity but the mother-in-law's death that emancipates the former, probably when she is old, and after all her

[66] Ibid., 181.

[67] Ibid., 184–185.

[68] Ibid., 186.

[69] Ibid., 238.

youthful yearnings and motherly sentiments have been smothered and even violated'.[70]

However, a remark by his cousin-uncle Mansukhram—that his opinions on the joint family were biased by his own existential experience and not really based on an impartial study of that institution—forces Govardhanram to re-evaluate his views.[71] Having oscillated between viewing the joint family as a 'joint nuisance' and as a 'joint insurance', in this enigmatic note of 25 April 1894, he suddenly turns to consider 'the brightest side of the joint family', which he says lies in its being '*Protective*'.[72] Comparing Western and Indian forms of social organisation, he says the former is territorial and 'spends its force in raising up individualism', while the latter is tribal and 'revels in destroying Individualism'.[73] The real strength of tribalism, he says, is that it protects its members 'whom it feeds and clothes and even saves from inclemency of all elements outside the hearth'.[74] He compares the joint family to an insurance society by citing examples from his own family. A system 'so holy and so invulnerable', which has provided 'indestructible vitality' and protection to 'society and even the nation' ever since the Aryans came to India, is under attack from territorial nations; therefore, one 'should pause and think a thousand times' before criticising such a superior social organisation which fulfills and furthers the aspirations of socialism, and in fact, 'It is *the* point which would solve many an inspiration of socialism'.[75]

'Joint Family ... provides the fatherless with fathers, the motherless with mothers, sonless with sons and daughterless with daughters, paupers with maintenance, the homeless with homes, the sick with nurses ... socialism never went the length of aspiring to so much.'[76]

[70] Ibid., 262.

[71] Ibid., 121.

[72] Ibid., 263; emphasis in the original.

[73] Ibid.

[74] Ibid., 264.

[75] Ibid.; emphasis in the original.

[76] Ibid., 266.

Given the situation of his own family, Govardhanram asks, 'Could I have left them cold, myself enjoying the warmth of my means? No, not for the world, so long as I was myself—*a Hindu and not a European*.'[77] He is even willing to forget his deep discomfort with his family members and says that all the suffering was not in vain. Having established the superiority of the Hindu (Indian) form of social organisation over the European form, he then cautions those seeking radical reorganisation of society. They can, he advises, 'attempt modifications and reasonable development', even attempt partitioning in a particular family—like his own—but in 'so far as the larger society and the nation of family goes, offer no quackery of medicine to the ignorant masses that are protected by their own old, nature-selected, instinct moulded ways of living, except by slow and well-judged alteration'.[78] Notwithstanding his harsh criticisms of his own family, he appears to largely accept the 'normative authority of the joint family'.[79] But these were in no respect his last words on the subject. Despite his resolve not to 'spoil' his notes by references to the family, during the next twelve years of his life, he did return again and again to the joint family.

Govardhanram grappled with the idea of the joint family with equal gravity in his novel. His fundamental ambivalence towards this institution, ranging from total condemnation and rejection to romantic idealisation and acceptance, is played out in *Sarasvatichandra* through two characters—Uddhatlal (as the name suggests, his response is marked by impudence) and Chandrakant, a dear friend of Sarasvatichandra.[80] Uddhatlal adopts the radical, abolitionist stance which Govardhanram had taken earlier, while Chandrakant provides an impassioned defence of the joint family, almost echoing the note of 25 April 1894. During their debate, they at times lapse into English from Gujarati to emphasise their rhetoric. Uddhatlal's trenchant criticism of the joint family is anchored in the argument

77 Ibid., 265; emphasis in the original.

78 Ibid., 266.

79 Chandra, 'A Nineteenth Century View of the Hindu Joint Family', 31.

80 Tripathi, *Sarasvatichandra*, Part IV, 145–165.

that tribal forms of social organisation—represented by the joint family—demand sacrifice of individual aspirations. Furthermore, he argues that no fundamental social reconstruction is possible until the root of the problem, the joint family, is abolished.

> Our joint family system has but a blasting influence on the growth of our individuals, on our economical and moral conditions, and even on our national and political growth. It has kept our beings stunted in intelligence and action ... And for any reform, woe be unto every idea of your social or domestic reconstruction or even improvement so long as you have not touched the root of the disease and said: Down with the joint family ...[81]

Chandrakant's reply to such severe criticism is more cautious. He argues that there is an element of truth in Uddhatlal's criticism, but that the picture he paints is an incomplete one. In an almost poetic re-articulation of Govardhanram's views in his note of 25 April 1894, Chandrakant asserts that the European solution to the oppressive tendencies of the family, which result in aggressive individualism, is undesirable. He refers to the aspect of social insurance that joint families provide and, at a national level, emphasises the need to preserve this ancient institution as it arouses feelings of patriotism. He articulates the familiar argument that families have socialist aspirations and that the Hindu ideal is superior to the Western one in so far as it aims to further such aspirations. 'The Hindu ideal is eminently socialist in life and practice ... The main feature of our Hindu socialism is that it is *Protective*. It protects the weak, the infants, the women, and the aged from starvation and its consequential crimes ... It protects and protects.'[82]

Chandrakant also shows an awareness that the joint family system in its pure form cannot survive the aggressive onslaught of individualism. And that the responsibility of his generation will be to make the necessary sacrifices to 'secure a combination of the two

[81] Ibid., 153.

[82] Ibid., 164; emphasis in the original.

boons, without their abuses.'[83] This harmony, he argues, cannot be achieved by an aggressive abolitionist stance. The harmonising process may take 'at least one generation' or even more and until then, the present generation will have to live in 'Poverty, patience, forbearance and even suffering.'[84]

To a reader of the novel, this almost unexpected and abrupt articulation of these two distinct positions on the joint family may appear unwarranted; but this exchange becomes more meaningful when read along with the *Scrap Books*. Uddhatlal and Chandrakant's distinct positions, when combined, evidence a direct resemblance to their creator's own complex and ambivalent attitude. Part II of the novel, *Gunasundari's Household*, is a larger and subtler unfolding of Govardhanram's views as presented in the *Scrap Books*. Gunasundari, the central character of this part, and Vidya Chatura were married as children. Vidya Chatura acquired formal education in Bombay while Gunasundari is 'naturally' virtuous, caring, intelligent and industrious. Vidya Chatura prepares her and educates her so that she can share his intellectual pleasures and appreciate the rich insights and delights of the printed word, of poetry, philosophy, and literature. Govardhanram then describes the circumstances in which more than fourteen members of Vidya Chatura's family come to inhabit their house. He creates a 'typical' joint family comprising Vidya Chatura's parents, Manchatura and Dharmalaxmi, his debauched and unemployed elder brother, his wife, their four children and a daughter-in-law, a sister-in-law widowed in her childhood, a widowed sister and her son, and yet another sister and her daughter whose husband had run away from home as he could not honour his multiple debts.

Their suddenly coming together in Gunasundari and Vidya Chatura's house not only places a tremendous burden on their household economy, it also brings to an abrupt end the joyous celebration of their newfound sensuous and intellectual 'conjugal love.' Henceforth, Gunasundari only aspires to keep the family contented

83 Ibid.

84 Ibid., 165.

and together. As an embodiment of the philosophy of consumption, she willingly makes all sacrifices and deprives herself of all pleasures and desires. She brings together these different individuals with disparate needs and peculiar characteristics into one cohesive whole. Despite her own consumption, her sacrifices and tireless efforts are neither recognised nor appreciated by the others, preoccupied as they are in furthering their own narrow self-interests.

Govardhanram describes with a touch of humour the complete anarchy which prevails in the household during Gunasundari's confinement after the birth of her first child, Kumud. During this period of ritual confinement, Gunasundari—like her creator Govardhanram—is forced to confront the oppressive reality of the joint family and critically evaluate those surrounding her.

> Oh God, guide me through this ocean! Until the other day, I believed that a joint family was a boon, a source of endless joy. But this is no joy—only conflict and endless blood-boil! Each one has a mind of their own; their true colours are different. Each one has a bad habit as large as a tree; and when their bad habits are curbed, I get all the blame! I have to care for all their desires, but there is no one to care for mine.[85]

Despite this indictment of the joint family, Gunasundari is not willing to absolve herself from her duties. It is the old patriarch, Manchatura, who in his empathy for his daughter-in-law realises that until Gunasundari and Vidya Chatura are relieved of the burden of the joint family, they will not be able to enjoy their youth and the others will never learn to manage for themselves and live independently, and it is Manchatura who eventually relocates all the family members. This is the solution also suggested by Govardhanram in his *Scrap Books*: minimise the jointness of the joint family without destroying the joint insurance and protection that it provides. In *Gunasundari's Household*, otherwise perceived in Gujarati literature to be a celebration of the Hindu joint family, Govardhanram's ambivalence towards the institution is evident.

[85] Tripathi, *Sarasvatichandra*, Part II, trans. Tridip Suhrud, 100.

As Sudhir Chandra has observed, it is perhaps futile to search for Govardhanram's final and definitive position on the issue of the Indian joint family.[86] Even so, it is possible to discern a dominant position. Govardhanram found the reality of his joint family oppressive, and he found members of his family undeserving of his presence and affection; this is quite evident from his chronic lamentations against his family which mark his *Scrap Books*. Although he found it necessary to address the civilisational issue and socialist aspirations while discussing the joint family, his dissatisfaction with his own family and his nuanced position in the novel are suggestive of his deep discomfort with normative aspects of the joint family.

VII

We are concerned not only with the fate of his societal endeavours, but also with the fate of Govardhanram and two other individuals irrevocably bound to him. Their minds and souls were the first that he tried to cultivate in accordance with his ideals and philosophy. These two were Lalita, Govardhanram's second wife, and Lilavati, their daughter. It is important for us to consider the fates of these three individuals not only because they were played out almost simultaneously to his public endeavour, but also because for Govardhanram there was no marked disjunction between giving his country a vision of an ideal society and of educating and 'raising' his wife and daughter. These two projects were essentially the same—both were integral to his personal dharma towards the country. And as Govardhanram himself put it, 'my country is a term which must be confined in the beginning and made to expand in course of time only'.[87]

Govardhanram shows a keen awareness of the intertwined fates of those inhabiting the inner worlds he created through his fiction, and of his own self and his family. At many places in the *Scrap Books*

[86] Chandra, 'A Nineteenth Century View of the Hindu Joint Family', 32.

[87] Pandya, Bakshi and Pandya, *Scrap Book* I, 51.

he draws parallels between his life and the novel, compares his wife to his heroine and asks his daughter to follow in the footsteps of Gunasundari. His life and his fiction seemed to him to mirror each other. Jayanti, another daughter of his, was betrothed at a tender age, a decision which upset him. Two days after the engagement he wrote: 'Curious coincidence! Jayanti betrothed on 25th, and I get the first proof of the second part of my novel on the 26th. The betrothal pinches me, and I compare myself to Vidya Chatura, who accepting in haste a woman's arguments, betrothed Kumud to Pramad, and dropped all talk of Sarasvatichandra.'[88] In a moment of rare passion, Govardhanram says: '*I only want their souls*.'[89] Moreover, the only source of deriving some understanding about the possible fate of his societal endeavour is from the lives of Govardhanram, Lilavati and Lalita, who tried to live a life of consumptive virtue. It is in their biographies that Govardhanram's 'grand project' unfolds itself completely.

Govardhanram's marriage to Harilaxmi was fixed before their birth. A close 'conjugal' relationship developed between the two. But the relationship between adolescent Harilaxmi and Govardhanram's dominating mother Shivkashi was one of constant conflict. Torn between love for his young wife and his sense of duty towards his mother, Govardhanram seriously contemplated running away from his conflict-ridden house to start life anew.[90] His first marriage ended tragically—Harilaxmi died in 1874 while giving birth to their child, who also died soon after. Govardhanram was to express his deep anguish and a sense of permanent loss in two verses—*Hridayruditshatakam* and *Snehmudra*—that he wrote in memory of Harilaxmi and in which he paid her glowing tributes.[91] Reflecting on his first marriage, he wrote in 1893: 'My first marriage was meant to be a cruel hoax which my wife lived and was eventually to leave me a

[88] Ibid., 93.

[89] Ibid., 27; emphasis in the original.

[90] Pandya, *Sriyut Govardhanram*, 16–17.

[91] *Hridayruditshatakam*, a long verse in Sanskrit, was written in 1875. *Snehmudra*, an adaption of the former, was published in 1889.

widower'.[92] Though delighted 'at the prospect of a living relieved from future marriage',[93] Govardhanram was married again to Lalitagauri in 1876. Years later, he complained: 'I was then married, under conditions to which I would have never assented, if I had not been kept ignorant of them, to a girl reputedly ill-bred ...'[94] Secure in his faith in the philosophy of 'consumption', he tried to cultivate in his 'ill-bred' wife the high ideals of this philosophy. 'My duty does not end with satisfying her poor ideals, but I am bound to enlarge them. This is my marital duty ...'[95] Govardhanram lists his 'duties' towards his wife as under: 'a) to train her up b) to raise her life c) to make her free d) to provide for her e) to fulfill her aspirations with such luxuries etc., as a husband in love and duty ought to give her'.[96] His primary obligation towards his wife was to 'train' her. By training he did not imply 'educating' her in the conventional sense of imparting literacy, as he time and again laments that he was not able to educate her.[97] Training for Govardhanram primarily meant imparting to her those virtues and ideals which would enable her to lead her life according to the tenets of his philosophy of consumption.

For Lalita, the first thirteen years of her life with Govardhanram were years of training under his constant guidance and close supervision. Not given to impassioned display of his feelings, he is nevertheless ecstatic in his praise of Lalita's moral strength to continuously lead a life of self-negation and self-inflicted deprivation. There are repeated references of Lalita's moral virtues and a life of self-sacrifice in his *Scrap Books* of this period. He writes:

> last thirteen years have been a life of training for her, and her life is high. Industrious to the fullest extent, virtuous and charitable, active and clever, enthusiastic and untiring in her domestic work

[92] Pandya, Bakshi and Pandya, *Scrap Book* I, 167.

[93] Ibid.

[94] Ibid., 167–68.

[95] Ibid., 64.

[96] Ibid., 61.

[97] Ibid., 62.

> and in the work of rendering me happy and all in the family, she has nobly – successfully – and touchingly borne, and willingly undertaken, the heaviest self-sacrifice for all this – the sacrifice of health, of liberty, of all luxuries, of all enjoyments – of her own wants and aspirations, and the most usual of worldly enjoyments, – of her tastes and temper – and of everything possible under the sun ...[98]

Govardhanram cannot hide his feelings of a personal success and achievement in training Lalita. 'I have trained wife from the beginning to do voluntary and loving service and sacrifice to my people. She has done it. She has worked like an ass for my people ...'[99] Lalita's sole aspiration of life becomes making Govardhanram and his family happy. For this she earns his unqualified praise. Her latest change of disposition compels Govardhanram 'to adore and make *arti* to her soul—to her goodness, to her virtue—to her understanding—and to her moral power'.[100] Lalita's sacrifice compels Govardhanram—who constantly lived with a feeling of his own moral and intellectual superiority—to put her on a pedestal even higher than himself. 'Her life is higher than mine.'[101] This was the greatest recognition that Govardhanram could have given to any one; he called her the 'Family's Angel'.[102] Lalita succeeds in acquiring respect even from the quarrelsome Shivkashi. Govardhanram compares Lalita to Gunasundari—the ideal and perfect embodiment of consumption created in *Sarasvatichandra*.[103]

But his 'heaven' does not last long. The familiar discord re-enters their lives. Govardhanram records instances of conflict between Lalita and Shivkashi, and Lalita and his brother's wife. He records, with some satisfaction, his own efforts to be an 'impartial judge' in these

[98] Ibid., 62–63.

[99] Ibid., 184–85.

[100] Ibid., 26.

[101] Ibid.

[102] Ibid.

[103] Ibid.

conflicts and reflects on 'Family misunderstandings and the way to remove them'.[104] As the conflicts and discord become deeper, he is forced to re-evaluate Lalita's morals and virtues and is ruthless in his condemnation: 'My wife is inadequate to be my heroine, alas, she falls far too short of my Gunasundari'.[105] Lalita's failure to continuously lead a life of consumption forced Govardhanram to grapple with a more fundamental question of how to successfully 'raise' our women. He also reflects on his own failure to do so.

> Are our women to be raised? How? Take a particular woman, and see, how? ... I have tried ... with my mother, my wife ... The result of my labours has been that both mother and wife have turned into discontented imperfect machines—square pegs in round holes—my mother the peg and my wife the hole![106]

Even this clear admission of failure does not introduce any element of doubt regarding his mission of cultivating minds and tempering the souls of his countrymen. Instead, quite characteristically, he sees in this failure a new raison d' etre for his endeavours: '99 out of 100 individuals will give up without thinking of the society,' he says, but 'my crucifixion in my own family must direct me to rise from this grave and try to relieve my countrymen from the troubles from which I could not relieve myself. *The next generation must always benefit by the adversities of its predecessors*'.[107]

Govardhanram was unwavering in his resolve to cultivate the minds of others, but by 1892 Lalita was not prepared to lead a life of continuous self-negation. Lalita becomes a victim of many physical and mental ailments: 'Mrs. has been suffering from premonitory symptoms of consumption ... she is doomed'.[108] As her physical condition further deteriorated, her mental health also suffered. She became a patient

[104] Ibid., 113–15.
[105] Ibid., 200.
[106] Ibid., 236–37.
[107] Ibid.; emphasis added.
[108] Ibid., 162.

of 'Monomania' and was admitted to a sanatorium at Sion.[109] Lalita's illness forced Govardhanram to examine the cause of her hysteria, which he does with clinical detachment, as is evident from his jottings in *Scrap Book* I:

> *Cure for wife's hysteria:*
> 1. Cause of hysteria: *Prolonged* and *compulsory* abstinence from natural tendencies and sentiments and sickness and agitations of soul and frequent irritations, etc., etc., caused by a sense of enduring injustice and ill-treatment, etc.
> 2. *Result*: Bodily hysteria, and abnormal and incessant irritability and pain of mind, and melancholia and hypochondria, etc.
> 3. *Remedy applied*: A general abstinence on my part from contradicting her and allowing free scope of her *will* and *frenzies* ... and showing sympathy for her real and imaginary miseries ...
> 4. *Shortcomings in the remedy*: I sometimes lose patience and temper, and sometimes fail to study her mind and mood.[110]

Despite care and medical treatment, Lalita's condition progressively worsened and she was faced with imminent death. 'Poor Lalita! Your life is hanging upon a most apparent uncertainty. Most people affected as you are die after lingering pains.'[111] The possibility of Lalita's death compels Govardhanram to articulate his own guilt: 'Poor beloved Lalita, sweet sharer of my cares, brave bearer of the heavy burdens that I have placed on thy frail personality, in this way am I bound to witness thy pangs and smoldering ...'[112] The Great Will willed otherwise, and Lalita survived. But hereafter, Govardhanram gave up his efforts to cultivate Lalita. After her illness, Lalita acquired the self-confidence to rebel against the regimentation imposed by Govardhanram. He indicates that she would frequently taunt him:

[109] Ibid., 166–68.

[110] Ibid., 182; emphases in the original.

[111] Ibid., 166.

[112] Ibid., 163–64.

> You taught me from childhood to love and serve your people; how do you ask at this stage and age, to be indifferent to their opinions and remarks, and their wounded feelings, simply on the ground that you agree with me in thinking they are mistaken? Why should they mistake? How can I change my nature now? My only way to bliss is to see them love me whatever the sacrifice.[113]

Govardhanram's philosophy had the resources to contain such rebellions. Centred as it was in the ideal of continuous self-negation, without an accompanying awareness of this sacrifice, his philosophy made Govardhanram respond to Lalita's questions in a characteristic manner: 'If she did not feel the sacrifice, she should be right'.[114]

Govardhanram may have been able to respond philosophically to Lalita's taunts but Lalita's life, her 'failure' to be the embodiment of 'consumption', her illness—hysteria which pushed her to the margins of insanity—posed fundamental questions to Govardhanram's philosophy of consumption and his declared mission to cultivate the minds and souls of his countrymen. Neither Govardhanram nor his philosophy had a creative response to this. His only response was silence. After his self-chosen retirement and final shift to Nadiad from Bombay to complete his novel and dedicate himself fully to contemplate the fate of his country and countrymen, there are no references either to Lalita's consumptive lungs, her mental illness, or her being the 'Family's Angel'. When Lalita entered Govardhanram's life, she was around twelve years old. She had received her primary *sanskara* [traditional mores and values]—for Govardhanram, 'ill-breeding'—from her natal home. And as Lalita herself so accurately posed the question: 'Is it possible to divert the branches of the tree at the fag end of their growth without breaking them?'[115]

[113] Ibid., 224.

[114] Ibid.

[115] Ibid.

VIII

In 1881 Lalita gave birth to their first child—daughter Lilavati. In 1885, Govardhanram started writing *Sarasvatichandra,* at the same time as Lilavati's education began. He assumed complete control of her education and upbringing. In Govardhanram's project neither chance nor *lila* had any play. Each action was to be based on proper study and intense reflection. This 'obsessive concern for clarity' is also reflected in the detailed curriculum that he worked out for Lilavati's education. Govardhanram believed that the sanskara of any individual is the sum total of the accumulated sanskara of her/his *swagotra,* the sanskara imparted at the natal home and the individual's own philosophy of life. Govardhanram did not have any control over Lilavati's accumulated sanskara, but he was determined and duty-bound to impart all those values to her which formed the core of his own philosophy.

Govardhanram believed that keeping girls completely unlettered was both a sin and a curse. His wisdom told him that education without a clear aim could be dangerous, especially for girls. To arrive at a decision regarding Lilavati's education he formulated a guiding principle: 'The decision must be made after considering the in-law's house, mental capacities of the girl and her future prospects'.[116] He defined, specifically for girls, the role of education: 'In the dark wintry night that this world is, there is no protection, support and light against the piercing blizzards comparable to good knowledge, to guide the helpless girls on the righteous path and give them warmth and solace'.[117]

Lilavati was admitted to a girl's school in Zaverbaug, Bombay, at the age of three. But Govardhanram soon realised the narrow vision of such institutions. After a few months he took his daughter out of the school, and 'keeping in mind her age, sex and body, appropriate

[116] Govardhanram Madhavram Tripathi, *Lilavati Jivankala,* 4th ed. (Bombay: N. M. Tripathi and Co., 1905, 1961), 57–58.

[117] Ibid.

facilities were created at home for her play and enjoyment'.[118] Lilavati was never to go to a school after this. This brief stay at a girls' school was to be her only excursion to the world outside—before marriage—without the ever present gaze of her father.

Govardhanram was seized by a sense of urgency about Lilavati's education, which he wanted completed before she was married and sent to live with her husband, as he firmly believed that there were too many obstacles in the path of education once a girl starts living with her husband.

Initially, Lilavati was given basic literacy in Gujarati. Govardhanram was conscious of the fact that his child was destined to live through the 'drama of transition' and hence, that she must be systematically exposed to both traditional Indian wisdom and knowledge systems as well as Western education. A private tutor was hired to teach Lilavati basic Sanskrit and English. She was taught Professor Bhandarkar's *Sanskritmargopadesika* and the English 'First Book'. Once she had acquired basic knowledge of Sanskrit, Govardhanram appointed Shastri Jivram Lallubhai (later Professor of Sanskrit, Elphinstone College, Bombay) to educate her in Sanskrit literature and the *shastras*. Before giving him the responsibility of his daughter's education, Govardhanram reminded Shastri of his obligations and the goals of knowledge.

> Shastriji, Lilavati is destined to live in a foreign environment. Neither I nor her mother will be able to guide her in good and bad times. Moreover, how are we—worldly beings—to provide her with wisdom? So, if you give her knowledge, give that type of Knowledge which will be a good friend of her intellect and constantly guide her, wherever she may be, on the right path.[119]

They decided to combine the knowledge of literature with that of the shastras because, 'Literature is useful in invoking and tempering higher desires and *rasas* of life while, development of the frail intellect requires

[118] Ibid., 61.

[119] Ibid., 4. For details of Lilavati's education, see 57–58.

the support of the *shastras*'.[120] Lilavati was too young to be exposed to *shringara* [an aesthetic of beauty pertaining to love]; hence, together they selected those parts of the texts which did not have shringara as the dominant *rasa* [aesthetic; flavour]. Shastriji taught her Bhartrhari's *Niti Sataka*, Aryashrenishvara's *Chandakaushik* and the fourth part of the *Shakuntal*. While she studied the *Savitri Natak* on her own, at a later stage she was allowed to study other parts of *Shakuntal* herself. Of the shastras, Lilavati was taught *Laghutark Kaumudi*, *Ishavasya* and *Ken Upanishad*, *Bhagvad Gita* and *Panchikaran*. As Lilavati went deeper into the Sanskrit tradition, she became disinterested in English education. Govardhanram allowed her to discontinue her English studies. In order to make sure she did not remain completely ignorant of Western life, she was given Karsandas Mulji's *Travels in England* (in Gujarati). To familiarise her with societal issues, she was made to read a daily, *Gujarati*, and some other journals. Through such complete education, 'the emotional and intellectual core' of Lilavati's life was formed.[121]

Govardhanram was aware that the prevailing social consciousness was inhospitable for a girl who was learned but did not have any housekeeping skills. Therefore, along with the training of her mind she was initiated into the intricacies of household work.

> In this training her mother was made her teacher. It is always desirable that a mother should initiate a daughter in this work because this training demands love and delicate tutoring while, at the same time, the teacher should have the right to punish. There is no other person who inspires the same level of confidence in a child as compared to her mother.[122]

From a tender age Lilavati was given the responsibility of cooking for the entire joint family of twelve or thirteen members. Lalita and other women of the house were given strict instructions not to interfere

[120] Ibid., 65.

[121] Ibid., 66.

[122] Ibid., 62.

in her work. Lilavati's mornings were spent doing the household work while the rest of the day was devoted to studies. Lilavati's education was comprehensive. No area was left untouched. So total was Govardhanram's involvement with Lilavati that he neglected his two other daughters, Jayanti and Jasu, and also his son Ramaniyaram's education and upbringing. In later years, he would often lament that in his own preoccupation with his literary and professional activities and total involvement with Lilavati, he had neglected his other children. Govardhanram notes that even Lilavati had noticed the wide gulf which separated her from her brother and sisters. She even questioned her father on this, and his meek defense left her unsatisfied.[123]

Lilavati was engaged to marry at the age of three or four. While choosing a husband for her, Govardhanram went against the established norm of his caste of choosing a family from his own native town Nadiad. She was engaged to Himatbhai, third son of Manilal Gangashankar of Petlad. Govardhanram's family was against Lilavati's betrothal to an impoverished and indebted family. But Govardhanram was uncompromising and argued that even his own family was indebted at the time of his marriage to Lalita, but that her parents had posed complete faith in their ability to overcome the crisis. He argued that they had no right to reject Himatbhai's family on grounds of indebtedness.[124] Lilavati's marriage to Himatbhai took place in 1891 when she was twelve years old. Her marriage at this tender age irked Govardhanram, but he eventually decided to go ahead with it, reasoning that her happiness had to be sought within the existing social structure, and that marriage was necessary to achieve that.[125]

[123] Ibid., 50. One incident captures this divide. Once while he was going to Bombay from Nadiad, Jayanti requested her father to get for her a book on religious and ritual observances, *Somvar Ni Katha*. After she left the room, Govardhanram expressed his sorrow and his sense of failure to his friend and relative, Chandrashankar Pandya. 'I could not educate this poor girl and therefore she has to ask for books like *Somvar Ni Katha*, otherwise like Lilavati she would have demanded excellent books.' Pandya, *Sriyut Govardhanram*, 207–08.

[124] Tripathi, *Lilavati Jivankala*, 16–17.

[125] Pandya, Bakshi and Pandya, *Scrap Book* I, 89.

Lilavati's education continued even after she was sent to live with her in-laws. Both Govardhanram and Lalita wrote her frequent letters, in which they counselled her in *grihinidharma*. In one such letter, Lalita wrote:

> You should not differentiate between the natal home and the house of your in-laws ... As long as you differentiate between the two families you shall never be happy. Therefore, it is your duty to consider them as your own and worship them like Gods. You once asked me, who was virtuous? Virtuous is one who considers the in-laws' house as her natal home and who treats all members—whether young or old—with utmost respect.[126]

Father Govardhanram urged her to follow the ideal and noble path of Gunasundari. 'Gunasundari was surrounded by all types of people and she made all of them her own through her *niti* and cleverness. Keep her in mind and follow her example. Notwithstanding the character of others we should always be good and virtuous because ultimately *Dharma* always emerges victorious.'[127] Reminding her of the education and wisdom he had imparted to her, he says: 'Make your mind so strong with the help of your knowledge that the unhappiness of this world does not generate any remorse in you.'[128]

Lilavati made this philosophy of life integral to her existence. She followed each tenet as the truth itself. Govardhanram lists many examples—and not without great satisfaction and some degree of pride—to prove that Lilavati had been worthy of all the knowledge he had given her and that she had completely internalised this knowledge and the principles of 'consumption'. Some rumours regarding her ill health and unhappiness prompted Govardhanram to write a rather concerned letter to her. In reply, Lilavati reminded her father of his swadharma, suggesting that it was his dharma not to be concerned about the wellbeing of a married daughter living with her parents-in-law. She quoted a verse from Govardhanram's own poem *Snehmudra*

126 Tripathi, *Lilavati Jivankala*, 6.

127 Ibid., 10.

128 Ibid., 11.

to remind him that when a bird leaves its nest, it flies on its own. Similarly, a girl leaves her father after marriage and is on her own. She further reminded him of a verse in *Shakuntal* in which Rishi Kanva says that a girl is another's property and the father is relieved by returning her to her husband,[129] prompting Govardhanram to observe: 'My sweet child admonished me in my own words and pointed the way to my happiness.'[130] By reminding her father of his swadharma, Lilavati showed that she had indeed internalised her education. Govardhanram notes many instances to reinforce that Lilavati lived her life in accordance with the two basic tenets of the philosophy of consumption: *yajmandharma* and *manojnadharma*.[131] His success in creating an embodiment of the principles of consumptive virtue through Lilavati was complete.

A writer can bring his literary creations to an ideal end, but life is rarely so kind. Lilavati lived in Junagadh, which suffered a series of epidemics. Her parents repeatedly asked her to come back to Nadiad. But Lilavati refused to leave her in-laws' house until she had nursed every member of the family to health. When Lilavati finally reached Nadiad, it was too late. She had in fact 'consumed' herself through self-inflicted privation; she was diagnosed as suffering from the 'disease of consumption', tuberculosis. She refused to blame anyone or even her fate in the face of imminent death. Reassuring her mother that she had fulfilled her grihinidharma, Lilavati said:

> Mother, in those days of fever epidemic there were only two possible outcomes. If I had pampered and loved myself and not cared to nurse others, someone else would have lost life. But I

[129] Ibid., 4.

[130] Pandya, Bakshi and Pandya, *Scrap Book* II, 230.

[131] Govardhanram defined virtue as consumption of the self in order to feed the world, while vice entailed feeding upon the flesh of the world. The dharma of the virtuous is to be a *yajman*, while those who feed on others are *atithi*. He imagined his ideal virtuous individual to be a follower of *yajmandharma*. The other quality of the virtuous is to know even the unarticulated feelings and desires of others and conduct their lives accordingly; he calls this *manojnadharma*. He attributed these qualities to the sadhvis of Sundargiri in *Sarasvatichandra*.

> did not do so, and I do not care what fate awaits me now. Either I could have saved my life or someone else's life, and it is desirable that I lose my life.[132]

Lilavati, the embodiment of consumption, sacrificed her life. Govardhanram wrote: 'Lilavati! By following the righteous path of *Dharma* as suggested by your parents, you sought, like Nachiketa, death. And death shall give you your fulfillment'.[133] Lilavati died at the age of twenty-one, on 8 January 1902. It is perhaps not a coincidence that the two projects which had taken complete hold of Govardhanram's life and being ended almost simultaneously. He completed the fourth and final part of *Sarasvatichandra* and it was published in 1901.

Govardhanram did one final act of duty towards the sacred memory of Lilavati and his country. He wrote her biography, *Lilavati Jivankala*. Even this final act was done not to glorify her memory, but to place before society an ideal life. 'I am not writing this book to glorify you. But I feel that your life, your philosophy and your actions have a message for the society. You are the real author of this work.'[134]

One question must be asked: Who or what was responsible for Lilavati's tragic and untimely death? Father Govardhanram, who assumed complete control of her existence and tried to create a real embodiment of his philosophy at the cost of her life? Or was it his philosophy which demanded a negation of the 'self'? Or should we hold Lilavati's husband and his parents responsible? Or was it perhaps the Great Will? *Lilavati Jivankala* does not provide any answers. We must turn to Govardhanram's *Scrap Books* to understand his real emotions. Initially, Govardhanram is tempted to attribute her pain and suffering to the desire of the Great Will.

> My best, Sweetest, meekest, wisest and most patient child, who has done nothing in this life to deserve this situation, a situation which can only be accounted for by a speculative desire of

132 Tripathi, *Lilavati Jivankala*, 28.

133 Ibid., 29.

134 Ibid., 3.

> Providence to kill her, or to test or toughen the 'Philosophy' of which alone her education and wealth consists.[135]

This attribution to the Great Will was only temporary. He feels that neither Lilavati's husband nor her parents-in-law deserved to have such a noble soul like Lilavati in their house. Emotions which are restrained in *Lilavati Jivankala* find free expression in *Scrap Book* II, where there are repeated references to the ill-treatment, agony and prolonged suffering that she was subjected to by her parents-in-law.

> Her services were not only accepted without the slightest effort at limiting her struggle to serve them, but she was taunted for her groans and complaints, which she could not have made except in extremities. Her complaints were belittled, she was allowed to pass latest hours of a coldest winter on a damp ground floor, working to do them superfluous service without being relieved. And when she had fever and shiverings and was in need of warm blankets to cover her, nobody looked to these things. She lay so, listening to talks with hard words about her making too much of her body.[136]

Govardhanram does not see any escape from this situation. If she were to live, she will have to go back to her husband. Only death can save his daughter from this misery, he feels, and he secretly desires her death.

> Not being able to see how the girl can be happy living with such people as those at her husband's, I have never been able to persuade myself to offer a single prayer for her life, and all that I could do in my affection, which cannot bear the idea of her death, has been to request the Great Will to do what is best for her welfare, and for his inscrutable objects, or to make her live, *provided* she is destined to be happy by living.[137]

Blaming others may have given temporary solace to Govardhanram the father, but the thinker in him is not convinced. He knows that the

[135] Pandya, Bakshi and Pandya, *Scrap Book* II, 191.

[136] Ibid., 224.

[137] Ibid., 213; emphasis in the original.

final decision regarding Lilavati's marriage was his, and that he had gone against both the norms of his community and express wishes of his family while taking this decision. He gives a long, agonising justification for his action.[138] Such post-facto wisdom does not however lessen his burden. His search for the truth finally leads him to the realisation: 'I am responsible'.[139] The realisation invokes in him a strong feeling of having sinned: 'I have to thank myself for my having committed this inexplicable sin against my poor child, by choosing for her an unsuitable family'.[140] With her death, this feeling of having sinned becomes magnified and possesses him.

> At 5.30 p.m. yesterday my poor Lilavati died after a stainless, spotless life of suffering. She was a martyr to the cause of our Hindu Social System, to her father's exercise of his power of disposing of her in early marriage ... and to the services she rendered to her mother-in-law and her father-in-law.[141]

Govardhanram's expiation and atonement can now lie only in 'realising my faults and weakness, and my sins against her life and merits'.[142] He also concludes that 'her soul and holiness were superior to *mine* and to that of every other person I see about me'.[143] Only one idea gives him solace: 'I can only feel proud to have had a child like this during my worldly sojourn, rewarded at the idea that I had the privilege of looking after the education and elevation of so aspiring a soul'.[144] His search for atonement leads him to examine the education and 'elevation' of her soul. 'In Lilavati's life, I and her mother always taught her the way to do her duty to her husband and his family, and to seek

[138] Ibid., 223.

[139] Ibid., 191.

[140] Ibid., 216.

[141] Ibid., 220.

[142] Ibid., 228.

[143] Ibid.; emphasis in the original.

[144] Ibid., 228.

reward and consolation in the idea of Duty. She was quite equal to her task and her body paid for it.'[145] He continues,

> and with the philosophy and sweetness that her education and innate powers were able to develop in her, her life became one of martyrdom, among other things, to her own very high sense of duty, in which point she outdistanced not only me and mine but all the characters that I have been able to spin out in my books.[146]

In the opening lines of *Sanskarkala-Shodashi*, a long poem on Lilavati, Govardhanram laments: 'I had conceived a Gunasundari in my head. In real life I fathered you, a better version of Gunasundari. You did penance like Gunasundari but unlike her, did not enjoy the fruit thereof. I produced a thesis, you sacrificed your life to prove it right!'[147] Aware that it was his education and his philosophy which was the cause of Lilavati's pain, suffering and ultimately, death, Govardhanram is forced to re-evaluate his project of cultivating minds and elevating souls.

> My daughter Lilavati suffered because of high virtues and would have fared better if she had not got the virtues! Is it right then to teach these virtues to our daughters? So many people tell my wife that she has killed Lilavati by making her virtuous; the charge comes home more to me. Is a parent right in educating his children in this way at their cost?[148]

He questions the idea of virtue itself. But he is not ready to give up either his project or his faith in the essential goodness and desirability of virtue. For one last time, he reasserts the validity of his principles of consumption: 'This question must be answered in *affirmative* for

[145] Ibid., 224.

[146] Govardhanram Tripathi to Janmanshankar Buch, in *Lilavati Jivankala*, 131.

[147] Govardhanram Madhavram Tripathi, 'Sanskarkala-Shodashi' in *Lilavati Jivankala*, 4th ed. (Bombay: N. M. Tripathi and Co., 1905, 1961), 133–55. The translated verse is from Sonal Shukla, 'Govardhanram's Women', *Economic and Political Weekly*, WS 65, 31 October 1987.

[148] Pandya, Bakshi and Pandya, *Scrap Book* II, 290–91.

people like *myself*; my children, like their father and mother, have been educated in virtue, *irrespective of its consequences*.'[149]

The power of his vision did not allow Govardhanram to abandon his project, but with Lilavati's death, his creative self died. He lived his final years lonely and miserable, seeking solace and strength from Lilavati's memory.

> No misery that will reach me now can be higher or more excruciating than that borne by my Lilavati, and I can do no better reverence to her sacred memory than by walking in her gentle and yet, firm, steady, virtuous and heroic footsteps in facing any circumstances that may befall me. [May] Her sweet and lofty virtues be my divine beacon-light in my mundane struggles henceforth! May her example inspire my soul and draw me closer unto hers wherever and whatsoever she now may be![150]

He died on 4 January 1907 after a long illness.

IX

While commenting on the high point that Gujarati poetry had achieved during the seventeenth century through Akho, Premanand and Samal, Govardhanram observed that the vocation of a writer is to expand the human nature by placing before the people 'purer and higher ideals of social life' in a 'beautiful and ennobling' manner. Akho, Premanand and Samal could achieve this only because they were 'above the society in which they live'.[151]

Govardhanram Tripathi's own mission as a writer, of influencing and improving contemporary society, was fulfilled, perhaps beyond his expectations, through *Sarasvatichandra*. 'The educated youth of Gujarat lived in the dreamland of Sarasvatichandra, Kumud and

149 Ibid.; emphases in the original.

150 Pandya, Bakshi and Pandya, *Scrap Book* II, 256.

151 Govardhanram Madhavram Tripathi, *Classical Poets of Gujarat and Their Influence on Society and Morals*, 3rd ed. (Bombay: Forbes Gujarati Sabha, 1894, 1958), 33–34.

Kusum ... No other book of fiction has made so powerful an impact on its contemporaries as *Sarasvatichandra* ...'[152] For over a hundred years, *Sarasvatichandra* has remained the canonical text of Gujarati literature; perhaps no other work of fiction has been able to match its range of concerns or popularity. 'No other event, before the arrival of Gandhi, had so captured the imagination of the society and had succeeded in moulding the minds of the people on the path of moral, civilised conduct as this epic novel.'[153]

Govardhanram's attempt was to create a new moral universe for the emerging middle class. As mediators of India's colonial encounter, this emerging class experienced deep uncertainties about the old order and felt ambivalent insecurities about new modes of thought, conduct, morality, faith, and culture, creating permanent disjunctions in their public and personal lives. Largely due to industrialisation, the distance between the public and domestic spheres increased, as people came in contact with new ideas and ideologies. This group was in search for new models of thought and conduct which would provide some sense of permanency in times of transition.

Govardhanram provided them with a new ideal through his 'graduate hero'. Sonal Shukla has beautifully captured the essence of this new ideal, which went on to become a dominant thematic category for Gujarat literature.

> He has done extremely well in his studies. He is sensitive and generous but also somewhat haughty and aloof. He has a mission, but no job. He usually belongs to a wealthy family, but does not mind living in poverty, although towards the end he is usually comfortably placed all over again. The novelist and his heroine admire this greatly. Sarasvatichandra is the first modern Gujarati hero of this type.[154]

[152] Mansukhlal Jhaveri, *History of Gujarati Literature* (New Delhi: Sahitya Akademi, 1978), 98.

[153] Vishnuprasad R. Trivedi, *Govardhanram: Chintak Ne Sarjak* (Bombay: N. M. Tripathi and Co., 1962), 95.

[154] Shukla, 'Govardhanram's Women', WS 63.

This acute awareness of having to provide anchors introduced caution in Govardhanram's enterprise. He is willing to question the assumptions and normative principles underlying social and political institutions; he is also willing to reject their moral superiority in some cases. Nevertheless, he does not consider it desirable to posit options which might fundamentally alter the old order and introduce new anxieties. This caution is quite evident in his attitudes towards widow remarriage. This overwhelming desire to provide anchors to society led him to the creation of a new idealised woman—the 'Domestic Angel'.[155] Govardhanram's personal life and the novel reflect a remarkable engagement with women and femininity. For a major part of his life he tried to 'educate' and 'raise' the virtues of his wife, Lalita. So complete and intense was his identification with his daughter Lilavati that he neglected his only male child Ramaniyaram. The novel *Sarasvatichandra* is anchored in the characters of women that he created—Gunasundari, Kumud and Kusum. What could be the reason for his intense encounter with womanhood?

For Govardhanram, tradition was to be 'the bedrock of social reconstruction through much of this transitional phase, when two civilisations confronted each other'.[156] In times of transition, women and womanhood became ideal embodiments of traditional virtues. Govardhanram introduced to Gujarat the Victorian ideal of the 'naturally virtuous woman'. Govardhanram established the moral and cultural superiority of women over men. For many, awareness of the colonial encounter and its social and cultural implications provoked deep insecurities regarding their own traditions and belief systems. In Govardhanram's moral vision, it was through women that harmony and virtue, in both family and society, were sought to be achieved. Women became the sites where the conflict between tradition and modernity was being played out. Govardhanram's philosophy of consumption also placed additional burden on women. Consumption with its emphasis on continuous self-denial, without an accompanying

[155] Ibid., WS 65–67.

[156] Chandra, *The Oppressive Present*, 82.

awareness of sacrifice, and valorisation of pain and humiliation as an ideal to be sought to further one's consumption, crushed womanhood.

Govardhanram Tripathi sought to create such an ideal woman in his life, as in his fiction. When his 'domestic angel'—his wife Lalita—became hysterical under his regimentation and ultimately gathered the courage to question his ideals, he made another attempt through his daughter Lilavati. Govardhanram's vision demanded, and received, heavy sacrifices from women. Gunasundari paid through her consumption, Kumud by submitting her desires to a higher ideal of ascetic renunciation, Lalita, through her hysteria, and Lilavati paid with her life. Little did he realise that it is impossible to create one ideal woman through two lives and one fiction.

Tridip Suhrud

Preface I[†]

With the third volume this narrative enters upon a different phase of its career. It still continues to be a mosaic or even blending of the actual and the ideal aspects of our life in these days, but the latter, henceforth, begin to acquire a distinct predominance over the former. It is eleven years since the first volume was published, and the progress of the reading classes during the interval has been equal to the writer's aspiration to interest them in the principal problems of the day.

This and the succeeding volume will bring this tale to a close. The labours of the writer will be sufficiently rewarded if this book will have stimulated, among the various classes of our society, an abiding interest in some of the great questions that make the young and the old in the country thrill with interchanging hopes and fears in all the varied matters which make up our life, and if it can enable them to follow with patience the solution which society is evolving upwards along a slow but sure gradient in relation to each of these pressing questions.

Each one of these problems is complicated and difficult, and the writer of a novel cannot be expected to do it the justice which a scientific or philosophical essayist can struggle for. An artist—and a novelist is no more—can only hope to give that simplicity to problems which the passive reader craves for, to bring out for his gaze the fascinations of

[†] Translator's note: This is the original 'English Preface' to the 1898 edition of *Sarasvatichandra*, Part III.

their lights and shades so as to recreate and not tax his eyes, and yet to hope that, humble as this province of the writer is, he may enable the reader to rise a stage higher than where he was. At the same time it is no object of the writer to do so with that partisan spirit which may fairly find room in polemical essays where he who has formed his convictions must strive to force them upon the erring world. To the artist the world is not so much a mass of errors as a prospect of beauty, even where it errs; and he can simply propose to draw upon the resources of his own soul to enlarge the vistas which he is picturing, only with a view to add to the beauty, and not to the logic of his work. As the Athenian believed, his beauty carries a silent logic more potent than reason and her quarrelsome ways.

What these problems are is a matter best left to the text itself. In the preface one can only attempt to introduce. Well, we are at present undergoing strange transition in matters domestic, social, religious, political and, what not? What with the laden atmosphere of our domestic difficulties, what with the currents of our social ideals and forces, what with the many-tongued voices of the religions which a multiform and party-coloured nation is singing into our ears, what with the constant upheavals of new and jarring worlds of political entities and nonentities rising within one's view whether he locates himself in one of the natives states or in any place in British India, one, standing in the midst of all this, is simply tempted to wish, like Cowper, "for a lodge in some vast wilderness," or for a transmigration back into the body of some quiet and retired Rishi of antiquity.

This universal jar and noise casts a gloomy shadow over many a wistful eye and disconcerts many a well-built hope. We shall leave it to other fields of learning to settle with conviction whether the world in India will survive this deluge of conflict or not, and we may be sure that, even in discussing that, men will differ and fall to quarrelling. The only place where we may safely look for a peaceful picture in spite of all transient facts is art and poetry. In the several volumes of this tale, the landing-places of our relief are sought to be pictured. We, no doubt, start even here with the jar and noise that surrounds us, and we hope to travel a good deal in the midst of these regions. But Progress and

Harmony at home, in society, in religion, and with Government, both in and outside British India peer overhead in the long run in spite of all this bewildering confusion: at least that is the postulate fundamental to our perspective. To look at these two cherubs of beauty and hope as they look at us is at least a vision of glory and happiness; and what is vision to-day may be reality to-morrow.

True it is that the realisation of this vision of the future taxes our patience, and we may never live to see it. Well may one grumble with the poet,

When will the hundred summers die,
And thought and time be born again,
And newer knowledge, drawing nigh,
Bring truth that sways the soul of men?
Here all things in their place remain,
As all were ordered, ages since.
Come, Care and Pleasure, Hope and Pain,
And bring the fated fairy prince.

But after all we may also have the privilege of seeing with him

Faint shadows, vapours lightly curl'd
Faint murmurs from the meadows come,
Like hints and echoes of the world
To spirits folded in the womb.‡

The vision is not altogether a dream. Transient hours will come and go. But the students of permanent elements and constant factors will be able to trace the birth and growth of an inward homogeneity in what is heterogeneous in the inception, and to hail the slow but sure triumph of Progress on lines which may not satisfy either theoretical, revolutionary and precipitate visionaries and reformers, or those who on the other hand wish to give an eternal rigidity to the to-day, whether of belief or of power and to dam out the influx of a sure and different to-morrow; for the lines of that Progress will certainly be such *gradual and harmonised resultants* of numerous currents of life

‡ Author's note: 'The Sleeping Palace', *The Sleeping Beauty*, Alfred Tennyson.

and facts as are still not dreamt of in our Horatio's philosophy. Such will be the *modus operandi* of the elements that do and shall vivify individuals, societies and governments with new forms of life, and our visions may be realised according to the extent that orthodoxy and reform, visionaries and practical people, Indians and Englishmen, and even Government and states and subjects—all on Indian soil—must yield to this irresistible process of reciprocal assimilation, at least as an inevitable duty in the working of the much talked about unity of all. And our vision will be able to resist yielding to this process in this way and to this end, more or less, sooner or later.

Dear reader, more were better left to the text.

Bombay, 1898 G. M. T.

Preface II[†]

Human destiny bears witness to the vicissitudes of riches and hardships; similarly, countries and human collectivities are also subject to the vagaries of fate. The adversities of many hues that have befallen this country are evident to all and beg no repetition. But these sufferings had caught the printing presses of Bombay in their grip. This piece of writing which was sent to the printing press a long time ago is being placed in the hands of readers only today. This novel, having passed through many tribulations, has demanded patience from its readers; it is quite natural to expect that such patience would be accorded to other subjects pertaining to the novel.

After publication of the third part, the plan is to write only one more part: the fourth part. If God has willed that the writer should have life till such time, the human desire is to bring this plan to fruition. I pray to God that this desire may be fulfilled and that all the readers live long to see its conclusion. The main inspiration behind this novel and the dear sister of the author has not lived long enough to see the novel end. Although this desire has remained unfulfilled, the author out of brotherly love has been compelled by fate to write an elegy for her. Dear reader, at a moment such as this, may the blessings that are part of the prayer be showered upon you.

[†]Translator's note: This is a translation of the original Gujarati preface to the 1898 edition of *Sarasvatichandra*, Part III.

It is intended to conclude this novel in the fourth part. The intention for writing this novel was briefly touched upon in the preface to the first part. The preface to the present volume presents one more opportunity to explicate it.

The light of the great and able writers of Sanskrit and English are beneficial to the people of this country in myriad ways. But the modern person may not find every resolution in this light. Because, just as there are many differences in thought and conduct between the English and the natives, similarly there are many differences between the thought and conduct prevalent in the Sanskrit period and our present day; and it is not possible for everyone to filter out the differences and savour the taste of the essence of that thought. A special purpose of this novel is to paint an imaginary picture of our future generations drawn from the colours of the contemporary—which is the condition of our people, our country, our times, our thoughts and conduct, and our trials and tribulations. Human beings cannot determine that the future would be as it is imagined. This picture is as imaginary as the calculations of future loss and gain made by merchants. It is the duty of the learned readers to discern the movement from one picture to another, to see the transformations therein and to reflect upon their purity and impurity. The intention of these pictures in words is to mix up and combine all the images, considering them to be transient, to cast their collective reflection in an ideal conception and to eventually draw up the horoscope of the generations to come.

In this endeavour, a purpose subsidiary to the imaginary construct being presented here, but otherwise principal, is to provide the support of high ideals, appropriate to the place and times, to the hearts of Arya men and women. What is the ground from which these high ideals—sometimes awash in and sometimes inspired by joys and sorrows of many hues—could emanate? Could they emerge from the exertions of each family, unique and yet shared by all those caught in the web of family relationships, known to all and yet kept secret from each other. The lonely hearts of individuals big and small suffering solitary mental agonies, the surging aspirations of persons desirous—albeit devoid of means—of self-improvement and the welfare of others, and natives states suffering from internal decay are also a source. High ideals could emerge from the constraining presence of the English power, which though stifling is capable of nurturing the golden egg of new life (with native princes, ministers, merchants, peasants, artisans representing various limbs of the body), and from the birthing pains of the new birth caused by the coming together of the old and the new. The seemingly disparate and contradictory amalgam of the pure and ancient knowledge of the land of the Aryas and the new and impulsive knowledge of Europe come together tumultuously like the Ganga and the Yamuna, re-shaping the forms of thought and conduct that are germane to this land, characterised by the desire to preserve and protect social norms and Western conduct arising out of foreign influences and the dazzle of the new age that aspires to foster individual freedom—in all these domains the painful condition of the present age of transition is evident. There is unease and anxiety regarding the present, dread and yet infatuation for the future to emerge from the whirl of time. And yet there are rays, few but everlasting, which could be discerned, incipient in an intellectual disposition that seeks to unify dissimilar influences.

The principal objective of this novel in four parts is to paint a picture of the present transition and provide an image of the future. In this drama of transition, light has been eclipsed from all those who are infatuated and yet dismayed by it. The old and the new, the young and the old, illiterate and literate, foolish and wise, meek and powerful, uncouth and cultivated, may all minds be imbued with the emerging rays and may reason prevail where unreason holds sway, may zeal replace melancholy—this purpose is central to all other objectives of all parts that make up this novel.

The author hopes and aspires that this objective would be realised, if not in full measure then partially, with the picture that would emerge in the fourth part, *The Dream-Land of Sarasvatichandra and the Culmination*.

'For man, mind is the cause of bondage and mind is the cause of liberation.' These words in themselves are a source of joy. My dear readers, the source of all your capabilities and aspirations is also in your minds. May this story be a source of bliss to all its readers.

Vikramsamvat 1954 G. M. T.
Bombay

Elegy for a Sister

The dream was thirty-two when Yama cut it short
The foolish wind unmade what was a vale of flowers
Sister, you were loved by our parents
From me you learnt things
Entrusted to a good gardener
You grew into a virtuous creeper
You blossomed and bore fruit
But all too soon, you withered
Leaving your dear ones bereft.
Your virtues were your wealth
This world is fragrant with them
My heart is full of pride for you
You died a fortunate woman.
Kalyani, you crossed the river of death
The flood is upon us, a Dark Age dawns
You escaped, you died when the world was still joyful.
At an innocent age I saw bliss in you
You were always my touchstone
I began this novel, and the ink had not yet dried
When you captured its golden truth
The fame of my book, though little
Appeared much to you.
In admiring endorsement, you smiled
And desired to see the third part
But leaving your brother in debt
You now reside at the feet of the Lord.
I understand, dear one

Elegy for a Sister

But I cannot help mourning
As the novel progresses, your memories flood my mind
Remembering your face, my touchstone
I make this gift of words to you:
Accept this heartfelt offering your brother makes
I have consigned to flames my joys and sorrows
Into this fire I pour the grief of a sister's death
This I do with dry eyes
As a stone-hearted brother must lay wood upon his sister's pyre.

But the age of chivalry is gone, that of sophisters, economists, and calculators has succeeded; and the glory of the country is extinguished for ever. Never, never more shall we behold that generous loyalty to rank and sex, that proud submission, that dignified obedience, that subordination of the heart which kept alive, even in servitude itself, the spirit of an exalted freedom. The unbought grace of life, the cheap defence of nations, the nurse of manly sentiments and heroic enterprise, is gone! It is gone, that sensibility of principle, that chastity of honour, which felt a stain like a wound, which inspired courage whilst it mitigated ferocity, which ennobled whatever it touched, and under which vice itself lost half its evil, by losing all its grossness.

—Edmund Burke

1 Sundargiri

He who had set out to experience the world and search the divine was blessed. In the dark forest of night he had experienced the fear of death. His unconsciousness, akin to death, had made him deaf to the bloodcurdling roars of the wild beasts. The great black serpent had brought him face to face with death. But the band of ascetics had at last freed Sarasvatichandra from all fear and rescued him. Mohanpuri had carried him on his broad shoulders through the raging forest fire to safety. The ascetics lived in a monastery on Yadu Shrunga, the third highest peak of Sundargiri. The path to the peak was treacherous. The steep climb easily tired ordinary persons; after two hours of arduous journey they would reach the top, out of breath. But the ascetics climbed the peak effortlessly within an hour. Sarasvatichandra was passed on from shoulder to sturdy shoulder and carried up the mountain. The ascetics reached the monastery one hour after midnight. As they climbed, the air became cooler. Although it was the month of Chaitra in summer, Sarasvatichandra's body felt the chill. The cool, clear mountain air revived his senses and infused him with new life. His weariness abated. He climbed down from the shoulders that carried him and looked around in astonishment, trying to grasp the meaning of this strange yet beautiful dream.

Glad to see the youth revive, the sadhus at once surrounded Sarasvatichandra. Their Guru, Vishnudas, had already arrived at Yadu Shrunga. A lamp had been lit at the entrance of the monastery; Sarasvatichandra's face was aglow in its soft light. Standing beside him, Mohanpuri gently rubbed his back and anxiously asked him, 'Bhai, are you now fully conscious? Does your body feel well?'

Sarasvatichandra, still uncertain if this was a dream or reality, asked him several questions in response, 'Who are you? What place is this? How did I come to be here? Is this a dream, or am I awake?'

Mohanpuri replied, 'Bhai, for your soul this is a dream, but for your illusory transient body this is wakefulness. You have neither gone anywhere, nor have you come. But it is we who carried your body here from the forest. In the kingdom of our Lord Krishna, all are equal. The land as far as human eyes can perceive is ruled by Maharaj Maniraj. You and we are one, not distinct, and all of us belong to the same kingdom. The land on which our feet rest is called Sundargiri. This is a monastery of Vishnudas and all of us are members of this monastery. But Bhai, do tell me, who are you?' Mohanpuri spoke in this manner to find out if the future as foretold by their Guruji would indeed come true. The other ascetics also realised this and they eagerly awaited his response.

As his senses revived, Sarasvatichandra, careworn as he was, felt extremely thirsty and hungry. The sadhu's speech jolted him into full awareness of his present circumstances and of the group of sadhus surrounding him. He replied in a language appropriate to the context. 'It is true—the darkness that surrounds us all has not yet been dispelled. You know who I am. Why then do you await my answer? To cut a long matter short, if you are an empowered member of this monastery, please give this famished body some sustenance and some place where it can rest, after which dream and wakefulness are but one.'

The ascetics were satisfied with this response. The truth of their Guruji's words both surprised and pleased them. They called out, 'Shri Krishna Paramatma ki Jai!' 'Shri Radhakrishna ki Jai!' Their faith in their Guruji's knowledge of the past, present and future was reaffirmed once more. They vied with each other to make their chosen guest comfortable. One of them brought food consecrated with basil leaf, another brought cool, pure water while the third made a bed for him on a raised platform under a neem tree. A light mattress was spread and covered by a clean, fresh sheet, free of creases. A fourth ascetic lit a small fire that dispelled the darkness and gave warmth. They wordlessly served food to their guest, and then retired to their respective places once he was asleep. Some smoked ganja, others chatted, some lay gazing at the clear night sky in silence while some others sang hymns. Finally they, too, fell asleep. Leaves rustled in the breeze. Stars twinkled in the sky. Nature was alive and awake while all else slumbered. Night reigned over all. The hours passed swiftly. It was almost four in the morning. The early risers awoke. The ascetics, like the tiger, had eyes that could see as clearly in the dark as in the light. They moved about doing their daily routine observances. Sarasvatichandra was awakened by their stealth-like movement. He remained in bed but allowed his ears to capture the soft sounds and muted voices floating around him. His ears focused on the conversation of two ascetics who slept just a few hand-spans away from him.

'Bhaiya, who is this guest of ours? From where did you bring him? And why has Guruji taken such a liking to him?'

'He was lying unconscious in the forest, from where he has been brought here. Guruji, in his state of meditation, said that this man is destined to be a mahatma, a great soul, and that one day he will bring glory to this monastery. Did you hear his responses to Mohanpuri's questions?'

Sarasvatichandra realised that it was he who was the subject of their conversation, and smiled when he heard the Guruji's prediction. He thought: This appears to be a peculiar land where predictions are made and believed. There must be something here for me to see and experience. As his ears picked up the conversation once again, his train of thoughts was halted.

'Yes, bhaiya, his intellect sparkles. What does Guruji intend for him?'

'That God alone knows. Guruji has commanded that the visitor be brought into his presence in the morning after he has completed his meditation. We have been instructed to look after the guest until then.'

'I feel that Guruji will ultimately reveal to him the mystic secret of our monastic order.'

'That would depend upon his adhikar, his capabilities. It is not easy to be in touch with the divine.'

'But surely, he must have that in him; or else there would have been no prediction.'

'Radhedas, whatever is to be, will be. Let us proceed for our daily discourse. The sun will soon rise.'

'What shall we discuss today, Viharpuri?'

'Has there been something troubling you since yesterday?'

'Yes.'

'What is it?'

'Yesterday as we were returning in the evening, we halted under a banyan tree to take rest. I was at Guruji's service. He recited a few verses. I sought explanation of their meaning. He said: "Child, not today. Meditate upon them and acquire the fitness to grasp their meaning. At present your capabilities extend only to hearing them. When you also acquire the fitness to receive their meaning, I shall discourse upon them."'

'It is true—everything depends upon one's awareness.'

'That is so. But their meaning may not be unknown to you, Viharpuri. Guruji will not bestow his gift on the undeserving; but you and I are fellow ascetics.'

'You spoke well. It is our duty to explain such things to each other. Tell me the verses.'

Radhedas thought for a while and then recited the first verse.

Gokul ma gokul chare, Gopalak Gopal;
Nandsadan Nandan thai, Madhuripu bhasat bāl.

The cows graze in Gokul, their cowherd is Gopal;
He took the form of Nand's son to slay Madhu the demon.

Viharpuri suddenly sat up and said, 'Oh! I have been taught the meaning of this verse—it is mystical! Its secret is almost magical. You are indeed fortunate that Guruji deemed you fit to hear this verse from his own lips. He must have recited some other verses as well?'

'He gave me three other verses.'

'Which ones?'

Radhedas sat up and recited:

Avani avani Madhupuri, Krishna Chandra avatār;
Shesha bhār uteri ne karat dharti uddhhār.

In Madhupuri on earth is manifest Shri Krishna incarnate;
Relieving Shesha Nag of his burden, He saved the earth.

Sarasvatichandra listened to them intently. Radhedas recited the remaining verses.

Paras sparshthi loh no thai swaroop vināsh,
Daitya hari amarata deija Sudarshan pāsh.
Pamar ma pamar dishe Gopalak Gopal,
Krishna bhakti vash bhasto bālak arthe bāl.

Just as a touch of the philosopher's stone can transform iron into gold,
To be slain by Sudarshan is to destroy the demon within and attain immortality.
In his devotion to Krishna, Gopal the cowherd appears gentle as a child.

'Guruji did not teach me any further,' said Viharpuri. 'And that is correct. Guruji has decreed that all those who have received the verses from him are permitted to consult fellow ascetics to glean their meanings. I will share with you the meaning of these magical verses. But you must not share it with anyone whom you think is yet to acquire the fitness to receive them. The teachings of the *Shastras* are of two kinds: one, those which can be understood by all and the second, those which are understood only by those initiated in the mysteries of a sect. A sword can protect, but it can also kill when wielded by one who is undeserving. Therefore it has been decreed that such sacred mysteries should be revealed only to the deserving. The sword should always be sheathed around children. The apparent meaning is called *semantic* meaning and the intended meaning is called *essential* meaning. Hence, that our Lord Krishna was the cowherd of Gokul is the apparent semantic meaning.'

'Does this mean that the semantic meaning is false?' Radhedas interjected.

'No. It is neither true nor false.'

'That is being non-committal.'

'No, it is not. Those who know the code can send a coded message through a messenger. The messenger cannot fathom the code but knows that his master has conveyed a secret message.'

'I see.'

'Now let us see, the term "go" has multiple meanings: in Sanskrit it means a cow; it also implies the senses, as well as the whole earth. Therefore, the apparent semantic meaning of *Gokul ma gokul chare* is: the cows graze in Gokul. But "Gokul" also means the entire human species that inhabits this earth. Thus, the essential hidden meaning of the stanza is that: sensory experiences abound on this earth.'

Radhedas was amazed. 'What else?'

'A "gopalak" is a keeper of cows, a cowherd. But at a deeper level, Brahma created the sensory universe, and Gopal, that is Lord Shri Krishna, rules over this world of senses—that is the mystical or metaphysical meaning of *Gopalak Gopal*.'

'Brother, this is truly miraculous!'

Viharpuri continued, 'Lord Krishna apparently manifested himself as a child in Nandji's house and slayed the demon Madhu. *Nandsadan Nandan thai* suggests that he assumed the form of a child, but that he is not a child.'

'That means that even semantic meaning is complex and what seems is in fact not.'

'That is correct. The term "Nand" is associated with Paramanand, Satchidanand: one whose abode is the entire universe. When the slayer of demons manifests himself as a child and assumes human form, he seems to be ignorant, that is, to others he seems bereft of knowledge; while in fact Gopal is knowledge Himself. This is the mystical meaning. Radhedas, do you comprehend?'

'How wonderful, Viharpuri! What profound mystical meanings are contained in Guruji's words! I will have to contemplate upon them seriously. Let us proceed.'

'Madhupuri, the abode of the demon Madhu, also refers to Mathura, or the earth. Shri Krishna was born in Mathura. Now let us consider the essential meaning. Burdened by evil, the earth is being crushed. It has become like Madhupuri, the abode of demons. Shri Krishna manifested Himself upon this earth in Mathura. What was his intention? The earth rests on the head of the great serpent Shesha. Can you decipher the meanings contained in the word "shesha"?'

Radhedas thought deeply for a few moments and replied, 'No'.

Viharpuri enthusiastically illuminated the mystery for him. 'Pay attention. This body is formed of five elements. The soul is neither tangible nor made of gross elements; it is neither subtle, nor is it the cause of anything. In this way we negate everything; what remains is shesha—this remainder is the soul. Have you been taught this?'

'Yes.'

'Just as the Shesha Nag bears the burdens of the earth, the soul or atman is also burdened by this neti neti "not this, not that" of the anatman—all that which is not the soul, is mere appearance, illusion, disguise, phantom. The Vedantis argue that this burden must be forsaken. While we the Alakhvadis—those who believe that the Creator is without form, without qualities or attributes and that creation is uncharacterised—argue that this earth itself is mere appearance and maya. But, our Lord Shri Krishna bears the burden of this earth, and so we must do likewise. What right have we to despise or reject something that Shri Krishna Himself bears? If we humans, who are also mere appearance and illusion, abrogate such rights, the earth itself would be destroyed.'

'Then what must we do?'

'That is the mystery of the Alakhvad. Dust assumes a higher form and becomes food; food becomes prana, the vital breath of life, and similarly the earth that bears us all also rises in the care of Shri Krishna and attains a higher state. Evil burdens the earth and pulls it down, which adds to the weight on Shesha Nag. But if we take the earth higher by our good and pious deeds, the burden on Shesha is reduced.'

'What do you mean?'

'We began with the illustration of dust and food. Similarly, Shri Krishna saves three kinds of illusory body. That is, he saves the soul which is crushed under the burden of earthly cares.'

Radhedas covered his ears with his palms and said, 'Bhai, this meaning is too difficult to grasp. At present, my shesha is crushed under the weight of its meaning.'

Viharpuri laughed and said, 'Fear not, even that burden shall be lightened by the grace of our Guru!' Then he solemnly added, 'It is for this reason that one needs to acquire the fitness to be initiated in the mystical meanings. The meaning will become clearer as you understand the remaining verses.'

'No!' said Radhedas, raising his hands in despair, 'I do not want to acquire the ability to comprehend them all today itself! I will ask you again tomorrow. Let me *ask* you—do not offer to explain before that. Let me first digest what has been given to me, or else I will get constipated.'

'Very well. The day is upon us. We must rise now, clean our teeth and bathe.'

'Should we wake up our guest as well?'

'Of course.'

'Brother, it is morning. Arise.' But Sarasvatichandra was sitting up before Radhedas could complete his sentence.

It was not yet five in the morning. It was the month of Chaitra when the dawn breaks early. They were on top of a mountain and the rays of the morning sun had already spread all around. It looked as if the eastern sky was donning a skirt made of light even as the night sky, clad in a garment of stars, shed its dress. Stars, witness to the passions of night, hid themselves. Even the cool mountain air was changing as the curtain of dark night was pierced and all life concealed by it came to light. Sarasvatichandra had spent the previous day and night in the forest; but when dawn broke he had found himself on this mountain. As you may recall dear reader, it was just the day before yesterday that he had witnessed the pomp and glory of Rana Bhupsinh's court in Suvarnapur. But the scenes now unfolding before his eager and astonished eyes were by far more dazzling, more glorious and even more baffling. He was surrounded by tall black mountains that stood like monstrous waves frozen in time. Even the boulders on the mountains seemed curious about this strange new visitor. Awed by the sight, Sarasvatichandra momentarily lost awareness of his immediate surroundings and of the tall, black-bodied sadhus of Sundargiri, who themselves resembled boulders. Just then, a song rose through the crisp dawn air. The monastery was some fifteen yards from where he stood.

Viharpuri said to Radhedas, 'Guruji has commenced his morning prayers. Do you hear him singing?' All ears were focused intently on the song. Vishnudas was an accomplished singer; his voice was cultivated, his singing robust and unrestrained; he sang with a tanpura. There was an idol of Yadunandan in the monastery. His prayer urged the god to rise.

I bow to Yadunandan
I bow to Thee who frees one from the cycle of birth and death
On this new dawn
I bow to Yadunandan
O' Hari, it is morning
Hari, a new dawn breaks

His voice and his fingers on the strings of the tanpura moved as one as his song rose from the very depths of his being.

It is dawn, O' Yadunandan—rise
What was concealed is now filled with light
The night is gone, the day is upon us
The day awaits You—O' Lord, arise!
The stars have set as the sun rises,
Hari, the peaks of Sundargiri rise in devotion to the Manifest
The sun pays obeisance to the sun of the Yadu family
Will my heart, too, bloom with the blossoming lotus?
This Vishnudas is powerless to comprehend
O Hari, it is now morning

Quite abruptly, Vishnudas stopped singing and his tanpura ceased to make music. Viharpuri kept his hand on Radhedas' shoulder and said, 'Guruji has entered a phase of intense meditation—he is now in samadhi.'

Radhedas exclaimed, 'What splendid powers our Guruji possesses! His singing! His asceticism! His teachings! Intellect, music, discourse, devotion, yoga, samadhi are all combined in his being—such qualities are without precedence.'

'Well spoken, Radhedas! Yes, it is indeed our good fortune that by service to such a master we seek the divine,' said Viharpuri. He turned towards Sarasvatichandra and said, 'O fortunate youth, you are a guest of this monastic order of Vishnudas. You are a recipient of his special love. We are his disciples and it is our duty, as also our right, to look after you. Hence, have no anxieties. You are in a space that is pure and pious. You seem unhappy. But by the power of the divine, by the grace of Yadunandan and by the blessings of Vishnudas, all your sorrows shall vanish. Therefore, leave all your cares behind and receive our hospitality. We shall get to know each other at leisure.'

Radhedas brought some water in a clean utensil and a neem twig for brushing the teeth and kept them on a rock for Sarasvatichandra. From this vantage point, the valley on the west far below could be seen stretching all the way to the sea. The sight of the sea brought back memories of Bombay and his father, and tears flowed from his eyes. He splashed some water on his face and eyes, but the tears flowed unabated. Viharpuri, who noticed this, said, 'Esteemed guest, leave behind your sorrows. By the grace of Shri Krishna, supreme bliss permeates Sundargiri. Your ordeal is also about to end,' and he recited an ancient Sanskrit verse:

> The white rays of the moon spread around the world like the windblown barren stalks devoid of chaff. They are split into shreds by the gentle breeze arising from the Lord's breath, which is the unfailing remedy for the three types of affliction.[1]

Sarasvatichandra had many friends from southern India in Bombay who could recite verses in Sanskrit. It was for the first time after leaving Bombay that he had the opportunity to hear the recitation of this familiar verse once again. Many pleasant memories came flooding back and took him away from the melancholy thoughts about his

[1] Translator's note: Translated from the Sanskrit for this volume by Arindam Chakrabarti. [Hereafter, except where otherwise specified, all notes are by the translator.]

father. Last night he had heard poetry in his own language, and this morning, in Sanskrit. It seemed that this place would provide him with the pleasures of both poetry and philosophical discourse, and this possibility made him happy. Sarasvatichandra was filled with affection for this tall, strong, scantily clad, black-bodied sadhu. He addressed Viharpuri affectionately, 'Yogi Raj, that was a fine verse you recited. But I could not understand how the rays of the moon can travel during the day! The hospitality that your monastery has bestowed upon me has purged my mind of its sorrows. And your Guruji's affection is certain to lift the burdens from my soul.'

'Well spoken, young man,' said Viharpuri, as he and Radhedas exchanged meaningful glances. They were amazed—this stranger was already initiated in the secrets of their sect! And he knew that Guruji was partial towards him. Moreover, he understood Sanskrit and even knew the mystical meaning of the burden of the soul! All this seemed most magical to Viharpuri and Radhedas. Their faith in their Guruji's prediction was reaffirmed. Viharpuri joyfully embraced Sarasvatichandra, and as he did, some of the sacred ash from his body got smeared on Sarasvatichandra. Viharpuri was delighted and laughing, said, 'Young man before I respond, do tell us your name.'

'My name is Navinchandra.'

'*Navinchandra*! Wonderful! What a beautiful name! Navinchandraji, you are our new moon. Shri Vishnudasji, our moon, represents the divine bliss of Shri Krishna. Vishnudasji's aura permeates everywhere. Those who come under its influence are healed and all their sorrows vanish. That supreme bliss will also alleviate your suffering, Navinchandraji. Do you comprehend?'

'Viharpuriji, your words are like nectar and they unburden my soul. Should it be any surprise then if the soft, soothing light of your Guruji gives my soul solace and peace?' responded Sarasvatichandra. It was his duty to show his gratitude towards those who had given him a new life. Love needs to be answered with love. Viharpuri was ecstatic. He said to Radhedas, 'With every passing moment, the true import of our Guruji's prediction is revealed. I will report this conversation verbatim to Guruji. We shall always be prepared to provide all hospitality to such a wise guest. Guruji will take some more time to get ready. Meanwhile, you give our guest a bird's eye view of all the sacred spots of Sundargiri. Also acquaint him with our monastery and the sublime power of our Guruji. Introduce him to all our fellow ascetics and do everything to please his mind. Until I return, this is your responsibility.' And saying so, Viharpuri walked away taking long strides.

Sarasvatichandra was left alone with Radhedas. The ascetic took him to different parts of the mountain and pointed out various sites in the magnificent scenery around them. The mountain range of Sundargiri comprised several hills. The monastery was situated on Yadu Shrunga. Right behind Yadu Shrunga was Tirtha Shrunga, which was the higher peak; some Jain caves and temples were located on it. Still higher was Matsyendra Shrunga, on which there were huts of Matsyendranath and Gorakhnath; only three or four yogis who practiced yoga shastra lived on this hill. In its thick forests there were monkeys, bears, snakes and tigers. The path to this hill was unpaved, steep, narrow and serpentine. One was required to negotiate sharp rocks at places and cut through tall prickly grass and thorny bushes. The winding path was flanked on one side by a deep gorge and by steep mountains on the other; one wrong step meant certain death. The chasms were so deep there was no chance of ever finding the body. It was said that many a traveller and pilgrim had lost their life on this path. Many would feel giddy and be compelled to turn back. But the faithful did persist on this treacherous path to pay their obeisance to the yogis and to seek their blessings. Radhedas pointed out these and several other peaks to Sarasvatichandra.

On one of the peaks lived ascetic scholars of the Vedanta who had taken a vow of silence. On another, pilgrims had built a monastery and a few huts for the use of itinerant mendicants. One hill had four Shiva temples, two of which were looked after by a brahmin priest and the other two by ascetics. Further away was a temple to Goddess Chandika where the worship was conducted by brahmin priests. The pilgrims had to walk from one holy place to another. They also made offerings at every place but of course the largest share was always reserved for their family deity. Ascetics, yogis, brahmins and mendicants were all provided for. The ascetics who lived in the farthest and most remote spots under harsh conditions were regarded superior to others. Very few pilgrims managed to reach their abode, but those who did believed that they had earned higher merit. Followers of all sects came to Sundargiri. On concluding their pilgrimage, they inevitably praised their own sect and decried the others. They often got into arguments with the followers of other sects. Sometimes these arguments even resulted in fist fights but they rarely went beyond little skirmishes. The pilgrims preferred to spend their energies in debates and discussion. Having narrated several such stories to Sarasvatichandra, Radhedas finally said, 'Navinchandraji, just like the sea, Sundargiri is also an abode of all kinds of living beings—but there is a difference. In the sea, animals prey upon each other; but on Sundargiri, Maharaj Maniraj's authority reigns supreme. His forces are not required even to police the place—everyone fears the king's authority. They feel that if any news of sectarian conflict were to reach Maniraj, the prestige of their sect would suffer and it would also pain the Maharaj. There has never been a duty-bound king like our Maharaj who gives equal respect to all religious. No one—neither a child nor an evil-minded person—wants to cause him any pain or trouble by their conduct. Maharaj is still young, but he is matchless in intellect, experience and statecraft.'

'Does the Maharaj ever visit Sundargiri?'

'Certainly. This place is so beautiful that every few years he visits us either in the month of Chaitra or Vaisakha. He is benevolent towards all sacred sites here. Our Guru, like the gurus of all other sects, pays him a visit every year. Every time our Guru Vishnudasji visits Ratnanagari, Maharaj Maniraj receives him personally and seeks new wisdom from him. Maharaj greatly values Guruji's blessings and is partial to all those religions that teach peace and morality. Just as Shri Krishna rules the hearts of gopis, Maharaj Maniraj rules the hearts of all the gurus.'

'Is the Maharaj a follower of your sect?' asked Sarasvatichandra.

'Maharaj follows his ancestral belief. How can we fault him for it? The *Gita* says: "Better is death in the discharge of one's duty; another's duty is fraught with danger." Each one must prefer his own duty above all else. One of the duties of the king is that he must protect and nurture every religion.'

Sarasvatichandra learnt much from this conversation with Radhedas. Statecraft has so many facets. One facet is the discharge of duties; another is splendour and glory. Action and the discharge of duties result in both affection and disaffection. A king must be loved by all his subjects. Hence, the king should act through his minister, the karbhari, and retain the ceremonial functions that accord splendour and glory to himself. The performance of kingly duties is far more difficult and dangerous as compared to the obligations of a minister. One who is responsible for the administration of the state must be prepared to face all types of criticism. Such a person is also in danger of losing his position and prestige. Therefore a trusted and devoted minister should shoulder the responsibility of administration while giving all credit, honour and glory to the king. Just as a warrior must be prepared to face death in battle, the minister must be prepared to face the consequences of his actions and decisions. The minister's duty is to sacrifice himself to protect the glory of the king; he should administer ably and correctly and ensure that all praise for it is due to the king. The object is not that the king should be praised but that the subjects must develop a feeling of affection, trust and loyalty towards their king. For example, in everyday commercial transactions or management of the household, the master of the house should always appear generous, and the charge of parsimony should fall upon the servants. Similarly in statecraft, splendour, honour and glory are the preserve of the king. This does not imply that the minister should not seek honour and glory or that the king should not perform any action or take any decisions. Action is the soul of the king while glory is the body. It is the responsibility of the king to protect his minister from the infamy that is heaped upon the minister in the discharge of his duties. It is the king's duty to be unselfish in this regard—only a king who fully understands and accepts this duty can separate statecraft from kingly glory. It is for such reasons that statecraft is divided between administrative functions and ceremonial pomp. But the division is only superficial;

at the core both functions are united—this is the first and essential principal of statecraft. In absence of this strong foundation the edifice is certain to be weak, which is detrimental to both the king and his subjects. This was the principle on which Vidya Chatura's statecraft was based; he had explained this to Sarasvatichandra in the course of a leisurely conversation one afternoon. Radhedas' comment refreshed Sarasvatichandra's memory. He also realised that these ideals were put in practice by Maniraj's minister. He remembered the Sanskrit verse:

Where king and friend in truth agree,
Fortune's favours love to dwell.[2]

He recognised that this saying was not just clever wordplay, it also drew upon experience. He thought, Maharaj Maniraj, your authority extends even over these ascetics who reside in this remote wilderness. Their love for you is deep; their fear of your authority is grave and their desire not to hurt or offend you so strong that they have no use for your police. Vidya Chatura, you have achieved such high glory and splendour for Maniraj! What deep trust and affection you must share with your king! It is certain that you have obtained this art from Gunasundari! Gunasundari! Kumud Sundari! The sudden memory of Kumud hurt like a knife wound and a painful, sorrowful world came before his mind's eye. But Radhedas took him away from this world of sorrows. He led Sarasvatichandra all the way to the top of the mountain through a narrow path strewn with stones, overgrown by weeds and shrubs. Once they reached the summit, they sat down on the smooth surface of a large rock to catch their breath. Sarasvatichandra stood up and looked all around. On the southern side was the teak forest; from the top of the mountain the tall teak trees looked small and shrub-like. Towards the east were Manoharpuri and the mango groves adjacent to it. The bright morning sun blinded him, forcing him to turn his gaze northwards. The various peaks of Sundargiri were awash with

[2] Romesh Chunder Dutt, trans. *Kirataarjunyam of Bharavi*, Verse 5, *Lays of Ancient India: Selections from Indian Poetry Rendered into English Verse* (London: Kegan Paul, 1894), 131.

light. As he turned towards the south, he saw the distant sea and the river Subhadra flowing from the east to meet the sea. It was a grand panorama that lay before Sarasvatichandra's eyes. Radhedas described the various points that made up the scene.

'Navinchandra, do you see that cluster of temples? It is an amazing spectacle during the four months of monsoon. A cloud-laden sky, water flowing from the mountain top to the foothills, the distant sea, these white temples in between, and the Subhadra flowing full at both the banks. The falling raindrops weave their tapestry, white silken clouds brush past us, the rain casts its spell, and all that water comes falling down! It is said that Gangaji emerged from the nail of Lord Narayana. These waterfalls give an illusion that they are flowing from our nails. Sundargiri is at its most magnificent during those four months. You must stay at Sundargiri forever and enjoy its abundant natural beauty—it is otherworldly. Those who have not seen it have wasted their life.'

A weeping child is distracted by a new toy; adults, even in moments of grief, are stunned by the beauty of nature and the flow of tears is arrested; past sorrows are momentarily erased by present joys. Sarasvatichandra's painful memories were erased by the scenic beauty of Sundargiri, by the vivid pictures painted by Radhedas, and the vision of the future he presented. 'Wonderful, Radhedas! Sundargiri is indeed beautiful! Who worships in these temples? What are those villages in the foothills?'

Radhedas had a bird's eye view of the temples. He said, 'Navinchandraji, those black spots in the distance are the homes of Surgram; it is a small village but it is a sacred place. Originally Surgram was situated where the temples are. These temples have the idols of all deities. There are as many different sects as there are hills on this mountain. The temples belong to all these various sects.'

'Radhedas, you are a devotee of Vishnu; you must not have entered the sanctum sanctorum of other deities.'

Radhedas laughed in response and said, 'It is an illusion that our God is separate from the gods of others. I think the fable of the blind men and the elephant is most appropriate for this world. You do understand, don't you? We are Vaishnava. But the followers of Shiva sing in their prayers:

Shiva and Vishnu are one
Do not consider them distinct
Do not take them to be different

'We, too, accept this view. When the Formless One decides to manifest Himself in the world, each one imagines Him according to the illumination of their hearts. Shiva, Vishnu, other deities and even the gods of other races are all manifestations of that one Formless One. It is all a matter of perception. Vishnu is the deity of our hearts. We worship Vishnu's incarnation as Krishna. But ultimately there is only the Formless One. The Vedantis describe him as Brahma.' Radhedas seemed to hesitate here. Sarasvatichandra sensed it and asked, 'Why did you hesitate? Were you about to say something more?'

'Should I say it? You are a householder and may find an illustration in the language of householders easier to grasp; but I am an ascetic, you see, and hence my hesitation.'

'Please do.'

'A beautiful woman: some are satisfied just by gazing at her face, some want her to sing and dance while others are not content until they have the pleasure of her touch. Some even desire playful sensuality, while someone may find in her a reflection of their own mother. Similarly, the formless and incorporeal, pure and unsullied one manifests in a myriad forms in the hearts of devotees.'

Radhedas' philosophical aspect was a revelation for Sarasvatichandra. The man who had successfully cleared all examinations to qualify as a counsellor was delighted to learn that the Indic religions also produced able advocates of its beliefs, and Sarasvatichandra was filled with patriotic pride. But he was tempted to test the abilities of these ascetics further. He took the position that many English educated take and asked, 'Radhedas, does idol worship also imply devotion to the unmanifest Formless One?'

For a moment, Radhedas was enraged by his question, but he remembered his Guruji's prediction and controlled his anger. He gravely said, 'Bhai, if you were to ask this question to anyone else in the monastery, they would take you for an atheist, and that would cause you pain. Please do not ask this question ever again. Our vision is bound by our faith in the Vedas and by our Guruji's commands. A question or argument that seeks to transgress these limits is for us intolerable.'

Sarasvatichandra realised the difference between this place and the intellectual freedom of Bombay. He was confounded by this combination of advocacy and religious conservatism. He knew that even by norms of English custom it was uncivil to criticise someone else's religion. He apologetically said, 'Forgive me, Radhedas. I did not realise that my question insulted your sensibility. I asked only as a disciple seeking deeper meaning.'

'Bhai, but was that a question at all? What deeper meaning could it possibly reveal?'

'Your Guruji has said: "In his devotion to Krishna, Gopal the cowherd appears gentle as a child." I feel that this must contain some mystical meaning about idol worship.'

Radhedas was taken aback. He has not only heard Guruji's saying, but he also comprehends it! Most certainly he is more advanced than I am, Radhedas thought. He politely said, 'Navinchandraji, forgive me. Only Viharpuriji or Guruji himself can satisfy your curiosity. My abilities are limited and much below yours. I cannot comprehend the deeper meaning of what you seek to know. You are indeed fortunate—it is certain that your heart is imbued with the presence of the Formless One.'

Wanting to change the topic, Sarasvatichandra made some queries about the natural beauty surrounding them. 'Radhedas, what is the name of the river that meets the sea? Where does it originate?'

'That is the Subhadra; it branches out from river Bhadra. The Bhadra meets the sea near Suvarnapur while Subhadra meets the sea near Surgram.'

Sarasvatichandra climbed up to a higher spot and followed the Subhadra's course from the east to the west. From that great distance and height, the river appeared like a meandering silver line, trees lining both its banks. He tried to locate the spot where he was robbed. He imagined Suvarnapur that was hidden from view. He imagined the teak forest infested with gangs of outlaws. Suddenly, in that broad light of day, he imagined a nightmarish scene—he vividly saw Kumud Sundari being captured by the outlaws at the very same spot where he had been robbed, and he was shaken. He saw a little white cloud floating by. He imagined Kumud's angelic form floating with that cloud. The song that he had heard from the old woman travelling with him in the cart taking him away from Suvarnapur came back to him. He imagined Kumud draped in a sari woven with sunrays, looking radiant and singing a song in that bright blue sky.

The melodious flute plays in Madhuvan
But the beloved slips away the moment he is espied
He teases mercilessly, setting hearts aflutter
The dark one hides in shadowy teak groves
The renunciate who once sought pleasure seeks it anew
The hidden one reveals himself

Sarasvatichandra rubbed his eyes and strained his ears. The little white cloud seemed ready to dive into the sea. He saw the cloud morph into Kumud. As Kumud dove to her death in the sea, she let out a soul-wrenching cry: 'Sarasvatichandra, you left me and ran away from Bombay. You abandoned me in Suvarnapur and ran away once again. This sin of my death is upon you, Sarasvatichandra!' And the apparition disappeared into the dark black waters. The dejection, the melancholy and utter desolation of the woman's heart and her searing curse singed Sarasvatichandra's being. He felt as if Kumud Sundari in her various forms was jumping to a fiery death in the funeral pyre that raged in his heart. Tears streamed down his eyes; even the bright sun could not dry them. In the distance, conch shells could be heard from the monastery.

Radhedas broke Sarasvatichandra's reverie. 'Navinchandraji, let us go. It is time to meet Guruji.' Radhedas had not seen his tears. As they began their descent from the summit, Radhedas observed Sarasvatichandra's fair complexion, his noble bearing and thought to himself: He is the troubled son of a wealthy father. His bearing and complexion betray his upbringing. His wandering into this place and his lost, distracted air suggest an unhappy past. His suffering must be grave. Shri Vishnudas will be his saviour. Who but a godly person like him could save him? Radhedas sang aloud:

Who but a man of religion can satiate the passions of the body?
Drink deeply of the Lord's cup, and you shall not suffer rebirth

Sarasvatichandra's eyes were still on that distant spot where Subhadra met the sea. He imagined Kumud in a 'jolly-boat', floating effortlessly down the Subhadra. He followed Radhedas' song with one of his own.

Subhadra, fair in name, be fair to me, too
If my beloved comes to you, counsel the one with the withered body
The cool breeze that blows over your banks also bears your fragrant dew
My beloved's heart is on fire: give her the peace and solace
To douse the fire in her heart and share with you its story
If she were to jump into your waters deep,
Like the creatures who reside there,
Hold her to your bosom
Save her, give her life from the nectar that flows in your heart
Kumud, the lotus, is born of water and shares its essence
If Kumud seeks your bosom, Subhadra be her friend

As he was composing this in his mind, Viharpuri, Mohanpuri and the other ascetics came up to meet Sarasvatichandra. He joined their group, firmly telling himself: I have gone mad. Kumud Sundari is happy in Suvarnapur. God's grace is upon her. I must not desire her. Some are separated by death, others by life. What is the difference? How is one human being to care for another? God Almighty shelters all. He found himself surrounded by the ascetics, who were being introduced to him one by one and making his acquaintance. But all at once, they seemed to diminish and vanish before his eyes—what remained were the mountains, the black boulders, the blinding rays of the sun, the distant sea, and the sparkling, rushing waters of the Subhadra. Everything else disappeared from his sight. Can the world become invisible at certain moments? Who knows? But Sarasvatichandra could only see the Subhadra as he sang,

She has become an apparition
The air is redolent with her fragrance
I shall be like the forest breeze, invisible but
Carrying aloft the fragrance called Kumud

He then saw myriad forms of Kumud floating around him in the sky—some danced, some sang songs that perhaps Vanleela would sing. Kumud seemed to be teasing him.

The renunciate who once sought pleasure seeks it anew
The aesthete who once sought knowledge seeks beauty anew
Standing atop Sundargiri, he muses on the Sundari etched on his heart
He hears her, he sees her, he pines for her anew
"Why did we love at all, Sundari?
Having loved, why did we forsake one another?
Having forsaken one other, why did I seek you anew, Sundari?
And having sought you again, why did I abandon you?"
As the melodious flute plays in your heart
Chandra and Kumud dance with abandon

He heard Kumud singing in several voices.

The flute plays, O' renunciate, for you the flute plays:
Come wait by the river bank
Bathing in that roaring sea, I see you, O' renunciate
And there again you stand by the temple door
Love may be blind, but it listens
Love hears a distant whisper
What is written in our fates cannot be undone
Even householders renounce their homes
You left the world behind, O' jogi
Dragging me along after you
Now be my teacher, O' jogi
Keep this jogini by your side
As you give learned discourses
This jogini will come and listen
The flute plays songs of love

Expressing what went unsaid
Its music sings of Brahman—it sings of our union
Contain the world in your flute, O' renunciate
And fill your song with bliss
Standing on the shores of the river of time
He plays his flute
Kumud, lost in pain and sorrow, is
Filled with the sounds of his flute

2 Maniraj and Vidya Chatura's Family in Manoharpuri

Soon after Manchatura left Manoharpuri in the company of soldiers to escort Kumud Sundari home safely, the rest of the family and Chandrakant lay down to rest; but sleep eluded them for long. Chandrakant finally fell asleep by three a.m., but he was haunted by dreams of Sarasvatichandra. Sundargauri cried herself to sleep. Gunasundari, troubled and anxious about her daughter, lay in bed staring vacantly at the walls. As the day broke, each of them got up and sought distraction in routine.

Young Kusum Sundari, who was given the charge of looking after their guest, brought Chandrakant his morning tea and milk. She engaged him in conversation to keep him amused. As he sat brooding alone in the veranda, she approached him with a few books and said, 'Chandrakantbhai, Gunial taught Kumud behn from these books, and she will be teaching them to me as well. Pitaji also likes them. Perhaps they might interest you, too.'

Chandrakant felt both happy and sad. This family's abiding love for learning and fondness for books gave him joy; but the fact that his dearest friend had broken all ties with such a worthy family pained him. Kusum, alert to his disappointment, said, 'Chandrakantbhai, I cannot blame Sarasvatichandra. I feel that perhaps he wanted to do something like Robinson Crusoe, and so he left home.'

Despite his gloomy mental state, Chandrakant was amused at this comment, and said, 'Behn, how did you suddenly remember Robinson Crusoe?'

'He left home to wander the world; Sarasvatichandra did likewise,' came the prompt reply.

'But was that wise?'

'I would also love to roam, to see the wide world. I tell Gunial every day—why should one be tied to the house? If you ask me, it was my idea to have this excursion to Bhadreshwar. I feel that Sarasvatichandra also wanted to see the world. The trouble in his family gave him the opportunity, and he left home to fulfill his desire.'

'But he could have done that even after marriage.'

'But that is like inviting trouble! Look at Kumud behn—all her problems are due to marriage, isn't it? Do I have a care in the world? Those who marry are certain to fall.'

'But behn, you shouldn't be saying this!'

Once I start talking, I have no control over my tongue, Kusum muttered coyly to herself. Then aloud, she said, 'I spoke in jest, Chandrakantbhai. But I can find no fault with Sarasvatichandra. He is an intelligent man and his decision was well considered. What can the outlaws possibly rob him of? I feel that this, too, he wished to experience.'

'How can anyone desire such a thing?'

'When he visited us, he was reading Shakespeare and he narrated to me the plot of a play. A gentleman called Valentine of Verona joined a band of thieves and became its leader. Couldn't Sarasvatichandra have also decided to do something similar? It would be such fun.'

'Do you think it is a good thing to join a band of thieves?'

'Are outlaws thieves?'

'Then what else?'

'No, they are relatives of the ruler. They become outlaws only when they are disaffected with the rulers. When kings kill in battle, it is not called murder, is it?'

This rather naïve and yet intelligent comment lessened Chandrakant's gloom somewhat. But before he could respond any further, there was a great commotion outside.

Kusum looked out. Mukhi, the head of the village, was galloping forth with glad tidings even as other men from the village followed in his wake, shouting with joy. In a short while they arrived; and Gunasundari, Chandrakant, Sundargauri and Kusum were given a detailed account of the encounter with the outlaws and the glorious victory over them. Gloom gave way to joy. Mukhi went back to join the soldiers. Now they all anxiously awaited the arrival of Manchatura and Kumud Sundari. Each moment seemed like a lifetime. Chandrakant went and stood on the veranda, staring at the horizon. The women waited inside the house.

Gunasundari suggested, 'Kusum, we are all by ourselves. Let's sing the song of the wasp; it would help us pass the time.'

Sundargauri said, 'Kusum should accompany you on the sarangi.' Kusum promptly went to fetch the sarangi. As she strummed its strings and tuned the instrument, she told Gunasundari, 'Gunial, I will sing the verses spoken by the lotus, and you take the part of the wasp.'

Chandrakant's reverie was broken by the sweet and melodious sounds of the sarangi. The veranda where he stood and the room where the women sat were separated by a grilled window. Through it, he could clearly see the pleasing scenes within. Sundargauri sat on a bed. Gunial sat beside her, her hand on Sundargauri's shoulder. Their glow merged into one another as if they were not two but one. Kusum stood facing them, resting one foot on a box. She looked as delicate as a tender plantain tree; the sarangi in her hands became the plantain leaf. Kusum's sweet voice merged with the sarangi as she sang.

Stay away, stay far away from me, wasp
I am a delicate flower
Your sting bites!
Stay far away from me, wasp
Lusting for nectar,
You think only of yourself
Stay away from me!

Kusum repeated the last line again and again. Sundargauri also joined in the singing. The sarangi played unrestrained. Gunasundari joined in with her melodious voice. Even the servants stopped working to listen to her sing.

O' delicate as lotus, you misunderstand me
In your haughtiness, you err
Night after night you imprison me
In your diamantine petals
Forsaking the forest of flowers
For the love of your lotus
I place your pollen on my head

All the three voices merged in the last line. Kusum swayed to the rhythm of the song. Her dancing form reminded one of the divine dance of Parvati. Before her statuesque mother and aunt, Kusum gushed forth like a fountain.

'Kusum, oh how well you dance! How wonderful! Let's call Chandrakant, too; let him also see your theatrics,' said Sundargauri. She got up and embraced Kusum and kissing her fondly on the head, asked, 'Who taught you this? When did you learn to dance like this, tell me?'

Kusum blushed and hid her face in Sundargauri's embrace. Still feeling shy, instead of responding, she went and sat next to Gunasundari. Her face had turned a warm red. Gunasundari caressed her affectionately and asked, 'Kusum, do tell us—from where did you learn to dance?'

Kusum would not look up but she mustered courage and said, 'Why? Is it such a lowly thing? Why do you ask?'

'No, no! It is high art!' said Sundargauri in jest.

'If it is such a lowly thing, then why did Malavika and Iravati learn how to dance? Ask Gunial about it!' Kusum was thoughtful for a while, then she added, 'And Samal Bhatt's heroine Vidyavilasini also learnt how to dance.'

'All that is fine, Kusum, but where did *you* learn this?' Gunasundari persisted.

'When we had invited the Maharaj to our house, we had organised a dance. I watched it from behind the curtains. You seem to have no memory of it,' Kusum replied, finally looking up.

'Oh, my God! Kusum, you learnt all this just by watching one dance! Such things never touched my Kumud,' said Sundargauri. Kusum's face showed some irritation.

Gunasundari winked at her sister-in-law and said to Kusum, 'That depends on one's abilities. But if you are fond of this art, I can ask your father and arrange for a teacher.'

At the mention of her father, Kusum hesitated. Gunasundari told her of the teacher that she had in mind for her. Kusum was taken aback. 'Who, that rand! Who is she to teach me? Gunial, you are impossible!' and she moved away from her mother to signal her displeasure.

'All right. We will do whatever you want.'

'If I want to learn, I shall do it on my own. Did I need a teacher to learn this much? Why do we need to inform Pitaji?'

'If not him, then whom will you tell—your in-laws?'

'Why? Aren't there things which neither parents nor in-laws know of?'

'Who else would know? Your husband!' her aunt shot back.

In response, Kusum brushed Sundargauri lightly on her shoulder and ran out of the room. Sundargauri said mockingly to the retreating Kusum,'Of course, some things you will only share with your husband. Now we know your answer!'

Gunasundari seemed concerned. 'What are you worried about, Bhabhi?' Sundargauri asked her.

'Kusum is so quick to learn; she listens carefully and she remembers; she is given to speaking her mind and she is hard to pin down and argumentative. As long as she is in our house, she is all right. But who knows what kind of a husband she will get? These very qualities of hers might be taken to be her weakness at her in-laws' house, and that would be a source of such misery for her. I wonder, how this delicate, doll-like daughter of mine will fare at her in-laws'?'

'Why worry about such things now, Bhabhi? Each one is bound to their own destiny.'

'Sundarbhabhi, are those days so far away in the distant future? How long can Kusum remain unmarried? Look at her—she grows with every passing day and night. She blossoms each day.'

Sundargauri saw Gunasundari's reason and flowed with it. 'That is true. She is younger than Kumud, yet she overshadows her.'

'And Kusum! She wants to be like Mirabai!'

'Yes, there is no match for your daughter.'

'She wants to be a Mira; she is unwilling to be homebound; she will even go to England if we let her. She learnt how to swim. And now she has taught herself to dance! To keep her safe and out of trouble is about as easy as carrying a bundle of snakes.'

'But, Bhabhi, she is still untouched by impure thoughts.'

'Yes, that is a relief. But she is not meek like Kumud. Kumud adjusts herself to the situation. Kusum is like a lioness; she needs a lion for a companion. Are they so easy to find?'

'That is true.'

'If we manage to trace Sarasvatichandra and could persuade him for this marriage ... But a man who gave up ten lakh rupees without a thought will not be easy to persuade.'

'Perhaps Chandrakant could do something.'

'Yes, and that is the reason I allow Kusum to mix freely with him.'

'You are doing the right thing.'

Chandrakant heaved a sigh. He could no longer bear to listen to this conversation. He got up and went to his room and lay down, despondent.

In a short while Kusum rushed in, saying, 'Chandrakantbhai! Chandrakantbhai, get up! Maharaj Maniraj is coming this way! We are going to put up a curtain here so that Gunial and all of us can see him. You sit on the other side and watch the procession.'

The servants put up a curtain. The women sat behind it, waiting for the royal procession. There was much excitement and bustle on the road. People waited impatiently. Then someone called out in the distance, 'He has come! The Maharaj has arrived!'

Kusum hid behind the curtain. She raised it slightly and peered from underneath it, unseen by those on the other side. Sundargauri gave her an affectionate pat on the back. Kusum brushed aside her aunt's hand and said, 'Kaki, we should not be seen by them. But there is nothing that says that we should not look at them.' Sundargauri whispered, 'But why raise the curtain?'

'All right. But you talk as if I don't know how to cheat a little. Tell me, what have I stolen from you? Have you any clue?'

'Little wretch, so you even know how to steal?' said Sundargauri, and got up to search.

'Now you can sit down. I only made you get up so I could have a little more space.'

'You could cheat even me! If Chandrakant were not around, I would have sat on your silly head!' her aunt retorted playfully.

'I take my chances. You can't say a thing to me. If Chandrakant weren't around, wouldn't I have sat in your lap instead?'

'Do sit quietly now. You are so difficult!'

Kusum spread herself contentedly. They had spoken so softly that Chandrakant had not caught a word of what they had said. The royal procession was now right at their door.

Maniraj, the ruler of Ratnanagari, was a young man of twenty or twenty-one. His father Mallaraj had died a few years ago. Vidya Chatura had become the prime minister during Mallaraj's reign. Maniraj had acquired a taste for hunting at a young age which had only grown with time. The forests around Sundargiri and Manoharpuri were ideal hunting grounds; human habitation there was sparse and the dense forests, saturated with wildlife. Maniraj took personal care to protect these forests. No trees could be cut without royal sanction. Maniraj liked the modern argument that thick forests are a guarantee against famine. Of course, forests also made hunting possible. But in an age when the old was fast disappearing under the onslaught of the new, Maniraj found it particularly pleasing when the old could be preserved with a modern argument.

This pure-blooded Rajput kshatriya was born with high aspirations, which were further cultivated by Vidya Chatura. Although a brahmin himself, Vidya Chatura believed that hunting was an appropriate means of inculcating the 'martial spirit' in these times. Following his counsel, Mallaraj had surrounded young prince Maniraj by the best and most valiant among the Rajputs. Under their watchful eye, he was imbued with the martial spirit. Vidya Chatura's wise counsel had endeared him even more to Mallaraj. Vidya Chatura had fulfilled Mallaraj's condition: 'Do not turn my son into a brahmin or a bania.' And yet, Vidya Chatura had never concealed his brahminhood. He ensured that Maniraj imbibed the qualities of Rajputs, but not their failings. Moreover, this arrangement also ensured that young Maniraj did not develop an attitude of ridicule towards Vidya Chatura's brahminhood and that he did not mistrust his counsel. Vidya Chatura demonstrated that he recognised the value of Rajput valour—this confidence was the basis of the mutual trust and respect between the king and his minister. The Rajputs in the administration had no opportunity to complain; in fact they were grateful to him for the opportunities that he created for them to be around Maniraj. Vidya Chatura ensured that the young prince met him as soon as he returned from a hunt. Maniraj always shared without any hesitation all that had transpired during the hunt, including what he had learnt in the company of other Rajput boys. This gave Vidya Chatura an opportunity to weed out any undesirable traits in young Maniraj as well as his companions. He had become a favourite teacher of not only the prince but also of many other Rajput youth. The young boys would in turn share their learning with their parents. Vidya Chatura had thus earned the affection and respect of many Rajput clans. The divide between the brahmins and the kshatriyas was to this extent bridged. Vidya Chatura rid Maniraj of all the undesirable facets of hunting and fostered the advantageous aspects. It is the duty of the king to protect the innocent and the weak and to punish the evil; this is also a mark of his valour. Vidya Chatura argued that this sense of justice and fairness should be extended not only to human beings but also to animals. Maniraj was taught that it was beneath his dignity to hunt harmless animals like deer and rabbits. He was encouraged to go after ferocious predators like tigers and lions. Vidya Chatura ensured that during hunts, these principles were adhered to. This maintained a balance in the forest by protecting the herbivorous population of the animal kingdom.

Summer months were ideal for hunting. The previous evening at around five, Maniraj had set out on a hunt. He was delighted that he had succeeded in hunting a lion. Thereafter, he had been informed of the activities of Sursinh and his band of outlaws. Not negligent of his responsibilities towards his people, Maniraj had immediately set out for Manoharpuri. The people of Manoharpuri were eager to welcome their ruler.

Gunasundari had sent out a soldier to bring back news of the king's arrival. The soldier returned and reported deferentially to her, 'The Maharaj and other Rajput royals are coming here directly from the hunt. The king and his attendants are in the front, followed by the riders.'

Gunasundari turned to Kusum and said, 'He is probably aware that we have camped here.' Kusum rushed inside the house swift as a foal. Gunasundari looked at Chandrakant. Satisfied that he was appropriately dressed to receive the king, she said, 'Chandrakantbhai, if the Maharaj seeks your company, be gracious in your response.' At this, Sundargauri looked questioningly at Gunasundari, who replied, 'Maharaj, though tired from the hunt, will invariably look for intelligent company even in this village. Who in Manoharpuri but this learned guest of your brother-in-law could fulfill that desire? Do you really think the Maharaj is unaware that Chandrakantbhai is our guest?' Meanwhile, Kusum came out all dressed in silken finery. She carried a large ornate tray made of gold and silver. On it she had kept flowers, incense, vermillion, an earthen lamp and various other things required to welcome the king. Her silk odhni with its border of red and green flowers was embroidered with gold and silver thread; it fluttered ever so lightly in the morning breeze. Her long flowing skirt with many gathers was the colour of embers and glowed like the soft rays of the morning sun. She looked delightful and fresh as a dewy flower. Her anklets tinkled softly, making musical announcement of her movements. She wore pure diamonds in her ears, on her neck and wrists, and a waistband made of pearls and precious stones which shone like the colours of a rainbow. She had read descriptions of adornments in Sanskrit texts and had persuaded her mother to get one made for her. Thus adorned, Kusum came and stood next to her mother.

Just then the bustle outside grew louder and more urgent. Everyone stood up. Gunasundari addressed Chandrakant, 'Chandrakantbhai, be prepared, Maharaj will be here any moment now. If you prefer, you could wait at the steps to receive him.' Chandrakant followed this good advice. A large crowd had gathered outside Gunasundari's veranda. People greeted the approaching king. 'Welcome! Welcome, Maharaj! May you rule till eternity!' Then suddenly, everyone became quiet and the crowd neatly parted into two and lined up on either side of the road—the royal procession now had a clear path. The Maharaj could now be seen approaching the house of his minister.

Maniraj and his companions walked on foot. The riders had also dismounted. Two covered carts made up the rear end of the procession. The carts were protected by Bhil tribals who walked bare-chested, their bows and arrows in readiness. A soldier carrying Maniraj's rifle preceded the royal procession. Maniraj was flanked by fully-armed Rajputs. They seemed relaxed and talked amongst themselves as they walked. All of them wore bright and colourful headgears, and tight pajamas which were clasped at the ankle with a button. Their upper garments were made of soft white mulmul suitable for the heat of Chaitra. They wore tight waistbands into which various weapons were tucked. Their bodies were sturdily built; some were dark-complexioned while others were fair. Their foreheads gave testimony to their courage. Their eyes were sharp as a tiger's. Their aquiline noses reminded Chandrakant of Roman sculptures. Some had thick lower lips, which they chewed on, their muscular arms eager and ready for daring tasks. There is a belief that some Rajput clans were the result of a union between the Aryas and the Shakas who came from the areas between China and the Caspian Sea. Watching these sturdily-built men stride together, Chandrakant relived this historical fantasy. Today, we the natives are the defeated and the English, the victorious foreigners. Some centuries ago, the Muslims were the victorious foreigners. The Mughals came after that. Before the Muslims came the Greeks and the Shakas. They, too, were foreign invaders. In ancient times the Arya kings and sages crossed the Indus and defeated the native Dasa inhabitants. They, too, were fair-skinned foreigners. This play of black and white, native and foreigner, the vanquished and the victorious has been going on since ancient times. But the definitions keep changing and they keep moving from one square to another in this gigantic game of chess. The sages and kings, the Shakas and the Muslims, even the Parsis who were once considered foreigners in this land of ancient tribals, have all become natives. The English, the new foreigners, will also become natives in the future. Time blurs all differences between the foreigner and the native; and once they disappear, all are coloured by the same hues. Maharaj Maniraj's procession was led by a Muslim; the Rajputs followed him and the tribals brought up the rear end. They were all different in some ways, but united by their devotion to the land and their ruler.

Maniraj had his mother's complexion and his father's stout frame and strength. His skin was the colour of gold, made ruddy with the pure Rajput blood and valour that flowed fiercely through his veins. His features were handsome and delicate, the power of authority apparent on his regal visage. Even those who did not know of his kingly status felt awed in his presence. In many native states, the dissensions between father and son are perceptible. In some instances these differences are out in open, while in others they simmer just below the surface. But those elders who had seen Mallaraj in his youth said that Maniraj was a mirror image of his father. His leonine stride, his deep, grave voice, his temperament and character reminded all of the young Mallaraj. A yogi who lived in seclusion at Sundargiri was unaware of Mallaraj's demise; when Maniraj went to Sundargiri to pay him his respects, the yogi addressed him as Mallaraj. The Raj Guru, Prassannath recited verses of Kalidas every morning.

> His majestic (or resplendent) form was the same, the valour the same, and the natural sublimity (or nobleness of nature) also the same; the new born prince did not differ from his generating cause (father) as [a] lamp lighted from another (does not differ from it).[1]

[1] M. R. Kale, trans. *The Raghuvamsa of Kalidasa*, Canto 5, Verse 37, 3rd ed. (Bombay: Gopal Narayan and Co., 1922), 137.

Maniraj, like his father, was about six inches taller than men of average height. His build resembled that of some Russian men. Vidya Chatura used to say that heroes of ancient ages like Ram, Krishna and the Pandavas must have been as tall as Maniraj, if not taller. Usually men are taller than women, but some of our men are shamefully shorter than the English madams. It is not surprising that the English sahibs are taller, broader and stronger than our men. But even the Europeans had to respect Maniraj's build. His imposing persona awed people the first time they saw him, and their respect for him would invariably grow on subsequent meetings. His people were proud of their ruler. As he walked towards Gunasundari's house, the people of Manoharpuri felt renewed pride in their king. Four women belonging to the community of bards, tall, dark and not very beautiful, made their way through the crowd. They greeted Maniraj and welcomed him with a song filled with affection for their ruler.

Welcome! We welcome you, Maharaj Maniraj!
The moustache is yet to grow thick and long, but you are the son of a lion
You hunt like the Lord of Death
The earth quivers as you step on it
And lions make way for you
You uphold the throne of your father
"Live long! Live long!" cry your people
"Live long! Live long!" cries the wind

They sang, they blessed him, and made way for Maniraj.

Maniraj said, 'Bhairvi, your blessings have reached me. Tell me, are your sons well?'

A group of boys came forward. Bhairvi's son bent low to salute the king and said, 'Maharaj, in a kingdom where even the deer and rabbits are happy, does one need to ask how Bhairvi's sons are? These are my brothers.' All of them bowed low to greet the king.

Maniraj asked them, 'How is your Talati?'

'Maharaj, you have so much concern for us, what more do we need? Please keep this Talati here forever.'

Bhairvi came forward and interjected, 'Son, you have still to learn the proper manner of speech. You should say: Please appoint such a Talati in our village. It is praise for the Talati as also a recommendation that he be appointed to a higher position. The Talati is a good and clever man. If he spends his entire life here, how will he move up?'

Maniraj was amused by this intervention and he smiled. Bhairvi noticed and, hesitating, said, 'Maharaj, have mercy. We villagers speak without really understanding the import of what we say. We have to be very careful while speaking in your presence. If we say anything unflattering about your officials, you will instantly have the matter investigated. And if you find a grain of truth in what we have said, you will punish even your favourite officials. Therefore, we have to weigh every word we speak, or else we might inadvertently commit a sin.'

Maniraj was amused. He asked, 'Bhairvi, tell me what kind of an administration would you like?'

Bhairvi was annoyed with herself. 'Maharaj, I have again made a mistake. Pray make no changes in your administration. If someone is punished because of something we have said, that person's sorrow affects us, too. If we speak more than is necessary, you must fathom the truth.'

'Should you not be speaking truth to me?'

'No, Bapaji, that is not what I meant. We are like your children. Why should we speak anything but the truth? We should conceal nothing from you. But you must be compassionate towards your officials. Are they any less deserving of your pity than the animals you hunt?'

'Bhairvi, what is it that you are implying?'

'Bapaji, we know that you have tears in your eyes every time you hunt a lion, because you have taken its life. You must show the same compassion for your officials when you punish them,' Bhairvi replied. Then she turned to her son and said, 'Recite what you have composed on Maharaj.'

Bhairvi's son came forward and recited:

Sword at his waist, gun in his hand
As the lord of this land takes aim

The lord of the forest wonders
Who is this brave man in the forest?
Who is this man? Why is he here?
Even as the lion ponders this
An unseen bullet pierces his head
Not knowing if the beast lives yet
The beaters quiver from afar
Maniraj strides forward fearlessly
And touches the lion's head
He who slayed the king of the forest
Now stands weeping:
"Vanraj is dead, the brave one is dead,
And the forest is bereft."

Bhairvi came forward and said, 'Maharaj, if we say anything more, we may say something inappropriate. Sukhashankar Maharaj will now speak about the shastras—pray listen to him.'

Sukhashankar came forward and said, 'Maharaj, anyone found harassing the innocent in your rule meets the same fate as those who approach a lioness playing with her cubs. And this is as it should be. The king and his people must have such abiding affection for each other. But we all pity that former Talati.'

'Did the Talati approach you after he was transferred from here?' asked Maniraj.

'No, Maharaj. Is your administration such that these things can be kept a secret?'

'But this woman grieves over his fate.'

'Bhairvi, would you like us to be more compassionate towards the Talati?'

'Yes, my King,' she replied gladly.

'All right, it shall be done.' Bhairvi touched Maniraj's feet and moved away. He was about to move forward when he found his path blocked by an ascetic. The sadhu, clad only in a loin cloth, addressed the king in chaste Hindustani, 'Maharaj, the shastras ordain that no one should approach the king without carrying a gift for him. But you have decreed that no one should present a gift to you. What is one to do? In one case we break the shastric regulations, and in the other, we break your royal decree. How is then one to approach you?'

Maniraj laughed and said, 'Sadhudasji, it is I who should make you an offering. I accept only blessings from ascetics like yourself. I cannot rightfully accept anything else.'

'Your wish, Maharaj. But you must accept some sandalwood paste—it is sacred. It was offered to Shri Thakorji. I cannot come to you without a gift, hence I have composed a poem in Gujarati. Please receive it as my offering, Maharaj.'

'Sadhudasji, please recite.'

The sadhu's tall, wiry frame was smeared with sandalwood paste. He raised a muscular arm and recited:

Brave and compassionate art thou, O' Maniraj
Shelter of virtue, all evil trembles at your sight
Beloved and feared art thou, O' Maniraj
Good to the righteous, all wrongs you smite
You inspire hope in the good and true
And from their hearts they bless you
With this love and goodwill, O' Maniraj
May your glorious reign last for ever
Steering you through every battlefield
Is Chatura the wise, your charioteer

In his Gujarati *Ramayana*, the poet Samal had made Angad recite a poem for Lord Ram; Sadhudas' recitation was reminiscent of that scene. As he was about to complete his recitation, Sadhudas became aware of a presence behind him. The Maharaj's gaze was on that person. The ascetic turned around and saw young Kusum standing with a tray, flanked by guards, waiting to welcome the king. Chandrakant was also with her. The ascetic realised that he had kept the minister's daughter waiting. He moved aside and said, 'Kusum behn, come forward and welcome the Maharaj with your flowers.'

Like the soft rays of the morning sun emerging from behind a mountain, Kusum stepped forward.

And like water-laden clouds bend to touch a river with hands of rain, Maniraj bent forward and took the tray full of fragrant flowers from Kusum's hands. Holding the tray in one hand, he picked up some flowers, gave a few to Chandrakant and to Kusum and kept some for himself. Then he handed the tray to a member of the royal procession and asking him to distribute the rest of the flowers to the others in his party and the villagers, Maniraj instantly struck up a conversation. 'Chandrakant, so you are here! Forgive me, I did not see you; you were right at the back. Kusum behn, your mother must have by now received news of the outlaws' defeat. Kumud behn will be with us soon.'

Kusum looked down bashfully and replied, 'One is blessed by the darshan of great men; but in your case even before one meets you, one is blessed by good news. Maharaj, Gunial has sent a message for you:

> First appears the flower and then the fruit; first the rising up of clouds, afterwards, the shower of water; this is the order of cause and effect; but prosperity comes before your favour.[2]

'Maharaj, I must say that Gunial is overcome with joy and gratitude for you.'

Both Maniraj and Chandrakant were moved by the message and unshed tears glistened in their eyes. Maniraj said, 'Kusum behn, please tell Gunialba that this is all the result of her good deeds. God always puts the virtuous through a trial, but he is generous in granting rewards at the end. Chandrakant, a mother's love is matchless. Gunialba must be delighted that the threat to Kumud behn has passed. She has loved me like a mother ever since I was a young boy. Kusum behn, please tell Gunialba that Pradhanji Vidya Chatura will be here shortly. But tell me, why did you wait right at the back?'

Kusum smiled and said, 'Maharaj, Pitaji once told me that Bhishma's advice to Yudhishthir, contained in the *Shanti Parva* of the *Mahabharata*, is very dear to you. He also said that one particular sentence is your favourite. As I saw you, I remembered that. I wanted to see for myself that advice being put into practice by you. But at the same time, I also know that to intervene while the king is performing his duties is to obstruct the kingly functions.'

[2] M. R. Kale, trans. *The Abhijnanasakuntalam of Kalidasa*, Act VII, Verse 30, 10th ed., 8th reprint (Delhi: Motilal Banarsidass, 1969, 2010), 289.

'Is that so? Tell me what that sentence is?' Maniraj asked eagerly.

Everyone present watched the enactment of this delightful drama, their unwavering gaze fixed on them. Gunasundari and Sundargauri looked on fondly from behind the curtain, their eyes on Kusum. Chandrakant was deeply vexed; in his mind he reprimanded his absent friend: Oh, Sarasvatichandra, you are ill-fated indeed! Who knows where your wandering has taken you? And here I am, following you without luck. Look at this precious jewel of a girl. You want to remain a brahmachari, and this one here wants to emulate Mirabai! How can that be? Because of the two of you, my legal practice has gone to seed!

This conversation with the king made Kusum feel very shy. She turned red with embarrassment and her eyes refused to lift from the ground. Finally she looked up and her lips parted softly like a blossoming bud, and she recited the verse.

> That king is the best in whose realm the people live without fear,
> just as the sons live without any fear in the house of their father.[3]

She continued, 'Maharaj, the people approached you just as children approach their father. Why would I not want to witness a scene of such joy and beauty?'

Maniraj was delighted. Kusum withdrew, and Maniraj sought Chandrakant's company. As they walked together, Maniraj spoke of his admiration for the *Shanti Parva*. 'Chandrakant, in fact I am yet to read a counsel to a king that has such gravity. You must have read many books. So tell me, in your readings have you ever come across the essence of the duties of a king as relevant as that which is contained in these verses?' Maniraj recited for Chandrakant.

> The king should always bear himself towards his subjects as a mother towards the child of her womb. Hear, O monarch, the reason why this becomes desirable. As the mother, disregarding those objects that are most cherished by her, seeks the good of

[3] Kisari Mohan Ganguli, trans. *The Mahabharata of Krishna-Dwaipayana Vyasa*, Book 12: *Shanti Parva*, Canto 66, Verse 33 (Calcutta: Pratap Chandra Roy, 1883–1896), 143.

> her child alone, even so, without doubt, should kings conduct themselves (towards their subjects).[4]

'I have placed these verses, etched in gold, in my bedroom as also in the hall of public audience.'

Maniraj and Chandrakant moved towards the royal tent that was pitched at the other end of the village. Others followed them. Kusum went inside the house and stood before her mother and aunt. Sundargauri was delighted with her beautifully adorned niece. Kusum's conversation with Maniraj had been both appropriate and charming. Sundargauri gathered Kusum in her embrace and kissed her. Gunasundari looked on affectionately at this lovely scene, thinking to herself: Just a moment ago, we were drowned in sorrows, while at this moment only joy prevails. How joyful are these two! Mysterious are the ways of God!

And truly, God's ways are mysterious. Joy follows sorrow, and behind joy lurks grief. Kusum, the embodiment of joy, was kissed by her widowed aunt who embodied sorrow. The moment she kissed Kusum, the two soldiers who had rushed to bring news of Kumud's drowning reached the house. They jumped down from their horses and, being granted entry into the house, breathlessly recounted the news of Kumud's drowning in the Subhadra. Everyone was stunned. A profound sorrow enveloped the house like a shroud. Gunasundari sat stupefied, unable to move or say anything as tears streamed down her eyes like rain. Sundargauri sat lamenting, 'Oh Kumud! What have you done? Oh my daughter, I raised you and loved you—you were the only one this poor wretch could call her own. How shall I bear this tragedy?' Young Kusum, with all her ornaments and finery still on her, collapsed onto the ground. She clutched Gunasundari and wept, 'Gunial, why are you so despondent? Why do you forget that we are under the protection of the Maharaj? At least have a message sent to him? Dadaji will not come back without Kumud behn. Pitaji will be here soon. Why have *you* have given up, Gunial?' Everyone sobbed and spoke incoherently. Finally, Kusum got up and came out

[4] Ganguli, *The Mahabharata*, Book 12: *Shanti Parva*, Canto 56, Verse 44–46, 116.

on the veranda. She saw a rider approaching in the distance, holding a bundle under one arm—you may remember dear reader, he was the messenger sent by Kumud's coachman with her belongings. Kusum rushed inside the house and excitedly said, 'Gunial, get up! There is a messenger on his way!' All rushed out anxiously. Kusum ran towards the approaching rider and asked, 'Has Kumud behn been rescued?'

The messenger replied, struggling to keep his voice even, 'It is God's will. The outlaws could not harm Kumud behn, but the river carried her away. These are all her belongings. Her coachman sent them with me. Vadil Manchatura and the other soldiers have gone in search of her. The coachman is waiting for them.'

Gunasundari's tears were unstoppable. She held on to the bundle and asked the messenger, 'Bhai, do you think she will be found? She had written to me yesterday. She wanted to talk to me about something; it has remained unsaid.'

The messenger tried to console her, 'Gunasundariba, it is pointless to worry. The river cannot be controlled by anyone. But have faith that your good deeds will bear fruit. It was not easy to defeat the outlaws. Who can harm the one whom Ram Himself protects? He is all merciful, and you have always done good to others. Kumud behn was worshipped like Goddess Lakshmi by her in-laws. The children of righteous parents have virtue. God will not turn his back on two such families.' The messenger, too, was weeping unabashedly by now.

His words gave little comfort to Gunasundari. Kumud, her first child, the sweetest fruit of her youth—and yet so uncared for! Gunasundari, crushed by the burdens of the family and by custom, had no time to love her, to fuss over her and shower her with affection. As if Kumud were motherless, she was given away to Sundargauri to raise! Gunasundari had no time for Kumud. Kumud, gentle and meek Kumud! She had never said an inappropriate word to anyone. Kumud, abandoned by Sarasvatichandra, was flung towards Pramaddhan by fate and haste. The misfortune of such a virtuous daughter made Gunasundari inconsolable. Nothing in the world could have given her solace. It was futile to hope that she could be rescued. Gunasundari collapsed weeping at the doorstep and sat there, numb and dazed.

No one knew how to console her. Her grief poured itself out in these words:

I could not love you enough, my daughter
And hence you faced such despair
I could not give you any joy, my daughter
Ask, now ask anything of me
O' woe betide—my Kumud is lost!
I rendered you motherless in infancy
I had no pity for you—how cruel could I be?
I placed heavy burdens on you, my daughter
O' woe is me—my Kumud has been crushed!
Daughter mine, you were most wise
You kept to yourself the burdens of your heart
Not even to your mother did you confide your woes
O' woe upon us—my bud-like Kumud has withered!
The river proved dearer to you than your mother
O' daughter mine, where have you gone?
That you chose the river puts a dagger through my heart
O' where is my precious Kumud?

Gunasundari hung her throbbing head in anguish. As she poured her heart out, she felt somewhat lighter and regained her fortitude. She wiped her tears and said, 'Kusum, open the bundle.' Kusum opened it. Vanleela's letter was on top. In it, Vanleela had narrated the doings of Pramaddhan, Krishnakalika and their lowly designs. Gunasundari read the letter, and was shocked. She said, 'Sundarbhabhi, if Kumud has indeed drowned in the river, consider that a cow has been rescued from an abattoir. Oh God! How could she have shared her pain with me?' Vanleela had composed a poem. Gunasundari read it.

My virtuous Kumud, do not be perturbed
The Lord will look after you; we walk in His shadow
The evil do not change their ways, as if blind to them
May they lose their sight and turn lame.
That black-hearted Kalika cast an evil eye
Not knowing that she was watched by me
I will not forgive her, for Kumud you are most dear to me
I pray no harm befalls you; be patient,

I will shame her publicly.
The minister will hear of this and Devi will know it all,
That whore will weep long and copious tears;
Alak will kick her out like she kicked Khalak
And rid her naïve brother of this witch's spell
She will send for you to return home.
Swear upon my head that you will fear nothing
You are clever, wise and God-fearing
Truth shall triumph, the untrue shall perish
Remembering her dear Vanleela,
Kumud must remain true to her word.

Gunasundari said, 'Sundarbhabhi, it is unimaginable—the cause of Kumud's sorrow is similar to what Chandikabhabhi faced. Oh, my daughter delicate as a flower, how could you ever bear this? This agony is so intense that one wants to give up life. It is now certain that Kumud did not drown in the river accidentally—she jumped to her death to be free of this pain.'

'My dearest daughter, couldn't you wait? Couldn't you at least talk to us once?' Sundargauri said as she wept. 'But the capacity to bear pain comes to those like me who are born to pain. And you were delicate as a flower. How did you bear this vajra-like blow? Kumud, I never once saw you cry. What all did you not suffer.'

Kusum also wept, but her pain with tinged with rage towards her brother-in-law.

Gunasundari read Vanleela's letter again to understand it better. She was shocked that Pramaddhan had in fact made accusations about Kumud's character. She read about Navinchandra. Her mind raised a few questions, but they did not persist long. She so longed to meet Kumud, to comfort her, to cradle in her arms and give her solace. Her mother's heart was torn between this intense desire to comfort her daughter, and an overwhelming sense of despondency and failure. This was perhaps the most unbearable of pains.

If Kumud's death were to become a certainty, Gunasundari decided she would invite Vanleela to Ratnanagari and learn all the details. It would pierce her heart and increase her pain a hundred-fold;

but that would be her way of repenting and doing penance for the sin of giving away her gentle and pure daughter to a family of butchers who slaughtered her, as a cow is slaughtered in an abattoir. But then Gunasundari realised that with the sole exception of Pramaddhan, all the others loved Kumud. She felt that she had been unfair in comparing them to a family of butchers. Saubhagya Devi, Alak Kishori and Buddhidhan were all good, pious individuals; the thought of them soothed her somewhat. And yet, Kumud's unspoken, unshared agony hovered above her like immense black clouds—no amount of wisdom or reasoning could alleviate her anguish. Gunasundari longed for Vidya Chatura, her soul companion who shared her joy and pain, ruled over her mind and heart and guided her in all her actions. Her heart cried out for him. Just then a maid came in and whispered to her that Pradhanji was on his way. Everyone got up to go and meet him. At that moment, Gunasundari saw a sliver of moonlight amidst the dark clouds; she heard his voice, and her aggrieved heart felt soothed as if touched by ambrosia.

> "You should know that even someone who lives far away would not be late for this festival!" Addressed by her relatives in this way with honest words a woman found peace, as if drinking amrta, as if from out in the woods she had heard the voice of her beloved.[5]

[5] Translated by Hank Heifetz from a translation in progress of Magha's *Shishupala Vadha*.

3 News from Bombay: Dhurtalal's Machinations

Dear reader, we must now turn our attention to Bombay to acquaint ourselves of the developments after Chandrakant's departure in search of Sarasvatichandra.

Old Sheth Laxminandan had realised that he was the cause of his son's disappearance and he was the reason why Sarasvatichandra had left home. This hurt him. He now longed for his son to return. A man in his youth feels passionately for his wife and sons. A youthful mind also has greater flexibility and suppleness to deal with separation from wife or son. The wounds heal faster. But as old age approaches, the mind grows feeble and one can hear the approaching steps of the God of Death. The possibility of final separation becomes vivid in imagination. Old age looms large not just over the ageing man but also over his sons; they need the assurance of their joys and of support in their sorrows. Laxminandan pined for his learned and intelligent son Sarasvatichandra and withered with every passing day. He was prepared to spend his inexhaustible wealth to search him out. He spent money everywhere, among the Bombay police, among the officials and businessmen, and gave money to his servants to further their efforts. He left no stone unturned. He sought advice from all quarters. He handed over the reins of the business to his wife's brother Dhurtalal and focused all his energies in looking for Sarasvatichandra. Food became tasteless, sleep deserted him. He would lie awake till the early hours of the morning preoccupied with only one thought—his lost son. Laxminandan became a wreck. He cried incessantly when he was alone. He even stopped bothering to wipe his tears. Sarasvatichandra's visage was etched on his mind's eye and Sarasvatichandra's voice haunted his ears. He could think of nothing else, speak of nothing else. In a few months the Sheth had withered and aged greatly; his eyes had become lustreless and protruded from their sockets. Everyone said that he would either go mad or die.

Almost everyone took pity on him. But his brother-in-law Dhurtalal was filled with a new zeal. He did not want Laxminandan to come out of his debilitating sorrow. Dhurtalal was quick to grasp that the Sheth had no affection left for his sister Guman; Laxminandan no longer had anything to do with her. Dhurtalal therefore no longer mentioned Guman to him. He tried to secure the Sheth's confidence by making a display of excessive humility, impeccable honesty, and a big show of doing everything within his powers to find Sarasvatichandra. He gained the old man's confidence and established control over all aspects of the business. The clerks working in Laxminandan's office accepted Dhurtalal's authority. He obtained the keys to the safe, the cash and all documents. He became the sole controller and master of the factory, and made sure that no complaint regarding his conduct ever reached Laxminandan. Mired in sorrow, old and feeble, Laxminandan was deceived.

Dhurtalal's treachery was played out behind the curtain of honesty. Dhurtalal accepted a nominal salary but he began to take a cut from every transaction. Apparently, there was no loss to Laxminandan as his arbitrage and commissions did not show any decline in revenue. But Dhurtalal took a part of these earnings for himself—he took a commission of two annas for every rupee of purchase made for the mill, the office and the household. The suppliers gave less and inferior quality of goods. Dhurtalal also took a commission on sales. He bribed Laxminandan's clerks and made them part of his scheme. He even threatened those who hesitated to join his plans.

But there were two individuals who did not join Dhurtalal. As long as Guman saw Sarasvatichandra as an adversary, she acted on her brother's advice. But with his disappearance, Guman's sole aim became to protect her son Dhananandan's interests—she wanted all of Laxminandan's wealth for her son. Dhurtalal, blinded by his own greed, had not anticipated this change. He assumed that his sister was still a partner in crime and he still shared with her his plans to strip Laxminandan of all his wealth. However, Guman had lately realised that her brother was in fact stealing money from her son. She had used him against Sarasvatichandra, true, but she now felt that Dhurtalal's next victim could be her own son. Guman was well aware of Dhurtalal's capacity for machination and guile. She grew to both fear and loath her brother. She now saw him as an adversary. Gradually, Guman put a distance between Dhurtalal and herself. Dhurtalal recognised this change. He began to threaten Guman of dire consequences on the one hand even as he gained the Sheth's confidence on the other. In front of Laxminandan, Dhurtalal showed great contempt for his sister and concern for Sarasvatichandra. But this had an unintended effect—Guman saw that her brother had turned arrogant, and she decided to take him on. Once Dhurtalal was firmly cast in the role of an adversary, jealousy and animosity stoked her fire. Guman resolved to herself: Watch out brother—I am your sister after all.

And so Guman kept herself out of her brother's group and his machinations. The only other person who resisted Dhurtalal was a clerk named Haridas. An experienced and honest bania from a good family, Haridas was an old employee of Laxminandan's firm; he was also quite attached to Sarasvatichandra. Haridas had a characteristic sense of self-preservation, cleverness, sweetness and patience. He did not challenge Dhurtalal openly; he remained close to Dhurtalal's men without implicating himself in their activities. He unobtrusively observed their activities and hoped that one day he would be able to prove himself true to his salt.

Dhurtalal's ascent seemed unchallenged. But he had no doubts that his reign was temporary, and that with the waning moon, it too would wane. The day Sarasvatichandra returned, or Sheth Laxminandan's interest in the business was reawakened, he was certain to lose his position. This fear stalked Dhurtalal day and night. He was determined to be wealthy before such a day came. He was also determined to extend his reign as long as possible. Propelled by this desire, he abandoned all considerations of good and bad, right and wrong and moved resolutely ahead to advance his goal, exploring every possible avenue to acquire ill-gotten wealth. He opened the flood gates. He stole not only from Laxminandan's business, he also starting cheating other firms with which he had dealings. He opened a business in partnership with some of his friends. They traded with Laxminandan's firm at arbitrary prices and borrowed money from the firm against promised delivery of goods. Once Dhurtalal's own business was established, he began to entice Laxminandan's clients. Many widows, religious institutions and other unsuspecting persons had deposited their savings with Laxminandan. Dhurtalal wanted to capture these deposits. Laxminandan had earned the reputation of a reliable 'trustee'. Dhurtalal believed that a trustee must flourish at the expense of others. He used Laxminandan's high reputation to acquire trusteeship. Like that cruel fisherman who wanted the entire season's catch in one day, Dhurtalal cast his net far and wide. He had begun to swim in dangerous waters.

Dhurtalal was not the kind whose greed was satisfied easily. His devilish mind plotted schemes to ensure that Sarasvatichandra was never traced and that Laxminandan's abilities were paralysed forever. Under pretence of assisting Laxminandan in his search for Sarasvatichandra, he bribed those carrying out the search to ensure that Sarasvatichandra's whereabouts were never traced—and that if he were ever traced, he should be killed immediately. Dhurtalal did not want to take any chances. He led Laxminandan towards a mirage, hoping that the old Sheth would get caught in the whirlpool of despair, hope, helplessness and confusion and lose his mental balance altogether. He kept Laxminandan's fears and anxieties alive and would not let him forget about his son even for a moment. Ultimately, Dhurtalal decided to take things in hand rather than just wait for things to happen.

One day, lonely and forlorn, Laxminandan visited Sarasvatichandra's bungalow in Walkeshwar. The doorman opened the house for him. He went and stood before Kumud Sundari's portrait. Haridas and Dhurtalal were with him. Laxminandan sat on a chair facing the portrait. Tears welled up in his eyes as he said, 'Haridas, this was to be the bride of my son. He left the house, and she was married to someone else. I lost two precious jewels. If I had not been so foolish and blind, all the riches and glories of the world would have been mine. But fate turned against me.' He put his head on Haridas' shoulder and wept aloud.

Haridas wiped his tears and said, 'Shethji, you must not punish yourself like this. Can you fight fate? It is not for lack of your efforts that Bhai cannot be found. We can make the efforts, but it is for God to grant us the fruits.'

Dhurtalal also butted in, 'Shethji, I am worried for you. You might lose your mental equilibrium. You have done all that one could for a son as deserving as yours. You are unable to pay any attention to the business. That may work against you in the future. I feel that you should plan for the future when you are in a position to do so.'

Laxminandan was startled. 'Haridas, do you think I am losing my mind?'

Haridas had observed the changing facial expressions of Dhurtalal. He softly said, 'Shethji, I believe that if you were to start taking interest in the business again, you shall never be in danger of losing your equilibrium. We should also know what plans Dhurtalal Sheth has for the future.'

Dhurtalal did not like this. He suspected Haridas and surmised that Haridas was either a fool or against him. He looked searchingly at the bania, and said, 'Shethji, just as I am concerned about my nephew, I am also concerned about Sarasvatichandra Bhai. I do not think like a woman in this respect, and you know that well. You should make arrangements such that it would protect the interests of both your sons. If I do not tell you that you have lost some of your equanimity, it would please you, but it would also harm the interests of your family. I would not be true to my salt if I say things just to please you, disregarding the real good of your family. That I cannot do, Shethji. But I am convinced that right now you are not in a position to take business decisions—you are torn between love for your son, and the pressures of running a vast business. And I am pained by your condition.'

Haridas thought, what a crook!

Sheth replied, 'Dhurtalal, you have to show me the way. I am preoccupied with thoughts of Bhai. I am incapable of any other thought.'

Dhurtalal was not one to let go of an opportunity presented to him. He eagerly said, 'That is what I am also saying, Shethji. I have already thought about it. You should make a document which gives the power of attorney to two persons—one who represents my nephew, and the other who could look after Sarasvatichandra Bhai's interests until he returns. This you should execute at a time when your mental capacities are not in question. If you fail to do this, at some point the matter will reach the courts, and all your wealth shall be wasted.'

Haridas quietly asked, 'Who could those two persons be?'

'If Shethji approves, I can represent my nephew Dhananandan and ...' Dhurtalal hesitated, 'Someone like Haridas could represent Sarasvatichandra Bhai.'

'No, I do not have such capabilities. Dhurtalal Sheth is capable of looking after the interests of both,' said Haridas. Laxminandan thought for a moment and said, 'We shall see,' and he got up and went to look at other rooms in the house. Dhurtalal was left alone with Haridas. He felt that Haridas' response had caused some uncertainty in Laxminandan. He decided to take Haridas into confidence.

'Haridas, you do not understand.'

'No, Sheth. I am a poor, small-minded bania. I don't have your intelligence.'

'Listen, if the Sheth follows my advice, both of us will be little princelings.'

'Both? Am I worthy of it, Sheth?'

'Do you think they were born wearing all their jewels and silks?'

'Bhai Sahib, I shall be guided by you.'

'Look here, in just two months I have filled my house with riches. Do you want that or not? How can anyone get rich on this measly salary!'

'That is true. But can anyone change his destiny?'

'Why worry about destiny? One should seize the moment. Old Sheth has lost his mind, and if he hasn't, we shall certify that he has—the day after he signs this document.'

'How?'

'There are many vaids and doctors available. A little money can make a slave of anyone.'

'But Sheth, I don't even have the money to buy poison.'

'Why are you so black-hearted, Haridas? The money is someone else's; the pen with which the doctor will certify him crazy will also be a borrowed one. We are only the beneficiaries. We shall use the Sheth's money to rob him. How come you are so daft!' Dhurtalal caught Haridas by the shoulders and shook him a little.

'I see. Now I understand. But both of us have eaten Shethji's salt.'

'Forget about being true to salt and all of that. Once the money starts pouring in, one can very well do without salt; we will have enough sweets to eat then.'

'But Sheth, I lack the courage to do this.'

'What a coward you are, Haridas! Come with me this evening, and I will provide you with the courage.'

'So what is to be done?'

'Once I leave, you must convince the Sheth of our plan. I will take you out in the evening. The Sheth has made out two-three promissory notes to me. I shall transfer them to you—that should give you the necessary courage.'

'Yes ...'

'Yes or no—don't botch it up, Haridas. In time, you will also learn to have fun.' Having said so, Dhurtalal proceeded towards his carriage, muttering to himself: I shall introduce the bania to some fun. I will take him to the prostitute Radhesani—Haridas will become my servant for life! The fool doesn't know that Bhai will have to die. Once he is gone, his share will go to my nephew Dhananandan. And then naturally, I shall remove the nephew, too. I shall be the sole owner. This brainless bania I will push out in no time. I want a power of attorney that states that once Sarasvatichandra is no more, his executor—this bania—will also have no say. But this Guman has become quite a nuisance! Bloody woman, why can't she be killed off as well? For a moment Dhurtalal was shocked that he actually wanted to kill his own sister, but it passed. He got into the carriage, thinking: Why should I care if she is my sister or my mother—all are secondary to my self-interest. How does it matter if it is ninety-nine or a hundred? I am going to kill so many mosquitoes, how will one more make any difference? The carriage moved on. He turned back and glanced at the bungalow. His conversation with himself continued: What if the Sheth refuses to sign the documents? But I will have my gang as the last resort, won't I? If he does not sign willingly, he will do so under duress. Failing everything, Padamji Parsi can forge the Sheth's signature even with his left hand. We will see what is to be done. The world can go to hell. Dhurtalal twirled his moustache, thrust out his chest and boxed the coachman, 'Rascal, why can't you move faster?' The coachman looked back, lashed out at the horse, and the carriage galloped out of sight. Haridas, dejected and despondent saw the coach disappear. He sat on a chair, ruminating.

Oh God! Oh Mother Earth! How can you bear such burdens? All this is beyond me. Once the brother-in-law takes control of this king's court, the old Sheth's business, Goddess Lakshmi is certain to vanish. Her place has been taken by strife and conflict. A precious jewel had to leave home because of the evil designs of this Dhurtalal. He turned Guman against the Sheth. He will now term the Sheth crazy. His evil ways have corrupted the old, trusted clerks. Now Sheth's sanity and his wealth are both about to desert him. All because of this Dhurtalal. Times have turned against the Sheth. The Sheth has realised his follies. But it is already too late. He now weeps and wails and Guman is frightened at the sight of her brother. After all they are brahmins—they only have hindsight. And could even Brahma put some sense into women's heads? If Sita had not compelled Laxman to follow Ram, she would not have been abducted. It is said that a woman's brains are in her ankles; it is not without substance. But such is fate. But Haridas, you are neither a brahmin nor a woman. You are a bania. Can you put your brains to some use? The Sheth is not about to change, the Shethani will remain what she is, and that rogue will do his roguery.

They will be who they are. It is you who have to somehow rescue the situation. This body of mine has been nourished by food provided by the Sheth. Now it is my turn to rescue him from the high seas—yes, that should be my life's purpose. Oh Haridas, God made you a bania. Now it is your turn to prove that you are in fact a bania.

Haridas closed his eyes and sat in quiet contemplation. A few moments of silence revived his brain. He calculated something on his fingers. He was about to say something aloud, but checked himself. His train of thought continued: It is dangerous to open my mouth. One should only speak to oneself. It is not wise to converse with the Sheth. He is not in control of his emotions and he might even blurt out my name to that rogue. Guman Shethani is in complete control of her faculties, but after all she has the tongue of a woman. There is no one in the house or the firm who has remained unsullied. I will have to put my life at stake. I will have to work alone. And then there is God. God is first; Haridas is his servant. God will back me up. The rest can go to hell.

Haridas, God is with you! He has renewed my hopes. He shows me the way. Chandrakant! Yes, very good. It's a good omen. But he has gone in search of Sarasvatichandra. All right, I will write to him. But can I wait that long? I will get a note of introduction from him to Bulwer Sahib, who is a friend of Bhai. But what am I to do until then? I will rob even the rogue. He has promised to pay me a bribe. I shall be greedy and take all that he has to offer. I will use his own shoes to beat him with. I am poor and without resources. I will use his bribe to pay the police and the lawyers. But will the boat sail on the steam of a poor bania like me? It may not, but even the stones float when Ram's name is invoked. So what if he is not with us, Sarasvatichandra Bhai's name still holds sway in this city. Just as a pedigree horse feels proud when an expert rider rides it, Haridas felt proud and his faculties grew sharper at the possibility of doing a good, selfless deed in service of his master, and he was filled with new vigour and hope. He had promised to meet Dhurtalal that evening. Haridas went inside the bungalow to seek Sheth Laxminandan's permission to leave. He found the Sheth standing near a window, gazing at the sea, his eyes searching for Sarasvatichandra. Laxminandan did not see or hear Haridas come in.

'Shethji ...' Haridas called softly to draw Sheth's attention. Laxminandan was startled. He turned around and shot a question, 'Haridas, where is Dhurtalal?'

'He has left.'

'Who else is in the bungalow?'

'Just the two of us.'

'Are you certain?'

'Absolutely.'

'Haridas?'

'Yes.'

'Haridas!' the Sheth repeated, looking intently at Haridas.

'Yes, Shethji.' Haridas saw inflamed passions simmering in old Laxminandan's eyes.

'Whose servant are you?'

'Yours.'

'Say that again.'

'Yours, Shethji. As long as there is life in this body, I am your servant, have no fear. I will remain faithful to you even if there is no one else left.'

'Who will protect my Sarasvatichandra?'

'That you alone will have to do, Shethji.'

'Liar! Go away! I don't need you.'

Haridas was shocked. He realised that the Sheth's rambling had a deeper meaning and he grew alert at once. 'Shethji, there was a time when you did not care for Sarasvatichandra Bhai. But now you do.'

'How long will this last, Haridas?'

'Shethji, as long as your heart remains in the right place.'

'If I accept Dhurtalal's suggestion, would I be thinking right?'

'That is for you to decide. But is he not a well-wisher of Bhai as well?'

'A man may err once. A man who makes the same mistake twice is a beast.'

'That has merit.'

'Either you consider me to be a beast, or you are a beast yourself.'

'I am a poor man, Shethji, more like a beast.'

'Stop it. Now listen to me. This is a pointless conversation. Dhurtalal has corrupted all my trusted men. If he has made even you his own, tell me so frankly right now and leave from my sight. He and you can both do whatever you like. But don't forget, Laxminandan still has some brains left. These ruins you see speak of a glorious past.'

Haridas was stunned by these clear words. He saw the former Laxminandan re-emerge before his eyes, and realised that his task had just become so much easier. His eyes welled up with tears of joy and relief.

Laxminandan was closely observing the fast-changing expressions on his face—his trust in Haridas was reaffirmed. 'Haridas, you need not say anything more. You are the only one from my firm who has remained faithful to me. All the others are scoundrels. I know you. You cannot be made to turn against me. You are not one of them. But take a pledge, touch my feet and swear that you are still worthy of my trust.'

Before Laxminandan could even complete the sentence, Haridas was at his feet. He clasped them and wept, 'Shri Vitthal is my witness, Shethji, if I ever turn against you, in thought or deed, I will incur the sin of killing a cow, a brahmin and a woman. Pray do reveal your mind to me.'

Laxminandan choked with emotion. He lifted Haridas up from the ground, gave him a seat adjacent and said, 'Haridas, tell me, what is on your mind?'

'Shethji, I will tell you everything. But I fear that if you were to lose your equilibrium and blurt out my name, no one will be able to find even a trace of my bones. I would lose my life, and you would lose the one man who is still faithful to you. Therefore, do not force me to reveal my mind. Have faith in me, and tell me all that you want to. You can put me on trial whenever you want. Open your heart to me—share with me all the secret burdens that you bear. But allow my lips to remain sealed. I will bring you all that you need from my store room. But if I handover the key to the room to you, Shethji, all shall be stolen.'

Laxminandan looked grave. He thought deeply for a while, then said, 'Haridas, you remain as truthful as ever. I am convinced that you have not crossed over to the other side. I trust you. Your advice is correct. I accept it just as a child obeys elders. You must give truthful replies to all that I ask.'

'I agree to that.'

'I was so perturbed by Bhai's disappearance that I lost my equilibrium and I was even prepared to do that which would have robbed Bhai of all his inheritance. This I realised only today—and I do not like what I have done at all. Tell me, is my caution misplaced?'

'Excellent, Shethji. What could be more auspicious than the day of marriage?'

'Today I realised that my brother-in-law has been cheating me. In my madness and despair, I have paid no mind to what he has been doing, but I did notice some things. When I think back on it, I know I have allowed him a free hand. I realise now that my brother-in-law is a complete rogue and a scoundrel.'

'Yes.'

'Just "Yes" won't do, Haridas. Tell me if I have thought it through or not?'

Haridas laughed. 'Shethji, today you have changed your opinion of him. What guarantee do I have that you will not change your mind again? Tomorrow is another day. Hence, do not ask me what he did. You tell me what *you* have decided to do, and I will respond. You must follow the condition that we agreed upon.'

'All right. I am not going to sign the document that has been drawn up by that rogue. It is like cutting my own wrist and making a gift of it to him. Am I right? You must respond to this; you have no choice.'

'Absolutely right, Shethji, you could not have been more correct. I say this without hesitation.'

'Fine. Tomorrow, I will come to the office after lunch. My intention is clear. I will take control of the treasury, the cash, the account books and all other business-related papers. I will then throw out my brother-in-law and warn him that he should never again step inside my house or my office.'

'That I agree. But you should consider if all that should be done tomorrow itself.'

'You might have a point there, Haridas. We shall think about it. Now the next thing. I have written some names on this paper; they are clerks in the office and the mill. They will be dismissed from their job tomorrow. Take this and read the list.'

'I will read the list, but we don't need to rush into it. They are lowly functionaries; they are moved by their hunger. If we provide them with enough to eat, they shall work with us.'

'All right. Once I drive this one out, you will have a major task to accomplish, Haridas.'

'What is that?'

'You must find Bhai. If it costs you a lakh of rupees, you must find him. If it costs you your life, you must find him. You must lead the search. But you must bring back Bhai—he *must* be brought back.' Laxminandan appeared somewhat unhinged as he spoke the last sentence.

Haridas became guarded. 'Shethji, that I will do. Chandrakant is already on Bhai's trail. Even Bulwer Sahib has some inkling of his whereabouts.'

'What? Is that so?'

'Yes. We should get a letter from Chandrakant in the next three to four days.'

'Haridas, this cunning rascal appropriated twenty-five thousand rupees of mine and made no effort to look for Bhai. And this Chandrakant took no money from me. You are right; Chandrakant genuinely feels for Bhai. But this rogue Dhurtalal was responsible for Bhai's disappearance. He did not want Bhai to return—why would he look for him? But without thinking I gave him the responsibility.'

'Shethji, that was fate. Now tell me, what else do we need to do?'

'I am still not in full possession of my senses. I don't know when I will lose it again. Therefore, we must have a trustee.'

'But just now you said that you would not sign the documents!'

'Let me complete. I will not sign any document prepared by that rascal. I want to make a document that makes Bhai the sole trustee of all my wealth. He will be the sole trustee—not you, not me.'

'Wonderful, Shethji. But will Shethani agree to it?'

'If she does not agree, let her be. I do not trust anyone but Bhai. I will hand over all my wealth to him. I will make him a trustee of Dhananandan's share as well. Bhai will be responsible for Dhan's mother. He will be Dhan's guardian. He will even be responsible for me.'

'But Shethji, Guman Shethani's consent is necessary. Don't be in such a mad hurry.'

Laxminandan got up and slapped Harilal. 'Bastard! Traitor! You want *her* consent? You want to please her? Go away! I have no use for you.'

Haridas caressed his cheek and said, 'Shethji, there was a time you wanted to please her to the point that you drove away Bhai. Am I so wrong in thinking about her pleasure in Bhai's absence?'

Laxminandan mellowed. 'You are right, Haridas. I won't curse you. But you know what Shethani told me? She said that she did not know that her brother was such a rogue. She said Bhai is like a son to her, too, and that he would care for her. She said Bhai would not be able to sleep if she were hungry. Shethani told me that if she had known of her brother's true character, she would never have allowed any of this to happen. Haridas, do you understand? Or is your brain slower than that of this woman?'

'Sheth, how can I, a poor clerk, aspire to the intelligence of a Shethani? But could she not have said this to test your intentions?'

'Stupid, you have still not understood. Dhurtalal gave some powder to his sister, which she was to administer to me. If she had done that, I would have either gone mad or died! Look, here it is.' Laxminandan took out the packet that contained the powder and showed it to Haridas.

Haridas was shocked. 'Dhurtalal! Oh, he is a demon in guise of a man. Sheth, now I understand things better. Did the Shethani give you this packet?'

'Who else? Do you think she fancies being a widow?'

'Oh God! Sheth, you are right.'

'Is there anything else?'

'No, but what shall we do till such time as Bhai returns?'

'I am around. I am still like a tiger. I shall have them for a meal.'

'That is true. But you are still not fully in control of yourself.'

'What if it persists? Do you think my abilities will be further eroded?'

'Shethji, who knows the will of God?'

'True, one cannot say what God wills. But if I were to lose my mental equilibrium, Chandrakant and Bulwer Sahib should take control of the business till such time that Bhai comes back.'

'Now everything is in place. I accept.'

'You can go now. Tomorrow at twelve noon I will be at the office. I will create a scene and drive out that rogue.'

Haridas realised that it was futile to restrain the Sheth any further. He decided to leave it in the hands of God. But he had to think about the next day's plan. 'All right, Shethji. I will see you tomorrow. Meanwhile, write me a note addressed to the Police Commissioner.'

'What for?'

'I want to ensure the presence of the police tomorrow at the office. That rogue will not give up so easily. He is certain to do some mischief.'

Laxminandan wrote a note to the police commissioner. He also wrote to Bulwer Sahib. He handed them both to Haridas and said, 'This one is for the chief of police, and this one is for Bulwer Sahib. I have requested him to come home tomorrow morning. We will draft the document together. I have to act fast. He will also bring some news of Bhai.'

Haridas took the notes, kept them carefully in his pocket, and waited. Laxminandan said, 'Now go. Go and bring back Bhai.'

Tears welled up in Haridas' eyes; the Sheth was not in full possession of himself. He repeated, 'Go, Haridas.'

'Tomorrow morning, Dhurtalal will enquire about the document. He will also want to know about our conversation. What will you tell him, Shethji?'

Laxminandan looked at him meekly and said, 'I will tell him whatever you want me to tell him.'

'Do not reveal your mind to him, Shethji. Just tell him that he should talk to me and that everything will be decided tomorrow afternoon.'

Laxminandan got up and hugged Haridas. 'Wonderful! You have the brains of a bania, Haridas. How do you think so fast? It's a perfect answer! I don't need to think about it at all. I need to tell him nothing! Now go—we will meet tomorrow at noon. Go. Until tomorrow noon. Nothing else.'

Haridas was torn between conflicting emotions. He felt burdened, pained, and yet he was happy at what he had accomplished. He felt hope and enthusiasm, as also fear. He told the gardener to look after Laxminandan and pleaded with God to take care of his Sheth. It was almost dark by the time he stepped out of the bungalow into the garden and on to the road. He had to meet Bulwer Sahib, the police commissioner and Dhurtalal. He hired a Victoria carriage. The road was deserted. The fading light of evening and the peaceful road allowed him to calm his excited mind. He said aloud, 'God, Your will is supreme. What a poor wretch like me could not have accomplished even with great effort will now be made possible because of a few words spoken by the Sheth, however unbalanced he might be—such is Your will. Morality and good shall emerge victorious and sin shall be vanquished.' These words lingered in the air, swirled around and finally merged with the falling dusk. Everything looked in its place, undisturbed as before.

Haridas went to the police commissioner's house first. The commissioner was well-disposed towards both Laxminandan and Sarasvatichandra. Dhurtalal knew of this, and he had used it to cultivate his own nexus in the police department. At times he would use the commissioner's name, at other times he used Laxminandan's contacts, and when necessary, he would bribe his way to favour. Haridas was aware of Dhurtalal's network among the subordinate policemen. He therefore thought it prudent to approach the commissioner directly. He gave Laxminandan's note to the commissioner. Haridas gave a detailed account of all the issues and individuals involved, and requested for police presence around the office for the next day at noon. The commissioner agreed. Next, Haridas met Bulwer Sahib and gave him the letter. The Sahib was pleased to hear about Laxminandan's decision, and he agreed to visit the Sheth's house the following morning.

Haridas went home, had his dinner, and without further delay hurried to Dhurtalal's house. Dhurtalal was waiting for him as impatiently as a farmer waiting for rains. Haridas told him that the Sheth was not immediately agreeable to signing the document but had promised to consider the matter the next day at a time when he intended to visit the office. This irked Dhurtalal considerably.

'Haridas, your help will be absolutely essential tomorrow. If the Sheth refuses to sign the document, we will have it forged, but we can't afford to wait any longer. Tomorrow afternoon, we shall declare him mad and have him sent to the mental hospital at Colaba with the help of the police. I have already warned the doctor at Colaba, but I need to tell him the exact time. I will give you a note, which you shall carry to him tomorrow morning.'

Haridas was stunned by Dhurtalal's brazen courage. He said, 'Very good. It's an unfailing remedy. Tomorrow afternoon we shall send the Sheth off to the mental hospital with his hands tied behind his back. What shall we do after that? How shall we get the police?'

'Take this note to Latif Khan Jamadar and Dhurkerao Havaldar. Tell them that the police must remain present at the appointed time.'

'All right. But who shall deliver that note?'

'You, who else? I am the end, and you are my means.'

'All right, Sheth; it will be done before twelve noon tomorrow.'

Haridas took three thousand rupees in cash from Dhurtalal to pay for all the arrangements. Dhurtalal took him to Radhesani's establishment. Radhesani gave him a bidi and sang a thumri for him. Haridas pocketed the bidi. Dhurtalal spoke freely. Haridas learnt all his secrets. He pretended to be shy and did not respond to Radhesani's advances. He left Dhurtalal in Radhesani's company and went home. He kept Dhurtalal's notes away safely. He went over the details of next day's plan in his mind once again and went to sleep late. The next day, Haridas went to the office just before noon. Dhurtalal arrived soon after, followed by Laxminandan a few minutes later. Haridas spoke to neither of them. He opened his desk, took out a ledger book and pretended to write in it. Some policemen were patrolling the street outside. Laxminandan thought that they had come at his request, while Dhurtalal took them to be his. Both believed that Haridas was their confidant; both were certain of final triumph and their confidence was apparent. Laxminandan walked in, his chest thrust out, and accepted the salutations from his staff. Dhurtalal sat on his seat twirling his moustache. Apart from Haridas, there were three or four other clerks sitting at their desks. Surprised by the Sheth's unexpected appearance after months, they made a great show of their diligence.

The brothers-in-law said nothing to each other for a while. Finally, Dhurtalal broke the silence. 'Wonderful, Sheth! Look how splendid the office looks just by your presence. Without you the office looks bald, like a head without a pagdi and an elephant without its palanquin.'

'But you have been present. Are we so different?' Sheth replied, concealing his impatience.

Dhurtalal leaned forward and asked, 'Shethji, did you think about what we discussed yesterday?'

'Hasn't Haridas told you already?'

'No, not everything.'

'It is just that I cannot make up my mind and until I am clear, I do not want to take any decision on it.'

'Sheth, you are mentally unstable. Therefore we should not postpone a good thing for another day.'

The Sheth sat down, put his feet up on his desk and said, 'You are right, I am unhinged. Hence, I order you to leave my office right now. You are dismissed.' Sheth turned towards the clerks and loudly said, 'Clerks, do any of you need to ask Dhurtalal anything? I have dismissed him.'

The clerks were stunned. Dhurtalal turned red in anger, but his words were calm and measured. 'Shethji, you are not completely stable. If you were in full possession of your mental faculties, you can dismiss me whenever you please—you are the master. But given your present condition, I have to act as a guardian to my sister and her son. I am also responsible for your wellbeing. I urge you to calm down.'

'Rogue! I dismiss you! I ask you to leave my premises this very moment. Come on, now get up and get lost!'

Dhurtalal got up and turned towards the clerks, 'Brothers, Shethji has lost all sense. It is indeed very sad. If we don't restrain him, he might harm himself.' No one moved or spoke. Then Laxminandan walked up briskly to Dhurtalal and gave him a shove, shouting, 'Clerks! Call my security guards or call the police. This rascal has no place in my office anymore!' Laxminandan looked towards Haridas.

Dhurtalal turned brazen. 'Haridas, go call the police. The Sheth has gone mad. Clerks, restrain him! What are you staring at my face for?'

A clerk named Thakordas was the first to get up, and the others followed his lead. They tried to restrain the Sheth, but Laxminandan pushed them away, enraged. They tried to tie him up with a cloth rope. Dhurtalal and the clerks shouted, 'The Sheth has gone mad! He is insane!'

Haridas quietly got up and signalled to the police to enter the office. Both Laxminandan and Dhurtalal were sure that the police was partisan. The police came in. They saw Dhurtalal and the clerks tie up Laxminandan. Dhurtalal told them, 'Haridas, the Sheth has gone mad; therefore I have tied him up. Take him away to Colaba or wherever you need to take him.'

One of the policemen asked in Marathi, 'You tied up the Sheth?'

Dhurtalal proudly replied, 'Yes, it was I who tied him up.'

The policeman ordered, 'Tukaji, first handcuff Dhurtalal, and then all these people. Untie the Sheth.'

Dhurtalal and the clerks were taken aback. In a moment the police had handcuffed Dhurtalal and his accomplices. The havaldar addressed his men, 'Tukaji, we can testify that these people illegally restrained Shethji. You take them to the Commissioner Sahib. I will follow.' The policemen dragged away Dhurtalal and his accomplices. Laxminandan, Haridas, the havaldar and a few policemen stayed back. The havaldar freed the Sheth and confiscated the cloth rope with which he was tied as evidence. The havaldar asked, 'Shethji, what are your orders for me?'

Laxminandan replied, 'Havaldar, I will follow you. I will meet the Sahib and file a complaint. You are free to go.'

The havaldar saluted Laxminandan and went away leaving him and Haridas alone.

Haridas said, 'Shethji, did you see the brazenness of the rascals?'

'Haridas, God was my saviour, and so were you. This rogue was determined to send me to the mental hospital.'

'Yes, I am aware of it. Here, read these notes.'

The news spread in the city. There was much excitement. As the Sheth read the notes written by Dhurtalal, Bulwer Sahib came to visit. Laxminandan got up, shook hands with him and offered him a chair to sit. The Sheth asked Haridas, 'Haridas, shall I show these notes to Sahib?'

Bulwer Sahib took his seat. He had met Laxminandan in the morning and learnt about Dhurtalal's treachery. They had decided to meet again in the afternoon. He read the two notes written by Dhurtalal; the plan to have the Sheth declared insane was apparent. Haridas produced the three thousand rupees that he had received from Dhurtalal the previous evening. Both gentlemen were pleased with the honest and dutiful employee. Bulwer Sahib was of the opinion that both the letters and money should be immediately deposited with the police commissioner and that the commissioner be made aware of all the details, but the plan of taking the case to its conclusion and eventual conviction should be left to the police. Bulwer Sahib approved the draft document prepared by Laxminandan, but they decided to seek the counsel of a senior barrister as they could not decide if the document should be signed immediately or if Laxminandan should wait until the criminal case against Dhurtalal was concluded. It was decided that Haridas should remain in Bombay until all these matters were resolved. Bulwer Sahib advised that Chandrakant should coordinate the efforts to find Sarasvatichandra and that the Sheth should give him all the financial assistance required. Laxminandan promptly sent three thousand rupees to Ratnanagari for Chandrakant. Bulwer Sahib returned to his house while Laxminandan and Haridas went to meet the police commissioner.

The police commissioner was a courteous and noble officer. He promptly arranged to have Laxminandan's formal complaint lodged. Haridas gave his testimony; so did the policemen who had witnessed the scene. He assigned the investigation to a trusted chief constable with an order that he should be immediately made aware of any development. Latif Khan and Dhurkerao met Dhurtalal in the prison with the letters he had written to them. They expressed their regret and said that they had received the letter somewhat late and had not understood its contents clearly. Dhurtalal explained to them his intent and read out the notes, thus admitting to his guilt. The serial numbers of the rupee notes that Dhurtalal had given to Haridas were registered in the account books of both Laxminandan and Dhurtalal, because the notes had been initially received by Laxminandan, who had passed them on to Dhurtalal. The police investigation thus moved at a brisk pace. All the news and rumours were reported in the newspapers. Dhurtalal and Laxminandan became the talk of the town. The newspapers also wrote movingly about Sarasvatichandra's disappearance and Laxminandan's state of mind. Bulwer Sahib was keen to publish such stories because he believed that no matter where Sarasvatichandra was, he would certainly be moved by his father's plight and would put aside his hurt and reach out to his father.

Bulwer Sahib printed short narratives and poems that described Sheth Laxminandan's sorrow. The poems, printed both in Gujarati and in English, were certain to touch Sarasvatichandra's heart, he believed. Laxminandan remembered a few lines of the poem that Sarasvatichandra had written to him when he left. A well-known poet, Tarang Shankar, used these lines to compose a poem, expressing Laxminandan's anguish and published them in the *Gurjar Vartik*.

> *What does your father care for your sorrows, you said*
> *He pines madly for you, of course*
> *He finds this earthly form burdensome*
> *The son may well have erred, the father took no offence;*
> *The father erred once, but the son's pride couldn't bear it.*
> *The world is home to many souls, but the father's life is invested in his son's*
> *He chants your name till his mouth runs dry*
> *He abuses Lakshmi: You robbed me of my son!*
> *He weeps so much he can barely see*
> *If the son is separated from his father,*
> *The father will surely die.*

Not content with the poem, Laxminandan decided to publish something under his own name.

> Bhai! Why are you so heartless? Have pity on my old age. I have no one else. Come back wherever you are. I can neither think nor breathe. For a month from today, I will wait for you. If you don't come back, I shall give up my life like Dashrathji. Bhai, what has made you so heartless? If you are not with me, to whom shall I turn in my old age?

The translation of this was read out to Bulwer Sahib by the editor of the newspaper where this was to be printed. Bulwer Sahib said, 'Print it under the Sheth's signature. If Sarasvatichandra reads it, he is sure to return. Just as the call of the hunter awakens a lion from its deep slumber, Sarasvatichandra's unreasonable and stubborn silence will vanish the moment he reads his father's heartfelt lament. Print it in bold type.'

4 News from Suvarnapur: The Guilty Son of the Karbhari

> Every good political institution must have a preventive operation as well as a remedial. It ought to have a natural tendency to exclude bad men from government, and not to trust for the safety of the state to subsequent punishment alone: punishment, which has ever been tardy and uncertain; and which, when power is suffered in bad hands, may chance to fall rather on the injured than the criminal.
>
> —Edmund Burke

The day that he had become the Karbhari of Suvarnapur, Buddhidhan had asked himself: what if people of his own faction and family were to turn tyrannical? Who would the people of Suvarnapur carry their woes to? Would they also face the predicament that had been his lot for so long? Who would be responsible for the sins of misrule? What if Pramaddhan or someone else in the intoxication of power were to begin oppressing the people? Would he, the Karbhari, be open to complaints against his own confidantes? These questions had troubled Buddhidhan the day he had assumed the powers of the Karbhari.[1] But at that time he had no inkling that soon this question would arise in his house, and that his own son would be the accused. And that let alone Krishna Kalika's husband, even his dear Kumud Sundari would not be able to put a charge on his son but, in fact,

[1] Author's note: See *Sarasvatichandra*, Part I: *Buddhidhan's Administration*, Chapter 18.

would herself stand accused. Such events awaken the conscience of karbharis and other officials—if indeed they do have a conscience—who soar high with the support of son, brother, friend and other close relatives. Not just that, if a conscientious official who is aware of his responsibilities were to take pride in the belief that he has the capacity to punish an old friend or a close relative, such instances expose their weakness and belittle their pride. As he gathered more information regarding Pramaddhan's doings, Buddhidhan was both shocked and greatly humbled. He could see shades of similarity between Shathrai who acted through his son Dushtarai, and himself who tolerated Pramaddhan's activities. This comparison pained him. He looked for strength that would enable him to remove the cause of that pain. Within just few days after assuming the Karbhar, Buddhidhan was perturbed by questions like: Am I any different from Shathrai? Will I be instrumental in inflicting the same pain on others which it was once my lot to suffer?

Events unfolded in quick succession which caused him immeasurable agony. Even before Navinchandra's departure, Vanleela shared some stories about Pramaddhan's doings with Saubhagya Devi and Alak Kishori, who in turn appraised Buddhidhan. We know that at the time of Navinchandra's departure, Buddhidhan was perturbed. What followed was much more painful. On the day of Kumud Sundari's departure, Vanleela spoke at length to Saubhagya Devi and Alak Kishori about Krishna Kalika and Pramaddhan. Mother and sister called Pramaddhan and without revealing their source or the details of his misdeeds, they reprimanded him for misdeeds which were certain to bring disrepute to his father. Pramaddhan's guilty mind sprang to his defence and he employed the guile taught to him by Krishna Kalika. He took out from his pocket some burnt pieces of paper and in a great show rage, he accused his wife Kumud of infidelity. This confirmed for mother and sister the validity of Vanleela's news.

Saubhagya Devi's eyes welled up with tears. 'Alak, the sins of my past lives have come to haunt me. I gave birth to a demon! Shiv! Shiv! Shiv! My daughter-in-law meek as a cow has this suffering in her fate! I am going away. I don't even want to look at the face of this son of mine! You deal with your brother. I, a daughter of poor parents, married your father who was destined for greatness. But does the fate of the wretched ever leave them? He got the Karbhar, and I lost my all.' Unable to bear the agony, Saubhagya Devi went and lay down in the parsal, covered herself from head to toe and wept her heart out.

Devi went away, but Alak Kishori pounced on her brother. She held him by his chin, looked him squarely in the face and said with eyes breathing fire, 'O wretch, I know that rand Kalika taught you what to say. She taught you this even before Bhabhi left. And now you have a black face. I loathe you! Have some shame!' Alak pushed her brother away and gave him a scathing look.

Pramaddhan was scared. He sought a way out of his predicament. He was one of those who could resort to a greater lie when caught lying. He turned brazen.

'Behn, you and Devi are simple-minded. I might be a liar, I might have done wrong, but you recognise this handwriting, don't you? Look at it, examine it closely and tell me if I have given you false evidence.'

Alak read the torn scraps of paper. 'Of course! Bhai, you forget that I have spent more years in my life than the number of days you have lived. Bhabhi composed these poems; but they are beyond your comprehension. Bhabhi would write such poems daily. How does that constitute any proof?'

'Behn, you are hasty. Take a closer look. This has not been written by your sister-in-law. This has been written by that Navinchandra.'

'You wretch! When one lie failed you, you advance another! Was Bhabhi so stupid as to hand you a letter that Navinchandra allegedly gave her?'

'No, I retrieved them from under your Bhabhi's table.'

'And you found them conveniently after she left, so that we would believe you and have no opportunity to hear Bhabhi's explanation, isn't it? Bhai, that rand Kalika has taught you all this. But your sister is a match for a hundred of those bitches. My brother can't be so vile.'

'I am vile, am I? Aren't you ashamed? Are you trying to shield your Bhabhi or that Navinchandra? Even I know of some things.'

This enraged Alak even more. 'Very good, Bhai! Who else but a brother can say such things? It is true—we become like the company we keep. How is it possible that you remain unsoiled by Kalika's loathsome depravities. Bhabhi has gone, but I pity Devi. Now go away from here!'

'Give back those scraps of paper to me.'

'As if I am a child!'

'What will you do with them?'

'I will show them to both Devi and Pitaji. He will judge you, me, Bhabhi and that Kalika of yours. You can tell Pitaji all that you have told me. And also tell that rand Kalika that she can do all that she is capable of—I will not rest until I have driven her away from this town.'

'I have evidence. What evidence do you have?'

'Forget your evidence; we will have enough evidence if we look for it. That rand was with you in your room, and you had thrown out her buttons from the window. You wouldn't remember it now, would you?' Alak retorted acidly.

That scene suddenly flashed before Pramaddhan's eyes. It was Kumud Sundari who had flung the buttons on a chain from Krishna Kalika's blouse and a flower fallen from her hair at Kalika in rage from the window.[2] Pramaddhan turned meek. He couldn't think. He realised that he had lost. He looked down and walked away, defeated.

The matter was reported to Buddhidhan. He maintained equanimity and heard all the charges. He sent Narbheram to his son to obtain answers.

Pramaddhan narrated his side of the story. In addition, following Krishna Kalika's advice he alleged that Navinchandra and Kumud had run away together because he had come to know of their relationship. Their joint departure, he argued, was further proof of their guilt. He said that the decision to run away was taken on the night when he had gone to Lilapur with a message for Russell Sahib. Kumud and Navinchandra were in adjacent rooms and the two educated lovers had planned their escape that night. Buddhidhan thought about it

[2] Author's note: See *Sarasvatichandra*, Part I: *Buddhidhan's Administration*, Chapter 17.

calmly; Pramaddhan's story did not appear to him beyond the realm of possibility. He thought about this all day long. The matter, he believed, could only be resolved if all the persons involved could be brought face to face; but he was apprehensive as to what that would reveal. He was also concerned that the matter would bring disrepute to the family. That evening his soldiers returned with the captive outlaw Sursinh. Later in the evening, around nine p.m., the coachman returned; he brought news of Kumud's drowning and reported on the futile search. The family was drowned in sorrow. Their affection and compassion for Kumud increased manyfold, while their anger against Pramaddhan and Krishna Kalika multiplied a hundredfold.

Late at night, Buddhidhan called Narbheram and sought his opinion. Narbheram said, 'Buddhidhanbhai, what has happened cannot be undone. If you stretch the matter, the Karbhar that you have obtained just a few days ago will slip out of your hands. It will be a blot on you. There is no greater stupidity than to declare one's own weaknesses—please don't commit this stupidity. Pramaddhan is scared of you and cannot face you. If he does something stupid out of shame and fear, you will repent later. You will blow this issue out of proportion and make a mountain out of a molehill. It will become public knowledge. I believe that your family was almost complete in every respect; it was too good to be true. Your family was certain to attract someone's evil eye and invite some calamity. You should consider that what could have been potentially a great misfortune is just a minor domestic problem. Thank God for it. Such things do happen in every other family. They were never a part of your domestic life, but now they are. Pramadbhai is a young man, and youth has to manifest itself in some form. Let me be frank, Buddhidhanbhai. If you are too harsh, or foolish, you will be left empty-handed. Your daughter-in-law is given up for dead. Now if something happens to your son, you will lose everything. Therefore, make sure that he is not forced into a misadventure.'

Buddhidhan said, 'I will keep what you say in mind. But you must come without fail tomorrow and bring along Vanleela and Krishna Kalika's husbands.'

'Why do you want them?'

'That you will know in the morning.'

'Your intention is not beyond my grasp. I will obey your command. But don't forget the saying: one should not act in haste.'

'I will do nothing without hearing your opinion, Narbheram. What shall we do about Kumud?'

'We must act swiftly. The coachman said that she drowned in the river and could not be traced even until late in the evening. He does not know anything more.'

'Did he also tell you that Kumud, overcome with grief, jumped into the river?'

'He can say what he likes.'

Buddhidhan sighed. 'All right. But before daybreak, send about twenty-five intelligent men to search for Kumud. They should also go and meet Vidya Chatura.'

'That is a good thing.'

'Oh, I just remembered that Vidya Chatura has sent a letter to me. Read it out to me.'

Narbheram read out the letter.

> Dear Buddhidhanbhai,
>
> I need not emphasise how glad we are that the evil-doers have been eclipsed, and that your Maharaja has recognised your true worth and bestowed the Karbhar on you. It is bound to do good to the king, the people of your state and yourself. This is a matter of great joy. A letter of congratulations written by our Maharaja Maniraj Shri to your Maharana Bhupsinhji is on the way.
>
> If I with my limited and shallow experience were to give any advice about administration to you, given your abilities and vast experience, it would most certainly be improper. But if I were to make some suggestions regarding Pramaddhan, it would not be out of place, given my relationship with him.
>
> It would benefit Pramaddhan greatly, I feel, if he were to spend some time as a student. Those with learning make much more out of the experiences of life. People like me, who have obtained an English education, believe that just as the minister has certain duties with regard to his king, he also has duties towards the

> state. A minister's primary responsibility is towards his king and then towards the state. I believe that a minister violates his duty towards the state if he appoints a son, a brother, a nephew or a son-in-law in high positions in the state. By doing so, a minister is constrained in the discharge of his duties towards the state. People fear greater injustice as justice is harder to obtain under such dispensation. It also harms the person we appoint. Their abilities and industriousness remain unexplored as they are encumbered by the burden of favour done to them. Hence, I believe you should consider sending Pramaddhanbhai to a place other than Ratnanagari and Suvarnapur. Let him learn to swim in strange waters. But of course, the final decision is yours.

The remaining part of the letter dealt with domestic matters. Narbheram read it hurriedly. He gave the letter back to Buddhidhan and remarked, 'Bhai Sahib, Vidya Chatura is a learned man. But our science and our reasoning is different.'

'Pramaddhan bears witness to the fact that Vidya Chatura's learning is not without merit,' Buddhidhan said cutting him short.

'Yes, that is possible. Just as you have learnt a lesson from your son, others, too, have learnt their lessons. Allow me to explain to you in vernacular idiom: your son's father-in-law is pedantic. I will give you another example. In a neighbouring kingdom, the karbhari was over-wise. He invited a Parsi, Jamshedji Manekji. Once the Parsi got a foothold, he got in Nasarvanji and several other Parsis. All the Parsis occupy high positions and ride horses, while that karbhari still walks to work. There are innumerable such examples. If you employ one Dakshini, more Dakshinis pour in after him; brahmins bring other brahmins and banias bring their own caste fellows. I don't blame them. This is the law of the land. Everyone follows this law; we do not need to reinvent this anew. Everyone likes a feast in someone else's house. I become your guest and feast on the choicest of sweets; but when you come to my house, you have to observe a fast! It is fine; we should certainly listen to what he has to say. If a liar admits to lying, he ceases to be liar. He will do what suits him, and we must do what is beneficial to us. We should let them say what they want; we should even agree with them but act only for our own benefit—the rest of the world can go to hell. Buddhidhanbhai, if we begin to accept all the advice that is given to us, those who give advice shall be considered wise, and we shall make fools of ourselves.'

For a moment, Buddhidhan forgot his troubles. He smiled and said, 'All right, Narbheram, you do that when you become the karbhari.'

'What is wrong with what I have said? Bhai Sahib, let me warn you. If you follow this pedantic advice and act stupidly and decide to give even the slightest of punishments to Pramaddhan, I will go to the Maharana myself and ask him to seek your resignation. I will tell him to appoint me in your place and give my position to Pramadbhai. Let me tell you, I will run the Karbhar very well and ensure that Pramadbhai succeeds me as the karbhari. Once he becomes the karbhari, you and I shall renounce the world, pretend that the world is an illusion, and set out in search of Brahma. But for the moment, our world consists of you, me and Pramadbhai; even Brahma is in this world of ours. All else is illusion, which we must shun!'

Buddhidhan could not contain his laughter. He pushed Narbheram away and lay down on the mattress. 'Is there more to it?'

'Yes. Now hear this:

> The wise seek the company of kings so that they can benefit their friends and harm their enemies. Who does not work to fill their stomach?

'This is the shastra. Allow me to compose a fitting reply to Vidya Chatura. Meanwhile, you must do as I have told you. Now I shall take your leave.'

Narbheram wore his pagdi and went down to talk to the women. Looking at his retreating figure, Buddhidhan thought, what a character! And how fate has brought the two of us together! His advice cannot be brushed aside. An intelligent man is one who learns even from inanimate things. Then why should I not listen to what Narbheram has to say? He is worldly-wise.

As he sat ruminating, Alak Kishori came up, followed closely by Vanleela who was almost hiding behind her. Alak looked like an enraged tigress; her eyes breathed fire, her lips trembled and her hands shook. She stood erect, her chest thrust out, and thundered, 'Pitaji, this is the limit!'

'Why? Has something else happened?' Buddhidhan asked calmly.

'Ever since the news of Bhabhi's drowning, Devi is laid up like a log, Pramadbhai is behaving like a beast, and you have done nothing to search for Bhabhi.'

'Alak, if I don't make efforts to search for your Bhabhi, what else am I good for then? Go and ask Narbheram, haven't I told him already that he should send out a search party early in the morning?'

'Who are you sending? Don't send anyone who keeps Pramadbhai's company. They will kill her.'

'Why would anyone do that?'

'You have fixed a salary of two hundred for Bhai. Have you ever asked him what he does with it?'

'No, what does he do with his money?'

'I am not like Bhabhi. Even if a fly were to come near me, I would crush it. But if a wasp were to attack Bhabhi, she would gently raise her garment to shield herself, taking care not to hurt the wasp. These two rands, Kalika and some prostitute called Padma, have squeezed Bhai dry. Bhabhi has done what she did to free herself from these two women and my brother. I am now certain that she jumped to her death. Pitaji, we have lost our most precious jewel!' Alak Kishori broke down and collapsed on the mattress. 'How can I bear to be alive?' she sobbed. Vanleela, also weeping, tried to hold Alak but fell on top of her and her hand was crushed under Alak's body. Buddhidhan helped them both get up.

Alak sat beside her father and composed herself. 'Pitaji, Devi is not herself. You are the only one who can save us. I can't bear the thought of Bhabhi's drowning. To top it, Bhai says whatever comes to his mind—it is like a thief punishing the police. Don't you give him a long rope, Pitaji! Bhabhi is incapable of hurting anyone, and this vile brother of mine accuses her even when she is gone! This fire will burn us all.'

'Behn, we will find a way out.'

'But Pitaji, what do you think?'

'We will see.'

'No, there is nothing more to be seen. Bhai will make up fantastic stories, and there is no one to tell you about Bhabhi's side of things. Therefore, you must ask me.' Alak Kishori relayed to her father the information that Vanleela had supplied her with. Of course, there was something that she could not share with him. Finally, the two women left, and Buddhidhan was once again left to his own thoughts.

O' God, this is not the way of the world, he thought. A sister came to defend her sister-in-law and put her own brother in the dock of an accused. Kumud Sundari, Goddess Lakshmi of my house! This is the result of your pure piety. Pramad did make an accusation that Navinchandra and Kumud both left Suvarnapur according to a predetermined plan. Is he right? No, what Alak said is correct. It was only after Navinchandra's departure that Kumud's visit to her parents was fixed. Navinchandra had no knowledge that Kumud was to go and meet her parents. They did not so much as lift their eyes to look at each other! And my house is always full of people. There was no scope that they ever met alone. No, all these accusations are pure fabrication.

Vanleela's story about Pramad and Krishna Kalika also came true. That thing about the buttons is also a fact. But, the handwriting on those pieces of paper was Navinchandra's. It said: I had a father! I had a brother! Does that not prove his innocence? My son is stupid to be suspicious. No, I don't think my son is so stupid. Then what is it? It is clear—it is a counter accusation to save himself from the charge. This ploy of putting a counter-charge on Kumud, who is as pure as Ganga herself, is the way of Shathrai's family. My son would not think of it; it is obviously something that Krishna Kalika has taught him—she is after all from Shathrai's family. I cannot be certain that only Kalika is to be blamed; but to the extent that Vanleela's reporting is correct, her guilt is established. The buttons from her blouse and her advice to accuse Kumud prove Krishna Kalika's involvement. It also proves that my son is debauched.

Buddhidhan, although a father, also had to be the judge. He was convinced of his son's guilt. He could feel Kumud's anguish. The injustice done to her was apparent. The father-judge was dejected. He realised that even Krishna Kalika's husband has been wronged and he grew more despondent. Kumud may or may not be traced alive, but to Buddhidhan it seemed plausible that Kumud had jumped into the river to free herself from the evil ways of his son. With this realisation, Buddhidhan's misery and gloom gave way to seething rage. He said aloud, 'Beast! I have vowed to punish even those who are nearest to me if they are proven guilty. Pramad—you cease to be my son, and I am no longer your father.'

But then again, Buddhidhan hesitated. He thought: Kumud was bound by fate to her husband; she had to share in his good deeds as also his sins. She, too, would suffer with him for no fault of hers. What could be that punitive action that would punish guilty Pramaddhan but not affect innocent Kumud? Buddhidhan was perplexed. He struck his hand on the mattress in frustration and thought aloud, Vidya Chatura, what you said was correct. If I act unjustly, the innocent will be punished; and if I seek to do justice, I will be punished! Why should one's administration be such? If we seek to do justice but do not want to be punished for wrongdoing, one's own conduct must be impeccable. One should not be in a situation where one is required to sit on judgement over one's own kin. One should be able to exercise control over one's friends and relatives. There is a saying: a man who asks after the host's origins after accepting hospitality is an ass. It is true, I have acted in an asinine way.

What if I resign? That would be punishment enough for me and my son. Don't I deserve to be punished? I can take steps for the future, but I can clearly see the implications of my past mistakes. I am certain that I am not even aware of the many mistakes that I have made. There may be others, like Krishna Kalika's husband, who may have been wronged. My statecraft is not unsullied. Who is responsible for all those mistakes, misdeeds and pain? Who is responsible for all those sins? Buddhidhan, *you* are responsible—who else? O' God! I have to account for all those sins. I have to accept punishment due to all others. It is said that those who rule end up in hell; this bears testimony to that wisdom.

Buddhidhan, you deserve punishment. What if I resign? But resignation is an escape from the battle-field, a ploy to save oneself from the real punishment. For all these years, I have prospered because of the Maharana. It is now my turn to be true to my salt. And if I wish to do so, I must stay on in the Karbhar, punish my son and bear the pain, accept the ignominy and disrepute that it would heap upon my family, and in so doing, lay down my duty. If it means that I have to face Kumud Sundari's suffering every day, that, too, I must endure. I must atone for the sins committed against Kumud. Whatever you may say, Narbheram, escaping the battlefield and deserting Maharana Bhupsinh is not atonement; the saying that you quoted misguides. It is wrong to aspire to authority to promote one's kin and punish the enemy. This aspiration befits only the lowly. It is sinful; it can only result in immorality. It is certain to lead good men astray. Vidya Chatura, now I appreciate your wise and good counsel. Devi, you have made my heart religious; I will not allow this irreligious thought to take root in it.

Tomorrow morning, I shall take the following actions. I shall dismiss Pramad from his position. He shall have no place in court. What about presenting him before the judge? Buddhidhan shuddered at the thought. Tears came to his eyes. He dried his tears and said to himself: All those who commit debauchery are punished by me. Why shouldn't Pramad be just because he is my son? A deep sigh escaped Buddhidhan and he said aloud, 'O' God! Your Will be done! I will do whatever you command tomorrow morning.'

God, You have robbed me of my pride. The fire of revenge that raged within me destroyed Shathrai's family. I avenged the insults borne by my mother and by Devi. But in my desire to take revenge and be proud of my achievements, I forgot how undeserving I am. I believed the force of that fire to be my own strength; without it I could not have obtained the Karbhar. But that fire is now doused. Will I retain this position of authority? O' God, the fire that I burnt with was Your fire, Your will, and for reasons known only to You, it raged within me. Now You have suddenly doused that fire—so I was only a receptacle for it. Shathrai, who was consumed by the fire, believed it was powerless to do him any harm. But I will not make the same mistake. I will not play with fire. An insult to that fire is to insult You. You have the power to annihilate the world. You can cause the great deluge. Why would You then be powerless to create such small fires?

But God, that fire is inanimate—You are the conscious one. I was a son of a poor widow. You gave me so much wealth. You gave me this family and prestige. This could only be done by Your grace. It is now my turn to perform my duties towards You. If I turn my back to You, would I not be ungrateful? Until You take away everything You have granted me, I am duty-bound. If this act of service is my duty, why should I grumble or be pained by it? Do I even have the right to do so?

Shathrai! Dushtarai! The edifice of administration that you created acted as a catalyst for me. I was moved and shaped by it. Hitherto, my Karbhar has been an imitation of the edifice that you created. But beginning tomorrow it will cease to resemble your administration, just as I will cease to resemble you; I will exorcise you, Shathrai. From tomorrow, my Karbhar will be determined by and run on one sole purpose—service to God, service to the people and service to the king to the extent that he remains pure. This purpose will define and guide my ministership. Without this purpose, I am a wretched man who needs a few yards of earth to sleep on and a few morsels of food to sustain this body.

With these thoughts, Buddhidhan at last fell asleep. It is said that a king and his minister remain sleepless. But that king and that minister who rule with a sense of duty and uphold dharma receive the boon of sleep. Buddhidhan fell into a deep and undisturbed sleep.

At this time, Pramaddhan was not at home. He did not come home even in the morning. The town was abuzz with rumours. A dead body was found floating in the sea. Some said that he had committed suicide. Some said that he was murdered. Some said that he had disappeared. There was speculation even among those close to him. Some said that the shock of Kumud Sundari's drowning had turned him insane. Some said that Pramaddhan had decided to pursue Kumud with the intention of killing her. Others said that he had followed Navinchandra with murderous intent. It was also said that he was driven by fear and shame. But no one was really certain. Upon his disappearance, many sentiments and statements were attributed to Buddhidhan. 'My son doesn't deserve a search party'; 'It is just as well that he has gone away'; 'I have nothing more to do with him'; 'I had already given him up for dead.'

Dear reader, why do we need to dwell further on what the people of Suvarnapur said or did? Suffice it to know that, 'Such is the atonement of the defeated.'

5 In the Presence of Vishnudas

Sundargiri and Surgram were favourite sacred spots for followers of many religions and sects. The temples and monasteries that dot its landscape provide testimony to this. Religion is a constitutive element of the Aryas who reside in the Indian subcontinent. There are at least four paths to religion: jnana (knowledge), yoga (self-concentration), karma (action) and bhakti (devotion). At various points in history, Sundargiri was the abode of all these paths. The followers of these paths created monuments to their faith. Sarasvatichandra was given a bird's-eye view of those sacred monuments. Once we know as to which of these four paths Vishnudas' monastery followed, we shall also acquire the fitness to know Vishnudas.

Yoga and karma have withered in our age, but the Aryas have a natural affinity for them. The path of karma is relatively easy to follow if the believer has faith and capability; hence this path still has a large following. The path of yoga is complex and its sadhana demands deep engagement; hence it is rare to find a master of this path. The few exponents who have attained mastery of yoga are greatly revered. The teachings of the path of jnana are accessible to all intelligent persons. The fruits of karma are long in coming; they manifest themselves only when the exponent is on the way to heaven. Unless the exponent experiences a mystical moment and obtains the fruits of his actions, the path of karma demands life-long patience. On the other hand, a follower of the path of knowledge receives the fruits of his learning during his lifetime itself. The preference for the path of knowledge in the age of English education is obviously for this reason. Ultimately the path of knowledge leads to Vedanta. The knowledge of Vedanta is mystical and can be obtained only after great effort. Hence, very few are able to realise this knowledge. For this reason, exponents of the path of knowledge are divided into two separate streams: one stream is for those with average intellectual capability and spiritual effort; the other is for those with mystical knowledge. The stream that demands average intelligence and effort is the more popular of the two; this is the one that supporters and critics of the path of knowledge usually refer to in their debates. The paths of knowledge, action and yoga all require capabilities and means. But among the Aryas, the path of devotion is not contingent upon cultivation of any means. It seeks to pave the way to heaven for the devoted. A devotee is not required to cultivate great learning. This path is imbued with the nectar of love and devotion. The devotees sing:

A woman bereft of all power
Can make him dance to her tunes;
The path of love is sublime.

Vishnudas had made profound study of all the four paths and sought to amalgamate them in the practices of his sect. Therefore those who wished to cultivate spiritual capability, whether they had the means for this attainment or not, became followers of his sect.

Before he took the vows of an ascetic and became known as Vishnudas Swami, he was a brahmin. He had studied grammar, literature, mathematics, the philosophies of Mimamsa, Nyaya and Vedanta in Kashi and Bengal. He had travelled through the sacred Himalayas and dabbled in yogic practices. He had also joined the devotees of Shiva, Vishnu and Shakti and tasted the power of devotion. He returned home to assume the responsibilities of a householder. Vishnudas lived the life of a householder and experienced both the pleasures and pains of a life with parents, brothers, sisters, wife and son. It did not take him long to acquire a mature understanding of life as a householder. He was about thirty-two. One evening he was at the village pond, offering his prayers, when a group of ascetics passed by. He began a conversation with the ascetics. Suddenly, he felt a strong urge to join them. He went home and made arrangements for the material needs of his family. He called his wife aside and said, 'I am going away never to return. God has given us enough to meet the family's needs. You have a son. My parents have my brother. I have done my duty towards all, and hence, it is no longer binding on me to be a householder. Therefore, I am going away.' His wife wailed. His family came to know of his resolve. They all cried. Vishnudas consoled them all; but late that night as the others slept he walked out—he had only a loin cloth on his body. Before daybreak he had joined the ascetics and left his home and family miles behind. He was conscious of the pain he had caused his family.

All journeys involve leaving and pain, Vishnudas reasoned with himself. But a traveller returns, and the promise of his return heals the pain faster. In my case it will take a little longer. But this pain is nothing in comparison to the pain they would have felt if I had died. Now they will never know of my death. I have saved them from the possibility of deeper sorrow. But my wife has become a widow even while her husband is alive in the bodily form. Vishnudas could not convince himself that he had not sinned against his wife; but his resolve was not to be undone. He accepted the vows of an ascetic for which he discarded the yajnopavit, the sacred thread worn by brahmin men. He wore his hair long, smeared his body with sacred ash and came to be called Vishnudas. In a short time his learning and experience elevated him to the position of the Guru—the master of the ascetics. As the master, he gained access to the mystical texts of the Yadunandan monastic order.

The monastic order and monastery of Yadu Shrunga was ancient. Some learned ascetics had been its gurus in the past. There were instances when the guru was of average accomplishments, but even these gurus had nurtured disciples of great talent and merit. The ascetics of this order were Alakhvadi; they also combined the worship of Yadunandan. The founders of the sect had composed texts to explain their philosophy. The ancient texts defined Alakh as formless, attributeless, Nirgun Brahman. One of the older texts demonstrated that in those days the Yadunandan monastic order was a firm believer in Vedanta; and as Vedantis they accepted the ultimate superiority of Brahman. At some point this monastic order got into a theological debate with Jain ascetics. The Jains argued that the Vedantis believed in a twin reality—one that was illusory and the other, real—and hence their notions of Brahman corresponded with this conception of reality. They further argued that to be non-dualistic and be a Vedanti was a contradiction in terms. The Vedantis entered the debate and argued their position through a nuanced argument drawn from the philosophy of Shankaracharya. They emerged victorious in the philosophical debate that ensued. But average followers did not understand the intricacies of the argument and many adopted Jain faith. The Vedanti ascetics realised that the tide had turned against them. They came up with an ingenious response—they introduced idol worship in their sect. Their sect, earlier called Alakhvad, was now called Alakh-Lakh-Vad. They argued that the Brahman is essentially formless, without any attributes and omnipresent, but that at points this Brahman manifests and assumes a name, a form and accepts attributes. In so doing, the Brahman bears witness to its own manifestations. This manifest form is recognised by different names such as God or Maya (illusion). Human beings may worship these manifest forms and through them recognise the ultimate reality of Brahman. This form of worship was more accessible to people. The ascetic community gained in strength once again. It was easy to incorporate the worship of Yadunandan, Brahma, Mahesh and Vishnu including their many incarnations in forms such as Krishna into the new faith. They drew average devotees through the path of bhakti into their fold and gradually helped them to attain an understanding of the philosophy of Brahman.

At the time when Vishnudas became paramount in the monastery of Yadu Shrunga, the charged debates and verbal battles between the various sects and beliefs had not entirely ceased. Some old debates between the Shaiva, the Shakta and the Vaishnava still remained. These debates were distasteful and often violent, and a lot of good people turned away from Sundargiri and Surgram because of them. If Vishnudas had not dealt with these issues with patience, tolerance, immense generosity and tact, the significance of the sacred mountain would have diminished. He propagated equality of all faiths and adopted the maxim that humility was the best means and that one's own qualities are revealed in one's appreciation of the qualities of others. Gradually, mutual tolerance and respect took the place of bitter sectarian conflicts. Vishnudas saved his monastic order by saving everyone. He gave equal respect to all sects and they in turn revered his sect. He worshipped their gods and they reciprocated by bowing their head at his shrine.

Sarasvatichandra was given these historical snippets of Sundargiri by his sadhu escorts. They praised the virtues of their Guru Vishnudas and spoke highly of his accomplishments. With all these new experiences, learnings and the vitality of his surroundings, thoughts of Kumud Sundari no longer occupied his mind as he approached the temple in company of the ascetics. Sarasvatichandra was now eager to meet this most famous and worthy guru. He was grateful to the ascetics for their hospitality and their learned conversation. He wondered what qualities the master possessed if his disciples were so worthy. He was eager to express his gratitude to the master. The deep sorrow that had enveloped him lifted and his face glowed with joy. As they approached the wide steps leading to the temple, all the ascetics hailed the vision of God, 'Jai Yadunandan! Jai Yadunandan.'

The temple was not built on the traditional plan of temples. It was part of a large monastery. The monastery was single-storied. A visitor passed through an otalo or platform built of lime stones and entered through a door. The door led to a covered veranda and a large quadrangle where the vedi or altar for performing fire sacrifices was located. A large holy basil plant grew near the vedi. The quadrangle led to the shrine, which was a spacious room. A large idol of Yadunandan was installed in the shrine. Vishnudas usually sat at the feet of the idol on a straw mat. The doors to the shrine were opened for people during the hours of darshan, but were kept closed at other times when Vishnudas sat in meditation. He also used a space in the open veranda to sleep. He gave his discourses there after his early morning prayers and meditation. After the discourse Vishnudas would sit down with all the ascetics and they would have their meal. After the meal, on most days, he went down to the neighbouring villages to spread the word of God. This was also the time when he, along with other ascetics, sought alms. They would return in the evening, offer their prayers, converse among themselves and sleep by midnight. If Vishnudas was late in returning on some days, some other ascetic would offer worship to Yadunandan in his place.

Vishnudas had divided his disciples into four categories. The lowest category was called anadhikari or the uninitiated. These novices were allowed to participate in the worship, have their meals with the master and seek clarifications during meals. The second rung comprised ascetics who had been initiated into the sect. These initiates were called the kanishtha adhikari and were invited to listen to Vishnudas' discourses twice a week. On other days they were required to read and reflect upon the scriptures. Vishnudas discoursed to them on the path of devotion. The third group, the middle order ascetics or the madhyam adhikaris also participated in these discourses on devotion and were also given lessons in yoga by the master twice a week. There were very few ascetics in the highest category of merit, the uttam adhikaris. They were allowed to participate in these discourses but they had special discourses on the Vedanta. Vishnudas would often introduce the ascetics to Nyaya, Mimamsa, mathematics and other such subjects during their excursions to villages or during moments of rest while travelling. He selected deserving candidates to move from the lower rung to the higher rung. The ascetic who was considered best among the highest category was invited to participate in Vishnudas' personal studies; he would treat such an ascetic as an equal and they would learn from each other.

The spaces in the monastery were divided according to these categories. The space closest to the temple was occupied by the ascetics of the highest order. The two large rooms on either side of the quadrangle were occupied by the kanishtha and the madhyam adhikaris. Those still uninitiated used the outer veranda. There were two rooms behind the temple. In one of them all materials required for worship and other rituals were stored. The other room was the repository of all the sacred texts of the monastery; all other precious material possessions of the monastery were also kept there. The space that Vishnudas used had a back door which led to his bath and toilet. This was a large area. On two sides, the ascetics had built walls using large boulders to create a spacious enclosure. There was a big cave which had its opening in the enclosure. A grand banyan tree stood at the mouth of the cave. A perennial fresh water spring provided pure, sweet water. The spring had created a beautiful pond in which lotuses with a hundred petals bloomed. The lotuses attracted bees. There were two large beehives on the mountain side abuzz with the humming of bees. Mango and banana trees grew in the enclosure. There were creepers and flowering plants as well. Swans and ducks swam in the pond created by the spring. Smaller birds like parrots and mynahs also nested in the enclosure. Deer and rabbits roamed around the enclosure, feeding on the lush green grass. It was a beautiful and serene space. The soft green grass, sweet birdsong, fragrant flowers, sparkling water, abundant fruits and the stunning view with the majestic mountains in the backdrop calmed the senses and lifted the pall of gloom even from melancholic minds. There was an all-pervasive feeling of tranquillity and joy. In this natural environment, all doubts disappeared and made way for good thoughts. Vishnudas had decided that this enclosed garden shall be the abode of Sarasvatichandra. Sarasvatichandra was led through the courtyard into the enclosure. Their guru's decision surprised his disciples, but they obeyed his command and led Sarasvatichandra respectfully into the garden. A deer skin was spread for him to sit under the shade of the banyan. Having seated him comfortably, Mohanpuri and Viharpuri went in to understand their guru's wishes.

Vishnudas was an accomplished astrologer and believed in the science of foretelling the future. He was approaching old age. He was in search of that great soul who could be his successor. He often consulted astrological charts and the position of stars to guide him in his search. His calculations had indicated that his search was nearing completion. His disciples had found Sarasvatichandra during the period indicated by his calculations. Vishnudas was convinced that Sarasvatichandra was that great soul who would succeed him. He was elated at this discovery. Viharpuri gave him an account of their early morning conversation with the guest. This account further affirmed Vishnudas' belief and filled him with new energy. He was now eager to put his guest through a trial.

Vishnudas had finished offering his prayers when Viharpuri and Mohanpuri approached him. He decreed: 'Bring him to the temple immediately. He knows Sanskrit. I will test his worth.'

Sarasvatichandra was brought into Vishnudas' presence without delay. Sarasvatichandra stood at the door of the temple and did namaskar to Vishnudas, but he did not fold his hands or pay obeisance to the idol of Yadunandan. The ascetics were surprised.

Vishnudas remained unperturbed. He looked at Sarasvatichandra and asked him in Sanskrit:

> O child! Who are you? Whose son are you? Where are you going? What is your name? From where have you come? O young one, please tell me what I have asked you, for the sake of my love, since you ever increase my love.[1]

Sarasvatichandra responded without hesitation:

> I am not a man, not even a divine being or a yaksha; not brahmin-kshatriya-vaishya-sudra; not a brahmachari, not a householder, not a forest dweller, not even a mendicant; I am the nature of Self-knowledge.[2]

He stood with his arms crossed over his chest and continued his conversation aloud with himself in English[3]: 'This is a correct answer, correct in a double sense, true to my philosophy, and true to myself—I alone know me and that I am. I belong to all castes or to none, and my stage of life comprehends all stages. I am my inner self and I know it. The words are true as they were first spoken and also as I speak them now.'

[1] Author's note: *Hastamalak Strotram of Adi Shankara*, Verse 1.

[2] Ibid., Verse 2.

[3] The English speech and musings of Sarasvatichandra and other characters have been retained from the original text throughout the novel.

'Very good. Well spoken,' Vishnudasji said in approval, and turning to his disciples, addressed them in Hindustani, 'Look, my prediction has come true.'

'Navinchandraji ...'

Sarasvatichandra was surprised that Vishnudas was aware of his assumed name. He waited for the next question.

'Navinchandraji, all those who enter the temple first bow to Yadunandan.'

'That is true, but I pay obeisance only to my personal god.'

'Who is your god?'

'The Eternal and the Formless One.'

'Navinchandraji, but a person and an idol are both manifestations of the Eternal and Formless One.'

'That is true. But you must be aware of what Tulsidasji had done.'

'What did Tulsidasji do?'

Sarasvatichandra responded enthusiastically, 'You are a learned man and also a devotee. Tulsidasji refused to bow before Shri Krishna and said: "Your image is powerful and enticing, but Tulsi will bow to you only when you hold bow and arrow in your hand."'

The ascetics were angry that Navinchandra had insulted their god, but his response set them thinking. Vishnudas was aware of their anger, and he also knew its remedy. He quickly said, 'Wonderful, Navinchandraji. Well said,' and turning to his disciples, he said, 'Listen, this man understands the nature of the Formless One. All that he needs to be taught is the unity of the manifest and the unmanifest. Navinchandraji proved himself superior even to Tulsidas. Navinchandraji would pay obeisance only if the manifest were to dissolve in him and become the Formless One. If Shri Krishna were to assume the form of Shri Ram, the unmanifest would become manifest. This wisdom is indicative of his superior capabilities. Isn't it so, Viharpuriji?'

'Absolutely true, Guruji! This is the resolve of a true devotee.'

The disciples were happy. Sarasvatichandra was also pleased. He said to himself silently in English: This man's pluck is equal to my wish. He has grasped my position and gracefully assisted me in extracting me from the perplexing conflict between my duty to my conscience and to such kind and gentle hosts as these. Far be it for me to speak a single syllable that will either be untrue for courtesy or for fear, or will happen to offend in the slightest degree the susceptibilities of such noble and innocent souls as these. Gracious God!

A disciple asked Vishnudas, 'Guruji, if this be the case, why not initiate Navinchandraji into our sect?'

Sarasvatichandra was frightened by this proposal. Vishnudas realised the disciple's naiveté as also his guest's quandary. He gave a response that satisfied both the disciple and assuaged Sarasvatichandra's fears. Vishnudas laughed aloud and said, 'Viharpuri, this disciple is still a novice. He has not yet received initiation and hence he does not understand what the lowest rung of initiates knows. But he is curious and has asked a question which must be responded to. All the initiates shall sing with me.'

Vishnudas stood up and sang the first stanza. All the initiates got up and joined him with gusto.

Do not torture yourself, child
Only the unseen is true
Whether you are white or ochre,
Or drape yourself in colourful finery,
Whether an ascetic or a householder,
A man or a woman,
The unseen has wrought the destiny of each:
What will be, will be
He who can awaken the unseen
Cannot escape an ash-smeared forehead

Everyone swayed to the rhythm of the song. The robust singing of the ascetics reverberated through the surrounding hills. The questioner stared meekly at the scene and sought forgiveness from the guru. Sarasvatichandra mused to himself in English: Look at this strong doctrine of toleration!

Finally, Vishnudas turned towards the novice who had asked the question and said, 'Child, have you understood? Who are we to offer the ash of renunciation to anyone? If someone does not become a renouncer, that is the play of the Unmanifest One. But if the Unmanifest One so desires, he shall become an ascetic for the welfare of others and shall renounce all—because the Unmanifest One so desires, not due to our persuasion. This ash is merely a symbol; the truth of it is internal. But to understand that you will have to acquire the highest capability. At this juncture it is enough for you to understand that all that is manifest and apparent is a reflection of that which is unmanifest. You should not treat any manifest thing with disdain. This disdain represents the arrogance of demonic illusion. The Unmanifest One has special love for a devotee who remains steadfast in his devotion and to his dharma. It was for this reason that Shri Krishna appeared before Tulsidasji in the form of Shri Ram. Navinchandraji is steadfast in his belief, but your faith is arrogant. I pardon you today, but the next time that demonic arrogance touches you, beware that you shall have no right to live under the protection of this monastery.'

Vishnudas addressed his disciples, 'Mohanpuri, we have concluded the morning prayers. Today is not a day of study and discourse. We shall spend the day talking about philosophical issues. Our guest can also participate. We shall go to the garden and sit there. All initiates are to remain present.' All the initiates went into the garden. Tiger and deer skins were spread on the ground. A tiger skin was spread on a flat rock for Vishnudas. A deer skin was spread on an adjacent rock for Sarasvatichandra. The disciples sat around them. Vishnudas turned towards Sarasvatichandra and said, 'The little that we know of you has pleased our hearts. But I have been told that deep within, your heart is wounded.'

At this Sarasvatichandra smiled and interrupted Vishnudas, 'Swamiji, that conclusion was based on their assumptions. But this assumption was not entirely without a basis either. Nevertheless, I see no harm in it. What if I were filled with sorrow? Without knowing sorrow we cannot value happiness. Without darkness we do not recognise the path of light. Sorrow often leads to renunciation. Sorrow arouses pity and pity leads to the service of another being. This act of service allows us to recognise that all beings are one. Joy is nothingness that we like and sorrow is nothingness that we do not like. Joy and sorrow both are nothingness. Nothingness is not distinct; then how can joy and sorrow be separate from one another? Like and dislike are constructs of our minds. Therefore, one cannot either aspire to happiness or shun sorrows. I welcome whatever comes my way. But I am partial to sorrows; they sharpen my intellect. If I had not sought out sorrows, I would never have gained this privilege of being in your presence.'

All the disciples were surprised by this opaque discourse. Viharpuri broke the silence and remarked, 'It is said that nothing by its nature is either pleasant or unpleasant. Navinchandraji, wonderful. Allow me to ask you a question. Assume that the following verses were addressed to you.'

Well hast thou in early age.
In these rites thy choice hast made;
Aged mortals like myself
Oft by worldly things are led.
And thy penance, noble youth,
Is endued with virtues fair,—
Handsome forms we often meet,
Handsome virtues,—they are rare!
Transient as the autumn clouds,
Pride and pomp of human kind;—
Pleasures please us for a day,
Bitter sorrows leave behind!
Mortals' days are full of evils,
Death cuts short our life's brief span;
Therefore in this fleeting world
Virtue seeks the holy man.
Wise and nobly thou hast chosen
Holy rites to virtue dear,
But, belying thy great penance,
Thy attire fills me with fear![4]

[4] Romesh Chunder Dutt, trans. *Kirataarjunyam of Bharavi*, Book VIII, 'The Advent of Indra', *Lays of Ancient India: Selections from Indian Poetry Rendered into English Verse* (London: Kegan Paul, 1894), 186–187.

'I am certain that you do not need the meaning of these verses explained,' Sarasvatichandra replied with a smile. 'Viharpuriji, these verses are from Bharavi's *Kirataarjunyam*. There were doubts regarding Arjun's appearance, which he resolved. But in response, I must state that I have many failings; consider this to be one more. To me, clothes, white or ochre, are all the same. This is my way of a response. Allow me to pose a question to you. You say that moksha or freedom is not possible without renunciation. But if you consider the manifest as a form of the Unmanifest One, why should it not be possible to attain moksha without renunciation? Please explain this. Moreover, if all that is manifest emanates from the unmanifest, their souls are one. The body is given to decay but the soul is eternal. If that is so, who needs moksha? Is the soul that desires moksha any different from that eternally free soul? What binds a soul to unfreedom? If the soul is eternal, how is it in bondage in the past and how shall it be free in the future? Please explain.'

All the disciples stared at each other in disbelief. It was certain that no one but the guru could provide an answer. Vishnudas looked pleased and eager to explain. 'What a wonderful question! Navinchandra, one who knows the answer to these questions is given the highest position in our order. The mystery of our philosophy, of the relation between the manifest and the unmanifest is contained in the response. Only those who belong to the highest cadre may stay; all the rest must leave.' Sarasvatichandra remained. Vishnudas turned towards a disciple and said, 'Alakhpuri, recite the Siddhant Mantra, the verses that explain the basic philosophical tenets, from the *Alakh Rahasya*.'

Alakhpuri said, 'Guruji, I obey your command' and he proceeded to recite.

> Neither am I born, nor do I die. I am neither in bondage, nor am I free. This world is akin to an arrow released from the bow.
>
> I am one, unique; I abide in me and outside of me. I assume a form and inhabit the world and when I cease to be manifest I still gaze at my manifest form.

One who neither likes nor dislikes either action or inaction is in essence without attributes and devoid of action.

A being out of reverence for the manifest one worships a form but retains awareness of the state of the Unmanifest One. Such a soul is self-aware and is intent upon the unmanifest.

A soul that inhabits the manifest arises in the unmanifest; why would that being not cause the unmanifest to become manifest? In this way the seeker of Alakh causes the being, the lord and the unmanifest Brahman to become one, indivisible.

This was the teaching of the greatest incarnation of the Manifest One, Shri Krishna to Arjun to urge him to perform his duty in war.

Doing verily one's work in the world one should wish to live a hundred years. Such is the saying of the Isa and the object of the manifest.

A yogi of Alakh inhabits this world through his soul with the Supreme soul. Is this not the self-illuminating unmanifest, eternally blissful One?

He is unattached, yet not free, neither a renunciate nor a householder, he is the Isa of the eternal nectar, He is the self-emanating Purusha.

Day is time and so is the night. People perceive the transient day and night; only the enlightened ones know the time in which they are immersed.

The ordinary person perceives the fiery manifestation and quiet repose of the manifest as distinct; they cannot perceive the non-duality as they comprehend only the transient.

The multitude of senses makes Him the one with a thousand senses and yet, He is self-immanent. The manifest abides in the unmanifest; this is not unwelcomed by the unmanifest.

Perceived only by the yogis but unrecognised by the uninitiated, the unmanifest surrounds us.

As Alakhpuri recited, the other disciples joined in the recitation.

Vishnudas discoursed at length on the meaning of the verses. 'We divide the Vedanta in two parts: the Shruti and the Shankar Vedanta. The Shruti is the source of all religious sects. The Shankar Vedanta considers renunciation as supreme and urges us to discard all attachments to the illusory world. We revere Shankaracharya. But our philosophy of the unmanifest Brahman differs from his philosophy. The differences will become clear as I explicate the meaning of the verses. The Shankar Vedanta creates a trinity of Being, God and Brahman. We accept this, but we prefer the dyad of the manifest and the unmanifest. This is clearer and pithier as a formulation. Both Being and God are limited by attributes and hence we place them in one category; while we place Brahma, which is without any attributes, in a separate category. Most uninitiated persons can grasp only attributes. Thus we describe Being and God as the Manifest One. Brahman is unseen and not grasped by most people; therefore we describe Brahman as the Unmanifest One. The world of humans is grasped by the mind and the world of gods is the world of illusion. These are integral attributes of Being and the divine. We do not consider them distinct and separate from the manifest. We do not consider illusion worthy of discarding, nor do we dismiss it. Acceptance and denial of a thing is also a sign of preference; it violates the idea of non-dualism. We therefore do not advocate either the acceptance or the rejection of either the world or that, which is illusory. We respect the non-dual philosophy of Janaka for this reason. This dyad has another advantage. We do not prefer to distinguish between the manifest Being and the manifest God. If the manifest Being were to militate against this arrangement, the whole system would collapse. Therefore, God, who governs the manifest world and the being that is so governed are regarded as non-distinct by us. We believe in unity of joy and sorrow as also in the life of a householder and a renouncer. This unity is the basis of non-duality. We do not privilege renunciation. We follow the manifest religion and worship Shri Krishna as the supreme presence of the manifest world. We aspire to understand the nature of the unmanifest through the path of devotion.

'When a spark is lit in the living being, he acquires knowledge, he receives divine vision, and the unmanifest that was hitherto latent comes to light. We call this the awakening of the unmanifest.

'The awareness of the manifest implies union of the being with the divine. This union is attained by devotion and performance of one's duties as a householder, as a king or as a woman. The performance of duties and the path of devotion do not exclude either the path of devotion or meditation on the unmanifest. Through these various means we awaken the unmanifest within us and thereby experience the union of the manifest and the unmanifest.

'In this grand cosmic play, being and God both are the manifest currents of the ocean of the unmanifest, which is Brahma. The unity of being and divine commences with the body and extends to the cosmic. We move towards this unity like an arrow released from the bow. This movement has both a beginning and an end. The body is composed of both the gross material aspect and the subtle aspect. Therefore, it is born and perishes; that is its destiny. It experiences rebirth eighty-four lakh times. This cycle of birth and death commenced with the birth of illusion at the moment of creation and it will cease with the great deluge that will cause the universe to perish. The state of unfreedom commenced with creation and ultimate freedom or moksha will be attained with the end of creation. But both the state of unfreedom and freedom belong to the realm of this world, or as some say, they are so perceived by the intellect. They may belong to this worldly reality or may be caused by the perception of the mind; but they are not attributes of the soul. There is no primeval cause for this state of freedom or unfreedom and therefore, there is no real salvation possible. They are integral and inseparable from the world but the soul has no relation to it. It is said that the soul attains moksha through renunciation and action that is free of desire. But we do not accept this argument; we believe that we human beings also experience the awakening of the unmanifest within us. Apart from this, there is no other condition described as either the state of unfreedom or freedom. Some Vedanta texts, like the commentary by Shri Gaudapadacharya, suggest that the soul is inherently and eternally free.'

Sarasvatichandra interjected, 'Are you and your disciples not renouncers?'

Vishnudas laughed and said, 'Good question, son. Listen to this. Alakhpuri, recite for him the essence of renunciation.'

Alakhpuri recited:

The mendicant leaves home to worship the lord of the gopis
He covers his body in ash and calls out to the unseen
He holds all Gokul in his sway
Through this world the itinerant sage
Carries the word of the unseen lord
He renders the unseen visible and changes the fate of eighty-four lakh lives
He ties this world into his matted locks
Attached and yet not—such is his asceticism
The unknowing sleep while the enlightened one is awake
Vishnudas on his perambulations awakens the unseen in us all

Sarasvatichandra requested Alakhpuri to repeat this three times, until he felt that he had grasped it. He thought to himself in English: This is true. Those are not apathetic to the world that show their right to live in it by being useful to their fellow men in some form; and the ascetic, that deluges the world with his poetry and philosophy without destroying it, does a duty; and if he does that, he is not bound to confine himself within the rooms where his father has left hoards of money and where his wife wants him to provide for her children. Duty is the best form; it is the motto of these men, and they are not bound to be home-keeping youths with homely wits. The point is Duty, and, in this case at least, asceticism does not murder Duty! Beautiful!

Vishnudas said, 'Navinchandra, we are neither mired in the world nor have we renounced the world; we are detached from it. But in practice renunciation and detachment are regarded as synonymous with each other. We have not renounced the world—it is contained in the locks of hair tied on our heads; we smear it in the form of ash on our bodies. And thus we awaken the unmanifest but we never forsake the manifest. Below the layers of ash lie smouldering embers. The unmanifest lies hidden under the manifest; we remove these layers and bring the unmanifest to light. In short, that is what we strive for. We worship the manifest but awaken the unmanifest. The life of householders is defined by desire. We aspire to a state of desirelessness and to symbolise that we smear our bodies with ash. The long hair tied in a knot that we keep symbolises the complex web of desires that we have knotted up. Both the ash and the long, unshorn hair are thus symbolic. Any great effort requires some uprooting of the old. Our effort is to awaken the unmanifest. We do not renounce the world to be free from sorrow. These symbols are indicative of our striving. We do not seek destruction of the manifest by a violent renunciation of the world. We are seekers; we renounce the state of the householder for the sake of our penance and roam the ignorant world much like the police that patrol the dark nights—as awakened beings making the realisation of the manifest possible. Navinchandra, we shall also awaken the unmanifest within you. All the initiates repeat after me: In this acrid world we smear ash and awaken the unmanifest.'

The disciples chanted these words. Those who were outside also echoed them. The praise of the unmanifest reverberated all around. As the chant subsided, Vishnudas placed a hand on Sarasvatichandra's shoulder, looked at him with a piercing gaze and asked, 'Tell me child, has the unmanifest stirred within you?'

Once again Vishnudas was disappointed. His guest had declined to bow before Yadunandan; even now he maintained a strange silence and appeared unmoved. Sarasvatichandra noticed the disappointment. He smiled and replied, 'Maharaj, I do not consider the unmanifest to be latent within me. Without that admission, can I experience the awakening of the unmanifest?'

Vishnudas appeared pained. Sarasvatichandra realised that he had hurt a good man and sought to assuage his sentiments. 'Swamiji, do forgive me as I have caused you pain. I heard the mystical verses of your philosophy today. How can I respond to them without proper deliberation? Allow me to ponder over their meaning, let me translate them for myself and then I shall pose my doubts to you. You will have the occasion to dispel my doubts. Through this process my thoughts will mature. Till such time there is no reason for you to be disappointed with me.'

Vishnudas seemed satisfied with this response. Just then the temple bells rang. It was time to offer food to Yadunandan. Vishnudas sent his disciples to participate in the ritual. Once Vishnudas and Navinchandra were left alone, Vishnudas spoke candidly. 'Navinchandra, before I joined the monastery I was a brahmin. I understand that a learned brahmin like you will only accept our philosophy of the unmanifest after due consideration. But I have to keep this group of ascetics under control. They obey my every command. But I also know when these temperamental ascetics are inclined to disobey me. I am cautious and don't allow for such occasions to arise. For some reason, I am partial towards you. But if they were to somehow feel that you do not deserve my favour, they will come to distrust my judgement and guidance and they may also cause you some harassment. According to them, those who do not believe in the unmanifest have no right to live in the monastery for a long period. I dislike this insistence of theirs, but that is besides the point. Your departure would cause me great sorrow. Therefore, please do not disregard my request.'

'And what would that be?' Sarasvatichandra asked anxiously.

'A renouncer cannot re-enter the state of a householder, but in our monastic order that is permissible. An initiate can become a householder among us. It is not mandatory that the ash be smeared on the entire body; it can also be applied on the forehead alone. We mix sandalwood paste in the ash. You may not bow before the idol of Yadunandan, so long as you do not show any disrespect. You may continue to wear your clothes, but they should be ochre coloured. You may continue to follow your own faith, but you should also worship the unmanifest. You can choose the category of initiates that you wish to belong to.

'An uttam adhikari is allowed to hold any philosophical belief. The monastery has no objection even to your marriage. In the adjacent monastery we have residences for married couples. They are a part of our order; they join us in prayers and we have meals together. If you desire to be a householder, you may also take up residence with them. I would like you to consider this. If, some day, you decide to return to your home and become a householder, do come and speak to me in confidence. But for now you will have to be initiated in the order. This initiation entails that you hear a formal discourse on the philosophy of the unmanifest. The acceptance of the philosophy will be deferred until you have had sufficient time to reflect on it. Please accept this request.'

Sarasvatichandra responded, 'If this will make you happy I shall do it, because you have given me a new life. But I cannot accept the philosophy of the unmanifest without reservations. It is contrary to my belief.'

'That we can tolerate. You have a period of reflection available to you. That period extends up to one year.' Vishnudas seemed satisfied. He went to the temple, allowing his guest to remain with his thoughts. On his way he said, 'After the meal we shall go out to seek alms. Some ascetics will stay behind. You may stay with them. In the evening you could go down and visit Surgram. Alakhpuri will give you a commentary on the philosophy of the unmanifest.'

Sarasvatichandra was left to himself. He walked around the garden for a while, quite content. Then he lay down on a boulder in the shade of the banyan tree. He thought of Chandrakant. He decided to write a letter to him, which could be posted from Surgram. His mind flitted to the verses that he had heard. He committed them to memory. He decided that the next morning he would have a discussion on them with Swami Vishnudas. He fell asleep. In his dream he saw Kumud Sundari seated beside him. His companion in dreams held his hand in hers and sang:

Now be my teacher, O' jogi
Keep this jogini by your side
Jogi, with knowledge may you also find beauty
May the vessel of the unseen you now hold be filled with light
May you swim in this delightful ocean of dreams
Jogi, stay true to your beloved

6 A Discourse on the Philosophy of the Manifest and the Unmanifest: Dream, Awakening, Dream

Sarasvatichandra surrendered to sleep. Soon after, Alakhpuri came with the text of the commentary. He placed dry leaves as a marker on the relevant pages, kept the text next to the sleeping man and left. Sarasvatichandra woke up, found the text and began to read it.[1]

> Now we shall reveal the secret of lakshya-alakshya, that is the relationship between the manifest and the unmanifest. What can be seen and perceived is the manifest and what cannot be perceived is the unmanifest. When we speak of perception or the lack of it, we speak of ordinary persons because the knowledgeable see and perceive much more. The statement: "When it is night for all others, the disciplined soul is awake" indicates this difference. Great souls have their sights fixed on goals that are diametrically opposite of those of the average individual. Great souls have higher perception. Those who can perceive even the unmanifest, the yogis, have been described in the verses.
>
> The first verse says: "Neither am I born, nor do I die." Just as the sky is distinct from space, we must recognise that the unmanifest soul is beyond birth and death. Similarly, it is neither in bondage nor free. It is only a figure of speech when

[1] The text of the following philosophical commentary, ending on p. 108, is in Sanskrit in the original.

we describe something as unfree and something else as free. In essence, there is no difference. In other words, it is the worldly being that is either bound or free, but not the soul. The Creator who is omnipotent appears in different forms. But these different forms are perceived as distinct by this-worldly, embodied beings. It is an illusion to say that an archer takes aim of the head and dislodges it from the body. In essence, the archer, the aim and the dislodging of the head are *all* manifestations of the unmanifest. Samsara, or living in this world, means to lead a good life. It has been described as akin to the movement of the arrow but not as the arrow itself. The moment of commencement of this movement is the moment of freedom. Being, universe, bondage and freedom are all illusory. The common element in them is termed the manifest. Similarly a body with hands and feet is either called purusha or being. A lump of clay can be moulded in many shapes and forms. Similarly, the manifest appears in countless forms and is made up of many such illusions. It is neither in a state of bondage nor in a state of freedom. It is said that each manifest being goes through many cycles of bondage and freedom. This implies that one is born again and again. This is a contradiction in terms. The world and the worldly being both are integral to the manifest, just as the state of dream is integral to the state of awakening. This is called illusion. Illusion is also a part of the manifest.

In verses two and three, the unity of the manifest and the unmanifest is established: "I am one," it is said. The unmanifest soul is cosmic and bears witness. What does the soul bear witness to? Its manifest form, that is, it bears witness to itself. This is the chitta or the conscious aspect of the soul. When the illusory movement ceases, it is the moment of shanti or repose or stillness which is seen as distinct from the illusory movement, but both are aspects of the manifest. Some prefer movement over repose while others prefer repose over movement. It is through likes and dislikes that a person acquires the three gunas or attributes which spur him into action. Some ascetic individuals, often called bhikshuk or mendicants, are no doubt learned and great souls, but they dislike illusion and prefer the moment of stillness. They accept a division between the two conditions. It is for this reason that they are unable to attain the sense of oneness. They are moved by the sense of apparent division and believe that some things are to be accepted, and others to be discarded. The sense of unity, of oneness is attained only through the philosophy of the manifest and the unmanifest. All other beliefs fail to achieve this sense of unity.

Philosophers of the Nyaya school classify matter according to its attributes. Other philosophies also have a notion of attributes. We consider it to be a part of the manifest. Some argue that just as the male and female principle are separate, so also being and divine are distinct—this is a false division. The soul bears witness to itself. The soul experiences the bliss of unity. Great souls are capable of experiencing the joys and sorrows of others. This is an obvious example. It proves that the manifest, in variegated forms, experiences itself in others. This unity and indivisibility is the source of bliss. This is true in any condition. Whenever the soul bears witness to itself, it involves birth. It is said that wherever there is mind, illusion persists; its play is apparent. There is no difference between an illusion and the one who conjures up the illusion, because they are contained in each other. The unmanifest extends this illusion through the soul and having extended it, the soul destroys it. In this play the unmanifest attains bliss. Some contend that the bliss so attained is temporal. But that is false, because like truth and consciousness bliss is also eternal and one, while action is temporal and temporary and hence not in-divisive. A yogi thus attains unity of the manifest and the unmanifest. It is asked if such a yogi sees attributes and actions as distinct from each other. We believe that for such a yogi, attributes and actions seem separate but this distinct orientation is like the movement in the world of dreams. But a yogi who has attained a sense of unity remains untouched by them. He is without attributes and indulges in no action. This spark of fire that is the manifest being experiences joy as he reaches out to the inanimate aspects of prakriti. In so doing it extends itself and follows the norms of the manifest, just as the fire that is inherent in the wood but which does not manifest itself. But when that fire is lit, it shows itself like any other matter that can be perceived by the eyes and felt by the skin. It has the same potential to give light and to burn as the cosmic fire. Similarly the enlightened one, in the form of being, appears to follow all conditions of the manifest. It is not sufficient that this spark of fire becomes manifest to others; it is also manifest to itself. It is only when this condition of being manifest both to others and to itself is fulfilled that the unity of one and many, of being and cosmos is attained. A being that aspires to this unity desires nothing else. Such a being is turned away from all other fruits of action. All his actions are good. He has no ego and hence all his actions are detached and selfless. All his actions are dedicated to the cosmic fire. By this dedication he fulfills the obligations of the manifest and of the relation between being and divine. This spark of fire thus attains the power of the cosmic fire and aspires to unity with the cosmic fire. And by this process the unity of being and divine is attained. Some describe it as karma yoga. The *Gita* says that the unity of being and divine is attained through action or karma yoga. The path of knowledge or jnana yoga attains the unity of being and Brahman. The unmanifest is Brahman. To enter the unmanifest implies knowledge of Brahman. The followers of Vedanta advocate the path of knowledge; they do not follow the path of action to the exclusion of all else. Just as day and night come together to form time, action and knowledge form a unity of approach. Only followers of the philosophy of the manifest follow this unified approach. Thereby, they attain the unity of being, divine and Brahman. All others seek either the unity of being and divine or of being and Brahman. That is, unity for them involves only two elements and to attain this they follow either the path of action or of knowledge. But none of them attain the unity of all the three. Some still argue that unity can only be of two elements and not of three. Such arguments are false because unity can be of many elements; unity does not signify a union of two or three elements only.

Now we shall understand the various meanings of the word karma. The shastras and the shrutis use the term in a variety of ways. When it is used along with the idea of fate or destiny, karma alludes to the destiny of an individual just as the term destiny is used as an equivalent of the term karma. Others use the term karma to denote action that is distinct from destiny. Many shastras contend that it is distinct from destiny. Many shastras contend that performance of rituals and offering of sacrifice is karma. The followers of Shankara contend that knowledge of meditation and ritual constitutes action. We believe that karma yoga as described earlier is most appropriate, because one can renounce the fruits of action but not action itself. It is a contradiction in terms to describe the renunciation of action as action. If action is added to the pursuit of knowledge, knowledge becomes temporary because action tends to be impermanent. The Shruti says that the one who knows the play of the atman knows the Brahman. The same is true for a karma yogi. The Shruti also enjoins us to be detached from the fruits of action. Renunciation of fruits of action leads to the dissolution of sorrow and desire. When a yogi becomes desire-less like the Creator, he also becomes free of sorrow. To that extent, such a yogi sits alongside the Creator. The path of knowledge allows for a unity with the Brahman but not with the divine. This unity can only be attained through the path of knowledge. The *Gita* is the living example of this. Shri Krishna is the supreme embodiment of our philosophy. Shri Krishna urged his beloved Arjun to perform his duties in the manifest world. The Lord reminded Arjun that he was his devotee and a friend and thus enjoined upon him the performance of his duties. This was done to uphold the law, not to destroy it. Shri Krishna's discourse to Arjun had a purpose—to convince Arjun that he must perform the duties enjoined upon him by the manifest world. The Lord said that this was the path to attain non-duality of the being and the divine. But for this purpose, Ved Vyasa would not have included the *Gita* in the *Mahabharata*. In absence of this purpose, the *Gita* would have become inappropriate and purposeless. Even in the *Yoga Vashistha,* Shri Krishna has taught us the same thing: that we should cultivate the bearing of the Brahman, that is, we should be imbued with His peace and perform our duties. The *Yoga Vashistha* propounds the karma yoga. The *Isha Upanishad* says: "Thus working, may you live a hundred years." It criticises those who are either steeped into knowledge or ignorance. This is also our view. Similarly, it also teaches us that we should not be mired in either the transcendental or the immanent to the exclusion of the other. It says true knowledge is the knowledge of the self which is attained by desire-less action. The *Isha Upanishad* urges us to forsake false knowledge which is illusion. Attachment to the fruits of action is the root of false knowledge. The pursuit of knowledge or of illusion, of the transcendental or the immanent, to the exclusion of the other, is a sign of duality. We who seek non-duality forsake this path. When we pursue one to the exclusion of the other, one enters the world of darkness. The *Isha Upanishad* clearly states that: "Those who combine action with meditation cross the sea of death through action and enter into immortality through the practice of meditation." It further states: "In the dark night live those for whom the Lord is only transcendent; in still darker night, for whom He is only immanent"; but those for whom He is both transcendent and immanent enter into immortality with the transcendental. Thus it states that only when we grasp the nature of illusion and of knowledge simultaneously and understand the essence of the transcendental and the immanent can we attain freedom. This is positive when action is desire-less and unattached. Our philosophy similarly advocates that only after we grasp the manifest can we understand the unmanifest. When the *Isha Upanishad* states: "Thus working, may you live a hundred years. Thus alone will you work in real freedom," it implies the same. Some argue that this is not knowledge of the self but of the divine. This contention is implausible because as the *Mandukya Upanishad* states, knowledge is that which leads to self-realisation. To argue that knowledge of Brahman is contrary to the path of action is incorrect. Because the knowledge of Brahman precludes the desire for the fruits of action, but not the action itself. It is not possible to forsake and renounce all action. Because the *Gita* states: "No one ever remains inactive even for a moment" and it further states: "Know that action springs from Brahman and Brahman from the imperishable." Therefore, we cannot ever be without action. Our philosophy of the non-duality of the manifest and the unmanifest is supported by the *Upanishads*. The *Isha* says: "The face of truth is hidden by your orb of gold, O sun; may you remove your orb so that I who adore the true may see the glory of truth."

The *Mundaka Upanishad* says: "In the golden city of the heart dwells the Lord of Love, without anchor, without blemish. Know Him as the radiant Light of Lights." The Brahman is concealed. The radiance of the Brahman is protected by that which envelopes it—and this is not to be discarded. When sorrow and desire dissolve, this protective cover is removed and Brahman shines further. If someone were to ask us, what is it that envelopes the Brahman, our answer would be karma yoga. This manifest world is like the golden orb that conceals the unmanifest Brahman. It is described as golden because it is as valuable as gold. Everything springs from the imperishable and will ultimately merge in the imperishable. The manifest is not to be destroyed because it springs from that which is imperishable.

The Shruti describes the nature of the manifest. Being or Jiva is not separate from Brahman. It is the spark of Purusha. The *Purusha Sukta* says: "A man has a thousand heads, a thousand eyes, a thousand feet. He pervades the earth on all sides and extends beyond it as far as ten fingers. It is man who is all this, whatever has been and whatever is to be. He is the ruler of immortality when he grows beyond everything through food"; food here means sacrificial offering. The *Mundaka Upanishad* says: "As hair grows from the body, even so the sages say, this universe springs from the deathless self, the source of life." Purusha springs from himself and withdraws into himself just like the web that is spun out of a spider and is withdrawn. The cosmic energy pervades both being and divine. Both finally merge with the unmanifest and eternal Brahman. The being is temporal while the unmanifest is eternal. The moment of creation is described as a sacrifice. The *Purusha Sukta* says: "When the gods began the sacrifice with man as the offering, spring was the clarified butter, summer the fuel, autumn the oblation. They anointed man—the sacrifice born at the beginning—upon the sacred grass. With him the gods, the sandhyas and the sages offered sacrifice." It further says: "With the sacrifice, the gods sacrificed to the sacrifice. These were the first ritual laws." The

> Purusha was the sacrifice and the one to be sacrificed. We do not advocate the sacrifice of animals. For us, sacrifice is to be taken in its original sense. The man with a thousand heads, a thousand eyes and a thousand feet is Purusha who manifests as Jiva, the Being. But the unmanifest purusha extends as far as ten fingers that are the ten directions. We seek the unity of the manifest and the unmanifest. This discourse, meant for the initiates of the highest category, awakens the unmanifest. What more need be said? The unmanifest is such that both mind and language fail to grasp it. The manifest is complete, so is the unmanifest. When fullness is taken from fullness, fullness still remains. Thus, our philosophy of the non-duality of the manifest and the unmanifest is complete. Because: "All this is full. All that is full. From fullness comes fullness. When fullness is taken from fullness, fullness still remains."

Sarasvatichandra read the commentary with great interest. He knew by heart the *Upanishads* and the *Purusha Sukta*. He had studied various commentaries on these texts, and yet he felt he had read an entirely new interpretation. Sarasvatichandra slipped into deep reverie and soon fell asleep.

Sleep brought back his earlier dream state. Kumud Sundari appeared in his dream. She sat close to him. But this girl had Kusum's face. Sarasvatichandra discoursed to her about the philosophy of the manifest and the unmanifest. The young woman heard him with interest and asked many questions. She floated up into the sky and asked, 'Sarasvatichandra, manifest or unmanifest? Pleasure or knowledge?' She touched his forehead fleetingly as if in play and sang:

> *My beloved is infatuated with beauty*
> *But awakened to knowledge*
> *You see the sorrows and joys of this world*
> *The wise jogi has claimed you*
> *Unseen by me, you worship the formless*
> *But your beloved also likes learned discourses*
> *We surrender all desires of the body*
> *Vraj is dense with tamal trees*
> *The sky is heavy with rain and dark as the night*

Radha seeks her dark lord
Searching for him she wearies and searches again
The flute plays further and still further away
The melody is heard but Krishna is unseen
The flute says, 'Listen Radha, O' mad one:
I sing from the lips of the one unseen
And inspire unnameable love in you.'
The invisible Krishna leaves no trace in the forest
O' you jogini of the invisible one, awaken this love
And play it out on the banks of Yamuna
Beloved do not forget that we are one
The one seeking knowledge reveres language
Maya is apparent, but Purusha is not
Their union produces this world—
It is surrounded by their coming together
Maya clings to the heart of Brahma
Beloved, these are the ways of love
O' you familiar with the ways of the unmanifest
Remember to also take delight in this world

Sarasvatichandra suddenly woke up and wondered, What is the meaning of this dream? Who governs the world of dreams? Who is responsible for the sins and merits committed in the world of dreams? Am I responsible? No! Why not? How is this world different from the life lived in dreams? Who is the doer? Who is the one to be consumed? Kumud Sundari, who abandoned you? When were you abandoned? Why do I repent? Whom do I repent for?

His eyes closed once more and he dreamt again. But this dream was different. He did not see any visions, but he heard a voice. His soul became omnipresent and his voice rang through in all directions. Sarasvatichandra heard the voice of his own conscience as if it were a voice from above.

Two birds:
Able of wing and far of sight,
Together in friendship and affection,
They found great joy.
Perched on the same tree branch,

One ate of the peepal's fruit, the other ate nothing
But was resplendent in dawn's first light;
One knew only pleasure, living godlessly,
While the other shone in His light.
He is the creator of the universe,
He is the Supreme Being, the bearer of divine light.
As the godless one grew aware of His glory,
He went beyond all sorrow
To leave behind this web of life,
Apprehending the non-dual, he became one with Him;
Transcending merit and sin,
Able of wing and far of sight,
That bird, he took flight.
Now replete with knowledge and imperishable,
He is not reborn—
He is the beloved of God.

With these words ringing in his ears, Sarasvatichandra woke up. But the world of dreams refused to recede or relinquish its hold on him. Kumud Sundari appeared before him dressed as an ascetic and posed philosophical questions. 'How have you become free of sorrow, Sarasvatichandra? How did you realise the Brahman? We are one, you and I—make my condition the same as yours. Free me from sorrow and help me realise myself!'

Chandrakant, too, entered the dream, saying, 'Dear friends, if the two of you are one, I am not separate from you. Let the three of us unite.'

Sarasvatichandra gave no response to either of them. He listened and allowed the dream to continue. A new dream emerged. Taking flight from the summit of the Sundargiri, Sarasvatichandra soared into the sky. He saw Chandrakant flying by his side. Chandrakant asked him in English: 'Where, my friend, dost thou fly like an angel upwards?'

Sarasvatichandra, thus halted in his flight, replied, 'Chandrakant, sweet philosophy brings me up into the heavens! I fly effortless like Dante in his Paradise!'

Kumud Sundari joined them. She held on to Sarasvatichandra's legs and said, 'Thou hast no right to rise without me! Am I not that Beatrice whose vision fills thy soul and flies as thou fliest?' Sarasvatichandra replied, 'Sweet angel of purity! Thou art—thou art! Fair ethereal spirit, guide us on! Thou shall rise and raise us all—come![2] The sky echoed Sarasvatichandra's words. The three of them flew through the skies, holding each other in a tight embrace, singing divine songs. But alas, we cannot fly with them into that land of dreams.

[2] The speech attributed to Chandrakant, Sarasvatichandra and Kumud in this passage is in English in the original.

7 Kings and Ministers of Ratnanagari

For hundreds of years, Ratnanagari had been blessed with great kings and able ministers. Given its turbulent history, this could only be considered an act of destiny. The kings were believed to have descended from the Sun God and as a marker of this they wore a gold anklet on one foot. From ancient times, every ruler of Ratnanagari had inculcated and nurtured this pride in the royal lineage and ancestral tradition, both as duty and their privilege. An eternal lamp, a sign of their devotion to the family deities, was worshipped by all kings. From a young age, heirs to the throne were also initiated into the responsibilities of kingly duties and royal traditions, which included devotion to the lamp and what it symbolised. This pride in ancestral traditions was embodied by many valorous reigning kings. It was also their custom to find suitable candidates as ministers, nurture their talents and appoint them to the position at an opportune time. The kings of Ratnanagari thus sought to perpetuate and further their traditions in these two ways.

The family tradition was neither complex nor elaborate. But its principles were firm, deep-rooted and allowed for superior practices to emerge. The king should relate to his subjects as a father would to his children. All wise kings realise that it is in their interest to protect their subjects, but the paternal sensibility cannot be cultivated in absence of an enduring affection for the people. The kings of Ratnanagari believed that in absence of this affection, their royal sun lineage cannot remain unsullied—this was the principle underlying all kingly conduct. A king must regard an enemy of his people as his own enemy. If someone, be it an official of the state or even a member of the royal family, were to act as an enemy of the people, that individual must be made to realise the maxim that 'a king has no friends.' From this followed the second norm that kings are attached to virtues and not to individuals. The third norm was that the resources of the state treasury should not be wasted and no one should be allowed to exploit the treasury for personal gains. The emphasis was on good and appropriate use of the resources and not on their accumulation. The army must always be battle-ready and its preparedness should be under constant surveillance. The king should always be the commander-in-chief of the army and he should prepare the heir to the throne to assume this responsibility. The king should always guard that his heir be pure-blooded; a child of a mixed marriage could not be appointed as heir as he would contaminate the royal throne. If a king did not have a male heir, he should adopt a male child of the royal household. Such a child should have a pure, uncontaminated lineage and possess all the kingly qualities. This was also a part of the royal tradition and was followed by every ruler of Ratnanagari, be he good or bad, virtuous or evil, wise or foolish. All rulers also looked for able men who could be their ministers. They ensured that the character of such potential ministers matched the disposition of the chosen heir and trained them into statecraft. They encouraged friendship between the heir apparent and the one chosen to be his chief minister.

The kingdom of Ratnanagari was ancient. Architectural monuments and coins dating back to the times of emperors like Ashok and Chandragupta had been found during excavations done around the capital, which indicated that the kingdom was prosperous even then. The rulers of Ratnanagari had fought several wars with the Shaka kings. After an initial triumph, they had lost the kingdom and there was a period during which the Shaka kings had ruled over the area. This history was found during excavations and studies of forts, temples, pillars and stepwells done during Vidya Chatura's ministership. There were also clear indicators that Buddhist, Jain and Vedic religions had flourished in the area. It was also borne out by the studies that during the medieval period the royal family was plagued by dissension, driven by jealousy and foolishness and there had been bitter internal feuds. Muslim rulers had made many expeditions to the kingdom; but the rulers of Ratnanagari had by a combination of diplomacy and valour retained their independence. In a way, God had been kind to the kingdom and had protected it. Towards the west of Ratnanagari were the sea and the hills of Sundargiri, while to its north, east and south were other Rajput kingdoms. The rulers of Ratnanagari maintained peaceful relations with these kings and in times of foreign invasion, they supported each other. The rulers knew that it was their combined strength which protected them. And hence, they did not indulge in displays of false pride with each other; rather they shared their intelligence and resources for mutual benefit. They ensured that no foreign invader could cast evil eyes on the kingdom. They placed so many obstacles in the path of potential invaders that, realising the heavy costs they would have to pay for an uncertain victory, such invaders were invariably deterred. The history of Ratnanagari during medieval times was filled with many such intrigues. It was not in the least difficult for this kingdom with fertile lands to satisfy the greed of the Marathas. The real downfall of the kingdom began when the British took control of the territories controlled by the Peshwas.

At the time of the decline of the Peshwa rule, Mallaraj's father Nagraj ruled over Ratnanagari. Nagraj had defeated the Peshwa's representative Sardar Vishwasrao. After the decline of the Peshwas, one Colonel Brave started carrying out military expeditions to establish the Company's authority in the area. With his small army, Nagaraj took on the might of the Company, engaging them in several skirmishes. He fought his last war with Colonel Brave's forces, a war which lasted six months and during which, the British came to admire both his war strategy and his diplomatic skills. Nagraj had built several fortifications around Ratnanagari. He first transferred all his important officials and wealthy citizens to the securer forts. He then established his headquarters on Sundargiri and from there, carried out periodic raids on the Company forces. Sometimes he attacked from the east, sometimes from the north and sometimes from the south. Twice or thrice he managed to destroy British canons; he also captured two canons and used them against the Company forces. Another time he attacked their supply lines. Always avoiding open and direct confrontation, Nagraj would prefer to launch surprise attacks on the Company forces. Colonel Brave realised that without a direct confrontation he would not be able to subdue Nagraj's forces. One day Colonel Brave got information that Nagraj's elder son Hastidant was on his way to Sundargiri along with his army. Brave's forces intercepted them at the foothills. Hastidant had a small army and his men were tired; but he had no choice but to engage in battle. He rallied his men for a fight to death and they charged on the Company forces. Nagraj was informed of the battle and he rushed down the Sundargiri with his small band of loyal soldiers. He decided to block the British from the rear. Colonel Brave's forces had more or less vanquished Hastidant's men by then; only Hastidant along with eight to ten men fiercely battled on, refusing to give in despite being surrounded. But the sudden, unexpected attack of Nagraj's forces took the British by surprise. It broke their spirit and Colonel Brave realised that his men were about to give in. He decided to attack Hastidant. Nagraj saw through this strategy, but before he could do anything, the Colonel took aim and shot at Hastidant. The bullet pierced his chest and the prince fell. The man who shot him was saddened by his death. But Nagraj did not lose heart. With an act of supreme will he jumped over a boulder two hand-spans high and five hand-spans wide, only to land on Hastidant. Nagraj leapt up from the chest of his fallen son with a war cry and like a flash of lightning cut Colonel Brave's second-in-command into two. Nagraj's men joined him and a fierce battle ensued, and they fought until the light in the sky had faded. At dusk, both armies retired to their respective camps. The battle was inconclusive—there was neither a victor, nor any vanquished. Both commandants took stock of their forces. Nagraj's army was almost destroyed, so were Colonel Brave's forces. Nagraj received information that the Company forces were likely to get re-enforcements. He had all the forts secured and asked the soldiers protecting the forts to be ready for battle. He then gave a call for all the Rajput men in the region, old and young, to join forces with him; they responded to his call to arms and came together to lay down their lives for their king. Before daybreak, Nagraj had a new army.

Colonel Brave knew that he had an upper hand. He also knew that Nagraj would not be able to put up resistance for very long. But the British officer was impressed by Nagraj's valour, his forbearance and his strategic intelligence. He also realised that the spirit and fierce pride of these kshatriyas was not easy to subdue and subjugate. He felt it would be in the long-term interests of the Company if such a strong ruler were to become a friend. Colonel Brave also believed that extending a hand in friendship was a sign of true valour. He sent an emissary to Nagraj; the emissary carried a letter from Colonel Brave.

> Dear brave Friend,
>
> If we continue to regard each other as enemies, it will result in the destruction of an ancient kingdom and its valorous king. That would be a sad day for me. If you so desire, I am willing to accept you as a friend and have this treaty of friendship ratified by the Company. I am not the Government, but my Government acts on the basis of its faith in the advice of men such as myself. You may wish to use the trust that my superiors repose in me and turn a war into peace and animosity into friendship. I shall await your response. But if you insist upon waging this war, the forces of the Company are prepared.
>
> Your friend, Brave.
>
> P.S.: I would not like it that you surrender. I have full faith in the power of your weapons, as in the strength of your words. —Brave.

Nagraj dictated a response: 'We would be blind if we did not recognise that the armies of the East India Company are like a river in flood. But we are like fire—anyone who touches us will be scalded. Not just fire, we also have light. If your flooding armies put out our smouldering embers, both the fire and the light will vanish in it. If you want that our light be preserved but want to extinguish our fire, that can never be. If that is your wish, war is the only option. But if our fire burns on, we shall never lose our light; even if it fades, it will glow again someday.

So we must keep your flood away from our fire. If that is not acceptable to you, we will engage with you in battle. Some will emerge victorious like Ram and others shall be defeated like Ravana. We are all fated to die one day. We do not fear death. All those who are born must die just as all who enter a battlefield must sustain wounds. It is up to you to consult your government. If you do wrong, the consultation is pointless; if you do right, there is no need to consult anyone to walk on the right path. We are strangers to your ways and are not bound to follow your rules. Please bear this in mind. As long as the Sun, our ancestor, shines on us and as long as there is life in us, not an inch of Ratnanagari's land will fall into foreign hands. We will never bow our heads to you. But we are not averse to friendship with you. We have goodwill for the Company. It is up to you to either further this goodwill or break these bonds.'

Nagraj sent some of his most trusted men to Colonel Brave with the reply. The negotiations also gave him an opportunity to consult with the rulers of the neighbouring kingdoms. He summoned his younger son Mallaraj and instructed him carefully. 'There are three neighbouring kingdoms. Go and meet their kings and tell them it is time that they wake up. Three bison together can drive out a lion; but if they go their separate ways the lion will kill each of them one after the other. Right now they are all watching the war between the foreigners and us, as if it is some farcical play being enacted for their entertainment. But once this play is over, the foreigners will turn towards them and others with similar attitude, and we shall watch their ignominy. There is still time. Tell them that we do not seek their assistance because we are afraid of death. But even a bania understands profit and loss; if we as rulers do not understand what is good for us, it would be fitting that the foreigners shall rule over our ancestral kingdoms. The throne is like Indrani, divine consort of Indra, the king of the gods; she is married to the occupant of the throne of heaven, and not to Indra. Our illustrious ancestors had established these kingdoms. We are not required to establish kingdoms, only to protect them from aggressors. If we are found wanting, the foreigners will rule over us, and that would serve us right. If you want to protect and preserve your kingdoms, please pay heed to my counsel. But if you do not wish to preserve them, you are masters of your own fate.'

With this message from his king and father, Mallaraj set out to meet the rulers of the three neighbouring kingdoms. There was mutual distrust and jealousy among these rulers, but Nagraj's words pierced them like arrows. They were shaken out of their inertia. Nagraj's ancestors had in the past managed to unite dissenting neighbouring rulers against common enemies. It was their combined efforts that had preserved their independence for so long. The same tradition continued. Nagraj's message, delivered by prince Mallaraj, bore fruit.

Colonel Brave received Nagraj's response to his letter. He read it carefully. He was delighted by it. But his superiors were not as generous as him. They wanted at least one-fourth part of the state's revenue, failing which a treaty that would benefit them. They did not want a treaty of friendship that gave them no material benefits; they saw this as a sign of foolishness and were not agreeable to it. Brave believed that the friendship of a valorous king was in itself a reward, but his superiors were not convinced. It was not possible for the Colonel to contradict his superiors; therefore he was forced to act against his wishes. He told Nagraj's minister, 'The Company does not want your land, but the Company now enjoys all the rights that the Peshwa had. Therefore, you must accept the Company's rights to collect land revenue.'

The minister responded, 'We were never subjugated by the Peshwas. We did not allow the Marathas to enter our territories. We do not recognise the rights of the Peshwas, but we are willing to extend our friendship to the Company.'

The claim was true, but Colonel Brave had to act within his authority. He was authorised to renew treaties on terms similar to the ones agreed to by the Peshwas. He was required to get specific sanctions from Bombay for any new treaty. The matter remained unresolved and the day passed. The following day, Mallaraj returned to the headquarters with reinforcements from the neighbouring kingdoms. These kings had also sent their leading men to confer with Nagraj. Statesmen of four kingdoms went as a delegation and met Colonel

Brave. Their unity convinced him that his earlier resolve was the right one, but he needed time to consult his superiors. Brave proposed a truce, which was accepted. He wrote to his superiors, saying, 'These Rajputs are valorous; they are noble, truthful and are not foolish, evil or wicked. If these rulers were to accept the Company's friendship, it would be beneficial to the Company in future.'

The treaty was signed. According to its terms the native states and the Company pledged support to each other in times of aggression. The native states accepted that in event of disputes, either among themselves or with the Company, they would accept the Company's arbitration and the chief arbitrator would be English. The treaty seemed innocuous. The rulers reasoned that they were not required to share any revenue with the Company, their territories were protected and their autonomy was guaranteed. But young Mallaraj remained unconvinced. He was unable to articulate his reservations and was hesitant to speak his mind before his father. At the conclusion of the treaty everyone rejoiced. But Mallaraj remained depressed. From today our state is under shackles, he lamented. Our kshatriyas have been widowed. Like women we, too, have worn bangles. We cannot wage a war. Just as we protect our women, now the English will protect us. We will have our land and our peace, but we shall be effeminate. Kshatriyahood has died. With such gloomy thoughts Mallaraj ascended the throne. Over time, he saw all the major native states drown in the flood that was the British. He remained neutral during the initial period of Nanasaheb's rebellion. The entire country was passing though a great churning similar to the mythical churning of the sea. He sought to learn from it. He realised that strength alone could not protect the country; statecraft was equally essential. Statecraft required the cultivation of compassion and forgiveness. He found his countrymen sorely lacking in these qualities, while the Englishmen had them. Mallaraj was disappointed and saddened. Vidya Chatura's maternal uncle Jarashankar had recently become his advisor. Jarashankar counselled him on the path of prosperity and happiness. He said, 'Maharaj, it is good to be on the side of the powerful and the virtuous. We should win their trust and we should also trust them. Every warrior is fond of his sword, but it cannot for that reason be put into one's stomach. It is wrong and foolish to support the natives if all they have to offer is the destruction of the country. Even righteous action is contextual. From what you have told me, I feel that the good of all the native states, and not just our state, lies in supporting these wise foreigners. They are compassionate and just. Ultimately, they will triumph. If the Muslims and the Marathas manage to defeat the English, they will turn against each other as soon as the common enemy is removed. Whoever triumphs in that conflict will tyrannise the native states. They are like wolves and jackals.'

Mallaraj looked at him sharply. 'There is little doubt in what you say, Jarashankar. But a brahmin like you will always search for peace, while a kshatriya like me will look for battle. If the English triumph, kshatriya valour will vanish forever. Does that concern you at all?'

'No.'

'What then?'

'Then, what? That would be an auspicious day. The people and the native rulers will both be at peace. I have faith in the English sense of justice.'

'Be careful! The English, too, are human. They, too, have their self-interest. They are like the banias. They will become the undisputed rulers of the country one day. No one can be as bad as an unchecked bania!'

'Maharaj, that may be so. But what option do we have? If the kshatriyas could unite, why would those seeking to drive out the British be called rebels? If we do not suffer from an incurable disease, the God of Death will not come knocking on our door.'

'Do you really think that we kshatriyas have become utterly useless?' asked Mallaraj with his hand on Jarashankar's shoulder, his eyes burning red with anger.

The brahmin laughed. 'Maharaj, if all kshatriyas were like you, they would not be considered useless. Among the Kauravas, there was Bhishma. But who remembers him today? There will be few like you. No matter whether the English win or lose, we shall see what the future has in store for us.'

'What will happen?'

'Maharaj, do you not see that many queens have taken up with banias and brahmins? Do you know how many queens have adopted the son of a cobbler or a miller as their prince? One of these robbers will become an emperor. He will either be a Muslim or a Marathi brahmin who are not faithful even to their masters. A time will come when persons of mixed and impure blood will ascend the thrones and pure, blue-blooded kshatriyas will be shamed into hiding.'

'What will happen if the English win?'

'It is better to have a wise enemy rather than a foolish friend. Maharaj, Ravana told the demon Marich that he should assume the form of a golden deer and be killed by Ram, failing which Ravana himself would kill him. Marich thought that if death were certain, it was better to die at the hands of Ram.'

Mallaraj took his sword and left the room. But he returned promptly, and this time his face betrayed a new resolve. He said, 'Jarashankar, write a letter to Brave Sahib and inform him that Mallaraj and his army are ready to defend the Company.'

Jarashankar cautioned, 'Maharaj, I think like a brahmin. You have decided to act upon my advice. But you should also consider it independently. Do not blame me later on.'

Mallaraj smiled and replied, 'Those who are in my employment should be ready to hear an assessment of both their qualities and shortcomings.'

'I do not deny that, Maharaj. But it is my duty to caution you as the implications of my advice will be felt by you and the entire state.'

'That is correct. The decision I have taken is not without attendant dangers. The English are like the banias. They will want to convert the Rajputs and make them into banias. The Rajputs will not be able to conduct themselves like banias and they will ultimately lose the game. But if our people emerge victorious, it would amount to placing an infant in the care of monkeys—the English will ill-treat all those who are weak.'

'Maharaj, my understanding is somewhat simplistic. The English are like rats. They will bite and soothe and thus corrode us, while our natives will pounce on us like a pack of wolves and decimate us.'

'In that case, we are not mistaken, Jarashankar. The English appear to be the lesser of the two evils. We should deal with them. We should remember, however, that the English are not sugary sweet but hot and pungent as pepper.'

Jarashankar got up to write the letter. He said to himself, Oh, how times have changed! The English will rule over the land of Rajputs! But my advice was appropriate. I acted according to the principles of statecraft. For,

> What can a spirited man, though strong, do if without a helper (allies)? Fire, kindled in a place where there is no wind, is extinguished of itself.[1]

Likewise, the good king Mallaraj is helpless. If these robbers were to take control of the state, how long would they remain friends of anyone?

> The comfort of clouds, the friendship of the vile, cooked food, women, youth and riches are capable of being enjoyed for a short period. Those who can distinguish between what is permanent and what is short-lived [are] hence able to take proper view of things.[2]

And what if they were to become the rulers, what would Ratnanagari be reduced to?

> Formerly a hare and Kapinjala (name of a sparrow) seeking justice and going to a mean judge for decision both met with destruction.[3]

Jarashankar, what if the English were to emerge superior? The Dutch, the Portuguese, the French, all accept their authority. The English

[1] M. R. Kale, trans. *Panchatantra of Visnusarman,* Tantra III, Verse 57 (Delhi: Motilal Banarsidass, 1912, 2008), 399.

[2] Ibid., Tantra II, Verse 117.

[3] Ibid., Tantra III, Verse 90.

have been equal to them and are likely to retain their superiority. They are a good protective cover for the small states.

> When there is a master, even at the mere mention of the name of the great before wicked men, good results at once.[4]

The English are members of an empire. But these robbers have no roots, no allegiance to anyone.

> One mighty king proves a blessing to the world. If there are many they lead to trouble (or destruction) as many suns at the end of a Yuga cause the destruction of the world.[5]

They have won some victories but the common enemy is still undefeated. Just a small victory has made them proud and haughty. What havoc would they wreak on the likes of Mallaraj and the people of the state if their victory were to be complete? The crow had said of the owl,

> What object shall we gain by making this owl which is frightful by nature, very fierce, cruel and of a repulsive aspect, a king?[6]

These robbers are no different. What does friendship of the Company entail? Mallaraj is certain to be eclipsed by the Company. He will become insignificant before a powerful force. We shall be forced to follow their dictates and be ruined.

> Friendship and marriage are proper between those whose wealth is equal and whose families are of equal rank, and not between the fat and the lean (rich and poor).[7]

Should I then advise Mallaraj to remain neutral? Should I advise him against this proposed alliance? Neutrality is the best policy when the outcome of a war is uncertain. One of the two is certain to be defeated. One will gain a friend but also make an enemy of someone. I, Jarashankar, do not have the capacity to predict the outcome of this

4 Ibid., Verse 80.

5 Ibid., Verse 79.

6 Ibid., Tantra III, Verse 78.

7 Ibid., Tantra II, Verse 28.

Great War, but Mallaraj estimates that the Company will emerge victorious. He has never been proven wrong. If we were to support the Company we shall stand to gain in two ways. If there is any doubt regarding their final victory, our throwing in our lot with them will definitely add to their strength. It is said that friendship with the mighty is not beneficial. But there is an exception to this. In moments of crisis the assistance given by the weak to the mighty is always remembered; the mighty remain grateful for life. Therefore the weaker party should never squander an opportunity. Both these are considerations for the future, and the wise are those who pull the future towards them. The mighty have use for the friendship of the weak.

> Wise men, even though endowed with fullness (abundance, opulence), should make friends: for the sea, though entirely full (of water), awaits the rise of the moon (to swell up).[8]

Hence, is it not a sign of stupidity if the weak forgo an opportunity to secure the affection of the powerful?

> From some cause one becomes a friend and also from a cause one becomes an enemy of another; therefore, a wise man should employ (form) friendship and not enmity in this world.[9]

Mallaraj's estimation of the English is unlikely to be wrong. He has the kshatriya's sharp sense. He does not know the English intimately, but the astute has to taste but one grain to know if the rice is cooked or not.

> Shrewd men know the mettle of a man although they see him but once; experts know accurately the measure of the pola by weighing a thing on (the palm of) their hand.[10]

Even a blind man can see that the English are clever. The eggs of a peacock need no decoration.

[8] Ibid., Tantra II, Verse 27.

[9] Ibid., Tantra II, Verse 32.

[10] Ibid., Verse 83.

> A young pea-cock that has not yet got its plumage, its distinguishing mark, can be known to be a pea-cock when moving away from a lake with stately steps backwards.[11]

Even if the English are destined to be defeated, one has to take this risk if one wants benefits of their possible victory. Even if the English prove to be ungrateful in victory and all our expectations remain unfulfilled, we would still have the benefit of knowing the flaws in their character. Knowledge of the weakness of the other is one path to victory.

> Having entered inside even through a very small hole, an enemy gradually destroys one afterwards, as does a flood of water a boat.[12]

Moreover,

> Timidly and timidly at first does an enemy move on the ground with gentle steps, but with great ease afterwards like a paramour of a beautiful woman.[13]

The English are experts at this game. This is our opportunity to use their game against them. It is not that we are going to be equal to them, but it is an opportunity nevertheless. We do not know what the future holds; our swords will come in use only if we have practiced our swordsmanship. This offers us that possibility. A treaty of friendship does not mean that we trust them implicitly. Distrust and scepticism must be kept alive. That is the first rule of politics.

> One should not repose confidence in one who is not trusted nor should one confide in one who has one's confidence; for fear arising from confidence nips off the very roots.
>
> One who never trusts (any one) although weak is not destroyed even by very powerful persons; but those who put confidence (in others) although strong are quickly destroyed even by the weak.[14]

11 Ibid., Verse 84.

12 Ibid., Verse 42.

13 Ibid., Verse 48.

14 Ibid., Tantra II, Verse 43–44.

In statecraft, friendship, gratitude and scepticism must all combine.

> The policy of good action advocated by Vishnugupta, of "the acquisition of friends" by Bhargava and of "distrust" by Brihaspati—thus threefold is the adoption of policy.[15]

Moreover,

> When an enemy is wicked and powerful one should deal with him distrustfully, taking one's stand on duplicity, now proposing peace, now fighting.[16]

This Company is as vast as the ocean. If we have to build embankments to contain it, the foundations of such embankments must reach the rock bottom and stay firm.

> Just as one can reach the bottom of water by means of a flight of steps, so the spies can penetrate the very heart of the enemy through the officials and know his secret plans.[17]

This will acquaint us with the weak points of the Company. If we are seen as friends, we shall use our friendship to get a better measure of their frailties. God willing, there shall not be any enmity between us. But even as friends, knowledge of their weaknesses would allow us to secure and guard our own interests better.

> Even a pearl, though exceedingly pure, unperforated, well rounded and very beautiful, gets confined (woven in a necklace) when bored through.[18]

This alliance will secure many benefits for us. The good of the king and the welfare of the people can both be secured by this alliance. It is a great effort. The bitter part is that we will be forced to betray the natives and embrace the foreigner. Jarashankar signed deeply. Tears glistened in his eyes. It is inordinately difficult to fulfill one's obligations towards the country. One is forced to alienate our near

[15] Ibid., Verse 45.

[16] Ibid., Tantra III, Verse 61.

[17] Ibid., Verse 70.

[18] Ibid., Tantra IV, Verse 108.

ones and embrace strangers. The only consideration must be the welfare of the state and its people. This welfare can be best secured if one has the five Pandavas as allies instead of seeking the company of a hundred Kauravas.

> One should not enter into an alliance with a man who is destitute of truthfulness and righteousness; for, although firmly allied, he, on account of his wickedness, will change before long.[19]

What even if one has to drink a cup of poison to ensure this?

> Even poison swallowed with the object of accomplishing an end acts like nectar, in the case of all creatures no hesitation should be made in such a case.[20]

Delayed decision-making and lengthy, unending debates in matters of state administration are both detrimental to it and akin to committing a sin.

> When a business to be promptly attended to arises and a man delays, the deities, being angry, undoubtedly put obstacles in his way.
>
> When any action, and especially one about to be attended with fruit, is not done at once, time saps its juice.[21]

And therefore,

> He who takes action before a thing comes to pass shines; he who does not provide for what is to happen comes to grief.[22]

And hence it is said: one must have foresight and act in time. I must act patiently.

> The enemy is killed; a friend is gained; the jewel necklace is not lost; and water was drunk by means of a lotus-stalk, well accomplished all this, oh monkey on the fig tree.[23]

19 Ibid., Tantra III, Verse 25.

20 Ibid., Verse 201.

21 Ibid., Verse 198–199.

22 Ibid., Tantra III, Verse 192.

23 Ibid., Tantra V, Verse 81.

After this lengthy deliberation with himself, Jarashankar the wise minister of Maharaj Mallaraj proceeded to compose the letter to Colonel Brave.

Meanwhile, Mallaraj had also reconsidered his decision, and it met with his approval. He thought to himself: In the final analysis, even kings are not attached to any particular piece of land. Which ruler does not have ancestors who were not foreign to the land they ruled? Which heirs to kings will be able to keep their kingdom as long as the sun and the moon shine in the sky? The duties of brahmins and kshatriyas are in some ways the same. The brahmins teach that the soul is immortal and it changes body just as we change clothes. For us our lineage is our soul and our kingdom our body. When one body has lived its life and dies, we must seek another body and nourish it.

Kings are not ultimately attached to their subjects either. The shastras say that a king has no friends. Jarashankar sometimes teases me that one should not trust a king. It is true. For parents, a son—be he mad, stupid or vile—is still a son; they cannot deny the blood ties. They also do not admit to the follies of their son. It is for this reason that sons tend to trust their parents. But a king relates only to virtue and he is an enemy of vice. He does not even regard his heir-apparent with complete trust, why would he trust his subjects? Everyone must understand that a king relates to their virtue, but not to their person. So long as the person remains virtuous and trustworthy, the king trusts him. There can be no other ground for trust. A king who considers his queen, his sons or ministers as his own is not a true king. The moment the virtues of a person wither, the king must remove him from his administration—just as one throws away a flower that has lost its fragrance—and punish him for his faults. If this logic were to hold, Mallaraj is not beholden to either the rebels or the people of India. Mallaraj is responsible only to his state and kingdom. The Company has captured the country and they know how to keep it; they are experts in statecraft; they know how to make and spend money; they know whom to please and how; they know the ways of the Muslims, the banias and the brahmins; they are adept at techniques of war and they know their diplomacy; they know how to protect their interests and have transformed a village like Bombay into a metropolis. Five thousand of them, relying only upon their intelligence and not force, can defeat an enemy force of fifteen thousand. They can be generous and thrifty; they are cunning and know how to plunder our wealth, and they know their self-interest as also the welfare of others. Their victory is certain. It is wise to be friends with them. This is also in accordance with my duties as a Rajput. If they do not win, I will have to battle to keep Ratnanagari. I may even lose my life in that battle. So what if I lose my life? If the English emerge victorious, my heirs will also gain some of their great virtues. Even Ratnanagari will produce great men. If all goes well, such will be the benefits. But if the plan fails, my body shall fall on the sands of the battlefield—that is its ultimate destiny and fulfillment. If this alliance proves detrimental, as alliances between the mighty and the weak can well be, my sons and ministers will battle them intellectually and they will learn to match intrigue with intrigue. This will sharpen their intellect. Whether the benefits accrue to all people or are squandered like flowers that grow in the wild will depend upon my heirs. That is how kings play.[24]

[24] Author's note: The Minister Azeem Ul Omrah 'had, however, no easy task to conquer the prejudices of his sovereign, the Nizam, against such an alliance; which, from the inequality of the parties, that monarch argued, would early terminate in rendering his dominions virtually dependent, for their future security, upon the British government. This the minister admitted, but contended ... that, as it was clear that the situation of the State of Hyderabad was such as to render it impossible to remain without the alliance of some one of those powers, it was assuredly wise to prefer a connexion with a government which brought with its protection the substantial blessings of security and peace, to the nominal friendship of states whose professed objects were plunder and conquest, and who had repeatedly shown that they held in contempt even the forms of public faith. The Nizam's prejudices and fears [were] at last subdued by this reasoning ...'

—*The Political History of India, from 1724 to 1823*, John Malcolm.

8 Mallaraj and His Jewels

Mallaraj was deep in thought the day he sent the letter to Colonel Brave. At a time when the foreigner could be driven away and the country could be ruled by natives, he had decided on an alliance with the foreigner. The alliance would soon become public knowledge and that was certain to bring condemnation and censure from the entire clan and community as well as other native states. The possible disgrace perturbed him. But he considered the possible gains of the future and felt less uneasy. This inner struggle made him weary.

The letter to Colonel Brave was sent in the afternoon. By dusk a messenger arrived in Ratnanagari. Mallaraj's favourite Bhayat, his cousin Samant Mulu accompanied the messenger to the king's presence. Mallaraj sat leaning against the bolsters, smoking his hookah, unmindful of the perspiration that soaked his forehead. He held the hookah in one hand and his sword in the other. The messenger and Samant came in and sat down, but Mallaraj remained oblivious of their presence. After some time Samant spoke, 'Maharaj, we still have time to reconsider. A fierce battle has broken out in Kanpur. The English judge of Fatehpur was tried, sentenced to death and his body was cut into small pieces which were thrown among the people. The Company's rule has disappeared.'

Mallaraj pursed his lips in anger and said, 'A judge is like their brahmin. Did these cowards kill a brahmin? Did the judge kill a few before being taken captive?'

'Can any Englishman be captured before he kills a few?'

'If their brahmins are so brave, what would happen when we fight their Rajputs? Tell me, was it a Rajput who cut up his dead body and threw away the pieces?'

'Can a Rajput ever be an enemy of the dead?'

Mallaraj reclined on his bolsters and, putting aside the hookah, said, 'Aren't Rajputs ashamed of the company of such irreligious men?'

'Maharaj, I did not realise that you would so brazenly take the side of the British. What has to happen shall happen. Tatya Tope's forces have camped outside the borders of Ratnanagari. Their leader has sent a message,' said Samant.

The messenger relayed the message: 'Maharaj, about three thousand of Tatya Tope's men have camped at a distance of about twenty furloughs outside Ratnanagari. Others are likely to join them soon. They demand grains for the men and fodder for the horses. They are willing to pay but claim that if grains and fodder are denied them for payment, they will forcibly seize them. It appears that by morning they will enter the capital.'

'Anything else?' Mallaraj asked impatiently.

'No. But I heard them talk among themselves. They say that they want friendship with the native states, but that they will capture any state that harbours foreigners.'

'Very well. You go back to your post and keep an eye on their movements. I want a report at midnight and before dawn.' The messenger retreated with a promise to obey the orders. Mallaraj stood up and addressed Samant. 'Samant, collect all the Bhayat present in the capital and bring them and the chief of our army to my presence immediately.'

Samant hesitated. Mallaraj was irked. 'What is the doubt? This is not a moment for doubts, Samant. It is necessary to take swift decisions.'

'Maharaj! The forces of Tatya Tope do not wish to battle with us; they seek our protection.'

'But they will fight us if we refuse to grant protection.'

'Is there a problem in granting them protection?'

'We will deal with that later. We shall consider all opinions. But for now we must be ready for battle. We cannot afford any delay. Now go.'

Samant stared at Mallaraj. His legs refused to move. It took him some effort to leave the king's presence.

Mallaraj ordered an attendant to call Jarashankar. But before the attendant could leave the room, Jarashankar sought permission to enter. Mallaraj was overjoyed. 'It is a good omen. Very good, Jarashankar! You heard the news and you came for consultations. What a minister! A rift in my forces is likely. I consider an alliance with the British desirable. Samant and some others prefer an alliance with the rebels. It would be disastrous if my forces turn against me at the time of battle. I will have to find a way out. A Rajput's word is non-negotiable. I have decided in favour of an alliance with the Company. I shall fight alongside them and also lay down my life. A promise has been given. This is not the occasion to reconsider its correctness. Mallaraj has given his word. Mount Meru that holds the earth might shake and the oceans might breach their shores, but Mallaraj will not renege on his promise. War is a certainty.' The possibility of war filled Mallaraj with new vigour. His legs were ready for action, his lips trembled with excitement and his right hand toyed with his sword as he paced up and down.

Jarashankar came in, and even before he could greet the king, Mallaraj placed a hand over his shoulder and said, 'Jarashankar, it is time for war, isn't it?'

'Maharaj, that is for you to decide.'

'But our decision has been made.'

'That is so, but your Bhayat think otherwise.'

'Who gave them these ideas?'

'Those whose interests will be served by it. The talk that you had with Samant is known to others also. You are ready to fight the natives. But all your Bhayat want to fight the foreigner. How can we raise an army without the Bhayat?'

Mallaraj put his hands on his waist, threw back his head and laughed aloud. 'You do not know my Bhayat. But a decision made and a word given will not change. That is not negotiable. Tell me, what is to be done.'

'Maharaj, Samant will soon be here with the Bhayat. If you were to seek their opinion in a congregation, they would all unite against you. It would be difficult to deal with them. It is advisable to deal with each one individually; call them aside and those who differ ...'

'Those who differ should be placed under house arrest or held captive in the palace. We should attack the rebels with our supporters.'

'Maharaj, that is just what I was going to suggest. How alike we—king and his minister, master and servant—think.'

Mallaraj laughed.

'Maharaj, this is a difficult moment, not one for laughter.'

'Fear not, Jarashankar, we will turn it into a joyous occasion. It is your responsibility to think. The "design" and "execution"[1] of a plan are also your responsibility. But when the execution of a design requires a war, that is not your terrain. Then one needs to be kshatriya. It is a game of chess. You step aside and let me play. You have to be a spectator. You watch me deal with my Bhayat. You watch me twirl my moustache. Mallaraj can never be treacherous towards his Bhayat. I cannot imprison them. They are my thoroughbred horses; you just watch me ride them.'

In no time the room was filled with Mallaraj's Bhayat. They came and took their place around Mallaraj. Mallaraj's seat was higher. Jarashankar sat behind him. Two torch-bearers of the barber caste stood behind Mallaraj. The light of the torches fell on the excited and eager faces of the Bhayat and allowed Mallaraj to gauge their inner feelings. No one spoke. The pregnant silence of the men merged with the silence of the night and filled the room.

Mallaraj broke the silence, 'Brothers!'

It was only at the time of war that the king addressed his Bhayat as 'brothers'—an address which carried all the connotations of honour, valour and unswerving loyalty to the king and the kingdom. It instantly captivated the Bhayat and they looked intently upon their king. As the

1 The words 'design' and 'execution' are in English in the original text.

words flowed from Mallaraj, their hearts filled with kshatriya pride and all the doubts harboured in their minds disappeared.

'Brothers, it is time for war! Samant Bha has brought news that Tatya Tope's forces have camped near Ratnanagari. Mallaraj does not wish to join them out of fear. They are petty robbers; the light of the sun lineage cannot mix with them. Brothers, our ancestor Nagraj had an alliance with Sugrivji, who was a devotee of Shri Ramji, who also belonged to the Suryavansh. In our Ratnanagari, a son does not break a promise made by his father. Similarly, the Bhayat do not break a promise given by their king. I, Mallaraj, am a son of Nagraj and you are my Bhayat. There is no doubt about this. It is given that I shall honour a promise made by Nagraj, and you shall honour my word. Should there be any doubt or discussion about this? Kshatriyas, rise! Give up this soft-hearted effusiveness of women and bania-like deliberations. Go and return with your forces. It is indeed an auspicious day when war is upon us. After many years. It is time to ride our horses and charge upon the enemy with our swords and guns. You are the protector of my honour. Goddess Lakshmi awaits us; her hands are smeared with the blood of our enemies.'

Mallaraj was charged by his own words. He got up and drew his sword and called out, 'Brothers! Come, let's show them who we are!' As soon as he stood up, all the Bhayat stood up as one man. One of them called out, 'Victory to Maharaj Mallaraj!' All doubts and misgivings disappeared and the loyal, brave soldiers trooped out to gather forces for their king.

Mallaraj and Jarashankar remained in the room. Samant followed the others up to the door, but once they had all left, he returned. He was soaked in perspiration. His eyes were blood-shot. It was difficult to tell whether he was angry or filled with valour. No words came out of him.

Mallaraj asked him, 'Samant, what doubts bring you back?'

Samant was seething with rage, but he spoke softly and succinctly. 'Maharaj, you have made a difficult choice. I called them to your presence with the hope that you would consult them. I did not know that you would command us to war. Maharaj, this is an adventure.'

The words came out stiff and heavy as if a shot-putter were throwing iron balls.

Mallaraj assuaged his feelings, 'Samant Bha, calm down. Sit down and breathe easy.'

Samant gave no response and turned his face away. The three of them sat down. Mallaraj continued, 'Samant, I have thought very carefully about this decision. I know that you would agree with my reasoning. But for a moment let us consider that we differ. Would you go your own way, or would you still follow me? Tell me honestly, what rights do I have over you? If I cannot claim rights over your devotion to the state and your love for me, I would be required to explain my position and I would need to convince you, wouldn't I?'

Samant became powerless before these words. He removed his pagdi from his head, placed it in Mallaraj's lap and said, 'Maharaj, please pardon me. If I do not obey you, whom shall I obey? I may hold a different opinion, but if I follow my own counsel in disobedience of your command, I should be considered a traitor and beheaded.' With folded hands he said, 'Maharaj, give me your command that I may follow the other Bhayat and prepare for battle.'

'Samant, my dear brother, you are a pillar of this state. You are the elephant that leads my forces. Ram obeyed Dashrath, and Laxman and Bharat obeyed Ram. In the same way, I will obey a command given by Raja Nagraj and you will keep the promise that I have made—such is the glorious tradition of the Suryavanshi kings.'

'Maharaj, command me. Why do you not allow me to show my obedience?'

'Samant, you are elder to me by four years. You occupy the position that Bhishma Pitamah occupied in the court of Duryodhana. I value your opinion as much as I trust your loyalty.'

Samant trembled, touched his ears as if to cover them and then touched Mallaraj's feet. 'Forgive me, Maharaj! Forgive me! I swear by the head of this pure and pious brahmin minister that not for a moment did I feel that your decision was like that of Duryodhana, irreligious and against righteous conduct.'

'Jarashankar, Karna was like a minister to Duryodhana, but you are a minister to me. How can I disbelieve if Samant swears by you?'

Samant was perturbed. 'Oh God! Maharaj, if you had awarded me a punishment that would have been my penance. But this is unbearable. I speak the truth. Jarashankar counselled you and you accepted the advice, which may have differed from my opinion. I firmly believe that any advice given to you—the protector of cows and brahmins—would have been righteous and in accordance with dharma. Even if this brahmin had advised you that I should be beheaded and you had accepted the minister's counsel, and for that reason if I were to even obliquely threaten your minister, it would not be true to my salt. Maharaj, it was not an act of treachery when I swore by Jarashankar.'

Mallaraj was happy. 'Samant, I am pleased with you. But you must listen to my reasoning.'

'Maharaj! Even though I hold a different opinion and know nothing of the reasons that prompted your decision, I have no desire to pry into the secrecy of the deliberations between my king and his minister. I must obey your command in total faith and in so doing I shall prove my loyalty. Please command me and I shall fulfill my duty with unstinting faith. Please grant me this favour.'

Mallaraj embraced Samant joyfully. 'Go, Bapu, go! As long as Ratnanagari is blessed with gems like you, God has granted me boons far greater than the favour that you seek from me.'

Samant Mulu stepped out of the palace at peace with himself and with renewed resolve to serve his king.

'Jarashankar, did you see the jewels of Ratnanagari? I have made you my minister so that in time you can test these jewels, and the day I become one with my ancestors you will teach my son to value these jewels among men. If there be such priceless individuals in other states, they should also be invited to make Ratnanagari their home. That is our duty. How can we neglect our own? Kings must know the art of assisting those men who have lost their sheen to rejuvenate themselves—so that their true worth and esteem grows and their light shines forth. You must learn this art and teach it to my heirs. You must appoint a capable minister for my heirs who can learn and appreciate and inculcate this art. Listen to me carefully. My body may fall in the battlefield, but you shall live longer than me and help Ratnanagari attain its destiny. Pay attention to my words, Jarashankar. It is kshatriya practice to confide in the minister at such moments so that nothing remains unsaid.'

Jarashankar grew tearful. Mallaraj continued: 'The varna division of brahmin-kshatriya-vaishya is an ancient one. It has one benefit. The kshatriyas are warriors while knowledge is the preserve of the brahmins. It is the duty of the kshatriya to lay down his life, while the brahmin must preserve life. There are trees which grow faster when pruned. Similarly among the kshatriyas when the father dies in battle, his sons are infused with even greater courage. When one body falls, from its seed arises a new body, but the seeds of knowledge and art cannot be sowed. Knowledge and art have to be preserved in a family from generation to generation like the sacred fire. What would the people do if the knowledge of statecraft and war strategies were to perish with the death of the king? If kings do not lay down their lives and if they cling on to dear life, why would the kshatriyas respect such cowardly kings? When kshatriya soldiers watch their king battle Yama the God of Death in the battlefield, their loyalty and valour are enhanced. Hence, kings must regard war as auspicious. If the king were to die in battle, his knowledge of statecraft and war strategy should not perish with him, especially if the heir to the throne is a minor. Therefore, the king must make his brahmin minister the repository of the knowledge of statecraft and the art of wielding weapons. The shastras prohibited the killing of the brahmin because he is the inexhaustible repository of knowledge and must be preserved for the welfare of mankind. Let me give you some examples: Dronacharya's knowledge of weapons and the statecraft of Chanakya. It was only because of Chanakaya that Chandragupta could defeat the mleccha. Even those born into royal lineage require the nurturance of a brahmin. It is only with vast experience that knowledge comes to light. Therefore, kings must have brahmin ministers who must gain experience by bearing witness to great events. The king must ensure a long life for his ministers; this is part of kingly duties. You should instruct my son accordingly, Jarashankar.

'Moreover, brahmins, kshatriyas and vaishyas should remain within their assigned status; there should be no compromise on this. But the times are changing and the varnashrama will also undergo changes. Do not get me wrong. There will come a time when the son of a brahmin will cease to perform priestly functions and hence his brahminhood will diminish. Under British rule the sons of kshatriyas will have no opportunity to go to war, and to that extent the varnashrama will be destroyed; with it, customs and conduct according to varna will also perish. It is imperative that you remain in tune with the times and that you teach the right conduct as per the varnashrama to others. However hard you might try but a brahmin will never acquire the qualities of a pure kshatriya just as a kshatriya can never become a brahmin. Sage Vishvamitra became a brahmarshi but could not divest himself of his customary disposition. The brahmin Peshwas born in the land of Parashuram may have learnt the art of war, but first they turned traitors to their king; later they turned against each other and now Nanasaheb, the grandson of Kaghoba, shall wreak havoc. Like Bhasmasur he will char himself to death. They fight because of their self-interest. Their actions are cruel. Nanasaheb does not know the generous and noble ways of the kshatriyas, nor will anyone in his lineage be equal to this task. They are not jewels among brahmins but men who will wreak havoc like wild fire. Jarashankar, remember my words even after I am gone. You must not encourage those who are unworthy like stones, hazardous like coal and fiery like embers among the various varnas. Customs and norms of varna are certain to be destroyed among them. Do not make futile attempts to prevent their destruction. Only after a careful examination of hearts and minds, invite the best among the brahmins, the kshatriyas and the vaishyas to Ratnanagari but dump the undesirable ones. Deal with each of them according to their varna. Jarashankar, the night is short and we have much to do. Instruct my heir accordingly.'

The brave men of the army had begun to gather outside. Their voices filtered inside the room. 'Jarashankar, I forgot to mention one important thing. When I say that you should collect the best among the men at Ratnanagari, do not take my words literally. Some jewels add to the beauty of our home while some shine forth when they are kept in the homes of others. A son and a kshatriya have to be kept at home. One should not trust an outsider with something. Do not forget this. A precious daughter has to be the jewel of someone else's house. You should also send the best of our brahmins out of the state to gain knowledge. At home their intellect will rust and grow dull, their experience shall remain restricted and they will become lazy; their impartiality and detachment also suffers as they become homebound, pick up internal fights and as a result a small state like ours would lose the few good men that it has. Consequently we would be forced to invite outsiders whose power and capability would be grudged by our worthless men. The money that we spent on worthless people would only bring injury and harm us. We would also not get the benefit of wise counsel in moments of crisis, the state would suffer setbacks and the people would be subject to tyranny. Jarashankar, you must bear all this in mind when you appoint officials and promote them.

'They might belong to any caste but they will have to do the work that brahmins did in earlier times. The only consideration in appointment should be their capability for the task. You should enable them to do even better. Do not appoint officers only from within the state; they would become bania-like—leonine at home but foxes outside. Remember the maxim that the true value of a person is recognised only when he travels outside. Such are the responsibilities of my ministers. You should cultivate the ingenuity of a bania to accomplish all these responsibilities.'

The clamour outside grew more insistent.

'That is all, Jarashankar. Our time is up. You must instruct and educate my heir. Before I plunge into battle and leave my beloved Ratnanagari, allow me one last expression of affection for this land. Recite the auspicious verse that tells us how Ratnanagari was named.'

Jarashankar recited:

> Ratnanagari is blessed with gems found in the mines of the mountains of Sundargiri. These gems adorn the fangs of great serpents. Mighty elephants and glorious lions inhabit this land. Its oceans are filled with pearls. Therefore, since times

immemorial this land has been called Ratnanagari. This land also gives birth to gems among men who bring imperishable glory to it.

Mallaraj looked up to the sky and said with folded hands, 'O Mother Ratnanagari! Your Sundargiri, your forests, your oceans, the animals of this land are precious as gems. We pray that the heirs of Mallaraj, their ministers and officers and the people of this land shall never bring disrepute to your name. Today, the best among your sons shall enter battle to protect your glory. We pray that God be with us!'

Just as he spoke these words, Samant Mulu entered with all the battle-ready Bhayat. He laid his sword at Mallaraj's feet and said, 'May God be with our righteous King Mallaraj. All of us, your brothers, await your command. We are prepared to lay down our lives. On behalf of all the Bhayat, Samant seeks your command.'

Mallaraj was overjoyed. He said, 'Samant, the devotion and affection that you and all other brothers have for me is unparalleled. I salute you! As long as I have brother like you, Samant, there is no danger to Ratnanagari. You shall lead the forces. You shall bring us glorious victory. My blessings are with you. Just as Kartikeya battled the demons on the instructions of Indra, I command you and all my brothers to attack the enemy forces and vanquish them. You shall ensure that they shall never again step inside the territories of Ratnanagari. My dear and brave brothers, return victorious before the sun rises. Brothers, give your all to Samant. Samant, you must send me a blow by blow account of the battle. Come, let me embrace you.'

The respect, the demonstration of trust and affectionate embrace of the king caused Samant Mulu's eyes to well up with tears. Mallaraj shook hands with each one of his brothers-in-arms as they took leave of their king one by one.

'Jarashankar, there can be no greater strength and fulfillment for the ruler of Ratnanagari than the true love and blessings of his Bhayat, his officials, his army and his people. This is part of our ancient history and you have witnessed it again today. You must teach this history to my son, if one were to be born to me, or to my heirs. Tell them that it does not matter if the English rule India or if someone else runs the empire. No harm shall come to them as long as they have the capacity to follow the ancient traditions and customs of our Suryavanshi family. The times may change, but their rule shall not.'

Mallaraj's trust in and love for the Bhayat and their devotion for the king had stunned Jarashankar into silence. Mallaraj's words brought tears to his eyes. He said, 'Maharaj, I am your culprit and I deserve punishment. I had advised you to neutralise your Bhayat. I think it was cruel on my part. If you did not have so much goodwill for these patriotic men, my advice would have led to evil consequences. I shall never forget your noble way of punishing Samant. You describe the Marathas as capable of thieving from the moment of their conception in their mother's womb. But you on the other hand were conceived as a great king. I am moved by your kingly qualities and delighted. I am proud that I serve a master such as you. Oh great king of the sun lineage, your words are etched in my heart and I shall instruct your heirs accordingly. But why do you feel that the time has come for you to give your final instructions?'

Mallaraj smiled. 'Jarashankar, a king and his ministers keep each other within limits. The king's family keeps the country united by providing continuity. As father, son, or grandson they are ultimately kings and hence they are one. Therefore, the king never dies and the wisdom of one generation is passed on to the next. The king looks upon his state and his subjects as part of his family. But he cannot remain abreast of all the developments taking place around him. He cannot gain all types of experience nor can he be acquainted with different forms of knowledge. He, therefore, needs to be associated with ministers who are both experienced and knowledgeable. It is against norms for a man to marry his sister; he must marry a woman outside his clan. Such are the norms of right conduct. Just as it is undesirable for a state to trouble and torment its Bhayat, it is equally undesirable that the Bhayat be appointed as ministers. When the son of the family marries a woman from another family, the relationship they share is different and personal; neither his father nor his brothers have a right to meddle in that relationship or to know what transpires between them. Similarly, the Bhayat have no right to know as to what transpires between a king and his ministers. Jarashankar, if a man were to be unduly and excessively attached to his mother, his wife is justified in seeking to wean him away and setting some limits. Similarly, if a king were to become unduly partial to his family, his minister must warn him. You were right to advise me.

'I know my brothers-in-arms. My affection for them ensures the desired outcome. I used my prerogative. But you must always fearlessly think and express yourself. We have to rectify each other's mistakes. You shall see that my Bhayat will now fight with greater courage, will and intelligence. Instead of leading the battle, I sent them. They will be more cautious. Samant made a mistake but he was rewarded with greater responsibility. I believe that he shall return victorious before the sun rises. But after all, battles are unpredictable; I may be called upon to join the battle and that would leave me no chance to have a word with you. It is said that in olden times warriors impregnated their wives before going into battle to ensure the continuity of their lineage. I am following the same tradition. I leave my thoughts to you to preserve, nurture and pass on. Women and brahmins cannot be killed in a war, but the kshatriyas do die. A seed planted in a woman's womb and thoughts planted in a brahmin's mind survive, flourish and come to light at the appropriate time. Who is that approaching us?'

It was Mallaraj's messenger. He said, 'Maharaj, two chiefs of Tatya Tope's army have accompanied me to the gates of the city. They desire an audience with you. At this moment they are waiting at the inn on the outskirts of town. If you so desire, I can bring them to your presence. I have given them my word that no harm shall come to them.'

'What is their caste?'

'One of them is a Maratha. He claims to be English educated. The other is an elderly brahmin and claims to be learned in the shastras. He has worked in a native state in Gujarat and has done his pilgrimage from Haridwar to Setubandh Rameshwar and from Jagannath to Dwarika.'

'Are they accompanied by other men?'

'Yes.'

'How many?'

'Only two; one of them is a Hindustani soldier and the other is a Muslim.'

'You go back. I will call for them after I have my meals.' The messenger left.

'Jarashankar, call them after Samant and his forces march out. These two have been promised that no harm shall come to them. But no such promise has been given to their army.' Jarashankar got up. The king continued, 'Jarashankar, I followed your advice regarding relations with the Company. When it came to the Bhayat I followed my instincts. But both of us will have to work together to deal with these two. You must return before they arrive.'

'As you desire,' replied Jarashankar and left. The king asked for his meals to be served. The food arrived in silver plates and glasses. It was tasty, simple and nourishing. He sat down to eat. The servants withdrew. Mallaraj's queen came in and sat before him. Her beautiful clothes were pleasing to the eyes. She was a tall, young woman of regal bearing. Her sensuality was suggestive. Her lineage was noble and she fulfilled her duties as a wife joyously and with ease. Her tastes were of the high-born. Her pride in being a kshatriya woman was apparent. She spoke sweetly; her voice had an unwavering clarity to it.

'Tell me, Mena Rani, what news do you bring?' Mallaraj asked her before picking up his first morsel of food.

'I have been told that before the day breaks, Maharaj will go to the battlefield. If this were true, does not the woman who shares your bed have a right to know?'

'You may have the right, you may not have it. A king has many queens. The battlefield, too, is a queen and she has the first right to share bed with us. When she calls, we forsake all other queens. If she allows us to come to you, we shall come and tell you about the war.'

'That is true. If a king like you does not have a passionate desire for the battlefield, who else will? But Maharaj, when you go to meet that beloved queen, it is my right to adorn you and hand you your sword.'

'I admit defeat. Yes, that right is indeed yours. Samant has set out with our army. I may or may not be required to lead the forces. But if that time comes, it will be anytime tonight. Now come, eat this morsel of milk, rice and sugar,' and the king placed the morsel in her mouth. She accepted it coyly. Mallaraj's hand grazed against her forehead ever so slightly. The queen fed a morsel to her husband in turn. After dinner the king, intent on love, took her hand and walked out on the terrace. A half-moon shone in the sky like the glowing face of Mena Rani leaning on her husband's shoulder. She longed to disappear into his powerful arms. Her eyes brimmed over. Mallaraj drew her closer. She sang a song for her husband as the tears streamed down her cheeks.

You are a Rajputani—harden your heart
So that when he who is intent upon the battlefield takes to it
Not a tear escapes your eyes
Take your husband into your embrace
For this brave will soon embark upon foreign lands
Hold him close tonight for tomorrow he must leave
If a tear were to fall today
An inauspicious omen it would be
And yet these wretched eyes weep,
Bathing him in my tears
O husband, return to me victorious
Our marital bed I will bedeck as I wait for you
Do not beat a retreat—you are blessed by the Goddess;
If you bleed on the battlefield,
Know that I will weep tears of blood
Thoughts riveted on the battlefield,
I will wait to hear your horse approach
If we find even a moment to embrace today,
My whole life will be contained in it
What sort of morning will dawn when you join battle?
Brahmin women find solace in Brahman;
The vaishya woman laments that her husband is away;
But I, a Rajputani, know not if my husband will keep me in sorrow or joy.

Mena Rani got a grip on her emotions and stood facing Mallaraj. She folded her hands and spoke, 'Mallaraj, our coming together is true, whether we shall meet or not is speculation. If you have the time, give me your command. I have not borne you a son, but I shall obey your command like a son who obeys his father.'

Tears gleamed in Mallaraj's eyes. He placed a hand over her head, drew her closer to him and said, 'You are the jewel of my house, Mena. One cannot predict the future. We Rajputs deal with things as they come. If I live, you and I need not worry about the future. But if I do not return alive and you need to consult someone, Jarashankar and Samant are my most trusted men. Apart from those two, you yourself are wise. The world knows that Rajput women are wiser than their men.'

'Maharaj, I shall obey your command like a son,' Mena said, easing herself out of his embrace.

'Of that I have no doubt. Rani, have no regrets that you bore no son of mine.'

'Maharaj, God will decide who your heir shall be. I have not sought that right when you are present, and I am not likely to assert my claim in your absence. Those kshatriya women who install children of others on the seat of their husbands deserve nothing but contempt. They are more fallen than prostitutes. Maharaj, a woman who has worldly desires even after her husband's death does so for two reasons: one, that there was something lacking in the life she shared with her husband; and two, that she belongs to an uncultured, lowly family. Maharaj, I have lacked nothing in my life with you. My family lineage is pure and high. Maharaj, what remains for a woman who has lost her husband? Why does she need a son or even a state? If I were to speak any further, it would be self-praise and that does not behove one such as me. Maharaj, I swear by your feet that I shall follow your instructions as dearly as I would care for a son. I will be true to my lineage. Maharaj, go and fight your battle with equanimity—your battlefield is my ornament.' Mena fell at his feet and kissed them.

Mallaraj lifted her up. 'Beloved queen, I trust your words. I know that women remain virtuous because they desire to remain so and not because of external pressure. Oh pure Rajput woman, I have full faith in your piety, your noble lineage and the words that were spoken from your heart.'

Just then, Jarashankar sought permission and entered. 'Maharaj, Samant and his army have commenced their march. I have instructed that only two of the four who seek audience with you should come. They will be here soon.' The queen left the room unobtrusively.

'Why did you permit only two?' asked Mallaraj.

'At such a late hour one should not deal with too many armed men. What they wish to accomplish can be done by one as well, but I have permitted two,' Jarashankar replied.

The messenger entered with two visitors. Mallaraj took his seat. Jarashankar took his place behind the king. The messenger and the two visitors stood facing Mallaraj. Mallaraj nodded in response to their salutations and pointed them to their seats. One of the two visitors wore a Maratha headgear while the other wore the pagdi typical of Dakshini brahmins. The messenger opened the conversation. 'Maharaj, this is Sardar Shubhaji Rao. And that is Shastri Keshav Pant. They will place before you their proposal. Shubhaji Rao, he is Jarashankar, our minister. There are no unauthorised outsiders here.'

Keshav Shastri was the first to speak.

'Srimant Sarkar Nanasaheb Peshwa knows that Maharaj Mallaraj is deeply patriotic, and therefore he has sent us to you.'

'So you carry a message from Nanasaheb? Do you also carry messages from someone else? What proof do you have that you are indeed Nanasaheb's messengers?' asked Mallaraj.

'Praise on your sharp intellect, Maharaj!' exclaimed Keshav Shastri. He turned to Shubhaji Rao and said, 'Shubhaji Rao, Maharaj's intellect is indeed as sharp as we were told. Maharaj, you know well that in the times of Emperor Alamgir, Shivaji Maharaj had undertaken a yagna, a sacrificial battle to defeat the mleccha. A similar sacrificial battle is being waged these days.'

'Even the Muslims are offering sacrifices nowadays and have become the officiating priests in this yagna,' Jarashankar interjected.

Keshav Shastri's displeasure at this interjection was visible. He changed the metaphor and said, 'Maharaj, it is like the mythical churning of the seas where the gods and the demons have come together.'

Mallaraj said in jest, 'Jarashankar, you cannot find fault with this metaphor. It was a futile attempt to spar with Shastri Maharaj.'

Keshav Shastri was delighted.

'I think that your metaphor carries a hidden meaning. During the churning of the seas, the gods deprived the demons of the nectar and other riches of the ocean. You intend to do something similar,' said Mallaraj.

'Maharaj, your understanding of politics deserves the highest praise. Your suggestion is most valid,' Shastri said with apparent excitement.

Mallaraj whispered to Jarashankar, 'Such treachery is typical of the Peshwas.' He turned again towards Shastri and said, 'Shastri, such treachery and ungratefulness are ingrained in the seed of politics.'

Shubhaji Rao felt that the whole display of intellect was misplaced. The discussion was getting waylaid. So he quickly took the proceedings in hand and said, 'Raja Saheb, Shastriji will present our case in a scholarly fashion, but I will come straight to the point. Just as you spoke frankly, I will also speak plain.'

Mallaraj approved and said, 'Speak without hesitation.'

'Raja Saheb, among all the foreigners who have invaded our country, the English are the most dangerous because they are most cunning of the lot.'

The argument found its mark. Shubhaji Rao was quick to realise that he had found a weak spot and pushed the argument further. He had by now realised that Mallaraj was no fool. He advanced the arguments that would appeal to someone with Mallaraj's intellect and experience. 'Saheb, some great men have found a way of bringing all the communities together. This news about the cartridges being greased with the fat of cows and pigs is nothing but a dangerous fiction. But the English army is made up of Hindu and Muslim soldiers; they are ignorant and easily swayed. This story has worked very well. During the times of Shivaji Maharaj we used to have a saying that, "The gods bowed down to the hills." The present story works similarly. There are many other fictions, but the message that we wish to convey to an experienced ruler like you is something else.

'Raja Saheb, the fact is that the English have lost their brains. This is a sign that their end is certain. If we do not wake up from our slumber and seize the moment when our enemy is weak, someone else will. Why should leonine kings such as you not seize the moment? The English have become wicked and unscrupulous. They do not even hesitate before causing a breach of trust. Hitherto they were hungry for money, but now their hunger has extended to land. All other types of greed and hunger can be satisfied, but the hunger for women and land can never be met. The English are now hungry for land. They are not going to allow adoption in royal families. Raja Saheb, the rule of our Peshwas is not very old, but see what they have done to Shivaji Maharaj's Satara—won't that hurt us? See what they have done to Jhansi, Jetpur, Baghat, Udaipur, Budawal, Tanjore, Orissa, Nagpur, Karnataka, Bihar, Awadh? How many more names shall I count? In some places they say that we shall not allow adoption; in other places they say that the native rulers have tyrannised the people. If we oppress our people, they will turn against us. But what injustice have we done unto the English? All these are mere excuses. It is like that story of the fox and the sheep—if you did not abuse us your father must have, but I am hungry and so for one reason or another, I shall make a meal out of you. The English have signed treaties. They were signed in the past as well; what validity do they carry now? Saheb, such are their ways. You must recognise that your state is not safe in their hands. You are of course free to join forces with them, but be aware that such opportunities do not present themselves every day. Tomorrow, you will be in the same condition that Satara finds itself in today. Saheb, we must unite and fight a common battle against the enemy. The people of the English-ruled territories have rebelled; their native soldiers have rebelled and many native princely states have also joined in the battle against them. Look, how fortunate we are—today, the Hindus and the Muslims have come together to drive out the English. Even the Emperor in Delhi has awakened from his slumber, but the reins of the empire are in the hands of the Hindus. In the past Mahadevji Scindia controlled the empire. Today, the Hindus control it. Have we not driven out the English? From Meerut, from Saharanpur,

Muzzafarnagar, Farooqabad, Kanpur and from many other places, the English have been driven away. I can count many more names. Sikhs, Marathas, Bengalis, Punjabis, Pathans, Purabias, Muslims and Mughals are united against them. The fire has spread far and wide. If you support us, the Emperor in Delhi will recognise you as the ruler and your rule shall become eternal. We shall give you more territories. If you do not help us and fight against us, our victory is certain and your destruction is guaranteed. Raja Saheb, it is *our* country, *our* religion and we are *one* people. We shall drive this pack of monkeys back across the seas. Such opportunities do not come every day.

'You ask us who our leaders are. The Emperor of Delhi leads the Muslims, while Nanasaheb leads the Hindus. Saheb, I am a Maratha; but for the sake of the country and religion I carry the flag of both the Muslim and the brahmin. The English shake with fear at the mere mention of Tatya Tope. Many other stars have clustered around the sun and the moon that Nanasaheb and Tatya Tope are. Do you want proof that I am their messenger? Take this—it is a decree of the Emperor. And if you still need more proof, there is an army waiting at the gates of your capital.' Shubhaji handed over the imperial decree to Mallaraj.

Mallaraj took it from him and asked without any excitement, 'I presume all you want from me is a monosyllabic Yes or No.'

'Yes, Raja Saheb. Whether you say yes or no, please do so without delay. You must remember that yes translates into riches, while a no would invite the wrath of our armies.'

'That we shall see. Messenger, please take these two great men to the adjoining room and look after their comfort. We shall duly consider your proposal and you shall have our response shortly.' The messenger and the two guests retreated to the adjoining room. Jarashankar walked them to the door, closed it and came and sat facing Mallaraj. Mallaraj twirled his moustache.

'Maharaj, what is your decision?' asked Jarashankar.

'What are your thoughts?' asked Mallaraj.

'Hope and threat, fear and affection—Shubhaji Rao's message was unambiguous.'

'Jarashankar, do you see this motley crowd fighting each other before too long?'

'It is obvious to everyone except them, Maharaj.'

'Would we look good in their company?'

'Only as good as a parrot in the company of crows,' came the prompt reply.

'Was it not you, Jarashankar, who had told me that story of how a foolish brahmin gave life to a dead lion?'

'Yes, Maharaj.'

'If we join them, we would be as wise as that brahmin.'

'There are many other wise men who would bring this lion back to life.'

Mallaraj laughed and said, 'No, it is not entirely so. Let me explain. Don't allow his namedropping to startle you. I have thought it through.'

'What have you thought?'

'Look at their factions. Let us count the states that support the English. Kapurthala, Jind, Patiala, Nabha, all our native states and the Punjab. In short, all the original royal families with pure Rajput blood are with the English. There are some fence-sitters, true, but they will join the English as soon as their fortunes turn. I keep an eye on developments even in far off Himachal.'

'Maharaj, you did not include the Gaikwad, Gwalior, Indore and the Nizam.'

'But you remembered. Only the old Rajput families come to my mind.'

'Do you see the English fortunes turning for the better? The fire has spread far and wide.'

'Jarashankar, you brahmins have a short memory. I told you that the English will emerge victorious. They have one failing—they go in a slumber like fools but when they awaken, they are undefeatable.'

'How so?'

'This issue of adoption is unnecessary. Everyone is greedy for land. The English are no exception. But they are foolish. To begin with they take pity; then they repent, turn cruel and lose their way. They get kicked around and when that happens they hit back, vanquish their enemies and then take pity on them all over again.'

'Maharaj, I still do not understand.'

Mallaraj clarified, 'I have thought about it carefully. The states in which they disallowed adoption were their own creations to begin with. The English had entered into these treaties either out of pity, greed or fear. Then they realised their mistake and wanted to take them back. So they began to swallow them up. But they have never interfered with the old states. As a result all the original states are in their camp. Those opposed to them are their own creations.'

'If they swallow their own creations, why would they be restrained while dealing with others?'

'If they become greedier, they will not show any restraint. The states they created or propped up are easy to gobble up; they say we created you and now we will destroy you. But that logic does not apply to the older states. However, if we give them a reason they will swallow us as well, just as bigger animals eat the smaller ones. But hitherto the English have not annexed any state without reason. They follow the divine rule of cause and effect. They wait for us to provide a reason. If we give them a reason, they shall become greedy for our state as well. But that would be our stupidity. If there is a tear in the fabric of our state, those monkeys will make it larger. They will bite any hand that comes out. So long as we do nothing to awaken the monkey in them, they will remain their noble selves. They will not annex any state without reason, because they are god-fearing and are cautious in taking bold steps. I do not fear them. But the actions of those who fear them are before you. Do you get it?'

Jarashankar replied, 'No, Maharaj.'

'Some cunning karbharis misled the Rajput women by putting in them the fear that the English would not allow adoption and annex their state. As a result these women passed off the sons of some Koli or Ganchi as their son and installed them on the throne. But these wretched women do not understand that the true heirs of their husband are men from his family, and not sons of Kolis or Ganchis. Once these ordinary men come to power, they will turn against the very women who gave them the throne. If a Rajput were to ascend the throne, he would never allow these women to be disgraced.'

'I see. What are we to do now? Those two are waiting for our response, Maharaj.'

'Let them wait. Samant will gain time over them. Jarashankar, our decision has been made. The English are not alone in this. All those whom one should side with are with the English. So we shall keep our word.'

'Shall I call them in, Maharaj?'

'Of course.'

Jarashankar called in the visitors and the messenger. Mallaraj stood up and hence the conversation took place standing. Mallaraj leaned on his sword and said, 'We have considered your proposal. We have given our word to the Company and we cannot go back on it. We considered the intent of your message seriously, but you have not been able to strike fear in our hearts. All other talk is insignificant. Hence, Ram Ram.'

Shubhaji Rao's forehead creased while Keshav Shastri appeared concerned. They were about to respond but Mallaraj stopped them and addressed the messenger, 'You gave them your word that no harm shall come to them. We honoured your word and granted them an audience. Now lead them out of our territories by the shortest possible way. Until they leave the boundaries, no harm shall come to them. Send some men to accompany them to our borders. If they choose to re-enter, they shall be dealt with in accordance with our laws. Jarashankar, it appears that their army is at our gates. They are here uninvited and intend to threaten us into submission. Our army will drive them out. All those who are captured should be handed over to the British so that we do not have to bear the cost of feeding them. You should also attach all the money they have. Robbers are not allowed to enter Ratnanagari. Let the world know that the king of Ratnanagari rules with his eyes wide open.' Mallaraj called out, 'Soldiers!'

Some Rajput soldiers promptly entered the room to carry out Mallaraj's orders. The visitors departed with the soldiers. The king and his minister stayed back. 'Jarashankar, ensure that all my orders are carried out. Do not hesitate to wake me up if the need arises. You can go home now.'

Jarashankar left. As Mallaraj moved towards his bed chamber, he reflected on the day's events. The smart ones get caught in their own smartness. The English are forced on the back foot because of the muddle they created out of the policy of adoption. The English understand the simple rule of chess that one should sacrifice a page to capture the bishop. But their ploy misfired. After all they are an army of monkeys. The king laughed at his own simile and continued with his reflections. But remember, if you are good, good people will harbour you. If you do wrong, you will teach others to do wrong. You will stumble and cause others to fall with you. We are pure-blooded kshatriya kings. All others might become sullied, but pure blood flows through our veins. We are ready to shed our blood, but on one condition: you must earn the right for us to shed our blood. You English, remain good and allow others to retain their goodness. Mallaraj recognises your virtues; you must learn to recognise the virtues of native states. We are precious for each other. The kshatriyas might have gathered some dust, but once that is wiped clean, sparkling gems lie underneath. These gems are valuable to you. The native states that support you in this moment of crisis are precious for you—do not apply your monkey justice on them.

But if you English behave like Sugriva's monkey army and step on these jewels, the choice is yours. Who can prevent you from being true to your monkey instincts! Even if you were to behave like monkeys, *we* shall remain human. Mallaraj could not suppress his laughter. He was near his bed chamber. Mena Rani heard his laughter and came to open the door. 'Do we have the right to know what amuses his highness so much?' she asked him with a smile as she wrapped her arm around him and led him in. She removed his finely woven headgear.

'Of course, my precious one!' chuckled the king, pulling her in. The doors closed behind them. We, too, dear reader, must bring the chapter to a close for the sake of decorum.

9 Mallaraj's Concerns

> Yet once more, in justice to this paragon of Heathen excellence, let us remember that Aurelius represents the decrepitude of this era. He is hopeless because the age is hopeless. He cannot rise beyond the sphere of ideas around him. The Heathen world looked for no renovation of a society which was visibly perishing before its face. And now when the popular notion of its degeneration was realised, it accepted its apparent destiny without a murmur.
>
> —Merivale

Shubhaji Rao had clear instructions that he should not waste his men and resources on recalcitrant native states. Their efforts had to be preserved for use against the English forces. For these reasons, Shubhaji Rao's forces did not engage Samant Mulu in a fierce or protracted battle. Mallaraj had permitted only Shubhaji Rao and Keshav Shastri to meet him. Their other associates meanwhile decided to take a look at life in Ratnanagari. They heard that Samant Mulu had set out with his forces. This was enough to indicate to them the fate of the meeting. One of them promptly returned to the inn, while the other rushed to inform the waiting army of the imminent attack. Shubhaji Rao's forces decided not to engage in battle and prepared to march out of Ratnanagari's territories. Samant Mulu did attack the retreating army; some men were captured as well. But Shubhaji Rao's forces made no attempt to either return fire or rescue their captured soldiers. Mallaraj's soldiers accompanied Shubhaji Rao and his three companions to the borders of the state through another route. The four met with their forces in the morning and abused Mallaraj and Jarashankar to their heart's content. Samant made sure that Shubhaji Rao had no surprises in store for him; having satisfied himself, he returned to the capital with his forces. Mallaraj released the captives because no war had been fought; he considered such captives to be equal to women.

The British captured Delhi, and the tide turned in their favour. The English emerged victorious. Queen Victoria became the Empress of India and made a liberal proclamation written in her own delicate hand. Mallaraj's predictions came true in every respect; his message to Colonel Brave and his response to Shubhaji Rao further cemented the ties between Ratnanagari and the English. This friendship gave the desired results to Ratnanagari.

For long years the king and his minister would remember those difficult and trying days; their memory was not a source of unsullied joy. Mallaraj's visage would turn sombre whenever he recalled them. Once he remarked, 'Jarashankar, God has granted us the expected fruits of our efforts. It is a mixed bag. Just as good things have happened, the things we dreaded would happen are also here for us to bear. When father signed the first treaty with the English, I realised that our Rajput valour was about to be widowed. At the time of Nanasaheb's rebellion, I considered the pros and the cons and further cemented the treaty. But the scales now seem to be tilting for the worse and they will tilt even further. Our thoughts and conduct towards them will have to change accordingly. Brave Sahib is no more; I outlived him. Very few Englishmen with the qualities of Brave Sahib will come to India. The English will not have to fight native states. They will have to draw their swords to punish robbers, cowards, the debauched and such like. But don't mistake that for a war; it will be like the game of cops and robbers that children play. The English and we alike will lose our valour. They will fight battles elsewhere in their great empire, which will train their armies. But we will not have any such opportunity. We have not surrendered our sword but it should be considered as good as surrendered. We will become vaishya-like. Our fate is to increase the productivity of this land. No matter what their character is elsewhere, the English will become mercantile in this land. They will earn their wealth here and take it away to their country. This will make people of their country develop similar mercantile tendencies. No one can fight destiny but the times have changed. Winds of the new age are blowing from every direction. Jarashankar, it is for you and me to think and act for these changing times. We shall have to consider what to do, how to conduct our affairs, what seeds to sow, how and where; what of the old to retain and what to discard, all these are now subjects of serious consideration for us.'

Jarashankar replied, 'Maharaj, you are absolutely correct. A new age is indeed upon us and we cannot join in its excitement unthinkingly. The old age still persists and we cannot begin to celebrate the new age. If the new age becomes inebriated and callous, it will be robbed of its glory just as some petty wayside robber defeating Arjun. If the new age forgets itself in the excitement of its newness, it will be like Parikshit who put a dead snake around a brahmin's neck in anger and then repented. It is clear that the kshatriyas have laid down their arms. Lord Shri Krishna was pledge-bound not to take up arms in the battle of Mahabharata; but unarmed as he was, he helped the Pandavas win a righteous battle. That story told by our sages is most instructive. And there is a message there for people like you. One should not act out of sorrow—this applies to brave men like yourself. Maharaj, do not allow sorrow to eclipse your mind.'

Mallaraj was deep in thought. As he listened intently to his minister speak, tears streamed down the eyes of this brave kshatriya though he seemed oblivious to them. He was biting his lips and they had turned bloodshot red. He twirled his moustache with the left hand. He was frowning hard and his forehead was damp with perspiration. Jarashankar attempted to break the king's reverie.

'Maharaj!'

Mallaraj looked up, his hand went to his sword and his visage turned severe. He suddenly got up and said, 'Brahmin, you speak the truth! For the present, the battlefield, the true beloved of all kshatriyas, has died. Until we mourn her, we shall have no peace. Go, go and tell my queen that her husband is no longer a battle-ready Rajput. He has been converted.' The king looked vacantly upwards.

Frightened by this state of his ruler, Jarashankar urgently called for the queen. Mena Rani rushed in, unmindful of the minister's presence. Her face was uncovered; she was out of breath. Jarashankar had never before seen the unveiled face of the queen, who was in obvious distress. Tears came to his eyes. With folded hands he addressed her respectfully, 'Mataji,' and he described to her the king's state of mind. The queen composed herself; she observed the king and thought with a clear mind. She asked Jarashankar to leave the room and close the door behind him. She went and stood before the king, who did not notice her. She touched his shoulder, but he did not stir. Mena Rani then gently caressed his head and face and said, 'Maharaj! Swaminath!' The king finally looked up at her. He put his hands on her shoulders and asked, 'Rani, what is it you want?'

'What can the queen want apart from her Maharaj's happiness? In your sadness I lose my all.'

'Where is Jarashankar?'

'He is waiting outside, saddened by your state.'

'When did you come?'

'I have been here for long, but so long as my Maharaj did not notice me, it cannot be said that I was present before you. Maharaj, what caused you such sadness?'

'Do you have the right to ask such questions?'

'I can partake of your joys only when you allow me to, but I have a right to share your sorrows since the day I married you. You cannot take away that right.'

The answer pleased Mallaraj. He sat down on his seat with his queen beside him and said, 'I am no longer sad. Does that not circumscribe your right?'

'Your love is immense, but I am not going to be cheated by it and forsake my right.'

'All right. For some reason I was deeply unhappy. But now I have found a solution, and hence the sadness, too, has disappeared. I will confer with Jarashankar and Samant. Tonight I shall be a captive of my Mena Rani and I will share with you all the details. As of now, the narration will be inconclusive. Tell me, what would you prefer?'

'Maharaj, I can only be a seeker before you. I do not have any preferences. You said that I exercise power over you at night. I shall then wait for the night. But do not adopt half measures in fulfilling your promise.'

'Very well.'

The queen left the room and went back to her quarters. As the king watched her receding figure, he called Jarashankar. Jarashankar came in accompanied by Samant.

'Samant, I was going to send for you, but I see that you are here already.'

'Maharaj, such is your grace; you think of me and I move.'

'Samant, tell me what brought you here?'

'I came because I was told that you were unhappy for some reason.'

'It is good that you came. Jarashankar, why did you go out? Did the queen throw you out?'

'Forgive me, Maharaj, but do not speak such words,' Jarashankar replied, keeping his hands over his ears. 'I failed to relieve you of your melancholy and hence I requested her intervention.'

'So she exercises greater authority over me, is it?' Mallaraj asked in jest.

'Maharaj, are words more important or deeds? I failed, but the queen removed the cause of your sadness and hence you are with us again; such is the power of her grace.'

'So the Rani is more effective than you?'

'Maharaj, efficacy depends upon context. During the day the sun shines bright, but at night it is the full moon that is resplendent; but on a moonless night the stars shine the brightest. Raja Dashrath had such power that Ram went to the forest to keep his promise. Dashrath, Kaushalya, Laxman and Sita, all four of them wished to accompany Ram to the forest. Shri Ramchandraji knew the laws and norms of right conduct. How fine and discerning was his judgement! He declined to entertain Kaushalya's request and told her that her right and duty were to be with Dashrath. He commanded her to stay with Dashrath. A son can command his mother so she can fulfill her righteous obligations. When a mother begins to act contrary to norms, a son, expert in normative conduct, must show her the right path. Dashrath was Ram's father and he, too, desired to accompany him to the forest. A son cannot command his father; hence Ram did not do so. But if Dashrath had followed Ram to the forest, he would have violated his duties as a king. Ram obeyed his father to the extent that he chose to go and live in the forest, but he disobeyed Dashrath's desire to accompany him to the forest as Ram did not wish to be the cause of the violation of kingly duties. Therefore, Ram left Ayodhya at night; such was his discernment. Laxman was devoted to Ram. Ram reasoned with him; when that failed he told Laxman that he was free to accompany him. He showed Sita the hardships of forest life and the comforts of living in the palace. A wife has the right to partake of her husband's hardships. She can exercise this right through anger, reason or force. A husband has no right to obstruct his wife in discharging her duties. Sita used her wrath to convince Ram that she would accompany him to the forest. Shri Ramchandra did not seek either Dashrath or Kaushalya's consent in this regard; he simply submitted to Sita's arguments. In certain matters the rights of a wife are supreme and cannot be curtailed either by the husband or the wife. She experiences this pain most intensely and a woman who assuages the husband's pain exercises unrestrained authority over him in this regard. Therefore, Maharaj if the virtuous queen frees you from pain and restores your joy to you, I cannot seek to undermine either her right or her authority in this regard. If I were to do so, I would be fit for a life in hell. Maharaj, I pray that both her right and her authority in this regard remain eternally undiminished. I also pray that you may come to us every day with your joy restored to you by the queen. I hope that this good fortune of ours will also remain undiminished.'

Mallaraj laughed aloud at this discourse and said to Samant, 'Did you notice how clever the minister is? He should keep me free of worries, but instead he has cleverly put the burden onto the queen. That should make both of them happy. Samant, I want to share my innermost thoughts with you. I need the minister's counsel, but more than him, I need your advice.'

Samant replied, 'Your servant awaits your words, Maharaj.'

'Jarashankar, bring two large sheets of paper. Samant will write on one and you shall write on the other.'

Both of them sat in readiness to take down the king's command. The king dictated: 'Write down. My state is composed of two bodies—one, my Bhayat, my brothers-in-arms, and the other, the Karbhari. The king and his Bhayat are one. Anyone from among the Bhayat can be chosen as the king. The Karbhari must ensure that all Bhayat acquire the fitness to rule so that on the decisive day, the blind and the unfit are not forced to be recognised as capable. Write that down.'

Jarashankar said, 'Every word has been taken down, Maharaj. The document is of the highest quality.'

'Don't interrupt. Write silently. The Bhayat must realise that the state belongs to the king. If they were to fight each other, the English will begin to interfere. Initially, they will go after the king but later they will also interfere in the work of the Bhayat. If the state is prosperous, the wealth will be shared by the Bhayat as well; but if the wealth is captured by the outsiders with their tiger-like hunger for wealth, neither the king nor the Bhayat will get anything.'

Samant looked up at the king in admiration. 'Maharaj, what you say is very true.'

Mallaraj said, 'Yes, what I say is true. But I fear that my Bhayat will not be able to deal with this truth and eventually, like other native states, the king and his Bhayat will fight each other in our state as well. The native states are staring at further disintegration. States do not multiply. There will be one state and one king, but the number of Bhayat will increase. Hitherto, the king and his Bhayat sought to increase the territories of the state to meet the Bhayat's demand for a greater share in the state revenue. You must write down everything I say. But now territorial expansion is not possible. The land is fixed and the number of Bhayat will increase. The state treasury will become empty and the states will become smaller. This will be the basic cause of dissension between the king and his Bhayat. The Bhayat will no longer be able to go to war and hence they will fight with words—spoken and written. They have no way with words; so the kayasthas and diplomats will earn at their expense. Ultimately, the judges will be English and we shall become supplicants before them; we shall try and please them with bribes. We will have to swallow their abuse and we shall fight like their puppets. We shall fight like the banias and not like kshatriyas. All kshatriyas, the king and his Bhayat will become paupers, while others will get rich at their expense. We shall become their slaves. Both of you take this down—I do *not* want such a fate for my state.

'I have narrated how the kshatriyas will become like banias. Now take down my words that kings will become brahmin-like. They will begin to relish their homes and property; they will prefer life over death; they will be a frightened lot. They will not know how to conduct the affairs of the state. They will lead debauched lives. Write down—I will *not* have such a king rule over my state. Once we forsake our love of arms and the battlefield, this fate is certain. Write that as well.

'Kshatriya men will behave like women. Take that down. Oh God! Why don't I have a son? They will worry about such matters. They will have no wars to fight and no one will come and narrate to them stories of valour; hence they will watch their women fight one another. A kshatriya man will marry many women; some of them will become his favourites and he will be indifferent to others. He will take sides, be partial to his favourite wife, act like her woman friend and deal with others like a mother-in-law. They will also harass former queens and the wives of his brothers. They will play games that women play and become womanly in the process. Both within and outside the house, kshatriya men will behave like women, while their women will seek virile men someplace else. These women would take other men, including household servants, as their men. Write that down.'

Samant could no longer write. Tears flowed from his eyes. 'Maharaj, I am afraid. I see the future you predict before my very eyes. All around us, the native states are already in such a condition. Maharaj, now ...'

'Samant, you are already behaving like a woman,' said Mallaraj, cutting him short.

Jarashankar said, 'Samant, Shri Krishna saw the destruction of the Yadav clan before he gave up his life. The kshatriyas will no longer be able to fight battles, but they must learn to be patient and deal with the problem with forbearance. Such is the duty of all men. Should the kshatriyas be any exception to this? Lord Narayan watched the great deluge take place before his very eyes.'

Mallaraj gave an encouraging slap on Jarashankar's back, 'Very well said, minister! Samant, write down what Jarashankar and you have said. Now stop weeping and be a man. *Write* it down.'

Samant gathered himself, picked up his pen again and wrote.

Mallaraj continued, 'Kshatriyas will become like shudras. They will not know how to read and write and will indulge in depraved acts. They will lead debauched lives. They will learn to plead and please others, revel in low intrigue and will kill and murder stealthily.

'Write, that the kshatriyas will become like the mleccha. All the vile acts of the mleccha that we hear of from Delhi and other such places will become habitual with the kshatriyas. They will abuse animals, will be evil and cruel. But the kshatriyas will not acquire any of the positive traits of the mleccha. Write that the kshatriyas will imbibe all the bad aspects of the brahmins, vaishyas, women and the shudras, but none of their good qualities.'

Once they had finished writing, Mallaraj said, 'Samant, now read it out to me.'

Samant read out the entire document. When he finished, Jarashankar said, 'Maharaj, this deluge, this end of the world that you predict will not come.'

Mallaraj retorted, 'What do you know? Many states are already living through such deluge. Ratnanagari is an exception where Satyug, the age of truth, prevails.'

Jarashankar said, 'And it will continue to prevail.'

Mallaraj said, 'Samant, the age of truth will prevail if all of you commit yourselves to it and if all of us strive together like men to sustain it. Shall I show you the way forward?'

Samant mournfully replied, 'Maharaj, the seas are breaching the barriers. What are mere men to do?'

'Come now, Samant, do not be so despondent! Write down what I say.'

'Maharaj, command us.'

'I will now show you the remedy for all these problems. First, write down that the kshatriyas may not be called upon to go to war, but if they do retain the art of war, it will come in handy, if not now, then two hundred years later. Jarashankar makes use of the wisdom of the *Ramayana* and the *Mahabharata*. The brahmins committed these things to memory for a thousand years and have found use for it in this day and age. We, the kshatriyas, should also adopt that method. We may not be able to fight other men, but our forests are full of lions and tigers and we should fight them. We should not come to love our lives so; we must keep alive the virtue of a death in the battlefield, by fighting the wild beasts of the forest. We must learn the use of new weapons. And for this reason, I grant to my Bhayat the privileged access to our forests. The Bhils, the Kolis or foreigners should not enter the forest with a view to hunt without the permission of the king or his Bhayat. The English will come as our guests and hospitality demands that we take them hunting. But they must be accompanied by my heirs or my Bhayat. My heirs should take the lead in hunting and never put life before valour. My Bhayat should be trained to take up kingly duties; they should retain their expertise in wielding weapons, and heirs must ensure that the Bhayat remain good warriors. My Bhayat shall not be called upon to war, but they must treat hunting as a new form of war and discharge their responsibility. My heirs should send the Bhayat to other states to learn the use of arms and join any battle that comes their way. The Bhayat must follow the lead of my heirs.'

Samant was delighted. 'Very good, Maharaj! Very good!'

But Jarashankar was clearly displeased. 'Maharaj! That your heirs and the Bhayat should treat the practice of hunting as war appears to me to be the wrong path, and one that will have disastrous consequences.'

Mallaraj lost his patience and cut him short, 'Stop it, brahmin! You would not understand such things. Just write down what I ask you to. You have to ensure that my orders are carried out in this regard. We are not here to debate these things. Make sure you write down everything and ensure their compliance.'

Jarashankar replied that his commands would be complied with.

Mallaraj continued, 'In case of a dispute among the Bhayat, they should approach the judicial officers of the state. In case of a dispute between the Bhayat and the state, a committee of arbitrators should be appointed. The minister should be the first arbitrator, the second arbitrator should be from the princely family but not a direct descendant of the king, and the third arbitrator should be a Bhayat nominated by the aggrieved party. The decision of the arbitrators should be unanimous and that would be final. In absence of unanimity among the arbitrators a new set of arbitrators should be appointed. The minister or his nominee should be one of the arbitrators. All the Bhayat should suggest names of ten elders among them, of whom two would be selected by the state to serve as arbitrators. If the arbitrators fail to arrive at a consensus then the majority decision should prevail. My Bhayat have to be discouraged from the tendency to fight like the vaishyas; this is the best remedy for that. Third, if their land holding becomes unviable for providing adequate compensation, my Bhayat are forbidden from either selling or pledging their land as collateral to anyone but the state. Fourth, the new garas or inheritance should not be of a land grant but in monetary terms, which should be double of the market price of the land grant.

'If a Bhayat deviates from the Rajput code of conduct or adopts ways of other castes or breaks the conditions mentioned in this document, he should be held accountable by the rest of the Bhayat and they, and not the state, should impose any punishment or sanctions. The Bhayat should impose a special tax on the errant Bhayat's lands. The same punishment should be awarded to those Bhayat who do not learn statecraft. The state retains its traditional right of confiscating the garas. And finally, all the customary taxes that the state levies on the Bhayat are stopped forthwith. In lieu of the customary taxes, the

Bhayat should pay a fiftieth part of their garas as taxes—this is their nazrana. If the Bhayat ensure a long life for the king, the taxes that he levies upon them will not increase. Apart from this new tax the state and the king shall place no other revenue demands on the Bhayat.

'That is all. Jarashankar, keep the original document in my records and place a copy of it in your records. It will be your responsibility to cultivate this sensibility and these norms in the future king and the future minister. Samant, I have no son. As of now, you are my heir apparent. But even you have not fathered a son. Let us see what the future holds for us. This scheme that I have outlined is to the advantage of all of us. It is your responsibility to get the assent of all the Bhayat. Please tell them that I am deeply concerned about the future; we are undergoing immense transitions and if we wish to preserve both kshatriyas and kshatriyahood in the new age, they should all give their assent to the proposal. Tell them that Mallaraj has no son and all his actions are motivated by a desire for the welfare of the kingdom and my Bhayat. Please also tell them that if they have any suspicion of my motives, I am ready to step down from the throne and they would be free to choose a king of their choice. Tell them that Mallaraj would be quite happy to serve as a Bhayat to the new king and would accept these and any other conditions that the new king might wish to impose for the betterment of the kingdom. But so long as I remain the king I would like this new proposal to be accepted by all. Mallaraj is willing to step down for the welfare of the kingdom and will serve as a Bhayat under Samant or any other Bhayat, even if the new king holds the lowest rank among the Bhayat today. Now go, Samant, hurry. Soon, we will be facing the prospect of the English interfering in the affairs of native states. They will tell a king that though he had a right to step down, the choice of the new king now rests with them. They might even bring such a state under their rule. But I still have the opportunity to make a gift of my kingdom. Allow me to use it and secure the future of the kingdom.'

'Maharaj, pray let things continue as they are ...'

'Jarashankar, stop it! My words must be a command for my officials even if it involves a great personal cost to me. It is *I* who have chosen to bear it, and I shall bear it happily for my brothers-in-arms. The Bhayat might not appreciate my reasoning and hence I have offered my kingdom. No one has a right to stop me from stepping down from the throne as long as my action is in the interest of the kingdom. Even my queen does not wish to exercise her authority in this respect. Samant, go and meet my brothers and I will hand over the kingdom to a man of their choice tomorrow when the dawn breaks.'

'Maharaj!'

'Samant, I do not want this moment of bliss to be delayed any further. Go, hurry.'

'But Maharaj ...'

'Go—that is an order.'

'Maharaj, unless I get a hearing, I shall not obey you. It is my right as a Bhayat.'

Mallaraj laughed and said, 'All right, speak your mind. But keep it short. Don't lecture me.'

'Maharaj, your Bhayat have unconditional faith in your words. They believe that no action of yours could be irreligious. But your proposal to seek their consent, your offer to step down from the throne and the insinuation that they no longer trust you amounts to questioning their devotion towards you. They have done nothing to merit such a charge. The Bhayat of Ratnanagari have always accepted what the kings have offered them and have always given what the king wanted from them. This has been a longstanding tradition. It is not correct to break this tradition and I should not be made instrumental in it. The Bhayat will consider me to be the evil one. We are happy to follow all your commands. Please remove these ideas of consent and conditions from our dealings with you.'

'Samant, just yesterday my brothers showed that they were willing to lay down their lives to honour my word. If I put a charge of disloyalty on them, I would be ungrateful. But I have carefully considered my proposal. Listen to me and try to understand, you don't need to write this down. People have to be cautious when the ruler changes, but in times of transition it is the ruler who must be vigilant. Each family has its tradition; similarly each age has norms that govern conduct appropriate to the time. Samant, you would recall that there are days when the sun is concealed by clouds. Days when it is difficult to tell if it is afternoon or evening, or tell the east from the west. In such bewildering times, a wise man stands and observes as to which side is the darkness denser and so discerns the east from the west. On such days one cannot rely upon the eternal sun to guide us. Similarly, in times of transition one cannot hope to be guided by tradition alone. In moments such as these one has to decide as to what shape the light or the darkness of the new age shall take. One has to find a way out of uncertain times. Because if one allows doubt to debilitate us, the darkness shall envelop all of us and we shall be stranded without a pathfinder. The wheels of fortune turn in a fraction of a moment. We, who have fought battles, ought to know this. We must be clear-sighted and prepared for any eventuality. We cannot always seek refuge in tradition. We cannot go looking for the wisdom of our forefathers when our house is on fire. Tell me, Samant, what do you think?'

'All right, Maharaj. We can forget our age-old family traditions for a while. But what is the reason for this charge and this apparent lack of confidence?'

'Samant, this new age will bring with it the vaishya way of fighting with paper and pen. Ratnanagari may not remain immune from it for too long. It will bring with itself new modes. What would prevent the charge that Mallaraj was a tyrannical ruler? If not today then tomorrow we will open ourselves to English influence. What kind of relations would the king and his Bhayat have in the future? Can we be certain that those would be relations of affection and trust? We should make sure that our mutual affection remains well-grounded even in these times of transition. This measure is in that direction.

'Samant, I do not have a son and you are my heir. One cannot be certain about matters of life and death. Therefore, I am letting you into the secret. Today you are a Bhayat, but tomorrow you could be king. You are the bridge that connects the king and his Bhayat. You are related to me and also to the Bhayat. The fortunes and misfortunes of either affect you equally. Therefore, you have to carry my message to the Bhayat. Is there anyone more capable and more devoted to me than you, Samant? By tomorrow morning, bring me the news that my command has been accepted.'

Samant did not respond and, with a frown of concern on his face, sought leave of the king.

'Jarashankar, you seem perturbed?' said Mallaraj.

'Yes, Maharaj. You have embarked on a most adventurous path.'

Mallaraj could not suppress his laughter. 'Which adventure? My offer to step down, or my attempt to cut the Bhayat to size?'

'Both.'

'Why should you worry if I cease to be king? We are always prepared to lay down our lives in the battlefield; similarly one should also be prepared to step down from the throne for a great cause. What does a man love more: life or wealth? Most would choose life over wealth. We kshatriyas do not love life and wealth is like the shoes we wear on our feet.'

'Maharaj, the shastras say that most men give considered thought to substantial issues. But one must also consider matters that appear insignificant. One must consider such matters like a scholar, one must think of its implications, because small matters when badly executed become a thorn in our side and cause permanent heartburn.'

Mallaraj asked him to repeat the verse. Jarashankar did so.

> A wise man bent on doing a thing, good or bad, should first carefully consider its consequences. The issue of actions done in hot haste becomes till death, like a dart, poignant to the heart.[1]

'Maharaj, your action will have grave implications. Shouldn't you have consulted me once?'

Mallaraj mellowed somewhat and replied, 'Jarashankar, you are right. I should have consulted you. That was obligatory upon me. I cannot deny that. Whose verse was it you recited?'

'Maharaj, that was from the wise sage Bhartrhari.'

[1] M. R. Kale, ed. and trans. *The Niti and Vairagya Satakas of Bhartrhari*, Verse 105, 2nd ed. (Delhi: Motilal Banarsidass, 1902, 2013), 131.

'I accept your view. But what has been done cannot be undone. Mallaraj never mourns his actions. Now tell me, what else have I done wrong?'

'I do not deny that your proposal, if accepted, will benefit the state, but there is an ancient practice. During war, whenever the gates of the enemy fortification had to be broken down, a camel was placed between the spiked gates and the elephant that charged to break down the gates. This killed the camel but saved the elephant.'

'Your example has no relevance to our discussion.'

'Maharaj, you are like the elephant and I, your minister, am like the camel. Maharaj, in your dealings with other kings or even with our own people there are moments when someone has to take the brickbats. You represent the royal personage and cannot be expected to face criticism and attacks. To do so would be against morality.[2] The royal personage has to be preserved like a precious jewel that is worn only on special occasions. But for everyday affairs, you need the shield of a camel like me so that even if the camel is sacrificed, a replacement can be obtained. A minister is a shield for the king; a minister who does not accept the blows intended for the king upon himself violates his duties and is an enemy of both the king and the state. You told me that Brave Sahib had explained to you the English doctrine that: "The king commits no sin." The king should only perform deeds that bring him glory. The king bestows honour, prestige, wealth and in return he is loved by all. In England, punishment is awarded by a judge; the queen is seen as merciful. All unpleasant matters that a

[2] Author's note:

The personalities of the present ministers are so insignificant, the covering shield they present is so transparent that the monarch himself always shines through them. It appears to me dangerous for the future of the monarchical idea for a ruler, even with the best intentions, to show himself too frequently in public without a decent ministerial covering. Because this danger seems to me imminent and a fight with men of straw has no charms for me, I say, like Chamisso when the French were in Germany, "*The situation was no sword for me.*"

—Bismarck

king wants conveyed to his people should be conveyed through his minister. Thereby, the world blames and abuses the minister, but never the king. The minister is the conduit and repository of all secrets and in the discharge of his duties he must face all the attacks and criticism. The people should have no clue as to what the view of the king is or whether he was even consulted in some decisions. When the king is so shielded, the people's affection for their king remains perennial and the royal personage remains undented. Maharaj, it was you who told me that the king and the royal family provide coherence and unity to a state. That lesson is etched in my heart. Maharaj, your family tree must be nourished and nurtured; it cannot be exposed to daily blows of axes. It is for this reason that a king needs a minister, and a king who becomes his own minister does damage the royal personage. The king is like a great tree that gives shelter to life. The king is required to weather great storms and not everyday skirmishes. Maharaj, why did you not think of using me as a front in your dealings with the Bhayat? Why did you expose yourself?'

Mallaraj heard this discourse with attention, enthusiasm, affection and joy. His affection for Jarashankar multiplied a hundred fold. 'Jarashankar, you are indeed a jewel among ministers. Your advice was of the highest order and what you say is very true. But I have considered all these while taking the step I have taken. It was for this very reason that I have put you as one of the arbitrators in all disputes with the Bhayat. The scheme is carefully devised so that the king is not required to sit on judgement on his Bhayat. Therefore, all judicial authority is vested in the minister. If the king had any role to play in adjudicating the disputes of the Bhayat, my heirs and my Bhayat would most certainly have come into conflict and that would have sowed the seeds of family disputes. Kings would have been subjected to ignominy. I have prevented such an eventuality. The task that I have undertaken is a grave one; even a hundred ministers cannot accomplish it. While for me it would be easy to accomplish, as easy as an elephant waving his trunk. Even if I lose a tusk it will grow back but remember that if this task is accomplished, the state of Ratnanagari would be secure for a hundred years.'

'You have left no scope for any further questions, Maharaj,' replied Jarashankar.

'Good. So go home now and watch things unfold. We have done enough for the day.'

Jarashankar left. Samant had to work hard and faced some difficulties in accomplishing the assigned task, but it was made easier by the fact that customary faith and affection for Mallaraj were still intact. Also, the traditional sense of kshatriya identity and devotion to the state were not vitiated by modern mercantile ways. Moreover, the Bhayat had not been influenced by modern methods of doubts and cynicism. Their hearts were uncomplicated. Samant's deeply affectionate relations with the Bhayat, Mallaraj's promise to abdicate the throne and the Bhayat's belief that Mallaraj would prove true to his words held sway. The Bhayat also recognised that Mallaraj's act was prompted by a desire to do good to the state. The Bhayat appreciated the glory of such acts. Their patriotic sense and devotion to the state increased manyfold and they competed with each other to offer even greater sacrifice. As a result of all these, Mallaraj's proposals were accepted by his good Bhayat without any amendment or dissent. As Mallaraj woke up the next morning, Mena Rani exercised her right and conveyed to him this good news sent to her by Samant.

The king met Samant and took him in his embrace and said, 'Samant, this is my last gift. Neither you nor I will ever again be called upon to accomplish something as significant as this. And even if we are required to perform such acts of duty, in this new age the king will not be as respected as I am today by my Bhayat. I will now hold court and express my gratitude to all the Bhayat. Neither the state of Ratnanagari nor her king can ever repay their gratitude.'

Mallaraj bid farewell to Samant and went back to his queen. He said, 'Rani, my minister would have spent a sleepless night. Send a message with our confidant Bhalji that both the camel and the elephant remained unharmed, and that the gates have been opened.' The queen went out to pass on the message. Mallaraj said to himself, Praise is due to the king while criticism is reserved for the minister! This is a new proposition. Like the camel, the minister faces criticism and harm.

What is his reward? Now I understand the tradition that the king should restrict his own powers and submit his will and authority to his minister and be like a student to the minister. It is impossible to use the minister as a shield where this tradition is not upheld. It is by following this tradition that a king recognises the value of his minister, expresses his gratitude and tries to reward the minister for his cares in whichever way possible. The minister is the camel-like shield in statecraft. And here comes the one who rules my household. I should submit to her authority as much as that of my minister.

Mena Rani approached him. The previous night Mallaraj had shared with her his concerns and his proposed solution. Explaining the metaphors of the camel and the elephant to her, he said, 'This camel is precious to the state. If I had used the camel as a shield, I am certain that the gates would have remained shut but the camel would have perished. The king must take care of his minister. A king who has no compassion for his minister is cruel. A minister with a character fault should be removed from office but a good minister must be protected and neither the king nor his family should add to the worries of the minister. A minister who restricts the powers of a king must also put limits on the king's family. It is for this reason that so often the minister and the royal family appear to be adversaries. This does not allow a minister to perform his duties well. Rani, you should ensure that no member of our family or our personal staff violates the commands of the minister. No one should act contrary to his advice.'

'Maharaj, the minister embodies your authority. He has all rights to know and to reform our follies. Please give him a free hand in the exercise of this authority and empower him that he should without hesitation discuss my misdemeanour with you,' said the queen.

'Rani, the minister has often expressed to me his gratitude towards you because you support his efforts and have never been an obstacle. Unlike in many other states, the queen is not opposed to the minister and does not enter into or encourage machinations against the minister. The minister is grateful that you have also accepted measures to bring about financial discipline in the royal household.'

'It would be a blot on my family if I do not learn your virtues, Maharaj.'

'When God is kind, everything else also falls in place; all act in good faith. Common people recognise this as fate. Rani, the good sense that you and my Bhayat have shown is a sign of God's grace.'

'Maharaj, you must reward the Bhayat for their good sense. Neither the king's anger nor his gift should be empty of substance.'

'There is no way I can repay the gratitude of my Bhayat. They have done a great deed.'

'But they have one unexpressed desire, Maharaj. You must fulfill this desire. It will give both them and me joy.'

'And what could that be?'

'Maharaj, first give me your word that my desire will be fulfilled.'

'In the Satyug, gods granted boons without enquiring about the nature of the boon sought. Brahma, occasionally and Shiva often granted such boons. But as the creator and the destroyer of the world, they could grant such boons. But Vishnu, the upholder of the universe, never granted such boons. We the kings, who uphold the righteous order, are embodiments of Vishnu. Moreover, by assuming the Vamana avatar, the demons taught a lesson to Vishnu that even he should not grant such boons. Shri Ramchandra wordlessly taught men that if they were to grant a boon unthinkingly in the heat of the moment, as Dashrath did to Kaikeyi, they, too, would come to grief. Rani, ours is the glorious Suryavansh. Would we not follow the example of Shri Ram, the epitome of Suryavansh?'

'Maharaj, in matters of love, you cannot take recourse to the *Puranas*.'

'Rani, if you are invoking love, tell me who has greater right—you or my principal queen? Can I grant you a boon without consulting my principal queen?'

'Maharaj, I was under the impression that I am your only queen.'

'I have never spoken to you about my principal queen in order to avoid a conflict.'

'You must tell me the name of my sister. You should test us and see if can live with each other without discord.'

'There are two-three other queens as well.'

'Without first making their acquaintance, I cannot accept any food.'

'But you know them already.'

'Maharaj, please tell me plainly.'

'The first among them is my intellect. She has been my principal queen since childhood; I can do nothing without consulting her. My second queen is Ratnanagari; I am neither allowed to compromise her, nor allowed to love you more. My third queen is the battlefield; I must respond to her call even if I have to leave you sleeping or waiting. These are your three elder sisters. If I were to grant you a boon without their consent they would turn away from me. They would throw a tantrum that would put even Satyabhama's tantrum to shame, and I do not have the skills of Shri Krishna to assuage their hurt and anger.'

'Maharaj, I should express myself clearly. Why should I seek something that is not made explicit?'

'Say it.'

'Apart from these three favourite queens, you should marry a fourth one. I shall be your fifth wife.'

'And who is she?'

Mena Rani spoke sombrely, 'Maharaj, Samantsinh sent a message through his wife. He wants me to request you that there is a tradition among kings to marry more than one woman from noble families to ensure that his lineage continues through a male heir. The shastras and our customs both sanctify such marriages. Maharaj should give the benefit of this tradition to Ratnanagari.'

'Rani, do you have anything to add to this message?'

'Maharaj, a woman who has been barren would naturally wish for her husband's lineage to continue and ensure the good of the kingdom, and she would wish for you to have all the worldly joys.'

'And thereby ensure that your own position is endangered.'

'This is not a farce, Maharaj. I have harboured this thought long before receiving Samantsinh's message.

Mallaraj mocked her, 'I, too, do not speak in jest. But pray do continue to harbour this thought until it rots and is destroyed.'

'Why do you make a mockery of me?'

'I do not mock you, Rani. But my three principal queens advise me that your proposal should be rejected. I will not act against their advice. Convey to Samant that I follow the vow of one wife that our Shri Ramchandraji followed. Mallaraj is not about to recognise the authority of either the shastras or customs and marry many women. Mallaraj will not act in an effeminate way. Tell Samant that he shall be king after me; he is free to marry as many women as he wants. Remind him of what I dictated to him just yesterday. I said that a man who marries more than one woman begins to act like a woman, like a mother-in-law or a sister-in-law. The document proscribes polygamy. Tell Samant's wife that she should act wisely and pass on some of her wisdom to her husband. Mena Rani, do you have anything more to say?'

'I have much to say, Maharaj, only if you would consider it.'

'Your ploy has failed. Do you have any more dice to throw?'

'The same.'

'My refusal stays.'

'No one can force a king.'

'All right then, I shall now visit the palaces of my principal wives.'

'Do grace me with your return, Maharaj.'

The king kissed his queen's forehead and left. The curtains came down on act one of Mallaraj's concerns.

10 Mallaraj's Mani and His Initiation into Statecraft

Mena Rani failed to convince Mallaraj. Samant made another attempt through Jarashankar. One day Jarashankar broached the issue. 'Maharaj, Samant appears unhappy with you.'

Mallaraj: 'What about?'

Jarashankar: 'He wished to convince you for a second marriage, and it is said that you dismissed the proposal with disdain.'

Mallaraj: 'Just that? Whose message are you carrying?'

Jarashankar: 'Samant himself informed me.'

Mallaraj: 'Did he tell you who his messenger was?'

Jarashankar: 'The queen.'

Mallaraj: 'Does he not deserve to be treated with disdain for this stupidity?'

Jarashankar: 'He wished to convey that even the queen agreed to this proposal.'

Mallaraj: 'Does Samant want me to remarry for the sake of Ratnanagari or for my worldly pleasures? If it was the latter that motivated Samant, he deserves to be treated with utmost disdain. The rulers of Ratnanagari are not moved by worldly pleasures, and if my heir believes that I desire such pleasures, I am pained both by his thinking and his estimation of me. If I were to accept this proposal, both he and I are unfit to be rulers. By my disdain, I showed him the path to acquire the capability to be a ruler. Moreover, he used the queen for something that would have been to her disadvantage. This is the other reason for my obvious disdain.'

Jarashankar: 'Maharaj, he was motivated by a desire to secure Ratnanagari's future. You appointed him as the heir apparent and used his mediation with the Bhayat. This idea probably came to him at that time.'

Mallaraj was thoughtful for a while. 'Yes, I understand. You are probably right. This proposal is the result of his devotion to the state. But I showed disdain for his devotion. I committed an error. Jarashankar you must rectify this mistake. Please explain my reasons to Samant and thank him for it.'

Jarashankar laughed. 'Maharaj, the king errs and the minister salvages the situation?'

Mallaraj: 'This happens every day in other states. For us, this is the first instance.'

Jarashankar: 'Maharaj, when a king takes a decision without consulting his minister, the king often repents. But if the minister is taken into confidence, even if it leads to repentance later, it is shared by the minister with his king.'

Mallaraj: 'Is this advocacy to expand the scope of your authority?'

Jarashankar: 'Yes, Maharaj!'

Mallaraj: 'I admire your autonomy and courage. How can I not accept my error? But tell me, was Samant not wrong in conveying the message through the queen instead of you? Was I wrong in decrying that choice? You tell me that Samant's counsel was in the interests of the state, and yet he chose the queen as messenger instead of my minister. Did I have an option but to push him out?'

Jarashankar: 'Maharaj, your argument has defeated me. But let me come to the main issue. Let us examine the merits of Samant's message. It has been held desirable that a king should marry more than one wife to have an heir and continue the royal lineage. Samant and the queen both are doing their duty by urging you to do so.'

Mallaraj: 'I have considered this. Let me give my arguments briefly. Something that fundamentally violates morality cannot become moral because either Samant or the queen considers it to be moral and part of their duty. A murder committed with the consent of the victim does not become less of a sin for that reason. A person who gives such consent is certainly noble but the one who seeks such consent is a lowly and evil person. One should weigh the costs and benefits of such actions. The costs would far outweigh any possible benefits. A kshatriya married to two or four women is likely to become womanly, and that to me is very harmful. I have decided that this practice must be stopped in the new age. I will set the example for my Bhayat.'

Jarashankar: 'But Maharaj, is not the destruction of the royal lineage a matter of grave concern?'

Mallaraj: 'A lion cohabits with one lioness; they have one cub. But a pig copulates with many females who give birth to multiple piglets. This destroys the potency of the semen. A lone lion cub is better able to protect the father's lineage than many piglets. Being with one wife also keeps the passion unsullied. Jarashankar, the kings of Ratnanagari are like lions.'

Jarashankar: 'Maharaj, this is not a response to my poser. The royal seed, even when dispersed, retains its potency—because it is nurtured in the royal household. Someone born in an average family cannot match that quality. Moreover, I did not suggest that you should sire many progeny. I suggested that you should have multiple wives, one of whom could give you a son.'

Mallaraj: 'A clean and smooth mirror gives the best reflection. Its clarity cannot be matched by a multifaceted mirror. Having many wives is like seeing your reflection in a faceted mirror. A progeny born out of a union of deep love for one's wife is the best.'

Jarashankar: 'If the best proves elusive, why should one not settle for something slightly inferior?'

Mallaraj: 'If I do not have a son, why can I not have an heir from among my Bhayat. Even they have royal lineage. The one who is closest of kin to the king should be his heir.'

Jarashankar: 'That may be so. But they do not have royal upbringing.'

Mallaraj: 'That lack has been adequately addressed in the document that the Bhayat have accepted. It will be the obligation of my heirs and my ministers to ensure that the Bhayat cultivate a regal attitude and that their kshatriyahood is strengthened.'

Jarashankar: 'There can be a situation where the heir is totally undeserving and is unfit to be educated in the discharge of royal duties. What then?'

Mallaraj: 'What prevents us from adopting a suitable heir, even if he were to be distantly related?'

Jarashankar: 'This opens up the possibility for intrigue and machinations. Not just that, if an adopted heir has to be selected after the king is deceased, the decision will be taken by women and others.'

Mallaraj: 'The right of adoption is only the king's. That is his sovereign right. If he, during his lifetime, does not adopt, it must be accepted that he wanted his heir to succeed him. No human agency can snatch the throne away from such an heir.'

Jarashankar: 'Maharaj, I am defeated.'

Mallaraj: 'Explain all this to Samant. Tell him that so long as I consider him fit to be my heir, I am not going to adopt anyone. So long as I am alive, I will not forsake or taint my kshatriyahood, my royal pride and my love for my queen by remarriage. If God has to grant me a son, my queen will bear that son. But if God has decided not to grant me a son, even the husband of a hundred queens will remain without an heir. Jarashankar, applaud Samant's devotion to the kingdom but tell him that brahmins and banias have insatiable desires for a son; it is not for me to have such desires. If the queen is destined to bear a son, she will give birth to one. But if that is not our destiny then I shall not do anything that insults the capability of my Bhayat. But the overriding reason is that I shall not respond to Mena Rani's love by doing her an injustice. She has sovereign right over my love and I shall not commit the sin of curtailing her right. I would not want to be a witness to injustice and sin committed by my own people. I, as their king, will never commit these sins. Until this point, you had a right to discuss these issues. But now that my principles are known to you, I do not want any further discussion, not even a word more about this. Any breach of this will be regarded as an act of disobedience which shall be punished. Jarashankar, this applies to you, Samant, the queen and all others. You must inform them of my resolve. And if you commit a breach, I will deal with you as sternly as Ram dealt with Laxman.'

Jarashankar: 'Maharaj!'

Mallaraj: 'I have vowed to remain faithful to my wife. No one shall come between my righteous and dutiful wife and me. The decision that we arrived at after consultations cannot be violated even by the king or his minister.'

Jarashankar: 'Maharaj!'

Mallaraj: 'I don't want to hear a word more. I have given my command.'

Jarashankar: 'Maharaj, I obey your command.'

Mallaraj: 'What were you about to say?'

Jarashankar: 'I was about to express my pleasure that it has been my good fortune to serve such a righteous king as you.'

Mallaraj: 'I was under the impression that it was the work of bards to sing praises of the king. That even ministers are required to praise the king I only learnt today.'

Jarashankar: 'Maharaj, please forgive me. It was a wrong choice of words. I am very pleased with your command.'

Mallaraj: 'That is better.'

Some years later, God rewarded the unsullied and pure love of Mallaraj and Mena Rani. The queen conceived. Mallaraj intended to inculcate the sanskar fit for a king to the unborn child. One day on his way to the queen's quarter he ruminated: A man, concerned with the welfare of the unborn child should consider the pregnant woman not as his wife but as a mother-to-be. Hence, he should observe abstinence from the moment of conception till the child is born. He should consider her body to be sacred and allow her to dedicate it fully to the service of the unborn child. The husband should aid her by becoming celibate. After the birth, till the time that the mother breastfeeds the baby the father must act in a way that does not deprive the child of nutrition. This is his duty, both as a father and as a husband. Among the brahmins and the banias, the customs of the elders ensure such conduct. Among them a pregnant woman goes to her natal home and spends the time of her confinement there. Thus, the woman remains free of her mother-in-law's nagging and the husband's sexual desires. And thus, she performs her duties towards the baby in the loving care of her mother. But the kings of Ratnanagari have their own traditions. For them the state of householder is not only for the satisfaction of carnal pleasures. They turn celibate whenever required. The king's mother has affection for his queen. The king's mother does not tend to be partial towards daughters and harsh on the daughter-in-law, like the commoners. Mallaraj, from today you have become celibate. Mena Rani will now reside in the temple-like palace of your mother.

Hastidant, Mallaraj's elder brother and heir apparent died in the war with Colonel Brave. His widow stayed with Mallaraj's mother. Hastidant was a martyr and therefore his glory was alive. Hastidant's widow, for this reason, did not adopt the traditional attire of a widow. On one hand she wore a bangle that signified her married status, but she broke the bangle on the other hand. She did not mourn the death of her husband but lived a sparse life devoid of luxuries. Her life was a complex mix of a woman who, though a widow, lived like a woman whose husband was still alive. She spent her days in prayer and in caring for her mother-in-law. She cultivated a detached attitude to life. Mallaraj's mother called him and the widowed daughter-in-law to her deathbed and said, 'Mallaraj, I have lived a life of duty. Now, I must follow your father and your brother to the other world. Do not mourn my death. Your sister-in-law, who has preserved the glory of your brother, should take my place. You and your queen should consider her to be your mother. You are like children to her. I do not have the strength to go on. But in short I have described your duties towards her. You should obey the command issued by me from my deathbed. This is the tradition of the Suryavansh and the royal family of Ratnanagari.' She then turned towards the young widow and said,

'Daughter, you must now take my place. We royal kshatriya women do not need any advice. I cannot speak anymore. Daughter, embrace me one last time. Mallaraj, give me your hand.'

Both obeyed her wish. The daughter-in-law embraced her and the son took her hand in his. The mother could speak no more. She seemed to take her daughter-in-law into her arms even as her eyes remained fixed on her son. Her fragile fingers clutched Mallaraj's hand, but she seemed hesitant to let go of life. Mallaraj said, 'Mother, I am Mallaraj and this is your daughter-in-law who will henceforth occupy a mother's place for me. Mother, this is not a moment to worry about anything or anyone. I am your son. I will care for the family and the people of this state just as my father Nagraj did. My brother laid down his life in the battlefield; my father battled on without mourning the loss of his son and when the moment of death came, he allowed his life to ebb away. We kshatriyas travel from this world to the other without any unfulfilled desires. Mother, this is a moment to take the name of our family deity, the sun, and of the God who governs all life. Cherish the moment of being one with their light. Mother, you are a kshatriya. It is our duty to receive Yama the God of Death with you. Mother, a death such as yours is auspicious.'

She looked at her son for one last time and closed her eyes. Her lips parted and people around her heard the faint utterance of the name of God. With that the king's mother gave up life. From that day on, Mallaraj addressed his sister-in-law as Mataji. He also commanded his queen to respect and care for her as she would for her mother-in-law.

Mallaraj was delighted with his idea that his pregnant wife should reside with Mataji. Mena Rani's unborn child will grow under the protective care of Mataji and imbibe the valour of my brave brother Hastidant, he thought. After years, memories of the elder brother flooded his mind and he was suddenly overwhelmed by sadness. Remembering Hastidant brought copious tears to Mallaraj's eyes and he wept in silence. Then, as he approached the door to the queen's quarters, the sadness at the loss of his brother gave way to the joy of fatherhood. The doors were closed. Laughter and banter could be heard. He waited outside and listened. He immediately recognised the voice of Mataji's personal maid. Mataji had named her Madhumakshika because she buzzed around like a bee. Among the servants she was known as Madhumakh.

Madhumakshika said to the queen, 'Rani Sahib, you must feign a temper tantrum and prepare for a long estrangement from Maharaj.'

'But I don't know how!'

'Radhaji had feigned estrangement from Hari. She said, "I will not speak to Hari. He called me Chandramukhi." You must do something similar.'

Mallaraj opened the door and stepped inside. The queen was on her bed while Madhumakshika sat facing her on the floor. Both stood up as he entered.

'Madhumakshika, why are you instigating conflict in my house?'

Madhumakshika laughed and said, 'Maharaj, the science that deals with man-woman relationships speaks of a lovers' quarrel. It is given to maids like me to spark such lovers' quarrels.'

'So, you do sting!'

'It is only by stinging that I give meaning to the name given to me by Mataji.'

'Now that you have invoked Mataji's authority, we will have to accept what you say.' The king sat down on the bed; the queen stood leaning against the side of the bed. Mallaraj said, 'Madhumakshika, why should Radhaji object to being called Chandramukhi?'

'Maharaj, the moon waxes and wanes. Its light also becomes faint. To call her moonfaced is to insult her. She does not want to wane.'

'You should not teach such playful estrangements to us of the sun lineage.'

'Maharaj, Raniji was born in the moon lineage; and when you accepted her in marriage you also accepted to partake of the joys of the intellectually pleasing banter that the moon lineage is known for.'

'Is that so? We will have to learn all that. We kings of the sun lineage are arid and know nothing of such matters!'

'Maharaj, the queens of the moon lineage have such light that their mere glance can kill kings of the sun lineage.'

'That is true. But Madhumakshika, why are you not with Mataji? What are you doing here?'

'Maharaj, I am here as Mataji's messenger.'

'And what is her command?'

'Yesterday Raniji visited Mataji, who by looking at Raniji's body and demeanour knew that she was pregnant and would give birth to a son. The royal astrologer has also come to the same conclusion after his calculations. Therefore, Maharaj, till such time that the queen is delivered of the child and feeds him at her breast, Raniji should come and reside with Mataji. Of course, your palace will always be in Raniji's heart. Mataji requests that you should permit Raniji to come and reside with her.'

'Madhumakshika, Mataji cares for me so much. I am indeed grateful to her. I see that her wish is an act of grace. We shall act upon her wish before the sun sets today.'

'Maharaj, the auspicious time for such a departure is only tomorrow. And therefore, I was trying to teach Raniji about a lovers' quarrel for tonight.'

'Have it your way. But if you taught her so much in the few moments that you had with her, what will you not teach her in the next two years that you will be around her?'

'Maharaj, I am a mere servant. All I can do is to hold up a lamp and light the path. A good kshatriya woman would see far into the distance with this light. Maharaj, your attendants can hand you the sword, but it is you who wield it with your might.'

'All right, what are the other commandments of Mataji?'

'Once Raniji shifts to Mataji's palace, you will have to regularly visit her to inculcate the values of the royal family in the unborn child. These visits are also necessary so that when Mataji is no longer alive, the traditional knowledge of care and nurture of pregnant royal women is carried forward. Maharaj, there is another purpose of these visits. For a kshatriya woman it is impossible to know which meeting with her husband will be her last one. Therefore, it is not advisable to deprive a kshatriya woman of the opportunity of seeing her husband, except when he is at war. Moreover, a pregnant woman craves to see her husband and receive his wisdom. When such craving is fulfilled the unborn child also receives the image of its father. Therefore, Maharaj, though you shall be celibate, to this limited extent you shall be a householder. According to Mataji, this is also a tradition of your family.'

'Madhumakshika, I will observe this family tradition.'

'Maharaj, the moon approaches Venus only when it is surrounded by other stars. Similarly, you should visit the pregnant queen only when she is surrounded by her maids.'

'I will follow this ritual perfectly.'

'Among the low-born, pregnant women have debased cravings because of the lowly company they keep. But Maharaj, in your family, ways of promoting noble cravings are adopted. By repeated darshan of the ascetics of Sundargiri, the soul of the foetus is ennobled. The pregnant queen is taken to the temples of Surgram. This pilgrimage to a beautiful and holy place gives a clear intellect to the foetus. Maharaj, when the pregnant queen looks up at the high ranges of Sundargiri, the foetus learns to aspire for higher things in life. When the pregnant queen breathes in the cool breeze of the ocean and looks out at the far horizon, the foetus acquires a sense of beauty, quiet equanimity and foresight. When she walks through your beautiful lush forests, breathing in the fragrance of flowers in bloom and listening to birdsong, the foetus experiences the joy as well. When the brave kshatriya woman hears the roars of lions and tigers, the foetus also acquires the first lessons in kshatriya valour. Maharaj, you must ensure that the pregnant queen is taken to all these places and that her comfort is ensured. You should also accompany the queen on these pilgrimages and visits whenever possible.'

'Madhumakshika, I will gladly obey all these commands. Please convey a request to Mataji: if possible you should be a constant companion to the queen during this period.'

'Mataji has already taken this decision, Maharaj. These were the main requests. But she has also made some other arrangements. I should inform you of them and seek your consent.'

'Mataji's decisions are always taken with our welfare in mind, hence I accept them even before you narrate them. But I do wish to learn about them and experience the joy I know it will bring.'

'There will be a few clever maids and a few who can remain in constant service of the queen. The elderly wife of Shastri Maharaj, the experienced wife of Samant Mulu, some three or four young wives of Bhayat and other maids will give the queen company and care for her. Mataji will of course be there. But she does not utter the name of any man other than your elder brother. When Subhadra was pregnant with Abhimanyu, Shri Krishna narrated stories of valour to her. Similarly, Mataji intends to narrate stories of your elder brother's valour to the queen. Maharaj, when Prahlad's mother was pregnant with him, Narad Muni also told stories of devotion to him. Maharaj, the character of the child is formed by the stories that are narrated to the pregnant mother.'

'Madhumakshika, how can I ever express my gratitude to Mataji? I do not remember my own mother having to worry so much about me. The care and concern shown by Mataji is a thousand-fold higher. Rani, whether I am alive or not, you shall never forget the debt of gratitude that we owe Mataji. You must ensure that our children also remember it always. Rani, what services can we offer Mataji? She must require so many things! We have appointed servants to care for her, but there must be many shortcomings that remain unseen. But the very qualities that enabled her to bear the separation from my brother also allow her to cope with all our shortcomings. Rani, Mataji's love for us is limitless.' Mallaraj wiped his tears.

Madhumakshika: 'Maharaj, it is your tender heart which has placed you in this condition. Your compassion is in keeping with the noblemen of this royal household. Maharaj, a Sanskrit verse aptly captures your noble character.

> Very few good men are there who, full of nectar of holiness in thought, word and action and pleasing the three worlds with

> numerous acts of beneficence, rejoice at heart in ever magnifying the minute good qualities of others.[1]

'Maharaj, Mataji is not doing you a favour. This unborn child is the future of Ratnanagari and to care for this child is the principal responsibility of the queen mother. Maharaj, from the day she entered this palace, Rani Sahib has cared for all of Mataji's needs. A kalpavriksha grants one a boon only when one seeks it, but Raniji's care goes much beyond that. Even before Mataji expresses a need, Raniji sees to it that it is met. This act of selfless service has melted Mataji's heart. Her love for Rani Sahib is inexhaustible. I am a witness to this, Maharaj. Mataji's concern for Raniji is like the rain giving back to the river the water which made rain possible.'

At the conclusion of this little speech, Madhumakshika sought the king's consent to return to Mataji's service. In due course of time, the queen gave birth to Maniraj. As the child began to walk and talk, the responsibility of his nurturance came to the men folk. Mallaraj relieved Mataji and Mena Rani of the responsibility and assumed direct charge of Maniraj's education.

Before handing over young Maniraj to his father the king, Mataji sent a message through Madhumakshika. The message was as follows: 'Maharaj, Mataji wishes you to be acquainted with the care and nurturance that Maniraj received so that you follow similar principles while raising him. This care began with his mother's milk. Maharaj, this young lion cub has been raised on the milk of his lioness-like royal mother. He has not been robbed of his right by being given the milk of women of inferior castes. Maharaj, eventually a child must leave his mother's womb and her breast. Now he will come under your care. He has the seeds of manly power. It is your responsibility to nurture, enhance and augment this power so that he grows up to possess powers and abilities greater than what you possess. Mataji requests you to ensure that no partial measures are taken in this effort. Maharaj, we, the worldly beings have to deal with joys and sorrows. This is inevitable. The youthful phase is the period when one must

[1] Kale, *The Niti and Vairagya Satakas of Bhartrhari*, Verse 78, 126–127.

learn to contend with sorrow. Maharaj, a man who wants an active day should spend a peaceful night undisturbed by nightmares. Similarly, this precious child of yours, who will have to wage difficult battles in his youth, should be exposed to nothing but joy as a child. Maharaj, Mataji has ensured that this kshatriya child does not shed a single tear, and has kept him away from tendencies common to women. These were her instructions to Raniji and all the maids in their service. Maharaj, she urges you to show even greater care. Do not allow this tender plant to wither away. Maharaj, a childhood free of worries and filled with joy is a right of every child. Do not please curtail this right in any form. Maharaj, hitherto Mataji and Raniji tended to this child just as a gardener tends his tender plants. A garden that is a responsibility of many gardeners can go untended. Similarly, a child who receives instructions from many cannot obey anyone. His heart is torn asunder. Maharaj, you are his father. Please appoint an affectionate tutor, and the two of you be his instructors and tend to him as a gardener would. Maharaj, it is said that a child's ears should be pierced by someone other than the mother. Therefore, assign these difficult tasks to this other person. The child should have no doubt that the other person's authority over him is not complete. But we observe among animals of the cat family that the mother carries the child in her mouth; no one else can do this delicate task. Therefore, the tutor that you appoint must also be under your constant vigil. You have to make sure that the tutor does not put his teeth on the tender skin of your son. Maharaj, you have to be as vigilant as a bird hatching her eggs. A royal child needs protection even from his tutor.

'Maharaj, even mature and intelligent adults fail to carry out all instructions fully. You will certainly not expect your tender-aged son to do so, but you have to resist similar expectations that others might have of him even in their dreams. Maharaj, a bitter pill has to be sugar coated. You must encourage everyone around him to follow this way. A child can be made to do his work by encouragement.

'Maharaj, do not allow ordinary men and servants to go anywhere near your son. We have not allowed maids to go close to him; you must also ensure the same. Women out of passionate desire for their husbands give the child away to their maids and the child then learns many undesirable traits from the maids. Your son has hitherto slept either with Raniji or Mataji. He has not spent a night away from either of them. He has not spent time unobserved with anyone else but me, because I am trusted by you. Maharaj, you will be occupied with matters of state and hence cannot be expected to watch over him all the time. But you must ensure that apart from his tutor, the young prince is not influenced by anyone else; he is like the son of Indra and needs the protection of Brihaspati. Maharaj, you can think of many things that we women have not been able to.'

Mallaraj took young prince Maniraj's hand. He sent a servant to call his minister. As they waited for Jarashankar, he engaged his young prince in playful conversation that also tested the boy's intelligence.

'Kumar, will you not miss Mataji?'

Maniraj: 'I will not like it, but just as you have to stay away from Mataji, I will also learn to do so.'

Madhumakshika: 'Maharaj, his answer lacks nothing. His response fulfills his obligation towards both you and Mataji; it reveals that as the king of Ratnanagari, he would be righteous and discerning.'

Mallaraj looked visibly pleased. He held on to his son and asked, 'I am required to look after the affairs of the state. And what will you do?'

Maniraj: 'Please allow me to be around you when you perform state duties. Please show me how one rules. I will accompany you; I will observe what you point out to me and I will obey your command.'

Madhumakshika: 'Maharaj, the young prince has asked that he be initiated into the intricate art of statecraft. You have to decide if you would like to grant him his wish.'

The young prince raised his hand and placed it over Madhumakshika's mouth and said, 'Madhumakh, who allowed you to butt in while I was speaking to Rajaji? You should not interrupt our conversation.'

Madhumakshika bent down to embrace the little prince. Tears filled her eyes. She said, 'Kumar, may you have a long life. Maharaj, just as the first rays of the sun break the spell of darkness, the young prince, even before commencing his education of statecraft, has conveyed to me that my rights over him are over. He has desired that a woman such as me will not exercise any influence over him.'

Maniraj: 'Madhumakh, you are still buzzing around. You don't follow instructions!' Maniraj turned to his father and said, 'Maharaj, Mataji told me that the king punishes all those who do wrong. Now it is up to you.'

Madhumakshika laughed and said, 'So, you have reached the limits of your power?'

Maniraj: 'I will not speak with you.'

Madhumakshika: 'Maharaj, the young prince understands that he can issue orders; he is intolerant of disobedience and he told you that it was your right to award punishment. And yet, he gave me the punishment that a child could give, by refusing to talk to me. Maharaj, the young prince has all the qualities required of a ruler. They have already begun to emerge in your presence, just as seeds sprout in sunlight.'

Maniraj: 'Maharaj, I put my view before you. You get this Madhumakh out of here or you order her to shut up and stop buzzing. Today, I wish to talk with you. I do not like what she says.'

Madhumakshika: 'Kumar, I will leave immediately if you ask me to.'

Maniraj: 'I am not throwing you out. You go into your hive and stop buzzing.'

Madhumakshika: 'All right. I will keep silent.'

Maniraj: 'That is good.'

Everyone was quiet. The young prince stared at Madhumakshika, who remained silent. Then he said, 'Madhumakh, why don't you speak?'

Madhumakshika just laughed.

Maniraj: 'Why don't you speak?'

Mallaraj: 'You forbade her. How can she speak?'

Maniraj: 'She should speak when I talk to her.'

Mallaraj: 'What do you want her to say?'

Maniraj: 'She told you everything that Mataji had told her to. But last night, Raniji and she had said something to me. About that she has not uttered a word.'

Mallaraj: 'And what was that?'

Maniraj: 'Madhumakh will tell you.'

Madhumakshika: 'I have forgotten.'

Maniraj: 'How can you forget? Say it! Raniji doesn't call you a liar for nothing!'

Madhumakshika: 'She only calls me jhoothi because I eat from her plate.'

Maniraj: 'Whatever it is. Say it.'

Madhumakshika: 'What am I to say? Give me a hint.'

Maniraj: 'That, a real horse and not a wooden play horse, and so on.'

Madhumakshika laughed. 'Yes, Maharaj, we have given a promise to the prince before he would allow himself to be brought here.'

Mallaraj: 'What is that promise?'

Meanwhile Jarashankar walked in. He sat beside the prince, gently lifted him into his lap and said, 'Maharaj, why are all these questions being posed to Kumarshri?'

Mallaraj: 'Kumar will no longer stay with Mataji. He has come to stay with us. But before coming here, he has sought some assurances, it seems.'

Jarashankar: 'Is that so? What has he sought?'

Maniraj: 'I will no longer play with my wooden horse. I should be given a real horse today.'

Jarashankar: 'Anything else?'

Maniraj: 'I will not play. I will learn to ride horses, wield a sword and I will give up the company of women. Instead, I will move about in the company of Pradhanji and Maharaj and I will also attend the court rituals.'

Jarashankar: 'Madhumakshika, was this the promise made?'

Madhumakshika: 'Yes, Pradhanji.'

Maniraj: 'From now on, I will have my meals with Maharaj.'

Jarashankar: 'For that you need his consent.'

Maniraj: 'Either you or Madhumakh get that consent. I will not ask.'

Jarashankar: 'Kumarshri, one needs to ask one's father.'

Maniraj: 'Mataji said that kshatriyas cannot be supplicants.'

Jarashankar: 'Then how do they obtain what they want?'

Maniraj: 'By their own effort, by the use of force and by wielding the sword.'

Jarashankar: 'Then you should also obtain it by those means.'

Maniraj: 'I have already obtained a promise from Madhumakh—if she does not get it for me, I will have nothing more to do with her. She will be forced to get it for me.'

Madhumakshika: 'Kumar, I will not be around you henceforth.'

Maniraj: 'Where do you think you are going? I will block your way if you leave without fulfilling your promise!'

Jarashankar: 'Kumar, Maharaj will honour your word.'

Maniraj: 'I will believe it only if he issues a command.'

Jarashankar: 'Take that command as given.'

Maniraj looked up expectantly at Mallaraj. The king could no longer contain his laughter.

Maniraj: 'Raniji told me that no one can take a single step without your order. Why is Pradhanji taking decisions without asking you, Maharaj?'

Mallaraj: 'You should ask him that.'

Jarashankar: 'Kumar, Maharaj's pleasure is a command in itself.'

Maniraj: 'All right. I will also please him. Then I shall be able to have my way with him.'

Jarashankar: 'That is correct.'

Madhumakshika: 'Maharaj, I now seek your permission to hand over Kumar to your care and take your leave.'

Maniraj: 'Madhumakh, Mataji taught me that a king and his prince must also learn to reward the services given to them. So, stay.'

Everyone looked on in surprise.

Maniraj: 'Maharaj, I wish to give all my toys to Madhumakh's son. With your permission I will go to Mataji's palace and hand them over to her.'

Mallaraj was pleased that his son had learnt gratitude. He took the young prince into his lap and said, 'Kumar, you must always remember what Mataji has taught you. Go with Madhumakshika and reward her appropriately. Madhumakshika, till such time that I make adequate arrangements for Kumar, let him stay with Mataji. I will call for him soon.'

Maniraj: 'Maharaj, I will not play with toys anymore.'

Mallaraj laughed and said, 'Of course, Kumar, you will no longer play with toys. You will have a horse to ride and swords and a bow and arrows to play with. Pradhanji will have them sent to you without delay.'

Maniraj: 'Who will teach me?'

Mallaraj: 'Even that shall be arranged.'

Maniraj: 'When will you call for me?'

Mallaraj: 'I will take you to the fort in the evening.'

Maniraj: 'Madhumakh, come, let's go. You go and fetch your son so that I can give him my toys.'

Madhumakshika: 'You can give them to me. I will hand them over to him.'

Maniraj: 'No. You will keep them in the house and not give them to him. You bring him to me so I can give them to him personally. If you take them away, I will deal with you harshly.'

Madhumakshika: 'Do what pleases you. Now we must take Maharaj's leave.'

Maniraj placed his hand over her mouth. Madhumakshika removed his hand and asked, 'What are you doing, Kumar? Don't you want to go?'

Maniraj: 'Stay here. We will leave after the Maharaj leaves.'

Madhumakshika: 'What shall we do till such time? Maharaj has to attend to other matters.'

Maniraj: 'We will listen to the conversation between Maharaj and Pradhanji.'

Madhumakshika: 'We are not permitted to listen to the secret talks of the Maharaj and his minister.'

Maniraj: 'All right. Then take his leave.'

Meanwhile the king and his minister had begun to attend to other matters. Madhumakshika said, 'Maharaj, I seek your permission to leave. I will take the prince with me for the time being, but before I go I wish to add—insignificant though I am—to the message that I carried from Mataji. I humbly urge you to listen.'

Mallaraj: 'Speak.'

Madhumakshika: 'Maharaj, even to ordinary folk, a son is precious. That a son should be prized and valued by a king is not surprising. The Shruti says, "Son, you are born of my body. Your place is in my heart. Son, you are my soul. Live a hundred springs."

'Maharaj, a son is an embodiment of his father. He must also be imbued with the father's heart. Just as a new banyan tree grows from the roots of the old tree, mother and father give birth to their progeny. Parents and progeny are of the same lineage. Not just that, they also share a common soul. The son acquires the characteristics of his father's soul. A son of the king acquires a kingly soul. This ancestral soul of the royal lineage is the true wealth of the king's people. The body and the soul are distinct, but the body exists because of the soul. The soul is unseen, the body is manifest. It grows and withers because of the soul. A lifeless seed cannot grow. But the seed of the body gives birth to another body because the seed is alive with the soul. This child, in due course, will attain maturity. Maharaj, do not consider the seed to be separate from the tree; do not consider the child as distinct from the adult form that he will acquire. The tree is contained in the seed and assumes its form in due course of time. The seed manifests itself in branches, in flowers and in their fragrance. The soul is concealed by the body; it is without form. But if one were to ask as to what the soul does, the answer would be that the roots that reach the sky and beyond and the seed that grows in the mother's womb are both manifestations of the soul. O Maharaj! Your son is a manifestation of that soul. The soul of this child is not the body of your son. You and he share a common soul. His soul is imbued with the light of your soul. This child is capable of spreading this light through this land and your populace. His light combines his royal lineage and his personal qualities. He is like a flower that embodies the full glory of the tree. Maharaj, this seed, this child, this light must be nurtured in its delicate stage. It is your duty. The brahmin sages join their soul with the souls of their disciples and create brahmatma. Similarly, a king should join his soul with the soul of his son and create rajatma, a kingly soul. This soul should inhabit the body politic. This can be attained by a self-aware king like you. Wretched though I be, Maharaj, I request you to strive towards this. Maharaj, I clearly see this young prince growing like a grand tree. It is incumbent upon you to ensure that he grows into a grand figure. It will be the result of the power of your soul. Maharaj, I have become verbose and loquacious, but it is my love for this light of yours which shines through your son that forces me to speak. Otherwise, I would never be so bold as to speak thus before you. Maharaj, I have said what I wanted to. I now seek your permission to take your son back to Mataji's palace.'

Maniraj listened attentively, his gaze shifting from the face of the maid to the faces of the king and his minister. When she had finished, even before Mallaraj could respond, he tugged at Madhumakshika's sari and said, 'Madhumakh, are you done?'

Madhumakshika: 'Yes. Do you have anything to add?'

Maniraj: 'Unless you give me your word, I will not accompany you.'

Madhumakshika: 'What word?'

Maniraj: 'When Bharat was engrossed in counting the teeth of a lion, Shakuntala and Dushyant forgot about him; neither of them spoke to Bharat.'

Madhumakshika: 'What about that?'

Maniraj: 'You should tell Raniji that I should not be placed in the situation of Bharat. She tells me stories of Luv-Kush and Bharat all day long.'

Everyone laughed.

Madhumakshika: 'Do I control Raniji? You should tell her yourself.'

Maniraj: 'When we came here, you spoke to Rajaji and got what I wanted. Now you claim that you have no influence over Raniji? Then why did you give me your word? I don't want to come back with you!'

This produced more laughter.

Mallaraj: 'Kumar, go with her. You should talk to Raniji yourself.'

Maniraj: 'I will not ask Raniji for anything. I am a prince and we get what we want by the power of our force. If you behave like King Dushyant, I will not like it at all. I would like you to talk to me.'

The king and his minister smiled. Madhumakshika also smiled bashfully and said, 'Kumar, you will bind me to a promise, but you will not make a request. Come, let us go. I will do what you want.'

Maniraj: 'Be careful. If you do not keep your word, I will deal with you appropriately.'

The two of them finally left, still deep in argument. The king's gaze followed them. The prince led the maid by her hand, forcing her to walk faster. The king followed them till they disappeared from view, his face glowing with pride.

The minister looked on with delight at the king's proud, indulgent gaze.

> As the king was looking intently at the lovely face of his son, with one eye as steady as lotus in a breezeless spot, his intense joy could not be contained in himself, like the flood of the great ocean at the appearance of the moon.[2]

[2] Kale, *The Raghuvamsa of Kalidasa*, Canto 3, Verse 17, 19–20.

The joy of watching one's son is similar. Jarashankar did not have a son, and for a moment, he was saddened by this lack. He had a nephew, Vidya Chatura, who was like a son to him. Vidya Chatura was both virtuous and intelligent. He considered the possibility of appointing Vidya Chatura as a tutor to Maniraj. This possibility allowed him to forget his sorrow. But it gave rise to a new concern. How could he recommend his own nephew? He thought of using the advice given by Madhumakshika to bring up this matter for discussion. But on second thoughts, Jarashankar discarded the idea. He said to himself: My responsibility is to serve the king according to the principles of Dharmashastra. I commit an act of treachery even if I entertain a selfish thought. I will not bring up the matter. I will wait till Maharaj himself has a use for Vidya Chatura.

Mallaraj interrupted his thoughts. 'Jarashankar, we cannot forget the commands of Mataji and the advice Madhumakshika gave us. A father has additional duty towards his son. I am concerned as to how Kumar should be trained in statecraft.'

'Maharaj, the mode of instructing the princes is part of our Shastras and have been practiced in your family for generations.'

'True, but the Shastras also give us an injunction to act according to the changing times. We must consider that as well.'

'Maharaj, hitherto the Muslims ruled over India. Even during those years, our ancient wisdom proved itself useful to your family.'

'And it will continue to be useful. But we must not consider knowledge that can be acquired only through our own language. Vidur saved the Pandavas in the palace of lacquer through the knowledge of the Mleccha language. Yudhishthir used the illusion of the demon Maya in his palace. Bhima married a demon and Arjun, a Naga woman. The brahmins think that knowledge can only be brahminical. But the kshatriyas accept knowledge of all people and all lands.'

'What is your suggestion, Maharaj?'

'The English will be the sovereign rulers of India. We must make use of their knowledge. The rulers of Ratnanagari must learn our traditional ancestral knowledge for the welfare of our people, but they must also learn English knowledge so that they do not become helpless in the face of change. This is their duty.'

Jarashankar appeared deep in thought.

'What are you thinking about?'

'Maharaj, statecraft is a complex subject.'

'How so?'

'Once they learn English, they will not submit to family traditions. They will become conceited.'

'Jarashankar, Rajputs must always look for victory. This is their duty. They should alter their ancient customs according to the times if necessary. Rajputs do not submit to anyone. Now if they become slaves to tradition, they will be reduced to slavery themselves. Rajputs sent their daughters to the zanana of the Mughal emperors. These marriages were intended to win over the Mughals. Many Rajput kings stayed in the outskirts of Delhi and held sway over the Mughal court in Delhi. Such Rajputs and Hindus are around even now.'

'That credit should go to Shivaji. But for Shivaji, everyone would have been converted to Islam.'

'No, Jarashankar. There were two other means as well. Persuasion, inducement, confidence and coercion are the old means. It is those who also acquire mastery over the new means who will ultimately emerge superior. The Rajputs lacked one of these means and they were forced to retreat. Shivaji also failed to use all the means possible and hence his state came to be ruled by the brahmins, and after them the English. Jarashankar, those who aspire to the knowledge of statecraft must garner all kinds of arms, ammunition and expertise in all kinds of means so that, if the need arises, they can use them at the opportune moment.'

'But, Maharaj, once we give up our ancient ways, we shall break all limits. If you decide to change the course, please ensure that it is contained within certain limits, or else we shall give rise to Bhasmasur, demons who will char all that they touch.'

'We of the Suryavansh fight demons with an army of monkeys and bears. Even Shivaji owed his success to such a plan.'

'If you go looking for monkeys and bears, what will your kshatriyas do?'

'My kshatriyas who have descended from the gods will not become monkeys just by dressing up like them. My heirs will use their English knowledge to build a bridge across the ocean and enter the abode of the monkeys. Jarashankar, I have thought it through.'

'But, Maharaj, you must secure the banks before the waters flow.'

'That is true. If they retain the good sense to work for the welfare of the people, that in itself would set limits to their actions. If the people change but not their king, it will lead to clashes. Therefore, everyone in my family and the state should learn English; but so long as we remain conscious that the objective is to grasp the intentions of the English, none of them shall imitate the ways of the English. This would secure our banks in one way. The other way of securing ourselves would be to take what is best and lasting from our age-old traditions. We need not impose any other limits. Jarashankar, that is it. I have made up my mind. Show me a way of educating Maniraj—that is your duty. Unless the kings of Ratnanagari are able to grasp the knowledge that comes their way from all the four directions, darkness will envelop them. That cannot be permitted at any cost.'

'Maharaj, when our children live with someone else they become like the foster family, and we lose control over them. A child reared on a foreign language will respect neither you nor your customs.'

'The sons of kshatriyas have to be acquainted with the land, the swords and the shields of the enemy. They have to learn the language and customs of the enemy. Women and brahmins stay at home and look after it, while kshatriyas have to protect the world outside the home.'

'That is correct. But it is undesirable that they become slaves to the ways of the enemy.'

'Of course! The danger is clear. One will come under the influence of the other when one learns their language and customs even for the purpose of self-protection; this danger is part of any diplomatic warfare. Those who enter the battlefield will either win or lose, will die or get wounded. Jarashankar, I have made up my mind. It is now your responsibility to ensure that my instructions are followed. Go, search for a Dronacharya for my Arjun.'

'Yes, it is my responsibility and duty to execute the commands of my king. But to find a brahmin-like Dronacharya to teach English is as easy as looking for a son born to a barren woman.'

Mallaraj laughed. 'Jarashankar, those who go out wailing come back with the news of someone's death. You will certainly not find a way for anything that goes against your opinion.'

'Maharaj, this accusation saddens me. But you will admit that it is impossible to find someone who is equally learned in English and our Shastras.'

'Drona was the teacher of the Kauravas. But the sons of Pandu learnt the art of war from him. My minister should be equal to such a task.'

'Maharaj, that is true. Your idea is best. But a man well versed in the knowledge of the enemy will occupy an undeserved position of influence in our state. The prince is very young and impressionable. If you want that his mind should be coloured by the contact with English knowledge and customs, then it is your desire. Arjun was mature enough to stealthily take the best out of Dronacharya. Dronacharya could not capture and subjugate Arjun's mind. Maharaj, Maniraj is still a child. Sitaji had become infatuated with the golden deer. You are a king, and kings can become adamant.'

'Jarashankar, I am pleased with your autonomous views and the accusations that you make to prevent me from taking my chosen path. I am pleased with you. You may ask for anything you like.'

'Maharaj, a lion does not allow his teeth to break and kshatriya kings do not tolerate any disobedience of their command.

> O you best of kings, eminent universal sovereigns like you, who are made by the Creator the receptacles of supreme valour, who, by their peculiar might, subdue kings having a large force of rut-shedding elephants, and who are distinguished by their sense of self-esteem and pride, do not put up with the infringement of their command for any reason whatsoever, just as the lords

> of beasts who are created by the Creator as the store-houses of strength, who by their fierce vigour conquer the rut-shedding leaders of elephant herds, and whose dignity and haughtiness are distinctly manifested, do not brook the breaking of their jaws on any account.[3]

'But Maharaj, you have shown exemplary patience. You permit me to disobey you. This is a sign of your grace and also of forbearance.'

'You have often recited that verse to me. A sovereign ruler cannot allow for disobedience. But we have a powerful ruler above us. I accepted their authority on your advice. Who but you could remind me that I am no longer a sovereign ruler by this act of disobedience?'

'Forgive me! Maharaj, please forgive me! I am but your servant and had no intention to hurt you by disobedience.'

'Then you must obey my instructions, Jarashankar. I will not be satisfied with my prince becoming a frog in the well. You were instrumental in the treaty that we signed with the English. If the acquisition of their knowledge is as difficult as crossing the black waters of the sea, the prince must do so. The prince must swim across the seas and enter the Lanka-like fortress of the English. It is up to him to drown or swim. We shall take precautions that he does not drown. But the rulers of Ratnanagari do not stop taking risks for the fear of drowning. Maniraj will learn from the teachers of our enemy.'

'Maharaj, I accept defeat. I will find a way of obeying your command and taking the necessary precautions.'

'You may or may not be able to find a way. But I can show you a way.'

'Your suggestion cannot but be the best.'

'Appoint your nephew Vidya Chatura. He has studied English; he will also obey you. He has made a good impression on me.'

Jarashankar was satisfied. It was good for both Vidya Chatura and Maniraj. Mallaraj's injunctions could also be adequately met by it. This seemed to be the best way. He said, 'Maharaj, you are very

[3] M. R. Kale, trans. *Mudrarakshasa of Visakhadatta*, Act 3, Verse 22, Reprint (Delhi: Motilal Banarsidass, 1911, 2011), 213.

kind. I do not know if the appointment of Vidya Chatura would be an act of obedience or an acceptance of your kindness. But if it is an act of kindness, Maharaj, please free me from it and I will give you an opportunity to test my obedience.'

'One should not argue about a king's order and an injunction of the Shastras. This is what our Shastras tell us. But you clearly disobey this injunction.'

'Very well, Maharaj,' and with that Jarashankar left.

Mallaraj thought: A king must ensure that the next generation is ready to take responsibility; this is a necessary obligation of the king. One would need a minister to take Jarashankar's place. The reasons why Maniraj must learn English, the new minister should also know English for the very same reasons. Vidya Chatura will benefit from Jarashankar's knowledge, experience and wisdom; he will mix as easily as sugar in milk. But that will not be so easy for others. Vidya Chatura is knowledgeable both in English and Sanskrit. It will not take him long to gain in experience like Jarashankar. The old days are swiftly passing us by. New times are upon us. In these times of transition we need a person who can keep note of all that which is passing us by and capture what is yet to come. Jarashankar, Vidya Chatura and I together will do this. The three of us together shall pave the way for Maniraj. We must ensure that he becomes capable of galloping on this path and that he acquires even greater intelligence and acumen than all of us. With such thoughts Mallaraj got engrossed in other matters of state.

11 The First Surge of Foreign Rule

Dear reader, in the second part of this novel you will recall that we read about the instructions that Mallaraj gave Vidya Chatura before he took charge as Maniraj's tutor.[1] Mallaraj was alert to ensure that these instructions were carried out. The king also followed the advice given by Madhumakshika. He gave complete autonomy to Vidya Chatura but ensured that this autonomy was not abused.

One day, Mallaraj took Kumar and Vidya Chatura on an excursion to Sundargiri. The king's tent was pitched on top of the hill and afforded a magnificent view. As Mallaraj reclined on a cushion embroidered with golden thread, his fingers toyed with his moustache and his gaze was fixed on the sea. At some distance from the king's tent Vidya Chatura and Maniraj strolled about; the young prince was holding Vidya Chatura's hand. Kumar pointed to the sea and asked, 'Chaturji, how big is the sea?'

'You have seen the map of India; the sea is almost twice as big as the landmass of India.'

'What comes after the sea?'

'Land.'

'Does it have people?'

'Yes.'

'What comes after that land?'

'The ocean.'

'What after that?'

[1] Tripathi, *Sarasvatichandra*, Part II, trans. Tridip Suhrud, 33–34.

'More land.'

'Even that land is populated?'

'Yes.'

'What kind of people are they?'

'The English Sahibs come from that land.'

'Do they have a king?'

'Yes.'

'Does their king have a prince?'

'Yes.'

'The Sahibs come to our land. Do our people go to theirs?'

'Very few.'

'Why do so many Sahibs come here, Chaturji?'

'To rule over us.'

'Please tell Maharaj that we should also go to their land and rule over them for a while.'

'You could tell him that yourself, Kumar.'

Mallaraj overheard this conversation with interest. Maniraj walked over to his father's tent followed by Vidya Chatura. He came up to the king and said, 'Maharaj, let us go to the land of the Sahibs to rule. I don't like it here.'

Mallaraj was deeply saddened, but he disguised his sadness with laughter and said, 'Kumar, I have grown old. But you could do that once you grow up. What do you say, Vidya Chatura?' Mallaraj's eyes had unshed tears as he said, 'Kshatriyahood has been widowed. The aspirations of Rajputs are no different from the desires of the son of a poor widow.'

Mallaraj took the prince into his lap and his eyes looked out to the sea, searching the horizon. His lips were pursed and he remained pensive for a while. Then quite abruptly, he stood up. Mallaraj walked up to the edge of the hill with his hand on his sword, his brows furrowed. Finally, he instructed Vidya Chatura in a grave voice, 'Vidya Chatura, get yourself a blank notebook which you must keep with you at all times. You will be required to write down what I dictate to you; Maniraj will read it once he attains maturity. The writing should be such that it touches his heart irrespective of whether I am alive or dead.

Secondly, the day we return to Ratnanagari, you will remind me to call my Bhayat, their sons, my son and Jarashankar. All of them and I will meet every day at an appointed time, and you shall tell us the story of the British people. We have been hearing stories from the *Ramayana*, the *Mahabharata* and accounts of the valour of our ancestors. This would be something like it. You can spend as much money as you want to acquire the books you need. You must read to us their story from the very beginning, from the time they were in the state of monkeys till the present times. Moreover, you shall read to us about the condition of the French, the Russians, the Dutch, the Portuguese and the Muslims. But your special focus should be on the descriptions of their wars, their methods of persuasion, inducement and conceit, their statecraft, the countries they visit or inhabit and their activities there as also about their enemies and friends, the people who wield influence among them, the condition of their people, their joys and sorrows, their methods of fabricating canons for war and industries for times of peace, and about their equivalents of our kshatriyas, brahmins and vaishyas. You must learn their secrets about all these things. You must steal the secrets of their arts and learn the way their mind works. Vidya Chatura you must learn, understand and steal all these things and narrate them to us in our language. And you must instruct the prince—the beacon of our hope—in their knowledge as per our instructions.

'Vidya Chatura, at the right time Kumar must be initiated in our traditional knowledge of the kshatriyas; but in this you cannot be his teacher. Whoever becomes his teacher—native or foreigner, friend or foe—the prince must learn the use of swords and canons alike; he must learn to duel with a brave warrior as also learn the art of commandeering an army similarly constituted. These arts might appear to be futile at present, but I want to ensure that my son and all Rajputs of his generation become experts in these arts. I want to keep the knowledge of these arts alive just as the sacrificial fire is kept alive eternally. I know that this difficult task cannot be accomplished without the help and cooperation of the English. Someday, I will explain to them that their self-interests and our interests are one and the same; the wise English will comprehend this. Vidya Chatura, by these actions we are verily sowing the seeds of a new statecraft. The sowing of the seeds is my responsibility; your duty, Vidya Chatura, will be to be a good minister to me and my son. I have no hesitation in sharing this secret with Jarashankar's nephew.

'For this vision to be realised, the sons of my Bhayat should surround my son and contribute to his light, just as the stars surround the moon. The country is passing through a dark night. The stars and the moon must shine together with each other's light. Vidya Chatura, hitherto my Bhayat have helped us in times of war, and we in turn have cared for them. They sacrificed their lives, and we awarded them land in the form of garas, their traditional inheritance. Now, under British rule, we no longer need their sacrifice and we will not be able to award them any garas; even holding on to the garas we have is going to be difficult. Previously, when Bhayat died in war, their garas was re-distributed to the new generation of Bhayat. Even when we shared our land with them, our own land share did not decline. Now, we will have to award garas to the new generation of Bhayat, but the land will not come back to us—because we will not lose our Bhayat to war. As a result the lands owned by us will diminish and with that our power will decline. Consequently, the British will become more powerful. I have taken certain other steps to arrest this dangerous process. But the wise have likened the mind to the fickleness of a courtesan. The king will have no dealings with Bhayat who fail to prove their usefulness. Selfish and inept Bhayat will not have the opportunity to serve the king—this is one of the weakest links in the state. One will find people who hold the two ends of the chain and make us dance like monkeys. Vidya Chatura, it is my duty to ensure that no foreigner takes control of this chain. You have to find bonds of affection that will act like glue between Kumar and the sons of the Bhayat so that we can mend this broken chain. There may come a time when we will have to wage a war for this country. Shalivahan made a battle-ready army out of soldiers of clay. If these new generations of kshatriyas are joined by bonds of affection, their ancestors will dance with you. Therefore, you must cultivate this clay well. For the present, the English have no use for my Bhayat. But a time will come when the English will feel entrapped by enemies and hostile neighbours. When their own people would have become like brahmins and vaishyas and would be useless in war. The English will feel isolated then. At such a time if my Bhayat have not become like statues and if they have any life left in them, they will go to the aid of the English. It is then that they will appreciate my foresight. Vidya Chatura, when their eyes open, the English will realise the true worth of the native states. Similarly, the kings will also realise the value of the English. But till such time, my Bhayat will be shunned. Till all parties learn to appreciate each other, unhappy times will prevail. You will have to teach my son patience and cultivate the Bhayat.

'You must remember that the kings of Ratnanagari marry only one queen. If they have no male heirs, the sons of Bhayat become rulers of the state. Thus, my Bhayat and their sons are potential rulers of the state. It will be your responsibility as the tutor of my prince to teach others as well.

'Vidya Chatura, there will come a time when kshatriyas will become farmers; they will cease to be Rajputs and will be called landlords. Even in those times, the principles I have enumerated must be kept alive like the eternal flame. That is my insistence ...'

The sentence remained incomplete, like the aspiration which was to remain unfulfilled, for just then a messenger rushed in with a letter from Jarashankar. Mallaraj opened the letter impatiently and read the message. His brows furrowed but he somehow retained his equanimity. He got up and walked to the edge of the hill, rolled up his sleeves and said, 'Hanuman has arrived from the army of monkeys.' He read some lines of the letter again. 'According to the terms of the treaty signed by Maharaj Nagraj, the British have a right to appoint an arbitrator to resolve disputes between the native states of the colony. In exercise of this right, their government has decided to appoint a representative. This representative will be called the Political Agent or the Resident. There will be one Political Agent for every four or five states. He will have diplomatic immunity and his residency will be designated as British territory. His task will be to act as an arbitrator among rulers and secure peace in the region. Suvarnapur, Ratnanagari and other native states will come under the Political Agent stationed at Malar Patan. He will appoint other outposts, one of which will be in Lilapur. A British officer, subordinate to the Political Agent will work from Lilapur.'

As Mallaraj folded up the letter, his mind was besieged. All my anxieties regarding the treaty signed by my father are proving to be true, he thought. A Hanuman from the army of monkeys has arrived. Now he will jump about and set fire to our golden Lanka. Now we are the demons and they are the monkeys. Our actions will be constituted as immoral and theirs as moral. The seed sown at the time of the treaty has suddenly sprouted in the form of this Resident. This action will spread fire. What is its remedy? These thoughts and questions passed through his mind like lightning. He chewed his lips as his hand played with his sword. Kumar expressed his desire to go to England and rule, and now the British have laid claims upon our territories! We have ceased to be kings. We are now a colony. The deluge that I apprehended is upon us! Mallaraj looked at his sword. Beloved sword, you have been rendered powerless. Now Rajputs should carry walking sticks instead.

Mallaraj turned to Vidya Chatura and said, 'Vidya Chatura, the pleasure of this excursion must end. We must proceed to Ratnanagari at ônce. I need to confer with my minister.' The king's order was complied with. The next day the king reached his palace and immediately sent for his minister.

'Jarashankar, write to Brave Sahib that we have no use for his Political Agent. He should be re-called immediately, otherwise ...'

'Otherwise we will go to war. Is that what you want me to write Maharaj?' Jarashankar said with laughter.

'This is no time for laughter. The treaty with Nagraj does not contain even a syllable about the Agent.'

'But the government is convinced that there is a full sentence about it.'

'Where is it?'

'Of course it is not there. But the government threatens us with its might and says that we must accept its interpretation, or else their army will show us our place.'

'If their sword is real, is my sword not real?' retorted Mallaraj.

'Maharaj, that question is for your sword,' replied Jarashankar.

'Are we their slaves?'

'No, Maharaj, we are free, but our sword is shut so tight that it will not open.'

Mallaraj was enraged. Blood rushed to his eyes. The old warrior was overcome with the desire to fight. He unsheathed his sword and began to wield it like a snake charmer showing off his snake. He rushed to the door and shouted, 'Samant! Samant! Who is there? Prepare the army! There will be war!' He kicked the floor and roared, 'Who says that my sword is enslaved!'

Jarashankar considered the situation calmly and urgently sent for the queen and Samant; each moment of waiting was as long as a year. The king stood still, leaning on his sword, his gaze fixed on the rafters of the ceiling. Then, as if he had woken up from a deep, meditative state, he looked around gravely and was surprised by the presence of so many persons. He asked, 'Why are you all here? Go back to your work. Don't you know that no one should enter the place where the king and his minister are in conference?'

Everyone went away astonished. The queen who was on her way also turned back. Samant came and joined the minister.

'Maharaj, you were in a state of intense and valiant excitement. Which is why everyone had rushed here,' Jarashankar clarified.

Mallaraj: 'Say it in plain tongue that I seemed mad.'

Jarashankar: 'Only Maharaj can describe his experience.'

Mallaraj: 'Samant, the minister knows how to speak the truth without being bitter.'

Samant: 'The fact that he has the courage to be so bold to your face speaks of your greatness, Maharaj.'

Jarashankar: 'You are right, Samant. Maharaj remembered you in his excited state. Hence, you were called.'

Mallaraj: 'Why did I want him here?'

Jarashankar: 'To have the appointment of the Political Agent annulled.'

Mallaraj: 'Apprise him of all the details.'

Jarashankar apprised Samant about the letter and the conversation that had led to the king's impassioned frenzy. Samant heard him in silence and gave no response.

Mallaraj: 'Samant, why don't you respond?'

Samant: 'Maharaj, your Bhayat no longer have a right to respond. When Tatya Tope's men came seeking your support, you decreed that the English were righteous and the Marathas immoral. You decided in favour of an alliance with the English. You also decreed that the Bhayat do not have the right to either question or disagree with a decision that the king had reached in consultation with the minister. My heart burns at your pain, but my intellect has forfeited its right to come to your aid.'

Mallaraj: 'Samant, that command was issued because we differed. Today when we are faced with the evil consequences of that decision, to remind me that your opinion was not honoured is the work of a dirty person. Your refusal to be either useful or give an opinion that is sought, just so that you can get even with me is like giving me a punishment. That you actually harboured this hurt for so long shows that you do not know all the duties of a statesman. To harbour hurt for a hundred years is characteristic of women. If you feel that you have been vindicated and have now emerged victorious because God has finally punished me for disregarding your opinion, you harbour within your heart the qualities of a traitor because you act like an enemy of the state. If you wish to throw barbs at me because you are victorious, your tongue is no different from that of a woman. Samant, you *are* my army. I have the right to rely upon you. I depend upon you more than I do on my army.'

Samant looked down. A tear fell from his eyes. He got up and went out. When he returned, he looked straight at the king and said, 'Maharaj, your generosity on this wretched self pierces more deeply than a sword would. Maharaj, I am your culprit. I am your servant who deserves punishment, but you treat me with generosity. My heart burns with the fire of expiation. Maharaj, please punish me. I introduced a falsehood in your truth, in your right conduct. I deserve the harshest of punishments.'

Mallaraj: 'Samant, my duty is not to destroy my army but to guide it onto the right path. You are my right hand, you are my pride, you are the pillar of my state, you are my army—any punishment to you is a punishment to myself.'

Samant: 'Maharaj, that army and this pillar are like a useless elephant who has to be fed for doing nothing. If you set the elephant free, it will crush your people, and if you keep it tied, its hunger will eat into your treasury. Maharaj, what use do you have for us now? What function is left for us to perform?' Samant sighed dejectedly, looking askance at Jarashankar whom he held responsible for the new politics that had rendered him and the other Bhayat obsolete. The minister ignored the barb and allowed the king and his Bhayat to converse uninterrupted.

Mallaraj: 'Samant, this is not the occasion for such talk. I want to know if we are free or not to resist the appointment of the Political Agent. It is your right to express yourself.'

Samant smiled vacantly. 'Maharaj, all things are appropriate in their right context. The time for wielding the sword is over; to bring out our sword at this moment is to invite death. The poet Samaldas has said: "Dissipated wealth shall return, ships will find their course; but an opportunity lost and a lifeless body shall never return." Maharaj, you chose to act on a brahmin's advice. We lost an opportunity and kshatriyahood lost its vitality, neither of which shall ever return. If this brahmin, Jarashankar, has the power to bring back lost opportunity and withered vitality, he should do so. But if you allow me, Maharaj, I will slay this brahmin and repay him for the desolation he has wreaked upon us.'

Jarashankar looked at the king, unperturbed. Mallaraj lost control over his temper. There comes a time when a lion stops roaring and uses his paws instead. The king had dealt with a personal insult with utmost generosity. He had in fact shown affection for Samant. That same king now nipped in the bud this opposition to his minister. He ceased to be a brother and spoke in the grave tones of a king: 'Samant, my minister is a part of me; he is integral to the royal body. You considered slaying him in my presence. For this you shall be punished. I order you to leave this city this moment. You shall not return to

Ratnanagari unless otherwise ordered by me. You shall also not enter within a five-mile radius of Ratnanagari or any other place where either I or my minister could be. Any disobedience will invite further and more severe punishment. Do not utter a word more and pollute the air around me further. Just leave this very moment.'

Jarashankar was shocked. 'Maharaj! ...'

'Silence! Samant, obey my command.'

Samant got up, bowed to the king and left, his body a prisoner of his sorrow and rage.

'Maharaj, this punishment was entirely inappropriate. You can punish me for speaking thus, but your act is unbecoming of you. You acted out of affection for me, but such punishment without consultation with the minister is inappropriate.'

'A king who feels insulted because of a contrary opinion has no right to rule. My command has nothing to do with my affection for you, Jarashankar. It is true that a king's command issued without consultation with his minister is invalid. But this norm does not apply when the minister is himself a party before the king.'

'Should the king act without the counsel of his minister in such matters?'

'It is my duty to protect my minister. Let my people know that just as I would hear any complaint regarding my own conduct, I would also hear grievances against my minister and do justice to them. If someone were to attack my person, I would even pardon them. But my queen, my prince, the Bhayat and my people should have no doubt that my officials are my weapons, and just as I would punish anyone who steals my sword, likewise anyone who seeks to curtail the authority of my minister shall receive harsh punishment. I will not show any mercy. In all matters pertaining to the scope of authority and the rights of my minister, I shall follow my own counsel. Jarashankar, issue a royal proclamation that I appoint Samant's son Mulu Bha as the commander of the army. So long as Mulu Bha is a minor, Samant will from a distance act in the name of his son and carry out my instructions. Samant does not have the right to enter into some areas; in such places he should act through a representative of his choice. The punishment I have awarded will also alert everyone to the meaning and power of my authority. Now let us deal with the issue of the Agent.'

'But Maharaj, I do have the right to point out to you the implications of your actions.'

'Why do you keep reminding me about implications? Can't you see that the politics that has rendered my Bhayat useless is being attributed to *you*? They blame you for influencing my judgement. They are enraged, and Samant is the instrument of their wrath. Would his sword have hesitated before coming down on you?'

'I understand very well that for many days now that sword has been hanging over my head, and also that your minister has remained unharmed only because of the shield of your grace. On the other hand, we can already hear the politics of the British at our doorstep; and if those predators were to learn of our internal dissensions, we would become easy prey to them. Maharaj, I have said this to you time and again that your minister is like that camel who should be sacrificed so that you can enter the enemy's fort. Maharaj, your family is about to be torn asunder, and if not, it shall certainly face divisive conflict. The British are certain to try and take advantage of this dissension. The easiest way of preventing such an eventuality is to place me, your minister, as the sacrificial camel. This would assuage the deep hurt of your Bhayat. This is also in the interests of the state. Maharaj, your Bhayat are neither traitors, nor have they turned against you; their anger is directed towards me personally. You need them and their army much more than you need me—this is a statement of fact. Maharaj, you will find many able ministers, but once you lose them you will not have such brothers-in-arms again. It is improper for you to punish them just for a few intemperate words. It is said: "A neem tree has bitter fruit but provides soothing shade; brothers are given to harsh words but they are like one's own arms."'

'Jarashankar, what you say is not without merit. Hence, the punishment to Samant is in essence a withdrawal of my affection. It involves no other harm. There is scope for him yet to repent and seek my pardon. Samant's heart is full of anger but not envy, and he is certain to repent. One day he will be with you again and work for the state with all his affection and loyalty restored. The punishment is both necessary and appropriate. Its outcome will be for the best. Only Rajputs understand Rajput temperament. But to sacrifice you would be both inappropriate and harmful. It was you who said, and quite truthfully, that now our swords are sheathed and our armies have been rendered useless. Now one clever and politically astute minister shall do what a thousand warriors cannot. He will act both as the sword and the shield of the king.'

'Maharaj has left the possibility of a pardon open and I do not wish to be instrumental in foreclosing that possibility. But I am surprised that you found this solution in response to the fact of your sword having been sheathed. It was the ineffectiveness of the sword that had perturbed you so deeply. Poor Samant was called here to assuage your feelings, and he ended up being punished.'

Mallaraj laughed. 'True. That was a strange fate. But even in the past such great events have produced such emotions within me. And yet once I bring my emotions under control, I also find a way out of the predicament. This is also a part of my disposition. But for you this seems to be a first experience of its kind.'

'Maharaj, my state is somewhat happier compared to yours because I find ways out of predicaments without succumbing to emotions.'

Mallaraj laughed again. 'That is correct. But in times of war such overpowering emotions are like a brother to a kshatriya. We are not so selfish that we would keep these emotions at a distance at other times. But you have no use for such powerful feelings; therefore, the wise among you keep away from them. *This* is the difference between us. And it is not in the interest of the state that this difference be obliterated. It is for this reason that it has been considered improper to appoint Bhayat as ministers. Jarashankar, we need your kind.'

'Then how has the Maharaj resolved the issue of the British Resident? Your heart has experienced an earthquake. So tell me how you have resolved this quandary.'

'Your and my opinions have become one.'

'I have not expressed my views hitherto.'

'But I have understood them.'

'Please illuminate.'

'First you express your views; then I will speak my mind.'

'Maharaj, it is better that your views prevail and not mine. I will speak my mind.'

'Tell me.'

'Maharaj, I still hold that the decision to have a treaty with the English was a correct one. But even if it were not, we are without any option. That treaty may be a gold mine or a bed of arrows, but the fact of it still remains. We must find ways to derive the maximum advantage from it. And we should not worry about what has not happened because it is not likely to happen.'

Mallaraj's face was grave. 'You spoke the truth.'

'Maharaj, just at present the circumstances are such that the English are in place of a mother-in-law, and you are in place of a daughter-in-law. They will employ newer means to curtail your authority. The treaty with them sowed a seed for the future, good or bad. If the result turns out to be good we should try to better it even further; but if the result be to our disadvantage we should bear with it anyhow and try to gradually improve our lot. One can entertain doubts while the matter is under consideration; but the time for doubts has passed. Doubt in moments of action is misplaced. It is said that those who harbour debilitating doubt are destroyed. The treaty with the English has been long concluded. Now we must deal with the results of our actions. In such moments the wise who have thought of the appropriate action say that good men do not forsake the fruits of actions that they were destined to do. What should be their conduct? It is said that a good man must, until the very end, deal with the consequences of his actions; this is also the norm that noble men uphold. Those who fail to uphold this are not considered worthy and good men. What does the upholder gain? The wise say that noble and worthy men always follow what has become a part of them. Those who succeed in doing so are fortunate; and they, too, consider themselves to be so. The throne that you occupy can be held only by men who are good and worthy; only the fortunate sit on it. This authority you understand much better than I do, Maharaj.

'Maharaj, all the considerations that one bore in mind at the time of taking a decision are often not remembered when one has to deal with the fruits of one's actions. One doesn't even recall the swift actions taken to implement one's thoughts. One would always consider all the obstacles before embarking upon a course of action. But the immediacy of those obstacles puts fear in one's mind. However, such fears are only because of attachment, which does not allow one to perform one's duties optimally. Such action is appropriate in case of someone like Samant who is experienced only in war. War itself is but a step in the implementation of a decision. The moment the duties of a warrior end, diplomacy commences for a king like you. Only a few like Mallaraj know how to swim against the current. Maharaj, at a time when we are faced with the momentous consequences of our actions, how can I, born to poor brahmins, instruct you, born in the royal house of Suryavansh, regarding matters of diplomacy! The traditions of your family would be far better at showing you the right path. Maharaj, your royal lineage will certainly produce some unique results—of that I am certain. Maharaj, in matters of diplomacy I am but your charioteer; you are the great warrior. I merely drive a chariot in the direction you prefer.'

'In short, you advise me to persist with the English, but how that should be done is to be determined by me.'

'Maharaj, that is correct. It is now your turn to express your opinion.'

Mallaraj laughed. 'Pradhan, you are a wily man. You spoke long, but left the burden of a decision on me. Are you scared of Samant before expressing another opinion?'

'Maharaj, even if I am scared, I am only a brahmin after all. A person who works under you cannot be afraid of fire. I have the courage to say that despite the knowledge that a weak and scared minister has no place in your service, you still retain me; and that you fail in your duty. I have this courage because of the trust I have in you.'

Mallaraj was very amused. He leaned his head back on the bolster and laughed aloud. 'Instead of telling a lie, Jarashankar, you have learnt to speak half-truth. I have already lost Samant; I would be foolish to lose you as well.'

'Maharaj, we have decided to persist with our treaty with the English. We have to, therefore, accept the Agent. The decision for us now is the proximity or distance that we would like to maintain from the cooking fire that he will light.'

'How so?'

'Should we allow him to start a fire as far as Bombay or as close as Lilapur?'

'They are already in Bombay.'

'We are too distant from it. We cannot tell whether the rice they cook remains uncooked or gets burnt. If they are in Lilapur, we will be able to keep an eye on them.'

Mallaraj sat up eager to listen. 'But if they light a fire in Lilapur, its sparks will fly in our direction, the ash and the smoke will cloud our vision as well. Moreover, we will also feel the heat. Is that an adequate price to pay to watch over what they cook?'

'Maharaj, you are a master in statecraft. You decided to get a measure of the English even before you spurned the advances of Shubhaji Rao. And in order to get a measure of our opponent, we have shown our hand as well. But that, too, is a means to an end.'

A major dilemma was resolved for Mallaraj. But some doubts still persisted. 'Jarashankar, that is correct. But what if we reveal too much of ourselves while trying to get a measure of them?'

'Maharaj, that fear is unfounded. The English know us well after the war that Nagraj fought. If they want to know us even more closely, we cannot prevent them. They will even remove our clothes and subject us to an examination. But they will employ cunning and not force to do so.'

'It seems as if we are going to bring the axe down on our own feet. Is there a reason for that? Why should we invite them so close to us?'

'Those states and rulers who have become devoid of any vitality and rendered effete due to various diseases that plague them must fear the proximity of the English. We look around us and we hardly find one state that is not diseased. They are hollow. The English will penetrate them with ease and drink their blood like a thirsty bear. Poison will flow through the veins of these states instead of blood. I do not think this is either an impossible or an undesirable scenario. Maharaj, there are rulers who prey upon their people, who do not devote even a small fraction of the day in thinking about and ensuring the welfare of their people, rulers who forsake their people and submit to debauched conduct to satiate their passions. If God has created an enemy to suppress such debauched rulers and corrupt realms, what is so improper about them? Maharaj, a king punishes his people, but God punishes even a king.'

Jarashankar caught his breath and continued, 'Maharaj, I do not know whether the proximity of the English would prove catastrophic for those states which have become hollow and corrupt. But even if it were to prove perilous, I would not regard it as undesirable. Even if such an outcome were to be considered disagreeable, the righteous and virtuous king of Ratnanagari has nothing to fear. Maharaj, as they come to have closer relations with you and your administration, your fragrance and the beauty of your administration will become even more apparent. Maharaj, you are like sandalwood—the more it is rubbed, the more fragrant it becomes. You are gold that glows brighter in fire.

> Again and again you rub sandalwood on the stone, it produces only a fragrant paste; cut the sugar cane again and again, it produces only sweetness. Burn again and again a piece of gold, it always shines. In the same way when noble people are put into different situations they do not change.[2]

'Maharaj, let alone the English, the whole world can try in vain. They can scrutinise the gems of Ratnanagari until they are satisfied. Our jewel-like men are not afraid of any test. If someone desires to observe our gems, we have nothing to fear. The English can see the treasury that our people are; they can do no harm. If these foreigners take a post at Lilapur, we would also have the benefit of knowing their arts and skills and we could learn some things from them. To me it seems

[2] Translated from the original Sanskrit for this volume by Arindam Chakrabarti.

that an opportunity has come looking for us. Maharaj, this is the best scenario for the present.'

Pleased with his minister, Mallaraj stood up, and so did Jarashankar. The enthused king patted his minister on the back and said, 'All right, Jarashankar. All my doubts have vanished. The gems of Ratnanagari are not under any threat. Go and ask Vidya Chatura to send a response. The progeny of Sugriva were dear to Sitaji. How can we, the descendants of Sitaji, keep them away from us? Those monkeys can sit on any tree they like and jump around as much as they want. They will eat some gram and nuts at most. But they are not capable of either breaking or chewing the gems of Ratnanagari. If they try to bite us, their teeth will break. Jarashankar, the monkeys of Mathura are greedy for gram; we shall be a match for them. If they jump around on our rooftops, they might break a few tiles, but we don't lack the mud to remake them.'

Jarashankar went home. The king walked towards the quarters of his queen. On his way there, he thought of Samant. Samant was a childhood friend, a companion of many wars and an heir to the throne after Maniraj. Separation from him was unbearable. Mallaraj felt his loss deeply. Tears streamed down his eyes. His heart felt a searing pain at the thought that he was the reason for Samant's departure and that he had grievously wounded his friend. He cursed himself: Curse on this kingship that forced me to wound a friend! Would it not have been better to have abdicated the throne rather than give up a friend?

Samant! Samant, my childhood friend! You were angry because you wanted to protect my interest. And see how I repaid you! A man who does not trust love is evil. It is for these reasons that the world does not trust the affection of a king. Kings are heartless. It is said that rulers end up in hell. This, too, is hell. Oh God! Strange are your ways.

Deep in such melancholic thoughts, Mallaraj entered the queen's quarter. The queen saw his withered and sad face. She knew the reason for his sadness. The news about Samant had spread through the woman's quarters. Everyone agreed that the punishment was heartless. People judged the king and decreed that the king had relied upon hearsay and not his own intellect while awarding punishment to a brave friend such as Samant. This was the first time that Mallaraj had been accused of such injustice. People said that the king's views had changed, which was also a sign of the changing times. The king could see that people behaved like strangers; it added fuel to the fire. But the power of Mallaraj was such that no one had the courage to even whisper of such things. The palace looked stricken by death. The queen shared the sentiments of the rest of the palace, but she was not about to mention this to Mallaraj. He had forbidden anyone from the women's quarters to express any opinion about matters of state; any disobedience would invite severe punishment. Samant's example left no doubt about that. But the queen took heart from the example of Laxman, who had not thought of punishment while allowing Rishi Durvasa to interrupt Ram's conversation with Yama, because such an act was in the interest of Ram. She gathered the courage to speak to the king. She decided on something that would relieve the king of his sorrow and give him pleasure as well. She hoped thus to meet two desirable ends by one action.

The king, weary of vain attempts to suppress love for his brother by reasons of state, placed his head on his queen's lap and lay down. The lamps spread soft light, not sorrow. The sea breeze wafting from the west soothed his body as he drifted into sleep. The rustle of leaves produced a pleasant sound. As his worries receded, his body relaxed and before sleep could overpower the king, the queen softly sang a song that she had composed for him earlier during the day, caressing him as she sang.

Mena pleads, my lord, your meek Mena beseeches you:
A brave man does not live by sword alone;
A valorous man does not harbour
The smouldering embers of wrath in his heart;
The conch-bearer who pierces the hearts of enemies
Is the lord of the three worlds
But to give solace to his devotees
He holds a lotus in his hand
He is the compassionate one who
Bore Bhrigu's blows

And incarnated on this earth, abided by its norms
Even a helpless woman like your Mena
Sees the times she lives in
For nine months have I borne our Mani in my womb.
O' husband mine, remember you are the devotee of such a lord.
You are enlightened: who can hold up
The lamp of compassion to you?

The king's sleep was disturbed. He turned to his side. The queen sang more lustily.

Samant, who ought to shine in your crown jewels, adorned your footwear

The king opened his eyes and stared at the queen.

My lord, you are the jewel on Samant's crown
Manidhar, stay forever compassionate

The king was startled. He sat up, his eyes reddening. The astute queen realised that the king was irate. She sang in a mellow voice:

Helpless woman that I am, I know I have no place near the throne;
Mine is the domain of pleasure and through it I seek subtle influence

Enacting the lines, Mena Rani pleaded with him with folded hands as she sang and tried to bury her face in his vast chest.

With folded hands and open heart,
Today your beloved beseeches you

The king took her face in his hands and waited for the next line. The queen sang:

My beloved, you are knowledgeable in the scriptures;
Give me deep and joyful pleasure
My beloved, you are knowledgeable in the art of war;
Bear with forgiveness the arrows of pleasure that I aim at you

The queen drew the king's attention to her body. Before he could take control of his desires, she seized the moment and launched an impassioned invitation to pleasure.

My lord, your brave Mena throws darts of love at you
My king, beware: your amorous queen attacks
Clever warrior, stay alert: this attack cannot be repulsed
My king, watch closely my hand
Playful one, catch me if you can

Even before the last word escaped her lips, Mena Rani flung herself passionately at the king. But Mallaraj brushed aside that beautiful body and got up. He walked towards the door of their bed chamber, and on his way out, he reproached her with scathing words: 'The king who punished Samant will also punish all those who take his side. Rani, you have transgressed your limits and sought to do something that is beyond your authority. A king forgets relationships while awarding punishment. Rani, I abandoned Samant. Now fate wills that I must forsake you as well.'

The king went out and disappeared into the dark. The queen followed him. She heard him converse with himself or someone else. Unseen in the dark, she sang:

O' beloved, surrender your anger
You are the bee and I, the flower,
How delightful is our union!
If we think of thorns,
How can there be pleasure?

She found no response. She took a lamp and went in search of the king. She caught up with him and said, 'My playmate won't play with me, my dearest!'

The king finally said, 'Rani, on second thoughts, I understand the meaning of what you said. Samant, is both a gem and also capable of poison like a snake; and hence one should forgive him. But I do not grant women authority in matters of state. What punishment should I award you?'

The queen fell at his feet. She held on to his right leg and said, 'Maharaj, I did not dabble in matters of state. I do not want to sully your reputation by my transgression. Other women may do so; but Mena is your subject and all my rights are those which you have yourself granted me.'

'Which right and which authority have you used?'

'If you venture into a place infested with snakes, Maharaj, I must alert you through words and if need be, even drag you away. I have had this right since the day I married you, Maharaj.'

'Do you think Samant is capable of a poisonous bite?'

'Samant will not do so. But your Bhayat are like Samant's fangs, and these fangs are venomous. Maharaj, your Bhayat are angry with your minister and you. If you pardon Samant, this poison will subside. You have to place the burden of holding up the earth upon the snake. This is one way of saving yourself.'

'Rani, I have heard your opinion; but that does not imply that you have not transgressed. I will give you light punishments. You will have to sleep without me tonight. I command you never again to meddle in the matters of state.'

The queen let go of the king's leg. She got up with tears in her eyes and said, 'Maharaj, your words are just and your command has both punishment and pardon. I do not have the heart to ever violate your command again. Maharaj, I am your subject. Please enter the bed chamber and sleep on the bed. I will sleep in the courtyard.'

The king lay down on the bed. The bed of love had turned thorny, and he passed a sleepless night. Yet he could not repent for the punishment that he as a king had awarded his beloved. Only a poet with the gifts of Bhavabhuti can capture the mental state of a king who has punished a friend like Samant and a queen like Mena.

> With an attentive mind he had to govern this world according to the rules of administration; his grief for his dear wife withers his body as heat does a flower; having himself abandoned her he cannot easily have the relief coming from lamentation, but today he can breathe a sigh of relief and thus, lamentation is, indeed a gain to him.[3]

[3] M. R. Kale, ed. and trans. *The Uttararamacharita of Bhavabhuti*, Act 3, Verse 30, 5th ed. (Delhi: Motilal Banarsidass, 1934, 2010), 35.

12 New Chapters and New Histories

> But no! The imperial theorist will live and die a martyr to his theory.
>
> —Merivale on Aurelius

The first shocks of foreign rule were felt through the entire administration of Mallaraj. His Bhayat, his army, his friends, the women's quarters in his palace, his love—all seemed to dissipate. His friends and relatives turned strangers. Difference of opinion finally led to disaffection among the loved ones. The treaty with the British rendered his kshatriya brethren obsolete, and they felt wounded by it. The Bhayat were enraged by the punishment awarded to Samant. Mallaraj was isolated. His trusted minister was seen by everyone as an enemy. The roots of dissension and machinations went deep. Formerly there was mutual trust, but it proved as unsteady as a stream of water. Mallaraj reclining alone in his chamber could see all this clearly before him. Late into the night he fell asleep. Before yielding to sleep, his thoughts were: A lion does not worry that he is solitary, helpless and alone in the forest.

The queen knew of his mental state. She peeped in from a window; for her this did not constitute a breach of the king's command. Seeing him asleep at last, she, too, went to sleep on the hard floor of the courtyard.

A year passed. The ruler of Virpur, a neighbouring state of Ratnanagari, died, and his young son Khachar ascended the throne.

Rana Khachar's father was a friend of Mallaraj. Ratnanagari and Virpur had together fought against common enemies in the past. The rulers of Ratnanagari believed in keeping their own state united, strong and well-administered. They did not crave for territories of other states. But they helped their Bhayat and Garasia satisfy their desire for acquiring garas in distant lands. The rulers of Virpur allowed their state to be subject to the desires of their Bhayat, while they themselves craved for territories outside their boundaries. The British presence precluded the possibility of wars as a means of acquiring territories, and hence the thirst for land could not be satiated. The Bhayat could no longer fight other armies and consequently, they began to harass the ruler. Young Khachar, thirsting for more land, found a way of grabbing the lands of friendly neighbours without taking recourse to war. The Bhayat became his instruments; instead of harassing Khachar, they turned like a pack of hungry dogs on the neighbours. The Garasia of Virpur began to grab land in the name of their ruler. The neighbouring states took their grievances to the newly appointed political agent. Khachar wanted to establish that he was not the only cause of all troubles. He took advantage of both the foolishness and greed of the Political Agent and filed suits against the neighbouring states. This disease spread to other states as well. The Political Agent's desire to become an arbitrator among native states was fulfilled. It was like the story of warring cats and a monkey. The scales of judgement went into British hands. For a time, Mallaraj saw this drama of change unfold from afar, and was deeply saddened by it. But he could not remain uninvolved for long; the wheels of time were also moving towards his state. He had managed to douse the fire that had reached as far as his queen's quarters. But soon flames erupted in neighbouring states and their sparks also flew in his direction. Khachar disregarded old friendship and opened a territorial dispute with Ratnanagari. Khachar's Garasia also began to plough land belonging to Ratnanagari. The Agent wrote to Mallaraj, soliciting explanations about the dispute raised by Khachar. Mallaraj challenged the authority of the Agent to seek such an explanation. A war of words ensued. Mallaraj called Jarashankar and Samant's son for confabulations.

'Jarashankar, the English have assumed the role of a judge in the dispute among kings; the foolish princes will cut each other's throats and present them to the English. In the times when battles were fought with arms, kings did not covet land; it is unlikely that the same rulers would hold sway when battles are being fought in mercenary fashion like the vaishyas. In times of armed conflict, it was in the interest of the Bhayat and the warriors that the rulers remained hungry for more territory; they sought conflicts to satisfy the warriors' hunger for land. Now when battles are being fought like the vaishyas, it is in the interest of the political advisors, including ministers that rulers remained hungry for land; and ongoing war through written documents satisfies the hunger of the class of writers. Jarashankar, in the past the jewels among our men were not sullied by greed and hunger. Like in the times gone by, we have among us unsullied, pure jewels among men; and your king does not exchange men of tinsel splendour for pure jewels. For generations, my ancestors have preferred the power of the men of Ratnanagari over the inanimate strength of land and wealth. Therefore, Jarashankar, you must commence a great yajna, a sacrifice to prevent the contagious disease that Khachar has contracted from spreading in this country. You are free to sacrifice as much land and money as required to ensure that this country does not burn in the fires of vaishya warfare and remains free from the subjugation of the monkeys who have usurped the role of the judge.

'Those times are gone when justice was that which was secured by the power of the sword! It has become a distant dream. Now justice among kings will be secured not by the sword but will be delivered by men! Jarashankar, as long as there is life in me, this Rajput will not allow these times to prevail upon this country. As long as I am alive, I will not permit my kingship to be usurped by the British and I will not accept their authority. What constitutes the loss of my kingly powers in accepting the superiority of the British, or in allowing my neighbourly kings to have their way and acceding to them some land—merely some dust, stones and trees? Jarashankar, rulers lose their powers by accepting the power of others. This has always been so. Let others accept the authority of the British. My ancestor Hastidant chose death over retreat in war, and a father like Nagraj did not hesitate to step on the body of a great warrior such as Hastidant. I, trained by those great souls, will not accept the power of others for the sake of mercenary vaishya-like warfare. Two of my ancestors departed from this earth right before my eyes. Why would I find it difficult to depart from this earth? I have accepted the friendship of the English, but not their justice. I would prefer to honourably accept some demands made by the progeny of those kings who supported me in the war against the English, rather than stand before the English with folded hands. This is what I desire. Go fulfill it.

'Jarashankar, I have shown you the end I desire. To find the means appropriate to that end is the responsibility of the minister. Mallaraj is not given to labouring over the question of means and the sacrifice involved in it. Put an end to these inconsequential quarrels by whatever means. You know well how to protect my interest and that of my state. In so doing if you were to make a mistake, I am capable of granting a pardon. Hence, go forth with my full authority, absolute trust and all the means at my disposal. Go fulfill the desired goal.

'But be careful. We must end all disputes. We must enter into treaties even with those with whom we have no quarrels at present, so that no quarrels about mud and stones arise later. Demarcate the boundaries of our state so carefully that even a child will not have any difficulty deciphering them, and even the most cunning person will not find a way of falsifying them. All disputes with other states must be so resolved that they never ever recur. We must bear any expense and even loss of some land, if need be, to ensure this. The sea naturally demarcates our territory on one side. The other three boundaries must be fixed permanently such that so long as the moon and the sun shine no one can raise any dispute regarding them. All outstanding issues must be settled for ever. Once this task is accomplished, no one will have the power to shorten the reigns of the rulers of Ratnanagari or be a hindrance in our pursuit to secure the welfare of our people.'

Mallaraj turned towards the adolescent Mulu Bha, held his hand and spoke with unbounded joy, 'Mulu Bha, just as Samant Bha is a pillar of my state, you, too, are fit to be a pillar of Maniraj's reign.

Samant Bha was by my side when I had to go to war. His intellect and love proved beneficial to me. Maniraj is still a child; but you have reached an age where you must learn and gather experience. Hence I have decided that you should accompany Jarashankar so that you become acquainted with matters of state and rulers of different lands. En route, go to Virpur and take your father along. You must obey him.'

Mulu Bha touched the king's feet. Mallaraj blessed him. Mulu Bha said, 'Maharaj, I can never repay the debt of gratitude for your mercy towards my wretched father. Your command is a sign of your grace, and I shall obey it. My father, who is unhappy to be separated from you, will experience the joy akin to having seen you when I shall relate your command to him.'

This response satisfied Mallaraj. He did not want to lose an opportune moment. 'Jarashankar, go with Mulu Bha and meet Samant. When you meet me next, Samant should be with the two of you.'

Jarashankar was clearly overjoyed. 'Of course, Maharaj! Can there be a moment of greater joy? You have granted Mulu Bha's request and shown great mercy for Samant. There can be no more auspicious beginning to this great task. The goal that you desire shall be attained. What can a master who has jewels like Samant and Mulu Bha lack?'

Jarashankar and Mulu took leave of Mallaraj. Mulu's family customarily wrote the father's name before that of the son. Thus, Mulu was known as Samant Mulu, and at times Mulu Samant. Mulu's heart was touched by the winds of a new age. He was greedy for land and power; he harboured anger for the insult meted out to his father, and nurtured jealousy and animosity towards the minister and his family. He was keen to fuel trouble for the kingdom. Such ghosts danced a macabre dance in Mulu's heart. He had inherited instrumental cruelty from his mother's side of the family. He had received nothing but intellect, imagination and valour from his father's family. With great effort, Mulu kept his ambitions secret. After he was gone, Mallaraj had a momentary apprehension that Mulu's speech hid his treachery, that his smile betrayed a secret weapon and that his heart was demonic. Mallaraj considered this apprehension unnecessary and turned his attention to other matters. Vidya Chatura will gather political experience and meet other men of politics, he surmised. As we have decided, he should be trained to take over Jarashankar's responsibilities; Maniraj and the state will stand to benefit. And so thinking, Mallaraj ordered Jarashankar to take Vidya Chatura as his assistant. For Jarashankar, it was as if the doctor had ordered what his heart most coveted.

This great task took many years to be accomplished. In the course of these years, they came to be acquainted with many rulers and British officials. The demeanour and the conduct of the British revenue officials changed over the years. Mallaraj prophesied that in the years to come they would herd the natives like a shepherd herding his cattle. The British government acted as a court of appeal in disputes among kings. Just as common people appeal over a judgement not in their favour, the rulers went in appeal over the orders of the Political Agent. Consequently the English courts came to be established above and over the rulers. Kings forgot their kshatriyahood and fought battles like vaishyas. They sought redress of their grievance in English courts and went in appeal to higher courts. They begged for justice, became supplicants, and the prestige of the English courts multiplied. This form of justice was formed on the evidence and testimonies of witnesses. The fates of kings came to be controlled by lowly witnesses. It was necessary to believe one evidence and testimony over the other. Consequently the prestige of kings and their ministers came to reside in the courts; with the loss of prestige, the glory of the kings inevitably declined. As their power and glory declined, the grip of the British administrators became firm. Sometimes the kings challenged their authority, but a weak challenge often only further strengthened the power and authority of the British. If a political agent was considered a just man, defeated rulers gambled with their chances and fell deeper into decline. The process of decline hastened if the agent was unjust. The inevitable decline of the rulers became a source of joy for some. Mallaraj keenly observed this and remarked to Jarashankar, 'Jarashankar, have you seen what pleasure this evil Fox Sahib derives from insulting and extracting money from this cunning and exploitative Thakore, who is a messenger of death for his people?'

Jarashankar replied, 'Maharaj, someone has said that it is cunning nature that brings at one place the ripe fruits of neem trees, a tongue that relishes their taste and a crow adept at eating the fruits. The person being punished is like Yamaduta, the messenger of death, and the one awarding the punishment is Fox Sahib; the Creator has thoughtfully made this pair.'

Mallaraj sighed, 'Jarashankar, because of one such ruler, all others will stand to lose. How many kingly powers has this messenger of death transferred to the English!'

'Maharaj, because of the inebriated, debauched Yadavs, a spear eventually killed Shri Krishna. That divine being lost his life because of his association with the Yadavs. If one like him can meet such a fate, who are we?'

'If the English officers were bad, one could blame the English for appointing them. But if our own kings and natives turn good officers into bad ones, how can we blame the English? It is certain that the English Sahibs are not as fallen as they are made out to be. It is our tendency to fight like vaishyas that is the cause of our downfall. A good wife can reform her evil husband. Would not our kings and ministers cultivate the art of reforming the Sahibs? Jarashankar this fire is raging; one cannot say when its flames will singe us. A forest fire engulfs not just dry trees but lush green ones as well. We must not allow this fire to burn us. We must not allow any weakness to creep into our state. It would be better to lose land, wealth, prestige and even this crown than allow debilitating weakness to corrode our state. If my progeny have any kingly glory, they will regain the state by the strength of their own acumen and ability. But those who seek to keep their rule but bargain away kingly glory will lose both their state and their glory forever.'

'That is the truth, Maharaj. A king is subject to temporal time. A king must overcome that through his endeavours. Your efforts will bear results.'

'It is because of the English that we native rulers fight amongst ourselves. They will play their game; but Mallaraj will watch their moves in this game of chess.' Mallaraj seemed delighted at this thought.

Virtue and shaping state policy for the welfare of the people is in itself a state of joy for a good king.

Over time, courts came to be established to adjudicate the disputes of native rulers. Laws were framed to govern the conduct of common people. Any attempt on part of the British to codify laws to govern the rulers would certainly have been seen as a clear sign of erosion of kingly authority. Hence the kings did not demand codified laws, and the British refrained from framing them. Therefore, the decisions of the courts became laws. This measure ostensibly adopted to protect the authority of the rulers became the source of many problems. In the absence of laws, judgement depended solely on the discretion of the judges and their predilections. There were not required to explain or assign reasons for their decisions. In this reign of darkness, the rulers stumbled around seeking favourable decisions. Often the judges were military men, and in such instances the real power of decision making was exercised by their lowly clerks. If the judges were learned men, they wrote reasoned judgements that could not be reversed even by the government. These judgements systematically eroded the authority of the rulers. The stories of such vaishya-like quarrels wafted into Ratnanagari like smoke from distant fires. It roused irritation in Mallaraj. At a time when other native rulers were subject to injustice and insult, Mallaraj drew his senses within himself and like a yogi meditating upon the eternal truth, he meditated upon the nature of kingly authority.

One day, Vidya Chatura opined, 'Maharaj, our native rulers have become corrupt. If the foreigners were to become equally corrupt, the rule of the Mughals would certainly return. But the norms of politics by which these foreigners are governed make it imperative for them to follow the norms of justice, even while furthering their self-interest. There are three reasons for the difficulty that native rulers face in securing justice. First, the laws are not entirely virtuous or in accordance with our customs. Second, the officials who implement these laws are either corrupt or inefficient; there are learned or effective men among them, but they are few in number. Third, even if we were to discount the evil among our rulers and their advisors, even the good ones do not have either the desire or the ability to remain abreast with the changing tides of time. We have no alternative but to bear the burden of the foreigner's self-interest. But these three factors can be ameliorated provided we are true to ourselves and our identity. Maharaj, it is impossible for all rulers to cultivate your attitude of non-possession, your generosity and self-control. It is not a small matter to deal with the kicks of our neighbours with equanimity. Hence, other rulers are unlikely to immediately acquire the ability to deal with these factors. The type of education that is being given to Maniraj ought to become common in all our royal households; only then they will acquire the ability to deal with difficult times. The path that you have adopted can become an infallible weapon, like the arrow of Ram, in the hands of noble rulers. No one can deny that. But Maharaj, there was only one Ram capable of wielding that infallible weapon!'

Mallaraj gave a patient hearing to the discourse of this young man.

Two or three years passed. A new chapter opened, and the nature of British adjudication changed. Disputes among the rulers were adjudicated by the British. This arrangement was tolerable, but there arose disputes between rulers and their subjects, which also went to the English courts. This unprecedented situation was not envisaged in the treaties between native rulers and the British. The native rulers had not imagined such an erosion of their authority even in their worst nightmares. They were for long years embroiled in disputes with each other, neglecting the welfare of their people. In the golden days, the kings ruled by their sword. They were always battle ready. They had no inclination to think of the welfare of their subjects. Kshatriya warriors were constantly at war with each other. They also tortured the people. Rulers lacked the courage to place limits on them. Inevitably, the people were crushed, just as trees fall when two elephants fight. But when subjected to torture, even the meekest of animals attack, cowards find courage and the foolish begin to find their intellect. By the same logic when subjected to injustice, the smouldering embers of discontent would suddenly turn into fire. Meek but clever banias would harass the rulers by going on strike and shake up the Rajputs, who were clueless about the world of business. The guild of traders was capable of shaking up the very foundation of the royal households. Similarly, the brahmins had cultivated the art of interfering in the royal household from a distance—much like causing the water to ripple by blowing air onto it through a pipe—by their hold over royal women, and it would create quite a storm that would blur the sight of men and women alike. In all castes and communities, from the highest to the lowest, from those doing customary manual work to those engaged in trade, in narrow streets, in large neighbourhoods, on the streets of brahmins, at the dharamshalas of banias, at the town squares of the Patels, in the otalas of the elderly, at the ponds and wells frequented by women, at the shops of petty traders, inside the barracks of soldiers and the huts of the lower class, everywhere the discontent of the people would simmer and the deafening noise of their combined whispers would rob the rulers of their sleep, as if the discontented held the garment of the goddess of sleep to prevent her from entering the royal households. But when rulers continued to remain indifferent to the pleading, pleasing and the treachery of their subjects, people would rise up in open rebellion and shake up the thrones of their rulers. At such times, to appease the rebellious subjects, rulers and their ferocious henchmen would dance to the tunes of their subjects like Mahadev before Chandi. In the early days of the British Empire the English gave a blanket assurance to the rulers, which turned the subject population effete, and the rulers and their cruel henchmen danced like ghosts over the fragile and withered bodies of the people. Some compassionate English officials were moved by the plight of the people. They realised that their protective treaties with the rulers had rendered the people powerless, and that the English were responsible for their plight. They felt that it was their duty to empower the people. Other selfish and power-hungry officials used this compassion to further their interests by robbing the rulers of their already frayed and withered authority. Selfishness and compassion became strange companions. The combined intellect of the good and the bad Englishman worked towards the same purpose. The question of means and ends was set aside, the only consideration being the efficacy of the means. The kings were like the slavish Pandavas, unable to fight Duryodhana having lost their all in the game of dice. The Political Agent played the role of Dushasana and robbed the royal authority of all vestiges of prestige. Like the Pandavas, the kings watched in silence. The English brazenly disregarded the sensibility of the mute elders just like Duryodhana who, disregarding the presence of Bhishma, Drona and Vidur, had invited Draupadi to sit on his thigh. The English invited the royal authority to sit on their lap and, like Duryodhana, said 'disrobe her'. The enfeebled royal authority did not possess enough life to say 'God, help the helpless.'

Mallaraj discussed this sorry state of affairs with Vidya Chatura and Jarashankar. 'It is the same country and the same lessons, but the times are not the same. The Pandavas were deserving of Panchali, but our kings are undeserving of royal authority. Jarashankar, when an Indra devoid of merit falls on earth from the heavens, Indrani accepts the new Indra as her new husband. Royal authority is like Indrani; it does not stay with an undeserving master. Royal authority is wedded to the virtue of the ruler. A king who tortures his subjects is no king. The moment the stench of the king's debauchery reaches the nostrils of royal authority, it deserts the king. If the English are more deserving, royal authority will come to them. On close and dispassionate examination, I for one certainly do not see this as inappropriate.'

Hitherto, Ratnanagari had remained untouched by raging fire, but a sudden gust of wind changed that, and the fire reached Mallaraj's palace. The state officials emerged from hibernation and stood up to face the challenge with all senses alert. Kumar Maniraj was in the direct line of succession to the throne. In the event of his death, Samant and then Mulu were second and third in line for the throne. It was customary in Ratnanagari that all potential heirs to the throne were trained to acquire the fitness to rule. Samant was trained by Nagraj in statecraft. It was with similar intent that Mallaraj had sent Mulu with Jarashankar on a political mission. At the same time care was taken that the direct heirs and the secondary heirs did not develop close proximity. This was done to ensure the personal safety of the direct heir and to curb jealousy or greed that the secondary heirs might develop. Yet, cordial and affectionate relations among the heirs were necessary for the welfare of the state. In times of peace the heirs were usually brought together to foster this. But Mulu Bha was discontented. The perceived insult of his father further fuelled his displeasure. He became unreasonable and impatient. He regarded Mallaraj as an enemy and interpreted Mallaraj's respect for him as a sign of appeasement by the weak. He thought of Maniraj as an effete, lustreless and stupid child. He rued Ratnanagari's fate in the hands of Maniraj. A thought took root in his mind that ultimately, it was Vidya Chatura who would wield authority. Such thoughts possessed his excited mind, but he lacked the courage to express them before his father who was a loyalist. Sometimes he spoke his mind to his mother, and received encouragement. One day, at a moment he felt was opportune, Mulu spoke to his father, albeit with hesitation. Samant instantly realised that a gun was being pointed at his master and he leapt up just as a ferociously loyal dog protects his master. Mulu grew sad and disheartened. Shunned at home, he sought solace and support outside. During his travels with Jarashankar, Mulu sought the friendship of Rana Khachar. He kept in touch with Khachar, and their friendship deepened. He passed on state secrets to Khachar, who found in Mulu a willing instrument of his machinations. Anonymous letters maligning Ratnanagari were sent to Fox Sahib, the Political Agent. A letter was sent to him, suggesting that Mallaraj's attempts to resolve disputes with other rulers were a clear sign of disrespect to the English. But a king has four eyes; before long Mallaraj became aware of these machinations. He remained calm and appeared indifferent, pretending to be a mere spectator in this affair. Both Mulu and Fox Sahib believed that their secret was intact. Jarashankar and Samant had secured an understanding with all the neighbouring rulers except Rana Khachar. Fox Sahib began an inquisitorial correspondence with Mallaraj; the response sent by Jarashankar proved ineffective. Fox Sahib insisted that all disputes between Mallaraj and Khachar be resolved immediately. Mallaraj had not shared his knowledge of Mulu's treachery with anyone, not even with Jarashankar who suspected Samant for the present trouble. Samant was aware of this suspicion, but did not make any attempts to correct Jarashankar's impression.

Before long, Fox Sahib, Mulu Bha and Rana Khachar became allies; they corresponded in secret code.

One day, Samant intercepted a letter from Fox Sahib to Mulu. This was Samant's opportunity to clear any suspicions regarding his loyalty. He took the letter to Mallaraj. The letter stated that Mallaraj was an enemy of the English Queen's representative, and that his attempt to forge a treaty with Rana Khachar was a part of this treachery. Mulu was asked to bear witness and provide evidence of Mallaraj's disloyalty. Samant wept as he placed this letter before Mallaraj. 'Maharaj, a traitor lives in my family. He is as destructive as fire. He has no right to live. Order his execution, and if there is any hesitation, allow me to bring you his head. Never before has Ratnanagari produced such a degenerate son.' Samant shook with anger and sorrow as he spoke, his eyes bloodshot.

Jarashankar said, 'Samant Bha is an epitome of loyalty. Loneliness in old age is not the reward for such loyalty. We cannot punish Mulu Bha on the basis of mere suspicion alone.'

Mallaraj smiled and said to Jarashankar, 'Explain to Samant the meaning of that verse cited by Vidya Chatura.'

Jarashankar recited:

> The elephants, whose temples are soiled with rut, are heard (to have run away) to the end of the quarters; the female elephants are an object of pity; while the deer are indeed not a footing of equality. Where should then this lord of the beasts exhibit the sharpness of his nails, the ends of which are incomparable.[1]

'The verse says that in the distant horizon where the earth and the sky meet, mighty elephants roar, flanked by the female of the species, and grazing deer idle. But who is there to equal the lion, and whom should he test his might against?

'Only Maharaj knows why he asked me to recount this verse to you, Samant Bha, but we have been reduced to little worms in the face of your fierce loyalty and the readiness to sacrifice your son. Mulu

[1] B. G. Bal, trans. *Bhaminivilasa of Pandit Jagannatha* (Bombay: Gopal Narayen and Co., 1895), 1.

Bha will also grow up to be a pillar of this state one day—this is a brahmin's blessing. Many Jarashankars will come and go, but only the house of Samant Mulu will gift loyal, lion-like men to the state.'

Samant paid scant attention to Jarashankar. His eyes were fixed on Mallaraj. No one spoke for a while. Then Samant broke the silence, 'Maharaj, I am not here to hear my praise. You have to give your assent to my request.'

Mallaraj: 'My response was that verse.'

Samant: 'I do not understand verses. Give me a straight response.'

Mallaraj: 'You will understand my response only if you comprehend that verse.'

Samant: 'It is your right to demand that I understand that verse.'

Mallaraj (laughing): 'You shall not be able to bring yourself to say, "Maharaj, please explain." I want you to comprehend it. In our times, the subject people are as helpless as the forest deer; to oppress them even more is like a man showing his might to a woman. Let other kings hunt female elephants; theirs is not the hunt of the brave. The English are like the mighty roaring elephants. Brave are those who match them in strength. Maharaja Nagraj showed them that the men of Ratnanagari were truly brave. We have to care for our meek subjects. Hunting deer is an act of cowardice, and that is what you ask of me. Do you have a response?'

Stunned, Samant stared at his master, at a loss for words. Then he said, 'Yes, we must protect our subjects, but that does not mean we should allow them to overpower us! Maharaj, if you make such norms, you will soon have to give up your throne and become a mendicant.'

Mallaraj smiled. 'What is wrong if a kshatriya king becomes a mendicant for the sake of his subjects?'

Samant: 'Maharaj forgive me, but I cannot see how this will secure the welfare of your subjects. This is your generosity, but generosity is often a foolish way of seeking popularity among subjects. Your generosity might turn the people brazen and instead of securing their welfare; it could cut the very branch that supports them.'

Mallaraj: 'Samant, you do not seem to realise that Mulu is not only my subject, he is as much a son to me as is Maniraj.'

Samant: 'If that is true, you ought to give him punishment that is a hundred-fold harsher than what you gave me. Maharaj, you do not want to punish him because you do *not* regard him as your own.'

Mallaraj: 'A father who distances his son so much that the son cannot approach him allows the son to behave as if he is not the son.'

Samant: 'Maharaj, I accept defeat. Then you must punish him wherever he ceases to act as if he is not your own.'

Mallaraj: '*Now* you speak intelligently, Samant, and not driven by rage. A king should not hear advice given in rage, nor should he act in rage or jealousy. Now that your intellect is unclouded by anger, you have acquired the fitness to discuss the matter. Justice is one of the responsibilities of a king. But statecraft occupies a place higher than justice; justice is only one of the instruments of statecraft. The sword of justice must always remain sharp so that subjects do not quarrel. But sometimes in case of conflict this weapon is used, but such use is rarely ever called for. The relationship between a ruler and his subjects is sometimes like that of a man and a woman; in such cases the man should deepen their love and union. At times their relationship is like that of a father and son; in such instances the ruler should deepen the trust between them; childlike subjects should remain in awe of the paternal power of the king. The king should nurture and nourish his subjects like a gardener tends his delicate plants. Infallible means are those which enhance, and not reduce, the power of the king. A king who does not choose means appropriate to the context and acts unreasonably, driven by rage or jealousy, also encourages others to walk the wrong path. Such a king merits hell. Samant, Mulu is intelligent. He has made an error, but we should not believe that he has been doing so for long. We must find a way wherein he is made to realise his mistake and give up the wrong path. Mulu should realise that the promised land contrived by the English and Khachar holds poison and not sugar; they have urged him to swallow poison. Mulu must acquire the discernment to distinguish between sugar and poison, and not seek the latter.'

Samant: 'Maharaj, I do not comprehend this roundabout way of speaking. Please talk to me straight.'

Mallaraj: 'Jarashankar, I have destroyed Samant's defences. It is your responsibility now to find suitable means and satisfy Samant's query.'

Jarashankar was deep in thought for a while as he searched for a way out of the quandary. When he spoke, his words were slow and deliberate; as he spoke his thoughts became clearer. 'Samantraj, the first hurdle in our intended treaty with Rana Khachar is Mulu Bha—this you have showed to us quite clearly. Khachar himself is an obstacle to our treaty. Agent Sahib is the third hurdle. Khachar does not stand to benefit from the delay because the treaty we have proposed is such that he is the sole beneficiary of it; in fact it is we who stand to lose. Khachar would gain both territory and wealth from the proposed treaty, but he shuns them. We have to ask whether this decision is due to his stubborn, unthinking nature. But Khachar is not stubborn, nor does he happen to be insistent. It is likely that he views our accommodative stance with suspicion. It is equally likely that the Agent has promised him something and that his actions are driven by greed. It is also likely that Khachar and Mulu Bha, being of the same age, are close friends and wish to use this friendship for mutual gain. These are the probable reasons for his conduct. Samantraj, I believe that you have forgiven me; but Mulu Bha still harbours a feeling of deep hurt and resentment. You know and are well capable of recognising that I as a minister had no role to play in the decision that Maharaj took in your case. However, it is but natural for young Mulu Bha to think otherwise. In such a state of mind, he will not take kindly to your loyalty to Maharaj. Hence, my first advice to you is that he should have no inkling whatsoever of our alliance.'

Samant bit his lips and said, 'What else?'

Jarashankar: 'You must become a close friend of Mulu Bha; he must come to trust you to the extent that he opens his heart to you. You have to ensure that he trusts you enough to reveal the machinations of the Agent and Khachar without any fear. Eventually, even Khachar should come to trust you. Samant Bha, an enemy's enemy is a friend—use this maxim and seek entry into their camp. Use Mulu Bha, who is clever enough to gain an entry into Khachar's house. We should not punish Mulu Bha but use him intelligently to secure the treaty with Khachar.'

As Samant's trust and comprehension grew, he seemed less agitated. He softly said, 'One acts either under duress, or with a hope for future gain. Mulu has nothing to fear as you have resolved not to punish him. What can he hope to gain from this?'

Jarashankar: 'Samantraj, at present, I am the eyes and ears of the Maharaj. But if Mulu Bha secures the treaty, he will take my place for the Maharaj. In the present scenario I occupy a position of prominence; but the future scenario erases me and paints Mulu Bha in bright, resplendent colours. This aspiration will be enough for him to trust you. Samantraj, for Mulu Bha friendship with Khachar is a means to acquire power in the state. Show him the way to power. Mulu Bha's tender heart is possessed by a ghost; he must be freed from this possession. With the intent of removing me from power, you, Mulu Bha, Khachar and ultimately the Maharaj should form an alliance and secure the treaty.'

Samant: 'What about the Agent? Eventually both Khachar and Mulu will remain dissatisfied and retaliate with even greater force. We will be back to the same quandary but with fewer options. Have you considered that?'

Jarashankar: 'Once we come together with Khachar, the Agent will be isolated. We will have a letter bearing his name, which may be true or may not be true. If it turns out that it is not the Agent's letter, any accusation from us will make us more vulnerable. He will have many instruments and occasions to cause us harm. Even if he is the author of this letter, he is not likely to admit it. His superiors will hold that he was right, and we were wrong. So he will not be hurt at all; it will be held that he is not the author of the letter. He will accuse us of disloyalty. If we accuse the Agent, we will have to fight a strong enemy openly and approach his seniors for justice. If we win, we get nothing but if we lose, we lose it all. If God has willed that we should take that course and go to war with the British, then so be it. But we should not bring it upon ourselves; it will be like cutting our own feet. And even if we were to succeed, what guarantee do we have that the new Agent will be any better than the present one? How can we be certain that the new official will not take revenge for his countrymen? If the new Agent were to start fresh proceedings against us, we will have to go in for an appeal. The superiors will come to believe that we complain habitually. Our situation is like that of the daughter-in-law who is blamed for all ills in the family of her in-laws. Samantraj, if Khachar can strike a deal with the Agent and we cannot, it is our inability. The best way out for us is to keep the matter of the letter a secret. At present, the Agent thinks that we are without any support, but once Khachar and we become allies, he will hesitate to strike at us. From being an arbitrator of the treaty, he will be reduced to being a mere registrar of it. This course will moderate animosity.'

Mallaraj: 'Samant, are you capable of this?'

Samant: 'I will learn and become capable of all that the Maharaj commands. I am not bothered about the Agent. But if that son of mine turns to devastation, I will have to raise this question once again. What about that? Maharaj, even a sage like Kashyap had a son like Hiranyakashyapu. My state is similar. Statecraft demands that an enemy be nipped in the bud. It would be stupid to let the enemy become powerful and then seek his destruction. Maharaj, I deserved the punishment you gave me for having insulted the minister. God is my witness that I harbour no other thought. That punishment saved me from grave fault. If I fail to express my gratitude to you for showing me the true nature of royal duty, it would be said that I did not deserve to be born in our glorious Suryavanshi family. Maharaj, I swear that I did not once grudge Jarashankar. If you and Jarashankar have truly forgiven me, allow me like Bharat of our glorious sun lineage, who abandoned his mother Kaikeyi, to both abandon and destroy the evil son born to me. Like Bharat who submitted to Shri Ram, I fall at your feet and swear that my conscience is pure.'

Just as a great storm subsides and surrenders to the lofty mountain, the powerfully built warrior fell at Mallaraj's feet, his head touching them. Samant's eyes rained tears and the lament of his saddened heart could be heard. Jarashankar was stunned; he stood petrified. Mallaraj melted. He bent down to raise his old friend and loyal Bhayat. At that moment, a song wafted in from Mena Rani's quarters.

My lord, you are the jewel in Samant's crown
Manidhar, stay forever compassionate
Helpless Mena begs of you

Mallaraj raised his brother and embraced him. Jarashankar watched the great warriors in tight embrace. His lips expressed what his heart felt, 'Maharaj, we pitiable brahmins can never rise up to such loyalty. Maharaj, today the son of this loyal friend has raised his head against you, but one day he shall fall at your feet with equal loyalty. The fruit of such seed can never be sour. Maharaj, do not forsake such men from your midst for the sake of this poor brahmin. Ministers will come and go, but such loyal, pure-blooded friends will come rarely.'

Mallaraj released Samant from his embrace. The three of them sat down. 'Samant, the duty of the king is so complex and unfathomable that he is often required to perform tasks repugnant to his conscience. The punishment that I awarded you was one such task.'

Samant interrupted the king and said, 'Maharaj, let us drop that matter. You must however decide upon my request.'

Mallaraj: 'Samant, you will not rest easy till I punish my child Mulu. But listen, he needs to be given a chance to reform himself. If God willed that he should have treacherous thoughts, the same God will also fill him with good sense. The fiery ordeal of today will allow him to cherish the cool shade of tomorrow. He will repent and that will be his punishment; you will know from your own experience that such repentance is in no way less than any punishment that I might award. And yet if Mulu fails to reform and constitutes himself to be an enemy of the state, we will use all our might to crush him.'

Samant: 'Maharaj, I cannot fathom your statecraft. I have come to believe that since you punished me, you hesitate to punish Mulu.'

Mallaraj: 'We have decided to use Mulu against his wish as a means of securing a treaty with Khachar, and in emerging victorious against the machinations of the Agent. But if Mulu remains treacherous even after we secure our goals, that will be his defeat and for a treacherous man, defeat is a punishment in itself.'

Samant: 'What then?'

Mallaraj: 'If any other punishment is required, I will have Samant punish Mulu.'

Samant: 'Is that certain?'

Mallaraj: 'Has Mallaraj ever been untrue to his words?'

Samant: 'Maharaj, consider your wish as good as fulfilled.'

Samant took his leave. Mallaraj said to Jarashankar, 'Some days ago Fox Sahib was my guest, and we went hunting in our forest. We spoke about a lot of things, but we could not bring up this matter. I knew that he wanted to raise this issue.'

Jarashankar: 'Maharaj, the power of your virtue is such that the evil-minded turns cowardly and retreats. Evil becomes powerless when faced with a great soul who combines virtue with valour. Let me remind you of a verse which I once told you. A king, while entering a forest inhabited by sages, said: "This forest has a quiet beauty but my heart treads softly." Even ferocious animals like lions and tigers turn tail when faced with a brave man who looks them in the eye. Why would a clever but evil Englishman not hesitate before expressing impure thoughts to you? If an Englishman ever succeeds in expressing lowly thoughts before a king, know that to be a measure of the withered authority and virtue of the king, and not a measure of the Englishman's character.'

Jarashankar took leave of Mallaraj. Samant accomplished the assigned task with faith and acumen. Days passed. Months went by. Samant gained Mulu's trust. Khachar and his associates submitted to the will of the ruler of Ratnanagari. The treaty with Khachar was signed. The Political Agent stood witness to the treaty and the British government confirmed it. All four boundaries of Mallaraj's kingdom came to be definitively demarcated. Young Mulu believed that all credit was due to him; even Khachar was no match for him. In this game of chaupat, there were four players: the Agent, Khachar, Mulu and Mallaraj. Mallaraj was the only player who secured all the houses. Mulu became proud of his success. The fall of the minister seemed imminent to him. He reckoned that he had earned the right to seek reward from Mallaraj and his father.

Samant's fears about Mulu seemed to be coming true. Mallaraj was keen to satisfy all of Mulu's aspirations. He was willing to shower all possible generosity over Mulu. But his desire and resolve to protect his minister were even greater. Samant had personal experience of this policy. He had come to regard both his personal banishment and the policy behind it as beneficial to the state. Mallaraj wanted his rule to benefit his Bhayat. He believed this was good for the state. At the same time he recognised that unchecked aspirations of his Bhayat would spell the demise of the authority of the state officials. Just as Ganga and Yamuna originate from the same source, the power of the Bhayat and the authority of the officials emanate from the same source—the person of the ruler. Yamuna merges in the Ganga and finds the sea. Similarly, the power of the Bhayat can be harnessed for the state only by the sagacity and authority of the officials. Therefore, Mallaraj remained alert that the unchecked, inebriated power of his Bhayat did not act to circumscribe the authority of his minister. Even if he so much as suspected his Bhayat of transgression, he came down on them like a lion on its prey. Samant, at one point, viewed this policy as detrimental, but with time and maturity he came to regard the policy as necessary and beneficial. Samant now wanted Mallaraj to use all possible force to curb his son, Mulu.

Mulu had proved himself useful to the king. The king made every possible effort to satisfy Mulu's aspirations. But a person consumed by the fire of animosity remains discontent even when all his aspirations are satisfied. While Samant had overcome his resentment about being punished and the resultant rage and had proved to be an example of loyalty, his son could not forgive Jarashankar for the same act. In his devotion to his father, Mulu destroyed all traces of loyalty towards the state that he might have felt. His statecraft was consumed by loathing. He had hoped that the treaty with Khachar would spell the doom of the powers of the brahmin minister, but his hopes were dashed. All other desires became insignificant compared to the desire to defeat Jarashankar, which possessed him. As Mulu failed even in this mission, frustrated rage took hold of him. Rage leads one to act indiscriminately in every sphere and it sullies every action. An enraged person is incapable of distinction; wrath destroys everything that it touches. Chandika in her rage danced on the body of Shiva. Mulu's anger towards Jarashankar inevitably turned into rage against Mallaraj. If Mallaraj does not get rid of the minister, why should one not get rid of Mallaraj, he asked himself. But this was not feasible in Ratnanagari. Mulu could not take such an issue to the Agent. Hence, he decided to finish off the minister rather than wait for his authority to be eclipsed.

Like a dog that sniffs its way around, Mulu sniffed around for some weakness of the minister. His search failed. Instead, he decided to cultivate a friendship with Jarashankar. Gradually, he gained entry into the house of Jarashankar and Vidya Chatura. Jarashankar, who had a measure of Mulu's mind, was not deceived. Their relationship did not grow beyond formal cordiality. Jarashankar, experienced as he was in palace politics, remained undeceived; but inexperienced Vidya Chatura accepted the offer of friendship from the king's nephew. This was enough of an opening for Mulu, who made his move with the dexterity of a warrior. Jarashankar warned Vidya Chatura, but Vidya Chatura, educated in English ways, did not agree with him. He could not distance Mulu completely.

Thus, Mulu retained some foothold in Vidya Chatura's house. His father, Manchatura, disliked Mulu and each time Mulu came visiting, Manchatura remained alert like a tiger. One day Manchatura was not at home. Mulu seized the opportunity and went to Vidya Chatura's house. All the servants were busy. Sundargauri was at the neighbour's house. Vidya Chatura had not yet come home. In the guise of playing with Kumud, Mulu sought Gunasundari's company. Gunasundari was quick to suspect Mulu's intentions. She trembled with fear but swiftly ran to the inner chambers and shut the door. She was concerned about little Kumud but reassured herself that it was more important to save herself and her family from ignominy. She left her daughter and the house to the care of the gods. Before long, Gunasundari regained her composure but still thought it prudent to stay behind closed doors. She peeped through an opening; Mulu, on the pretext of handing over Kumud to her mother, had entered the house and was looking around. Just then, Manchatura returned. He was quick to grasp the situation and he could imagine Gunasundari's state. He took Kumud in his arms and, in his brief exchange with Mulu, ensured that such a situation would never again arise in the future. Manchatura said, 'Mulu Bha, you are a scion of the royal household. When you visit our poor home, it creates complications and people get a chance to talk ill about you. Hence, all that you need to do is to send a message, and Vidya Chatura will present himself before you. In any case you will find him at the palace daily. Therefore, you should not trouble yourself by coming here. It is in the fitness of things that Vidya Chatura should come and visit you. You are a wise man, Mulu Bha. If you were to ask Samant Bha, his advice to you would be the same.'

Mulu's guilty conscience enabled him to understand the true import of this statement. Mulu lacked the courage to give a retort to the elderly but robust Manchatura. He looked down, mumbled, 'That is true,' and left. Manchatura called out to Gunasundari. His words were clearly audible to the retreating Mulu. He said, 'Gunasundari, the evil one has left. From tomorrow onwards, appoint Arab guards to protect you so that such an evil incident does not recur.'

Gunasundari came out and said meekly to her father-in-law, 'Pitaji, I have told you more than once that the custom of a joint family is good. In a joint family, such difficulties do not arise. When Mataji, my sisters-in-law, brother-in-law and his family all lived here, no stranger, no matter how powerful or evil, ever had the courage to so much as peep inside our house. I do not know what wrong I have done that you have to go and live in Manoharpuri every now and then.'

Manchatura laughed and said, 'Then we will appoint Arab guards, won't we? Those who learn English must live like the English in separate households.'

Gunasundari sat down, and somewhat dejectedly said, 'You are our elder, Pitaji, and can say what you like. But God is my witness.

A mere blow of air from the mouth of an Englishman is enough to destroy a mountain. Even kings tremble in their presence. English madams can live in forests all by themselves, and our men will be afraid to even glance at them. If, like them, we, too, kept an open house, every passerby and even dogs would want to enter. When our families disperse, we lose our protection. Elders like you are our fortification, and when these forts are breached, women like me and all else that is precious in our households will be robbed in broad daylight.'

'Gunasundari, I provoked you because I wanted to hear these words from you. You speak like wizened elders. But these days, young people sing to a different tune in which the elderly cannot join in. You will find your words falling on deaf ears. In our household, I am the elder and all of you are the young ones. It is good that our household has remained untouched by new-fangled notions. But who can foretell the future? Do we know even the present? Therefore, we will have Arab guards. And I am of course around as long as there is life in me.' Manchatura changed the subject and made Gunasundari feel lighter.

Angered by his failure, Mulu walked towards his pleasure garden outside the city. Gunasundari had proved smarter than him. He had to swallow Manchatura's insult; he felt humiliated. He was also afraid that now Vidya Chatura, Jarashankar and the Maharaj would come to know of his misadventures. As he walked on dejectedly, he passed by a market. People had gathered around a brahmin, who entertained them with a song. Hoping to lighten his heavy heart, Mulu joined the crowd.

She whom the world calls 'helpless' makes
A man dance to her tunes,
Compels even one born of a queen
To stand as her water-bearer
Such are the scenes of this Kalyug.
She draws the debauched even deeper,
Drowns the very scriptures of the priests,
Entices the most accomplished yogis,
Blindfolds the wise—
Even the sages and seers have succumbed to her spell:

The woman's sinful body ensnares them all
Such is the blazing Kalyug.
All the Satis have descended into the netherworld
The debauched have become the high-priestesses;
Their gaze entraps all those
Who come into their line of vision;
The brahmin's verses have become their charms,
The Rajput's weapons, their toys.

Someone went up to the brahmin and asked, 'Is your woman like the one you described?' There ensued a scuffle. Young lads tossed around the brahmin's headgear. Mulu got the brahmin out of the melee, and he went on his way, the words of the song still ringing in his ears. '*She ... Compels even one born of a queen to stand as her water-bearer ... The Rajput's weapons, their toys*.' This is so true! No! No! There *are* pure unsullied women. It is we the Rajputs who have become debauched. Mulu's excitement ebbed. He reasoned: There can't be anyone as stupid as me. I went the wrong way. War can only be among equals. This Jarashankar and Vidya Chatura—mere brahmins! Ministers are after all servants of the king. I harboured animosity against the lowly, and I was driven to low means. What would I have gained even if I had succeeded? I failed, and lost face. One must fight an equal.

Mulu walked on, deep in thought. A new plot came to his mind. Excited, he twirled his moustache and said to himself: A Rajput is one who breaks norms given by the brahmins. My grandfather was two years younger to Nagraj, and he was for that reason denied the kingdom. Such are the rules of the devious brahmins! But I, his grandson, have the capacity to make the living join the dead. The day this effete Maniraj dies, Mulu will be crowned king! All he needs is one blow of my sword. Why should this Rajput not act like one? Why deal with the brahmin? Whom should a Rajput fear? The man who deserves to be king shall be crowned king!

This calamitous thought that came to him at an inauspicious moment took possession of Mulu. He was caught in a whirlwind. Maniraj was now an adolescent, and was being trained to hunt in the large forests of Ratnanagari. Scions of royal households accompanied him on the hunt. Mulu decided to take advantage of such an expedition. Samant had become a confidante of his son. Before long, he became aware of Mulu's machinations. Samant had Mulu seized, placed him under arrest and put guards to watch over Mulu. Samant was not in the least surprised by the evil designs of his son. He now understood Mallaraj's reluctance to punish Mulu. He knew that Mulu had a short time to live; he wanted the enemy of his king dead. Samant was delighted that Maniraj was unharmed and safe forever. He felt proud that his forecast had come true. This Rajput father felt no remorse or sadness at the certain death of his son. He set forth for the palace, resplendent as the noon sun, to hold the king to his promise. Samant lodged a complaint against Mulu, accusing him of plotting to kill the prince and heir apparent. Mallaraj gave him a patient hearing. Samant demanded death for Mulu. Mallaraj promised to consider the request.

Samant said, 'What is the need to deliberate in a matter as clear as this? What could be a greater crime? You must remain true to your promise, Maharaj.'

Mallaraj considered the matter and ordered Jarashankar, 'Both Samant and you are aware of the resolution under which such matters are to be placed before a tribunal of the Bhayat. Read the resolution again and appoint a tribunal as per its terms. That tribunal will decide the charges against Mulu.'

Samant: 'Does that mean that you will not sit on judgement? The resolution does not cover criminal offences.'

Mallaraj: 'Read the resolution carefully. It clearly states that in case of any dispute with the state, the tribunal should be constituted. It is incorrect for me to sit on judgement in any matter that involves Maniraj. If you want my justice, withdraw your complaint and set Mulu free.'

Samant: 'He will be released only in the next life. You are bound by your pledge to me.'

Mallaraj: 'In that case, the tribunal, to which you and other Bhayat have committed to, will adjudicate the matter.'

Samant: 'Maharaj, in that case, the tribunal will also award punishment. I am entitled to be a member of that tribunal.'

Mallaraj: 'You are not impartial, Samant. You are the complainant. You are not fit to sit on judgement.'

Samant: 'I am also the father of the accused. Maharaj, the other Bhayat will be torn between conflicting loyalties and will not award punishment that is deserved. As per your promise, I am entitled to be on that tribunal, failing which it will be a breach of your promise.'

Jarashankar: 'Maharaj, it is for such reasons that I had said that such a resolution should require the consent of the minister.'

Mallaraj: 'You brahmins are wise in the hindsight; you will not understand such things. Samant, I authorise you to be on that tribunal. I am bound by my promise. But read and act according to the terms of the resolution, so that I am not constrained to appoint another tribunal to review your decision.'

The tribunal was constituted; it held Mulu guilty of the conspiracy to murder Maniraj and awarded him death penalty. The king refused to abide by this extreme punishment. A fresh debate ensued between Samant and Mallaraj. The king asked Mulu, 'Mulu Bha, it was my attempt to satisfy all your desires. But I failed. I take pity on you. For that, I am chided by your father. Have either Maniraj or I done a personal wrong to you?'

Mulu was in shackles. He raised himself to his full height, looked up straight at the king and said, 'Maharaj, but for your treaty with the English, we would not have seen such sorry days. You signed the treaty. You were misguided by this brahmin. If you had stripped him of his powers, I would not have been forced to act as I did. So be it. You proved to be a weakling in moments of political crisis. You are mesmerised by this lowly brahmin, and so long as you do not free yourself from his snare, I consider you undeserving of this throne. I have the courage and the capacity of shouldering the burden that you are incapable of. I chose the path that would give me the responsibility of the state. I have done no wrong. In this world there are many undeserving and ineffective rulers such as you who take the lives of capable men to perpetuate their rule. You can do the same and take my life. I am ready to die.'

Samant was enraged. He got up and hit his fist hard on Mulu's forehead. Blood flowed. The king restrained Samant. Mallaraj said, 'Mulu Bha, your father's anger and punishment must bring back memories of childhood. Hear me out. I am happy that you became my judge before I could judge your conduct. Mulu Bha, you admit to the charges levelled against you, but the veracity of the charges that you place upon me can only be decided by time. You require the maturity that comes with experience to realise this. If I give you death penalty and shorten your life, you would never gain this experience, and I would never have the opportunity to be freed from the charges levelled against me. Given my desire to be freed from those charges, I cannot award you death penalty.'

Samant jumped up and said, 'What? Maharaj, that cannot be! You have to accept the punishment decided by the tribunal of the Bhayat.'

Mallaraj: 'Samant, be patient. We will give you the opportunity to be heard. Mulu Bha, no one in your family has been as depraved as you. This is a sign of our times. One day you will acquire the fitness to be a member of our family, and till such time, I do not have the right to take your life. Only a criminal who cannot be reformed deserves death penalty. I have not yet given up hope. Hence, you do not deserve to die. Mulu Bha, you have insulted this throne, and for that reason you are a criminal in the eyes of God. But I cannot say that this throne will never need someone like you. And it is my duty to see to it that you have a long life only for such an eventuality. Mulu Bha, you were intent on taking Maniraj's life. Someday, Maniraj will occupy this throne, and at that time he may decide to pardon you. I hope he will have the generosity to forgive you, and I do not wish to forsake that hope by taking your life. Therefore, Samant, Mulu will be placed in your custody today. Tomorrow, we shall decide on his punishment in a way that respects the decision of the tribunal, and also my hope.'

Samant put Mulu into the prison and returned to be with the king. Mallaraj, Jarashankar and Samant sat together to reflect on the fate of the royal household.

Mallaraj: 'Jarashankar, you heard the judgement of the Bhayat. They are authorised to adjudicate on the crime but cannot award punishment. I felt that their decision was extreme and so I gave a punishment that he deserves. It is your responsibility to think of ways of executing that punishment.

Samant: 'Do I have the right to know the reasons underlying your decision?'

Mallaraj: 'Of course. The reason is the same as what I told Mulu.'

Samant: 'But I am not satisfied. Such generosity towards an enemy is stupidity. This snake does not deserve to be cared for and raised. He will become a baharvatiya—he will form a band of outlaws and evil-doers from among our people, our Bhayat and the English; he will foster many enemies of the state. Maharaj, I clearly say that Mulu does not deserve to live. Death is the least punishment for those who seek to poison the state.'

Mallaraj: 'You should recall that it was because of the threat of English presence that we decided that Bhayat should sit in judgement over other Bhayat.'

Samant: 'Yes.'

Mallaraj: 'We gave juridical powers to the Bhayat in order to fortify our state even further.'

Samant: 'Yes.'

Mallaraj: 'The English might use some of the Bhayat to attack us, and at that time our Bhayat should have the strength to defend the state. This arrangement was made with the consent of the Bhayat.'

Samant: 'That is true.'

Mallaraj: 'The English and Mulu may use their combined strength to attack the state; this would also show up our weakness, and when that happens, you, Samant, will be authorised to use every possible force to meet with such a challenge.'

Samant: 'All that is there. But I do not like this way of inviting the axe to chop our feet.'

Mallaraj: 'The present arrangement will save our feet from being chopped. Think of a time when neither you, nor I, nor even Maniraj are alive. At that time, the man we consider the enemy of our state will become its master and protector. If we were to finish him off now, we would have acted as enemies of the state.'

After long deliberation, the validity of Mallaraj's decision was accepted by the other two. It was decided that Mulu be banished from the state and be allowed to live in exile in a place of his choosing; he was to be provided with enough resources to meet his needs. It was also decided that after Samant's death, his garas would vest in the state. If Mulu were to run away from his place of exile or act against the interests of Ratnanagari, his annuity would be stopped. If he were to enter the territory of Ratnanagari, he would be arrested and imprisoned for life. Maniraj was authorised to commute any part of this sentence, or pardon Mulu altogether. Mulu wanted to live in exile in Rana Khachar's state. His wish was granted. The tribunal of the Bhayat signed the document.

Mulu was banished from the state, but he left behind many burning issues. The Agent was informed of this banishment; he wrote a letter to Mallaraj, seeking information. Samant was quick to accuse Mulu of conspiring through the Agent. In response, Ratnanagari asked the Agent as to who had initiated this inquiry, for what reason and under what authority.

The Agent responded, 'It is the office of the Political Agent that wishes to be informed of the events. If the information about Mulu's banishment is correct, it is likely that he would become an outlaw. This would threaten the peace and security of the country. It is in this exercise of the sovereign powers vested in the British government that this information is sought. In matters of peace and security of the country, the interests of the native rulers, subjects and the sovereign power are one.' In conclusion, the Agent made a personal appeal to Mallaraj, saying, 'I regard you as a friend, and as a friend, I urge you that a virtuous king like you should have no hesitation in accepting the power of the British government. If you were to defy this power, it would needlessly sow the seeds of suspicion. I do wish to inform you that the British government has the power to seek compliance of its desire.'

Mallaraj was enraged by this letter. 'Initially, the Agent assumed the powers of arbitration. Now he wants to police the state. Jarashankar, this is the outcome of your statecraft.'

Jarashankar, keen to observe Samant's reaction, looked towards him. Samant realised this. He spoke not impatiently but in a grave tone, 'Maharaj, if this is the outcome of the minister's statecraft, its resolution also lies within it.'

'Samant, have you jumped from the king's chariot to that of the minister? Am I awake or in sleep? Is this *you*?' Mallaraj spoke with genuine surprise.

Samant smiled and said, 'Maharaj, how can I say that you were asleep? Earlier, whenever issues of statecraft were discussed, the two of us were on the same side as brothers. But eventually you would go across to the brahmin's way of thinking, and I would be left holding on to the earlier opinion. I have learnt from my experience. I have decided to join the party that you are eventually going to join.'

Mallaraj shook with laughter. 'Samant, the punishment has clearly been beneficial to you. You have to speak your mind. I do not want you to conceal your opinion.'

Samant: 'Maharaj, if I were to speak a lie, either because of fear or for any other reason, I would disqualify myself to be your brother. Maharaj, during the period of banishment, I had the opportunity of quiet reflection. I have become a devout follower of the statecraft of Jarashankar. Therefore, I have the courage today to defend his statecraft against the charge that you place on it.'

Mallaraj: 'How so?'

Samant: 'Maharaj, the minister has given us the broad contours of the policy of our times. The British government is in the mood of feasting at our expense; it will have many desires. It will insist that some of these be satisfied whether they are just or unjust. It will use force or persuasion to secure our compliance. We cannot engage them in battle. We can only carry on a war of words, which will cause ripples in quiet waters. We will have to oppose a force far superior to us; each time we oppose them, we are likely to lose and we will come to be regarded as an enemy. We would decline and eventually, we will have to give in to their demands. Maharaj, I do not think that we should bring upon ourselves this situation. It is better to abdicate the throne than commit this folly.'

Mallaraj: 'What should we do?'

Samant: 'We should enter into a war of words with the British government only when we think they are ready to accept our point of view; we can decide then either to sweet-talk them in a friendly way, or use some bitter remedy. Whenever the government places a new demand, we should ask ourselves if in the final instance compliance with it is inevitable or negotiable. If the demand is one on which negotiation is possible, we should oppose it. We should not resist inevitable demands; we should comply with such demands as friends, and not be forced into submission as weak opponents. This will earn us their friendship and even their gratitude. Maharaj, those like us who learnt to swim in different waters will not feel comfortable with the new situation. I prefer death to this submission; but Maharaj for kings and kshatriyas, adherence to duty is much greater than personal emotion. It is the royal duty to submit to the demands of the time and seek space for manoeuvre within that.'

Mallaraj, mesmerised by these words, carried on the discussion with Samant, disregarding Jarashankar. 'Samant, your words today have the depth and wisdom of experience that even our minister cannot match; Jarashankar would agree to that. So tell me, what are we to do with this desire of their government to police our homes? The British government might want that when their dogs bark at us, we do not even shoo them away. Would you consider such a demand as inevitable or negotiable?' Mallaraj was so full of anger that his eyes had turned red and his body was bathed in perspiration.

Samant fully sympathised with this kshatriya sentiment. He said, 'Maharaj, you were born to command and rule; you do not know what it is to carry out orders. In former times, the emperor of Delhi or his governor or the Peshwa of Poona or his officials used to lay siege and coerce the rulers to accept their demands. Today, the British government keeps its forces in the barracks and sends out their Political Agent, who is still backed by their military might. Rulers have no means to fight this coercion and must submit to it while retaining whatever autonomous authority they can. You have operated under similar constraints ever since you sat on the saddle.'

'Samant, you are right. I, too, had foreseen this day when we signed the treaty with the British. But clearly, my body and mind have become feeble with age. Both my intellect and authority have withered. Old age has made you wiser, but my mind has become blurred. Jarashankar, so long as Samant was opposed to your views, in order to protect you, I considered it my duty to shoulder the responsibility of the state. You no longer need my protection; Samant is with you, not opposed to you. Maniraj is still a child and cannot shoulder the responsibility of the state. I am old and hence incapable of ruling. From today onwards, you and Samant have to think of the welfare of the state. Leave me to think of God.'

Both Samant and Jarashankar were overcome with emotion but did not allow the tears welling up in their eyes to roll down. No one could speak for a while. Samant wiped his blurred eyes and broke the silence, 'Maharaj, all these years we have lived in the protection of a great banyan tree. We are incapable of providing that kind of shelter to the state. Maharaj, we are fit to obey. You are the soul of this kingdom. Only you can infuse life into this state, not us.'

Mallaraj stood up. He appeared as tall and sturdy as the pillars of the palace. Hitherto, his bearing had the visage of valour and authority; today he seemed detached and unconcerned. Religious quest had replaced royal authority. His gaze seemed to have turned inwards; his ears seemed eager to listen to a hitherto unheard voice. Mallaraj seemed uncertain of the path that awaited him. Samant and Jarashankar also stood up. The minister appeared to have found a way of fulfilling the new aspiration of the king, as also a way of ensuring that he continued to discharge his duties.

Jarashankar: 'Maharaj, if you have decided to withdraw from worldly life and accept Vanaprastha, I am willing to follow you into the forest.

Hitherto, I have advised you on statecraft; henceforth, I shall join you in deliberations on the matters of the soul. But when the hour of death approaches, each one of us is required to perform one final duty: the one about to die must ensure the welfare of the living.'

Mallaraj smiled and said, 'All right. That shall be done. You and Samant think of a solution. I am not about to run away like a truant child. I am open to all kinds of suggestions except one.'

Jarashankar: 'We will think about it and implement it with your consent.'

Mallaraj: 'This means that you will involve me in the final decision. This is not part of the duty of a man ready to meet his maker.'

Jarashankar: 'Only you can decide whether our decision is in accordance with your religious duty.'

Mallaraj: 'Is that so?'

Jarashankar: 'It simply means that you will have to participate in the discussion and decide for yourself as to what constitutes your duty.'

Mallaraj: 'If I have to participate in the discussion and decide regarding my duty, what will the two of you do?'

Jarashankar: 'Maharaj, who are we to decide for you?'

Mallaraj: 'Samant, don't you think our Pradhan is cunning? He got me to agree to his proposal against my wish. Now he persuades me to change my mind without even opposing me!'

Samant: 'Maharaj, it is for this very reason that he is fit to be your minister. There are ministers who plead and please their kings, garner benefits and consider their duty fulfilled. They do not have the interest of the king or of the people at heart. They never speak their mind. Moved by greed for wealth or power, they deceive their master. They tell lies. They have no regards for their masters, whom they consider to be fools. These treacherous ministers are enemies of both the king and the people. Maharaj, such ministers deserve to be thrown into the gutter.'

Mallaraj: 'But even Jarashankar did not speak his mind freely. He took a circuitous route, he deceived me and he finally got me to agree to what he wanted of me.'

Samant: 'That is the correct thing to do. One cannot be brazen and call one's mother as our father's wife. Maharaj, once upon a time I was brazen. The minister spoke the truth in a civil and courteous way. This is a sign of his acumen, and my brazenness was a sign of my stupidity. It is the duty of a minister to speak the truth in an agreeable manner.'

Mallaraj: 'Then he could speak an agreeable lie as well.'

Samant: 'No, the scriptures do not encourage a lie. The scriptural injunction is to speak the truth that is both agreeable and in the interest of the listener—which I interpret to mean a clear disavowal of a lie. It also suggests that a truth that is not in the interest of the listener, or one that is disagreeable, should not be spoken. A minister proves his worth by speaking the truth that is both agreeable and in the interest of the king.'

Mallaraj: 'Jarashankar, is that so?'

Jarashankar: 'Maharaj, when I have a pleader as clever as Samant, why should I complicate matters by speaking for myself?'

Mallaraj: 'Do you think that kings are incapable of hearing the truth?'

Jarashankar: 'Maharaj, you know what your capacity is. Your wrath was unbearable when the functionary of a powerful sovereign asked a question. Would I have the strength to remain steadfast in the face of your wrath? Maharaj, I know my weakness, you know your strength.'

Mallaraj: 'Is it desirable that the king be possessed of such capacity?'

Jarashankar: 'Maharaj, the answer is contingent upon time and context. In the *Shanti Parva* of the *Mahabharata*, Bhishma's counsel to Yudhishthir was that in times to come, kings will be surpassed by their advisors.'

Mallaraj: 'And what is the injunction of our times?'

Jarashankar smiled and said: 'You are determined that I should speak my mind. I cannot go contrary to your wish. Maharaj is well seized of the imperatives of our times. Our context would depend upon whether you are angry, excited or possessed of equanimity as also whether I am moved by selfishness or act out of consideration of your interest. If a king has to deliberate on all such matters, it is burdensome and it can also be dangerous. Hence it is good for both the king and the counsellor to remain steadfast to the advice of Bhishma.'

Mallaraj: 'What should the king do?'

Jarashankar: 'A king must encourage his counsellor to speak the truth that is both agreeable and beneficial; he should be intolerant of untruth and yet not crave for agreeable counsel. He should at the same time not accept brazenness. A king should not tolerate any insult and must punish any transgression immediately. The authority of the king should be such that his counsellors and servants do not deviate from their duty. These qualities are necessary for a king, regardless of whether they be regarded as strength or weakness. Maharaj, I have spoken fearlessly.'

Mallaraj heard his minister attentively and said, 'Jarashankar, you gave us a long discourse, and I shall imbibe these qualities. Tell me, what should we do about the Agent?'

Jarashankar: 'Maharaj, our responsibility is confined to our state. The British have to keep an eye over hundreds of native rulers of India. It is the duty of the sovereign to be seized of all developments, however insignificant, in their territory. They have to observe what tiny kingdoms and petty rulers cannot see. They have to institute processes for a common good and also protect and further their larger interests. It is the duty of the sovereign to be alert, inquisitive and informed. They also have to keep native rulers on their guard. In order to meet with different situations, they will have to assume more powers. We have to ensure that they do not get any opportunity to exercise more power over us. In a given situation, we should, according to Samantraj's advice, decide if the outcome is predetermined or if it can be negotiated to our advantage. We committed a mistake by raising a question on the authority of the Agent. He seized the opportunity and gave a cunning response. We shall not commit such mistakes in the future; we shall also try and undo this harm. A king who has no weakness has nothing to fear from prying eyes.'

Samant: 'Maharaj, let us drop this long-winded discussion. This problem has been created by that wretched son of mine. For me he is dead and I have already performed his last rites. Now our cry announcing his death should be heard by that Agent. Maharaj, Jarashankar is right. Our authority will not be compromised. We should send copies of the tribunal's decision and the final punishment awarded by you, to the Agent. Jarashankar and I will take care of the rest. We must announce that Mulu is dead for us, and if the Agent still wants to be possessed by his ghost, we know how to deal with possessions. For the present, we must announce Mulu's death. Jarashankar, let's go.'

All three men got up. Samant followed Jarashankar. Samant's anger was evident from his demeanour; he bit his lips and clenched his teeth; his hand seemed poised to draw out his dagger, but sheathed it. Mallaraj observed this as he saw his minister and Bhayat walk away.

13 Mallaraj's Retirement and Maniraj's Youthful Reign

The day passed. Night fell. All of a sudden Mena Rani came running, out of breath, to Mallaraj. She apprised him of the latest developments. Samant recognised that Mulu had instigated the Agent to fight his battle, and this was just the beginning of trouble. He feared that both Mallaraj's throne and Maniraj's life were in danger. Samant was also troubled by the anxiety that the Agent had caused Mallaraj; he did not want his ruler to be anxious. He saw his path clearly before him—his evil son had to die. He did not want to wait for any royal decree. He saw no violation of duty if the murder of his son was committed in the territory of another state. For him, the punishment for such a crime was as glorious as death in battle. At eight o' clock that evening, he took five trusted men, fully armed, and set off towards Rana Khachar's state. Mulu's mother got wind of her husband's intentions. The certain prospect of her son's death gave her the courage to approach Mena Rani to seek her intervention. The queen ran to the king and informed him of the developments. The king set out in the dark and caught up with Samant. Samant was angry but powerless before the king. The king took a promise from him that he would not set out on such an adventure without royal command. Samant returned home, but resolved that he would not so much as look at his wife from that day on.

Days turned to months, and months into years. Samant's men kept a watch over Mulu. Mallaraj relied more and more on Samant and Jarashankar, and kept Maniraj by his side. Mallaraj placed more and more responsibilities on Vidya Chatura. Jarashankar retained the title of minister, while Vidya Chatura performed all the duties of the minister. As Vidya Chatura grew in stature, he was made the minister. Maniraj was appointed the crown prince and he performed all royal duties. The king and the former minister kept a distant watch on the new minister and the crown prince, while they spent their days in spiritual quest. Jarashankar became his counsellor even in this quest. They studied the scriptures and drew upon their wisdom gained through statecraft to enlighten their path. They sought the company and guidance of scholars and ascetics. Loss of royal power appears hellish to most people, but for these two it became heaven. The crown prince and his minister also benefited from this wisdom and aspired to have similar experiences at appropriate stages in their lives. While Jarashankar and Mallaraj retired from worldly affairs, Samant had other desires. It was Samant's duty to look after the welfare of the crown prince and the new minister. He knew that Mulu was a constant threat, and that his destruction was the only guarantee of their security. Samant constantly thought of ways to eliminate this enemy. Hitherto, Samant had been unable to eliminate Mulu entirely because of the king's order. He made several attempts to seek Mallaraj's permission, which he never could secure. Mallaraj did not entertain any discussion about eliminating Mulu. This irritated Samant, who could not bring himself to disobey the king.

Mulu also remained disaffected. He kept close watch over Maniraj's movements. Sometimes he roamed the banks of the Subhadra in the company of outlaws; Sursinh of Suvarnapur was his companion. Mulu enjoyed his company and relished the hardships of the life of a baharvatiya. Rana Khachar also instigated and encouraged him. Samant kept himself informed of Mulu's movements and appraised Mallaraj of the developments. Despite the knowledge of Mulu's intentions, Mallaraj refused to order his execution. Samant thought of giving a false sense of security to Mulu. He allowed him to enter and roam within the territory of Ratnanagari without apprehension. Samant's plan was to ambush Mulu and kill him in battle, or at least capture him alive. According to the decree, Mulu was to be given life imprisonment if he violated the code of conduct. However, despite Samant's efforts, Mulu remained free. Khachar supported him, and Mulu's distrust of his father ran deep. Mulu openly associated with Sursinh's band of outlaws. Samant appealed to Mallaraj that the annuity paid to Mulu be discontinued as he had joined the baharvatiyas. Mallaraj laughed off the matter by saying that Mulu would learn to yield weapons and become brave in the company of the baharvatiyas. Mallaraj eventually asked Maniraj to capture Mulu, because Mulu had questioned Maniraj's capacity as a ruler. Samant did not approve of this plan, but he had no choice. Henceforth, he accompanied Maniraj on all his expeditions. This matter did not remain secret from Mulu, who saw this as his chance to eliminate Maniraj. He began to frequent the territories of Ratnanagari and robbed people in open defiance of royal authority. Complaints were also sent to the Political Agent that Mallaraj lacked the capacity to capture the baharvatiyas. The Agency in turn posed questions to Ratnanagari. The problems seemed to multiply for Ratnanagari. The terrain was suitable for the outlaws to operate at will. Jadsinh and Shathrai of Suvarnapur harboured antipathy towards Ratnanagari and gave their support to the enemies of the state. It was not possible for the forces of Ratnanagari to chase the baharvatiyas once they entered British territory.

Meanwhile, Mallaraj took ill. His days seemed numbered. Once again Samant sought permission from the ailing king to kill Mulu in Khachar's state. He was even willing to be hanged by Khachar for his crime. Mallaraj not only refused the request, he obtained a pledge from Samant that he would never ever attempt such a thing. Samant had no choice but to give his word of honour to the ailing ruler. Samant came up another plan. He proposed to give his daughter in marriage to Rana Khachar. In return, he wanted Khachar to hand over Mulu to Ratnanagari. Samant obtained the support of some greedy courtiers of Khachar's court. Khachar accepted the proposal of marriage, but broke his promise subsequently and refused to hand over Mulu. Samant's daughter also took her mother's side. Samant felt cheated.

These failed machinations of Samant amused the ailing Mallaraj. But Samant was not one to accept defeat. He bribed the baharvatiyas and some of Khachar's men. They were willing to lead Mulu into a trap. Mulu had no inkling that a new plan had been hatched. Mulu was secure in his abilities; he considered himself superior to any machinations of inferior men.

Samant and Maniraj keenly followed every move that Mulu made. One day they had camped near Manoharpuri when they received information that Mulu had also camped nearby. Some of Mulu's men had shifted their loyalty to Samant. Samant, Maniraj and their forces moved swiftly towards Mulu's camp. Mulu received information that Maniraj was leading the charge. He decided to move ahead and face Maniraj. Those of his men who had turned disloyal broke off and went in the other direction. Mulu's remaining forces were taken aback by this development and their movement became uncertain and slow; the group scattered because of this change. Samant pursued the breakaway group, believing that Mulu was part of that group. Meanwhile, Mulu, who had gone a long way ahead, was isolated from his men but pressed on in anticipation of meeting Maniraj. Maniraj and his men charged at Mulu. Mulu knew the forest well and he moved his horse onto a treacherous trail. Maniraj followed after him. The chase continued for three-four miles. Mulu jumped over a deep gorge. Maniraj crossed the gorge from another point and continued his pursuit. Mulu rode up to a steep rock precipice and stopped. From this high ground, he looked below for those pursuing him. He saw no one; all he could hear was the trotting of a lone horse. Before Mulu could decide on his next move, Maniraj took his position on a rock facing him. Maniraj fired a bullet, which pierced Mulu's horse. Both rider and horse tumbled into the gorge. Mulu's leg got entangled in the stirrup and he fell along with his horse, losing his weapons in the fall. Some were swept away by the force of the water. Maniraj watched Mulu fall. Mulu somehow managed to disentangle himself from his horse and slowly got up. He had miraculously survived the fall; but his horse was dead and his weapons useless or lost. He looked up and saw Maniraj standing high above him. Mulu shouted a challenge, 'Maniraj you are armed; I have lost all my weapons. I am ready to fight. But if you have the courage for a righteous battle, discard all your weapons and fight me with your bare hands.'

Maniraj replied, 'Muluraj, there is no escape for you. Your life and death are at the mercy of my weapons. Do not make a show of your courage. The choice is not yours, but mine. I am ready to dismount and fight you with bare hands. But I do not trust you. I am not going to send away my horse along with my weapons. If you want to fight, come up, and I shall engage you in a duel. Maharaj Mallaraj has authorised me to kill you or capture you. I am eager to follow his command.'

Mulu climbed up. Maniraj dismounted and faced him. For a while they matched each other in strength and skill. Finally, Mulu fell and, pinning him down, Maniraj sat astride his chest. 'Muluraj, you are my prisoner. It is your choice whether you wish to come along without further resistance, or force me to use my weapons and take you captive. You have lost the duel.'

Mulu had concealed a dagger in the folds of his clothes. He made an attempt to push the dagger into Maniraj, but before he could do so, Maniraj unsheathed his sword and cut off Mulu's hand. Blood gushed out. Mulu made one last attempt and kicked Maniraj. Maniraj flew into the air and, landing expertly on his hands, in one swift movement of his leg sent Mulu tumbling down the rock and into the gorge. Mulu fell unconscious. The stream turned red with his blood.

Meanwhile, Samant realised his mistake. He gave up pursuing Mulu's men and went in search of Mulu and Maniraj. Samant divided his men into two groups, which went in separate directions. One of these groups, not led by Samant, witnessed the duel. For a moment, fear gripped them when Mulu kicked Maniraj. They went down the ravines to capture Mulu. In a short time Maniraj also reached the spot where Mulu lay unconscious, bleeding to death. Maniraj's eyes welled up with tears to see Mulu's plight. He ordered his men to immediately arrange for Mulu's treatment. Samant, Maniraj and their troops came together at Manoharpuri. They sang praises of Maniraj's bravery. Samant was overjoyed. Maniraj had fulfilled his duty. Samant and his troops marched triumphantly towards Ratnanagari with Mulu as their prisoner. Maniraj expressed his intention to go on a hunting expedition in the forest of Sundargiri and Subhadra.

Maniraj and his hunting party roamed the hills, the forests and the banks of river Subhadra. He feasted on the beauty of nature, felt awe in its grandeur. He walked and rode in the forest from dawn to dusk, drenched in sweat, hunting wild animals. One day, as he stood exhausted under a large tree, gazing at the distant mountains, he saw a great eagle soar with a small animal clutched in its claws. Suddenly he heard a gunshot. The bullet found its mark; the wounded bird let go its prey and fell on the mountain top. These were royal grounds where hunting was prohibited unless sanctioned by the king or the crown prince. Maniraj was surprised. He wondered if there was a trespasser or some member of the royal family or some English officer who had come to hunt in the forest with the king's permission. He galloped in the direction from which the gunshot had come. He reached the banks of Subhadra. There was a lovely grove of trees on the river bank. Wind wafting over the river water cooled the grove. Its coolness soothed one even at the height of a summer noon.

Maniraj saw some foot marks. He followed them. The grove was so thick that it was not possible to ride a horse. He dismounted; he looked closely at the footmarks. They were made by a group of persons walking bare feet. They were small and delicate as if made by children or dainty women. He reasoned that a man out on a hunt was likely to be wearing heavy boots. His curiosity was aroused. What were women doing in a place like this? Could they be young boys? He tied his horse to a tree trunk and moved silently ahead. Then he saw them—it was a group of three or four young women. They were led by a nubile beauty of fifteen or sixteen. The group seemed to be her friends and servants.

'Ratni, I am tired. Let's sit and soothe our feet awhile in the flowing water,' said that nubile beauty.

'Kamalaba, what if there are crocodiles in the river?'

'We shall deal with it when we see one. Let us sit, and don't forget to bring the flowers,' said Kamala.

They sat on the bank, dangling their feet in the flowing water. Maniraj watched them in raptures of pleasure. Though he was a young man now, he had hitherto exercised great control over his passions. But today he was curious about these women and wanted to watch them at play. These women are like the beautiful and meek deer which play fearlessly in the forest, unmindful of the predatory tiger, he said to himself; it is wrong to disrupt their play. Maniraj hid behind a tree and watched them. But he felt a sudden pang of guilt; a man who watches unknown women at play is unfit to be a ruler, he thought. He changed his position. Now he could see their backs, but not their faces. He murmured to himself:

In public spots my dignity I show,
On high-born dames I hesitate to gaze.[1]

He could hear them talk.

Kamala's hands rested on the shoulders of her friends as her feet played with the water. She looked admiringly at her own feet. 'Ratni, how do my legs look?' she asked.

'Your legs are as smooth and delicate as the stem of a lotus flower, the soles of your feet as radiant as the lotus and your toes are as beautifully formed as lotus petals.'

'And this water?' Kamala asked as she played with the water.

'It is as clear as the dew that gathers on lotus leaves.'

A friend chirpily said, 'Kamalaba, do sing us a song!'

Kamala continued to admire her feet splashing in the water. 'What do you want me to sing?'

'The one which you have composed.'

Kamala sang her song.

I don't want a beloved delicate as a jasmine
I must have a rose
Not for me the smooth lotus
I desire the thorns of the ketak flower
Friend, go tell mother

[1] Arthur William Ryder, trans. *The Mrichchhakatika of Sudraka*, Act VIII, Verse 15, *The Little Clay Cart* (Cambridge, Massachusetts: Harvard University, 1905), 115.

Friend, do tell father
Hear me, mother and father
This I have resolved:
My beloved must be like a rose
Like a kevda
I cannot abide a good, soft husband—
Everyone, calling him 'good,' will want to touch him!
A prickly husband must I have
Attractive and fragrant
But able to prick anyone who comes too close
He will yield himself only to
A clever gardener like me—
All mine to enjoy his fragrance and colour
Other women shall be jealous
Such a husband I call a rose or a kevda
For the sake of Kamala
He must be born of the Suryavansh

'Why don't you pluck one such flower yourself?' teased one of her companions.

'I, too, am a flower. I will marry the one who can come close to me and pluck me,' Kamala replied.

'What kind of a flower are you? And why is it difficult to pluck you?'

'I am the lotus that blooms in the delicate rays of the moon. I open up on solitary nights—the one who wants to pluck me must approach me at night, breathe in my fragrance and take delight in my beauty.'

At that very moment, Maniraj leapt out like a tiger, lifted Kamala in his arms and carried her away from the water. Her retinue of companions looked on in bewilderment. Just then a crocodile raised its head at the water's edge.

Maniraj lowered Kamala on her feet. 'Your splashing feet and your song attracted that crocodile to you. I saw it and carried you to safety before it could devour you. Forgive me that I carried you in my arms.'

Kamala blushed and could not utter a word. She could not bring herself to look up at his face; her eyes furtively gazed at the strong hands that had carried her to safety. Her friend Ratna spoke up, 'We are grateful to you. We wish to know our saviour, his name, family and lineage.'

'I am Maniraj, son of Mallaraj, the ruler of Ratnanagari. My code of conduct forbids me to be inquisitive about women. I can be your guide and take you to safety out of this dense forest.'

'Prince, we do not need an escort. Our Kamalaba rides and wields weapons. Her father, Maharaja Khachar, is a guest of your state. His camp is nearby. We know the shortest way to the camp. We can be your guide, if you wish to come and pay your respects to him.'

'Has Kamala Kumari used her weapons in this forest?' inquired Maniraj.

'Yes, she shot an eagle that was preying on a lamb.'

'In that case, she has violated the laws of this state. I will have to arrest her,' Maniraj said, smiling mischievously.

Kamala's retinue of women did not know what to say. Kamala spoke up, 'Is there a law in your state that I should be arrested twice?'

'No, only once.'

'You held me captive just a while ago, and then set me free!'

'Of course, we shall not arrest you again. How do we know that you committed this crime? We have not heard of women who use guns.'

'That is right. I am ready for a test, provided you agree to compete with me.'

Kamala's friends and servants quietly withdrew, leaving them to their banter.

Rana Khachar had two queens. Kamala was the daughter of the elder queen. Samant's daughter, the younger queen, had proposed marriage between Kamala and Maniraj in the hope that this alliance would put an end to the longstanding animosity between Samant, Khachar, Mulu and Mallaraj. She sang praises of Maniraj's qualities to Kamala. She told her that in Mallaraj's family, the men remained faithful to their wives and Kamala would never have to share her husband with another woman. Kamala was thus infatuated with Maniraj even before they met. She was a brave and pure kshatriya woman. Her father showered affection on her. But Khachar was against the idea of giving his daughter to an enemy. And Kamala was determined that she would marry none else but Maniraj and refused all other alliances. After Mulu's arrest, Khachar's younger queen and Mulu's sister persuaded him to visit Ratnanagari as a state guest. For years Khachar had harboured animosity and hatred towards the rulers of Ratnanagari. With maturity and experience, however, he had come to appreciate the nobility of Mallaraj and wished to learn from the grand old king. He accepted the suggestion of his younger queen. They were on their way to Ratnanagari and had camped in the forest for rest. It was these fortuitous circumstances that brought Kamala face to face with Maniraj. This was Maniraj's first experience of being alone with a young woman; he felt the excitement of it. Kamala was the daughter of the enemy of Ratnanagari; he wondered if he should trust her or maintain cautious distance. The words of her lovesick song were fresh in his mind and they removed all traces of mistrust. He was secure in his valour and had nothing to fear from Khachar. He leaned on his gun, stole glances at her and asked, 'Where have your friends gone?'

'They went away to present you with an opportunity to hold me captive.'

'That was just a joke. I do not stay alone with a woman not known to me. If you do not need me any longer, allow me to go.'

Kamala leaned against a tree and wept, 'Crown prince, I am not someone else's woman. Hitherto, I have not accepted anyone in marriage, and I shall be the wife of none else but you, Maniraj. You say that I should allow you to go if I do not need you. Maniraj, I need you till the very end of my life. How can I allow you to go when I want to draw you nearer?'

Maniraj felt pity for her. 'Princess, you are unmarried. It is your duty to marry a man chosen by your parents.'

Kamala sighed with dejection. 'Maniraj, just as Rukmini had given herself to Shri Krishna, I have given myself to you. You are capable of accepting me in marriage just as Shri Krishna accepted Rukmini.' She looked at him, her gaze expectant, infatuated and hopeful; her eyes filled with tears. Maniraj held her gaze.

'Kamala Kumari, your father considers us his enemy. If you think that I have the qualities of the rose and kevda, you pluck me and make me your own. I do not ask for anything. How can I ask your father for your hand?'

'Kumar, when you permit me to enter your garden, I will pluck my rose. You have to take the initiative and pick this lotus from her pond. Marry me, like Shri Krishna married Rukmini.' Kamala came forward and rested her head on his shoulder. Maniraj's instinct was to push her away, but hesitated lest she should fall. Her touch was exciting and delightful. Kamala took his hand in hers and intertwined her fingers with his; they both felt surging desire.

Torn between a sense of rectitude and desire, Maniraj caught her by her shoulders and held her at some distance from himself. He spoke gently but firmly, 'Kamala, we have already transgressed all limits. We are not yet married. A man destined to be king must obey all norms of rectitude. Who shall uphold the norms if we, the rulers, break them? Hence ...' But before Maniraj could say, 'stay away,' Kamala leaned forward and held him in a tight embrace. She concealed her face in his broad chest and said, 'You could have asked me to stay away so long as you were not my husband. But both our bodies have felt the same surge of desire and passion. We are joined by the same fire. We are now married. I am no longer my father's daughter; I am now your wife, Maniraj. My dear husband, you must now take me with you, as Shri Krishna took Rukmini.'

Maniraj was speechless. A conflict raged within him. He had not sought his father's permission. A part of him wanted to push her away. Mallaraj had received many proposals of marriage for Maniraj. In each case, Mallaraj's response was unambiguous. 'According to the custom of our family, a man upon maturity selects his own wife. You must wait for my son to grow up.' It occurred to Maniraj that his father's consent would not be a problem. He saw their meeting as an act of providence. He had won the heart of the enemy's daughter. It would be politically beneficial if this alliance could result in friendship between the two families. By all measures, this was a favourable alliance. Maniraj was not guided by reason alone; his passions, too, came into play. Kamala was a pure-blooded kshatriya woman, brave and an expert shot! She appealed to his sense of valour. He gently lifted her face and looked at her, but did not know what else to do. He held her close. She was tall and voluptuous; he liked the feel of her body against him. He surrendered to desire. Kamala responded passionately, holding him close and leaning over him. At length, Maniraj caressed her back and said, 'Kamala Rani, please return to your father now. We shall decide on the future course once you reach Ratnanagari.'

In a day or so, both parties reached Ratnanagari. The decision regarding Mulu awaited the crown prince. The decree of punishment was clear. Mulu had to be awarded imprisonment for life. Samant could not appreciate the uncertainty and hesitation. He urged Mallaraj to issue the orders. Mallaraj declined, saying that he had cultivated detachment from worldly affairs, and left the final decision to Maniraj.

Rana Khachar met Mallaraj and benefited from his Bhishma-like wisdom. Khachar felt a newfound reverence for Mallaraj. Meanwhile, Maniraj reached Ratnanagari. Khachar met Mulu, who informed him about the circumstances that led to his defeat and capture; Maniraj had won their duel in every sense—in strategy, in strength, in rectitude and in forgiveness. Hitherto, Mulu had always held that Maniraj was effete and unworthy of the throne. He now accepted Maniraj's superiority. He felt humbled and deeply repented that he had turned against such a noble state when he should have, in fact, been its strength. Mulu shared his feelings with Khachar, who laughed and mocked him. Khachar had to revise his opinion of Maniraj, but he viewed Mulu's attribution of superior virtue to Maniraj as a sign of the weakness of a wounded and defeated person. Khachar said that Maniraj had missed his mark, and the bullet from his gun had killed the horse and not Mulu. He categorically expressed that the day Maniraj assumes the throne of Ratnanagari, it would indeed be an unfortunate day for the state.

Samant demanded that Maniraj agree to life imprisonment for Mulu, as per the punishment decreed. Maniraj sought time to decide on the matter and called Mulu's mother and sister for a meeting. He told them that Mulu had to choose between life imprisonment in

Ratnanagari and life as a free man in Khachar's state. He asked them to get a clear response from Mulu.

Mulu told his mother and sister, 'Please tell Maniraj that hitherto I had a low opinion of his abilities, but now my views have changed. In my encounter with him, I learnt about his strengths, his statecraft, his generosity and intellect. My pride and hatred have melted—I am humbled. I have sinned against the state by supporting its enemies. I can never be free of this sin. Tell the crown prince that Khachar is their enemy, and it is for that reason he was my friend. He remains an enemy of Ratnanagari, and for the very same reason I do not wish to even look at his face. Imprisonment would be my reparation. I prefer incarceration to a life of ignominy. But, on the other hand, I also feel that I should work to establish friendly relations with Khachar and weaken his animosity towards Ratnanagari. I can do this service to the state, which I can render only if I were to live freely in Khachar's state. The decision rests with Maniraj. Please tell him that he should not set me free and allow me to live in Ratnanagari. I would never be able to live with such an act of generosity. Moreover, the two brahmins—Jarashankar and Vidya Chatura—are dear to him; but I will always remain their enemy. If I were to live freely in this state, someday I will commit the crime of killing not one, but two brahmins.'

Maniraj left the choice to Mulu's mother and sister. They asked that Mulu be allowed to live as a free man in Khachar's state. Maniraj cautioned them, 'I will set him free on your guarantee that henceforth, he will not do anything to harm the state or participate in intrigues against the state.' The two women gave their word of honour. Maniraj further said, 'One of you is my aunt, and the other, my sister. I must fulfill your desire. Samantraj insists that we should take guarantees from both Khachar and Mulu Bha; but tell Mulu Bha that your word of honour carries greater value for me. Mulu Bha has said that Khachar is our enemy, and for that reason, even his. We would not ask an enemy to stand guarantee. What greater guarantee can a kshatriya have than the word of honour of his aunt, his sister and brother? If and when there is a breach of such trust, the kshatriyas will face each other with whatever strength they are capable of. I accept your promise. Please tell Mulu Bha that expectations lead to despair; I have none from him. I have been true to myself. Now it is up to him to be true to himself.'

Having decided Mulu's fate, Maniraj went straight to the palace of his mother, Mena Rani. Kamala Kumari had gone there to meet the queen, but her eyes pined for Maniraj. Maniraj saw his opportunity, called his mother aside and briefly narrated to her his encounter with Kamala. Seeing Mena Rani hesitate, Maniraj told her, 'Mother, there is no scope for either hesitation or deliberation. I have given my word and accepted Kamala as my wife. Father cannot have any objection as he has left the decision to me. Hence, Kamala will stay in your palace. Please tell her that she is not to go back to her father, even if he were to command her to do so.'

Mena Rani was surprised. 'Kumar, you can marry anyone of your choice. But this is abduction. The British government is watching over us.'

'Mother, it would have been a different matter if we had abducted her against her will. But in this case, the woman herself says that she has accepted me as her husband. Her abduction—if it is that—has become necessary only because her father is our enemy. Both she and you come from the moon lineage, and since the time of Krishna, it is customary among you of the Chandravansh to abduct women as wives.'

'What if your enemy complain to the British, and they harass you? You should consult the minister.'

'Mother, Kamala will not hesitate to give her testimony to the British, but we must help her. Let us see what Khachar does. We will consult the minister and others as well.'

Till late that evening, Kamala did not return to her father's quarters. Khachar sent word that it was time for her to return. She replied, 'My Chhoti Ma will apprise my father of all the developments. How can I leave my husband's house? My husband has not placed any restrictions on me. I will come when I wish to.'

Khachar was enraged. He was given the details of all that had happened. He went to meet Mallaraj and complained to him. Mallaraj gave him a patient hearing, but could not help laughing. 'Ranaji, your daughter appears willing and has given her consent.'

Khachar: 'Maharaj so what? These two have deceived me.'

Mallaraj: 'You! Deceived by mere children! Ranaji, please do not say this to anyone else.'

Khachar: 'You of course cannot see that your son has done anything wrong, but I have to take some steps.'

Mallaraj: 'Ranaji, if you will kindly regain your composure and become a little less agitated, I will say something to you.'

Khachar: 'All right.'

Mallaraj: 'You claim that these children have deceived you. But Ranaji, Maniraj has not sought my consent either for this marriage. Let that be. Do you consider this a suitable match or not?'

Khachar: 'No, it is not suitable.'

Mallaraj: 'How so?'

Khachar: 'First, Maniraj is not adept in the use of weapons, while my daughter is an expert.'

Mallaraj: 'What else?'

Khachar: 'Maniraj is naïve. He does not have the cunning mind required of a ruler.'

Mallaraj: 'And what else?'

Khachar: 'Nothing else. He is suitable in all other respects.'

The two rulers were in Mallaraj's garden. A lake separated this garden from that of Maniraj's. Mallaraj pointed towards Maniraj's garden and said, 'That one is Maniraj's garden. He is likely to be there. Let us go there incognito, and you might get a chance to test his ability. What if he emerges triumphant and you lose?'

Khachar: 'I will accept the relationship.'

Both rulers changed their appearance and assumed the dress of Kabulis and walked towards Maniraj's garden. The guards stopped them. They pleaded with the guards, 'We would like to see the garden and also meet Prince Maniraj. Please go and obtain permission for us.'

The guard replied, 'The crown prince and his queen are in the garden. I cannot permit you to go in, nor can I go in to seek their permission.'

The garden was fortified, but not on all sides. Mallaraj and Khachar went to a corner where the fortification gave way to a hedge. The hedge was made of a thicket of thorny branches and trees. The hedge was impenetrable. They could not see inside the garden, but voices from within were audible. The voices came nearer.

'Crown prince, you showed me the garden, but did not talk about an important matter.'

'Which one?'

'When a man holds a woman captive, it is considered to be a rakshasa vivah. You forbade me from going back to my father. Does your custom approve of such a demonic marriage?'

Maniraj laughed and said, 'You wanted me to accept you in marriage and so we came together in gandharva vivah, a union akin to that of celestial lovers. Moreover, it is just to take the enemy's daughter in a rakshasa vivah once a gandharva vivah has been consummated. Kamala Rani, it is our family custom to show our demonic power to our enemy.'

'Kumar, I had also challenged you to a test of marksmanship. You are yet to meet that challenge.' At that moment, a bird flew up from the lake with a fish held in its beak. Two gun shots were fired; one of them hit its mark, and the other missed it. The two kings heard Kamala laugh. 'Fortune favours men. Crown prince, never before has my bullet missed its mark. But today I missed.'

'That is not the case. If my bullet had not hit the bird, yours would have. You did not calculate the distance between my bullet and yours as also the flight of the bird. If you had done so, yours too would have found its mark.'

'You are right. But I am not as good a shot as you are, Maniraj.'

'There is some movement behind that thicket; it could be some men. The guards must have been negligent.'

'There is someone or something there.'

Khachar and Mallaraj grew alert. 'Let them be. What can they do to us?' Kamala said.

'No, that cannot be allowed. They could also be thieves. Do they think I do not know how to be on my guard?'

'What is impossible for a man who can deceive Rana Khachar and hold his daughter captive?' teased Kamala with an alluring smile.

Mallaraj could not suppress a chuckle and whispered, 'Rana, you called my son naïve, but your daughter thinks he is cleverer than you. She knows both you and him, and she has expressed her opinion.'

Rana Khachar urgently signalled to Mallaraj with a finger on his lips that he must keep absolutely quiet. He pulled Mallaraj to a more secure place.

Maniraj asked a gardener to bring him a sickle attached to a long bamboo rod. He pushed and poked in the hedge, making any movement difficult for the two rulers dressed as Kabulis. When no one came out, he pushed the sharp sickle into the hedge. Rana Khachar tried to hold onto it, but Maniraj pulled hard. The sickle came out strained with blood. Maniraj alerted the guards at once. Mallaraj and Khachar jumped into the lake and swam back to safety. They hurriedly changed into their regal clothes and sat ponderously in Mallaraj's garden. Maniraj's guards returned empty-handed.

Maniraj went over to his father's garden. In a corner of the garden, thrown in a heap behind a hedge, he saw wet Kabuli dresses; he also noticed injuries on Rana Khachar's fingers. He instantly understood who the intruders were. He came back to the palace and informed Samant about the curious happenings. They went over with some guards to Mallaraj's garden. Maniraj addressed his father, 'Maharaj, two thieves tried to enter my garden just now. One of them is the master of this land. But the other thief deserves punishment. I request you to hand him over to me.'

'What is the identification of that thief?'

Samant replied, 'Maharaj, Aniruddha's grandfather had cut off Bana's hands. But our Aniruddha has himself cut Bana's fingers. This Bana does not have a thousand hands. What are we to do? When

Aniruddha's father himself has become an accomplice of Bana, Aniruddha has to take matters in his hands.'

Khachar was defeated and felt ashamed. He accepted his daughter's choice. Mallaraj came to be regarded as fortunate in every respect. He had a brave son and an able heir. Mulu was conclusively defeated. Khachar gladly gave his daughter in marriage to Maniraj; his animosity gave way to genuine affection. Moreover, Fox Sahib was transferred and the good Buskin Sahib, who held the position at Lilapur, became the new Political Agent. Buskin Sahib was an old friend of Brave Sahib. The Agency ceased to be a source of trouble or anxiety. Maniraj, Vidya Chatura and Samant ably administered the state. Mallaraj moved out of the palace and made the garden his dwelling. The old king and Jarashankar passed their days in spiritual quest.

One day, the king felt that the hour of his death was approaching. He called his family and counsellors by his bedside. The king lived in a bamboo hut. Its floor was made of mud and cow dung. He slept on a simple string cot. He had worn a dhoti and a loose kurta. Despite his weakness, Mallaraj had bathed early in the morning. He was too weak to sit up and hence lay in his bed. His once stout body had withered and he looked emaciated. He had smeared ash over his large forehead. His long white hair was neatly tied; his moustaches had turned white and pale. His eyes shone with light. His speech was clear and measured as ever. Mena Rani sat on the floor by his side; she was inconsolable. A vaidya sat on the other side, measuring the pulse and administering medicinal preparations to the king. Maniraj visited his father every day, sometimes four or five times, and spent the night by his father's side, sleeping on the floor. He was called. He came and stood watching the life ebb out of his father. Samant, Jarashankar and Vidya Chatura also rushed to the king's side.

The king signalled to Samant to approach his bed. Samant bent down to hear the king's last wish. Mallaraj said, 'Brother, you have been an integral part of Ratnanagari's statecraft. Look after Maniraj, and ensure that Mulu takes your place. I am ready to meet my Maker. Send Vidya Chatura.'

Samant wept, choking on his words, 'Maharaj, please do not worry. Do not worry about the state, the ministers, your people and even Maniraj.' Turning to Vidya Chatura, Samant said, 'Maharaj would like to speak with you.'

Vidya Chatura approached the king's bedside. Samant said to himself: What a great soul! He showed grace and generosity towards that evil Mulu even at the moment of death. Maharaj, you will not forsake your nobility, but that Mulu will not abandon his evil ways. God has summoned this great soul, while that rascal lives a living death. What more trouble won't he cause! Oh God! Why did I father him? Samant wept.

Mallaraj spoke to Vidya Chatura, 'Vidya Chatura, you are the gardener. You must take such care that not one plant withers. I have nurtured you as one nurtures a plant. Don't forget that. What more can I say from my death bed? I have withered. This is the age of the British. I have accepted their friendship. I cannot think clearly anymore.'

Vidya Chatura spoke soothingly, 'Maharaj, my body and intellect are dedicated to you. Your soul is immortal. You have led a life of virtue and done good deeds. Your heir is equally worthy and virtuous.'

Mallaraj signalled Maniraj to approach nearer, and said, 'Maniraj, all my energies were spent in dealing with the enemies of our state and making it secure. In all this, I have not cared for our people. I give you a state that has no enemies. You must work for the welfare of its people. The people are meek; they are silent. But do not forget that I have not been able to do anything for them. You must give up the pleasures of food, drink and the body and work for your people. It is your responsibility to care for your subjects.' Mallaraj felt all his strength ebbing from him. His eyes turned misty and he closed them. Everyone in the room wept.

Mallaraj stretched a feeble hand towards his queen and mumbled, 'Mena ... Mena.' Mena Rani came forward, took his hand in hers and said, 'Yes, Maharaj.' Mallaraj opened his eyes and looked at her. 'I punished you that night for no fault of yours.' The Rani somehow managed to say, 'No, Maharaj. I was at fault. You did the right thing.'

'Now Kumar is the king. You must obey him.'

'Of course, Maharaj. Kumar will be the king, and I his subject. My conduct towards him will be like that of your mother towards you, once you assumed the throne.'

'And Kamala will get precedence over you, Rani,' the king said, extending his hand as if seeking a promise.

The queen put her hand in his and said, 'Maharaj, you are my god. I promise that I have no claims on the state now. In my childhood I obeyed my father, and after marriage I obeyed you. Like your widowed mother obeyed your wishes, it is my duty to obey the wishes of the new king and queen. I am blessed that they are my son and daughter-in-law.' With these words, the distraught queen fell unconscious. But before his mother could fall to the ground, Maniraj caught her in his arms. Mallaraj had closed his eyes and did not see the plight of his queen. He murmured, 'I have spoken my last words. Is there anything else?'

Jarashankar came forward and said, 'Maharaj, Raghu's journey to the forest!' The king had sought guidance from the conduct of the Raghu dynasty. These verses were very dear to him. Jarashankar stood close by the king and recited:

> Now the king Raghu, finding that his son was firmly established among his (ministers) and subjects, became indifferent to the objects of pleasure, even though situated in heaven, which are perishable by nature.
>
> For verily the descendants of Dilipa's race, when they grew old, transferred by royal fortune to their accomplished sons, and curbing their passions, betook themselves to the life of anchorites, wearing garments of the bark of trees.
>
> The son with his head adorned with royal turban, prostrated at the feet of his father who was about to repair to the forest, and begged that he should not be abandoned.
>
> Raghu, who tenderly loved his son, granted that desire of him whose face was covered with tears, but did not resume his kingly fortune, once abandoned, just as a serpent does not put on the slough it has once cast off.
>
> He, having entered the last stage of life, lived, it is said, in a convent outside the city, where he was served, his senses not

being affected, by the goddess of the royal fortune, as by a daughter-in-law, enjoyable only by his son.

The illustrious (royal) family, with the old king leading a life of spiritual tranquillity, and the new king just entered upon his kingly career, was comparable to the sky with the moon almost set and sun newly risen.

Raghu and his son, being (respectively) the emblems of the ascetic and the king, seemed to the people like the portions of the two dharmas, come down to the earth, whose rewards are final emancipation and earthly glory.

For the acquisition of what was (yet) unconquered, Aja took for his companions ministers well-versed in politics, while Raghu, in order to reach the state which is not subject to decay (salvation), associated himself with the contemplative ascetic who had got true insight into Yoga and whoever spoke the truth.

The youthful king took his judgement seat in order to look into (the affairs of) his subjects; while the aged monarch seated himself, in solitude, on the holy seat of kusa grass, in order to practice the abstract contemplation of the mind.

The one (Aja) by the super eminence of his sovereign power reduced to submission the neighbouring princes; while the other (Raghu) by virtue of his constant metaphysical exercises brought under control the five vital airs existing in the body.

The new king completely foiled the efforts of his enemies; while the old one engaged himself in burning down, by means of [the] fire of knowledge, the fruits of his own actions.

Aja employed the six expedients beginning with peace, with a due regard to their results; Raghu, on his part, who regarded gold and clod of earth as equal, established his mastery over the three primary principles, the constituents of Prakriti.

The new lord, steady in action, did never desist from his undertakings until they bore fruit; nor did the lord other than the new one, firm in mind, desist from the practice of holy meditation, until he obtained a vision of the Supreme Spirit.

Thus the two (Aja and Raghu) who were watchful of the enemies and the senses (respectively) whose course was checked, and who were bent on (attaining) prosperity and absolution, obtained their (respective) desired objects.

> Then Raghu who regarded all beings with equal eye passed some years out of regard for (the desire of) Aja and then obtained, by means of profound contemplation, the Supreme Spirit that is imperishable and that is beyond mental darkness.[2]

The visage of the dying king was saturated with peace and joy. As the last verse was being recited, Mallaraj murmured, 'Shiv, Shiv ...' Then all speech ceased. His hand fell limp on Jarashankar's shoulder, and life left his body.

The king's body was consigned to the sacred fire. His hut and his state felt his absence. It was only after a few days that Mena Rani and Maniraj could begin to mourn his loss. In a few months, Maharaj Mallaraj became a part of fading memory. What remained were the fruits of his actions, the benefits of his statecraft, the lessons that he had taught. The seeds he had sown grew into trees. Like the many sacred basil plants and Shiva temples erected in his memory, the good deeds of Mallaraj's statecraft remained for posterity.

[2] Kale, *The Raghuvamsa of Kalidasa*, Canto 8, Verses 10–24, 61–63.

14 Maniraj's Sorrow and the Vision of His Father

O star of strength! I see thee stand
And smile upon my pain;
Thou beckonest with thy mailed hand,
And I am strong again.

—H. W. Longfellow

Maniraj, devoted to his father, decided not to assume the throne. He felt that he should place his father's footwear on the throne and rule in his name. He conveyed his decision to all the officials of the state. The period of ritual mourning came to an end, but the dark shadow of sorrow continued to mark his face. The crown prince refused to fix an auspicious time for his accession to the throne. Maniraj wrote to Buskin Sahib, informing him of Mallaraj's death, but made no mention of the new ruler. He gave no response to the repeated entreaties of Samant, Jarashankar, Vidya Chatura and Kamala Rani. The saying: 'The king is dead, long live the king!' proved false in his case. If anyone dared to address him as 'Maharaj', that person was certain to be insulted.

Buskin Sahib was informed of these happenings. He wrote an affectionate letter to Maniraj and urged him to shoulder his royal duties. Buskin Sahib reminded him that the Father in Heaven does not die and urged Maniraj to perform his duties by submitting all his actions to that father. It was Maniraj's duty to abide by both his mortal father and the Immortal One, Buskin Sahib wrote. The letter also mentioned that Buskin Sahib would attend the ceremony of Maniraj's ascension to the throne of Ratnanagari.

Maniraj read the letter and put it into his pocket. He reclined on an easy chair. It was seven in the evening. His mind was full of his father, and he wept silent tears. Weeping, he fell asleep and dreamt that he was in a small boat in the middle of a stormy sea. The boat rose and fell with the high waves and was tossed about by the strong gales, but it somehow remained afloat. The moon shone brightly. Unperturbed by the storm, Maniraj lay watching the moon. A figure emerged from the moon and sat facing him on the boat. It was Mallaraj. He took Maniraj into his arms and spoke lovingly, 'Kumar, Samant was present at the time of my death, and hence I could not share all my secrets with you. I have come to you in this moment of solitude. I chose to remain silent as I did not want any ill feelings at the time of my death. I have come to share some secrets of my statecraft with you. Listen carefully.

'Maniraj, you must retain your affection for Samant and Muluraj. But they do not know the reason for our relationship with the English; I share this with you from the heavens. Agnidev, the God of Fire, handed over Sitaji to Ram after her trial by fire. As she prepared to leave Ayodhya for her heavenly abode, Sugriva, Angad and Hanumanji approached her with folded hands and asked her as to what should be done to the bridge that they had built across the ocean. Sitaji said, "Son, the bridge has no further use. It must be destroyed so that no one else can cross the sea and attack Vibhishana's kingdom. Only a portion of that bridge should be preserved so that the bridge of dharma and rectitude does not perish from memory. That portion will survive as long as the sun and the moon shine. It will be sacred to all religions." As they sought her leave, Sitaji gave them a boon and said, "You are divine beings; in this life you will build a bridge of dharma and help establish the righteous order. In the Kali Yuga, you will be born as men and establish a new Ram Rajya in this land."

'Maniraj, Shri Krishna married Jambuvati, a daughter of the king of bears. The flag on Arjun's chariot has the sign of a monkey. Wherever you find that flag—the kapidhwaja—dharma and victory prevail.

Shri Krishna became the charioteer of the kapidhwaja. Maniraj, it was foretold that fair people shall rule in Kali Yuga. That was also the boon given by Sitaji. It has come true, and the English now rule over this land. The monkeys of Sugriva's army were the progeny of gods; the English are the bearers of the same divine seed.

'You may ask: How did I recognise them? When we ruled this land, it was the reign of untruth and fratricidal war. Like the ten-headed Ravana, thousands of Ravanas ruled this land and perpetuated falsehood. The earth trembled under their terror. Maniraj, you have no idea of those terrible times, but I have lived through them. I saw monkeys and bears who had received Sitaji's grace emerge triumphant over those Ravanas. Have you seen rulers without an emperor? I have seen a community of traders become rulers! Who was Ram and who was Sugriva? Monkeys and bears rushed to the aid of Ram. Similarly, a community of traders came to the aid of dharma in this land.

'Maniraj, Samant will say something quite to the contrary. But on this one matter, do not take his counsel. The new monkeys and bears have slayed a thousand-headed Ravana and established a new Ram Rajya! Why did I sign a treaty of friendship with these foreigners of a different race? Why did I trust them over fellow countrymen? You might ask me all these questions. Samant will lead you on the wrong path; hence do not pose these questions to him.

'Maniraj, what is greater—one's brothers or one's religion? Is mother earth more precious or is dharma? If you really want to know who is a brother, ask Vibhishana, ask Bharat. Ask any great soul, ask the scriptures, ask the philosophers. Remember, where there is dharma, there is victory. Ramji believed so. Vibhishana, too, believed the same. The Pandavas held the same faith. And Shri Krishna taught the same truth.

'Maniraj, how did I divine that the English will emerge victorious? At the time of the war of Mahabharata, when two great armies clashed, how were dharma and victory decided? Maniraj, the victory of the kapidhwaja was certain—I, too, saw the victory of the new bearers of that standard. Samant could not see it, but I did. You might want to ask if the English have never done any wrong. Maniraj, in this world what matters is a wrong which is the cause of things, not an action done as a consequence of that wrong. Disrobing Draupadi was wrong, not Bhima's act of breaking Duryodhana's thigh. The Pandavas accepted banishment because they were bound by a promise; that is right conduct. Their final victory was the triumph of dharma.

'Maniraj, do you think these monkeys and bears do not trouble me? Have I not been perplexed by them? Samant will cite my example and mislead you; do not take his advice. I, too, was startled by their presence just as children are frightened by monkeys jumping around. But those who lost their all to the monkeys were wrongdoers and perpetrators of adharma. I was merely frightened by the strange sight of bears, but the wrongdoers were vanquished. The monkeys and bears have emerged victorious; there is no conceit in them. They have become humble in victory.

'Maniraj, the bridge of dharma near Lanka was destroyed. But a new bridge is coming up in our land; stones will float on the water, and the army of monkeys will cross over it. Our rulers want to get on to that bridge; they want to run after that monkey flag. The enemies of the English are your enemies, and your enemies will be the enemy of the English—Maharaja Nagraj taught us that lesson. Maniraj, do not be stingy like a bania nor should you live like a brahmin. Victory is guaranteed if you climb onto that bridge and fight under the kapidhwaja. Maniraj, do not show your teeth to the monkey—play with them and win them over.

'Maniraj, do not follow Samant's advice on this. But take his son along with you and make him run by your side. If Mulu does not have life enough in him, become his Shalivahan and breathe life into him. Fight those who fight against the warriors of the new monkey army; you will benefit by associating with them. If you cannot run with them, you are certain to be left behind. But if you run with them and feel tired during the run, they will carry you on their shoulders and run.'

With these words, Mallaraj's form faded and disappeared. The boat disappeared; the stormy sea disappeared. Maniraj woke up from his dream and reflected on it. The words 'kapidhwaja' and 'dharma' echoed in his mind. He recalled the poem about Akbar's dream. He got up and recited it to himself.

Me too the black-wing'd Azrael overcame,
But Death had ears and eyes; I watch'd my son,
And those that follow'd, loosen, stone from stone,
All my fair work; and from the ruin arose
The shriek and curse of trampled millions, even
As in the time before; but while I groan'd,
From out the sunset pour'd an alien race,
Who fitted stone to stone again, and Truth,
Peace, Love and Justice, came and dwelt therein[1]

'Maharaj, give me the command to perform my duty and build the bridge of righteousness,' Maniraj said aloud, beseeching his father and king. His reverie was broken when he saw Kamala.

Approaching him, Kamala said, 'Mother's sorrow has deepened seeing your condition. Instead of alleviating her sorrow, you have drowned in yours. There is no one to give her succour.'

'You are right. Her bond with the Maharaj was much deeper than what I could ever cultivate. Maharaj had taught me that it was the duty of the one whose sorrow is less to console the one whose grief is deeper; a son must console his mother, and a man his woman.'

Kamala came closer and placed her hand on his shoulder. Maniraj permitted her this proximity after many days. Encouraged, she said, 'I am told that Sahib is to come tomorrow morning to commiserate with Maharaj in his times of sorrow.'

Maniraj did not show displeasure at being addressed as 'Maharaj'. He sat down and made Kamala sit beside him. He said, 'I feel that I have been lax in my duty and have not met Mataji as often as I should have.'

'That is correct. It not only provides solace to both of you, it also gives us a sense of relief.'

1 Author's note: 'Akbar's Dream,' Alfred Tennyson.

'Kamala Rani, it is also your duty to ensure that I do not deviate from the performance of my duties,' said Maniraj, getting up, a vacant, distant expression in his eyes.

Kamala held his hand and gently guided him towards their conjugal bed. 'Maharaj is preoccupied with something.'

Maniraj did not respond for a while. Then he said, 'Do you see our shadows at play?'

'Yes. Even our shadows are playing a game of love.'

'Our limbs appear disproportionately elongated or fat. Look at that hand!'

'Yes.'

'Our heads appear large and disfigured.'

'Such is the illusion created by God. Look at that, now our headless bodies are moving.'[2]

Maniraj stared at the shadows. 'Rani, the illusions of the dream world are similar,' he said, reflecting on his dream.

'Maharaj, even this real world is like that.' Kamala had no inkling of Maniraj's dream. Her endeavour was only to help him forget his sorrow.

'In a dream, things appear disproportionately significant. It often lacks context, and it is difficult to decipher its meaning.'

'Even in this world a lie masquerades as truth, Maharaj.'

[2] Author's note:

... His slanting ray
Slides ineffectual down the snowy vale,
And ... From every herb and every spiry blade
Stretches a length of shadow o'er the field.
Mine, spindling into longitude immense, ...
Provokes me to a smile. With eye askance
I view the muscular proportioned limb
Transformed to a lean shank. The shapeless pair,
As they designed to mock me, at my side
Take step for step; and, as I near approach
The cottage, walk along the plastered wall,
Preposterous sight! the legs without the man.

—'The Winter Morning Walk,' William Cowper.

'The world of dreams is shadowy.'

'The world is as intricate a trap as a spider's web.'

'Kamala, a dream is constructed like a beehive; but when you wake up, there are neither bees nor honey. What remains is an empty shell of a few lingering memories.'

'The world as it is today is not what it was yesterday and it will not be the same tomorrow.'

'Yes, one cannot remember a dream that one had just a while ago.'

Kamala led Maniraj towards a large swing which was shaped like a bed. He lay down in her lap. As she fondly caressed his body, he said, 'Even faces appear strange in dreams.'

'People change their minds in a flash, Maharaj, and so their appearance also changes. Especially, the features of children change often.'

'The dead sometimes appear in a dream and say things which they never said while alive.'

'Maharaj, do not let such dreams trouble your heart.'

'Rani, sometimes the sweetness of dreams is preferable to the wakeful state.' Maniraj's eyelids grew heavy with sleep. Kamala moved her hand over his body, wishing for him a dreamless sleep. She sang him to sleep.

Beloved, may you dream sweetly
Know that I dream of you often
You played in the laps of your parents
Like the monsoon cloud in the month of Ashad
Your father was a yogi and an ascetic:
He was the supreme bearer of compassion
He has now ascended to the heavens
Leaving deep wounds in the queen's heart
King, you have been devoted to your parents
Contain now your tears
One cannot forget the virtues of your parents
Their like is impossible to find
Beloved, at a time such as this, remember your duties
Know the will of God
Your father entrusted you with caring for the people

But the King's subjects stand orphaned
Mourn no more
Hold firmly the reins of your kingdom
Draw your mother and your people
Out of their sorrow
Establish peace and prosperity instead
Bee-like one, roam the forests and flowers
Seek the nectar sweet
Mountains, seas, forests and palaces
Saints and sages, people of all four castes
Men and women
They are each thirsting for your benevolence
They wait for you—
Wake up and arise my king
Enthuse your people
And receive their blessings

15 A Look Back at Sarasvatichandra and Kumud

It was the third year of Maniraj's reign. A small but beautiful Shiva temple called Malleshwar was built in the garden where Mallaraj had lived his last days. Ratnanagari's rulers were devotees of Shiva. Large parts of the population followed the Vaishnava sect. The rulers respected their faith and as a sign of this respect, numerous plants of the sacred basil, the tulsi, were planted in the garden.

Mena Rani lived in that garden. She slept on the floor of the hut in which Mallaraj's soul had left his body. She refused to entertain any talk about the state or worldly affairs. She ate one sparse meal daily. With the exception of Maniraj and some gardeners, no male was permitted to enter the garden. Every day she woke up early, remembered her departed husband and wept, prayed to be united with him in the other world and sought solace in the recitation of God's name. At sunrise she worshipped Malleshwar and watered the tulsi plants. Soon after, Maniraj and Kamala Rani would come to visit her. They would touch her feet, sit on the ground and seek religious advice and her blessings. Maniraj would return to the palace to attend to his royal duties, but Kamala would stay back, prepare Mena Rani's meals, clean her hut, wash her clothes and try to alleviate her sorrow; only then would she go back to the palace to serve her husband and king.

Every afternoon, Madhumakshika would go to Mena Rani, read to her from the *Puranas* and discuss scriptural matters. Kamala and other women from the palace would gather at the hut to hear stories of the virtuous royal women of Ratnanagari from the old queen. Mena Rani would invariably speak of the greatness of Mallaraj, which would fill Kamala with pride and she would often weep, moved by her mother-in-law's pain. Kamala would stay with her till she was asked to leave. Mena often wondered if she deserved such doting care and affection of her virtuous children, and would invariably retire to bed in tears. She neither knew nor cared whether her bed was hard or soft. She would lie awake, talking to herself: How generous Maharaj was towards me! He left for his heavenly abode, while I cling on to life! I did not deserve his love and affection. I gave him nothing but sorrow. Eventually, sleep would take pity on this grieving royal widow.

After receiving the news of Kumud Sundari's drowning, Vidya Chatura and Gunasundari returned to Ratnanagari from Manoharpuri. Vidya Chatura's attempts to console Gunasundari proved futile; she could not bear the weight of her sorrow. Maniraj and Vidya Chatura decided to send her to Mena Rani. They reasoned that the intense mourning of the widow would help Gunasundari forget her own pain. At seven in the morning Gunasundari arrived at the garden, accompanied by Sundargauri and Kusum Sundari. They saw Mena Rani deep in thought, leaning against a platform on which grew a tulsi plant; the water from her pitcher had drenched her clothes, but she seemed oblivious of it. She had worn a borderless black sari. Her body had withered and appeared fragile, as if about to snap under the weight of her sorrows. Kamala Rani had given clear orders that Mena Rani was never to be left alone under any circumstances. Female servants followed her everywhere, ensuring her comfort and safety at all times. Their constant hovering presence often irritated Mena and she would often ask them to leave her alone. That day, too, she had told the servants that she wanted to be left alone. She was deep in remembrance of her departed husband. In her mind's eye, she saw his form; her eyes were shut tight as if to capture that fleeting image. Her body was so emaciated that her bones could be counted. The constant flow of tears had made deep lines from her eyes to her sunken cheeks. Her face had turned pale, her skin was deeply furrowed, and her lips had become parched and white. She felt faint and looked as if she would collapse any moment. Anyone who saw her was certain to be moved to tears.

The servants came out from their hiding places behind the trees and shrubs. Mena Rani often experienced such fainting spells. The servants took care that she did not fall and hurt herself, but they had orders that they were to make no attempt to revive her. Mena had composed many devotional songs. Being a widow, she did not sing, but she had taught these songs to the servants. Kamala Rani had instructed the servants to sing these compositions and play the tanpura whenever Mena Rani experienced her fainting spells. A servant signalled to Gunasundari, Sundargauri and Kusum to stay out of sight. One of the servants approached Mena Rani and stood close to her. She plucked the strings of the tanpura and began to sing.

Tell the world there is but one God:
The one who lives in Vaikunth is the one who resides in Kailash
Brahma and Hari are the same omnipotent Purusha
The unknowing see the difference
But their devotion is the same
He who seeks differences in the One
Is only fit for hell
Knowing the divine to be One
I have chosen a personal god
In the palace of Ratnanagari, Shankar is the presiding deity
For those who aspire to death on the battlefield
Must draw their strength from Him
Mallaraj worshipped Shiva, Vishnu and Shakti alike
He treated destitute beggars and queens alike
His rule, his vision and his devotion were all one
The Rajyogi has departed, but his God remains with us
He whose devotion was steadfast has gone
But he has charged Mena with the worship of Shankar

Mena Rani seemed to revive with the last lines. She opened her eyes, but they closed again. Just then Kamala arrived. She was told in hushed tones what had happened. She took the tanpura from the servant and began to sing another song. The servants also joined in.

Shankar, who is both formless and not
Entices the world
His presence permeates the universe
Even as he remains steady, unmoving
He resides in the crematorium
Bearing witness to the destruction of the world
This equitous god drinks the poison of the world
The serpent that spews venom wraps itself around
Shankar's body
The purveyor of destruction destroys all differences
Subsuming them into one formless being
Mallaraj, who worshipped him, has
Now merged into the formless Shankar
Leaving behind the body of Mena

As she sang the last lines with difficulty, Kamala, too, felt faint with sorrow.

My husband has become one with God
Leaving this world a crematorium
Mena is alone here
Singing to her Lord

Kamala fell at the feet of her mother in-law. The strings of the tanpura broke. Her song, her soulful rendering and her touch revived Mena Rani. She opened her eyes and saw Kamala prostrate at her feet. She bent down and picked Kamala up and held her in fond embrace.

Kamala said, 'Mataji, after Pitaji's demise, you are our elder. Do not rob us of this shelter. Please forget your sorrow for a while and give us succour. Maharaj has become one with the divine; you are his earthly representative. You are a great devotee of Malleshwar; you embody him. All of us are your children and subjects. I beg you to rain upon us like a shower of mercy.'

'Kamala Rani ...' Mena murmured.

'No, Mataji, I am your subject. If you love me, please call me Kamala. Laugh with us, spend time with us. Give me orders; I rejoice in your service, in obeying your commands. I shudder at the thought of giving anyone an order. I feel inadequate to shoulder this burden.

Mataji, the one who has to obey has to think of only one thing, but the one who commands has to think of many. Please keep the burden of issuing commands and directing all of us in your holy and pious hands. Please free me from this burden, at least for a few days. I will observe and learn from you.'

This noble kshatriya woman made an attempt to reinstate her widowed mother-in-law with all the authority and responsibilities of a queen. She hoped that this enormous responsibility would help alleviate Mena's suffering. But if Kamala was determined to engage her mother-in-law in worldly affairs, Mena was equally determined to follow in letter and spirit her late husband's advice and the promise she had given him. She touched Kamala's face and said, 'Kamala, you are devoted to your husband. Why then do you ask me to break the promise given to one who was the head of our family? Let us forget that. I see that Gunasundari has come. Let us go and receive her.'

Everyone got up. Pain and sorrow were momentarily forgotten as they engaged with practical matters of worldly affairs. 'Gunasundari, come let us go to my ashram.' They walked in a row, side by side, Mena, Gunasundari, Kamala holding Kusum's hand and finally Sundargauri. The female servants walked behind them. They broke up this formation only when dense trees narrowed the path, but as soon as the path widened they would re-group. Mena said to Gunasundari, 'Gunasundari, the pain of a diseased person or someone like me is apparent. You saw my condition a while ago. I am an old woman; you are young. What ails you?'

Gunasundari: 'Mataji, Pradhanji sent me to you, so that I could share your grief.'

Mena: 'For a kshatriya woman death is preferable to the pity of others.'

Gunasundari: 'Mataji, our sorrow is fleeting. We should understand what you are going through so that we do not wallow in our pain. Mataji, the news of Kumud's drowning has been a source of great shock and grief for us; her father's words did nothing to lessen my anguish. He advised me that my pain was insignificant compared to your deep suffering and that I should come to you and seek solace.'

Mena was shocked to learn about Kumud's drowning. Gunasundari told her about the mishap. Just then a Jain arja, a woman ascetic, came, followed by Samant's wife. They, too, heard Gunasundari's narration. Samant's wife said, 'Gunasundariba, this is how the world is. You moan the loss of a virtuous daughter, while I bemoan the fact that my wicked son is still alive.' Her interjection was disregarded. They continued talking, until they had nothing more to say. Samant's wife pleaded attention. 'Mataji, you are aware of my condition.'

'A woman who prefers the son over the husband is not regarded as devoted to her husband and does not deserve her husband's love. Thakurani, I have no sympathy for you.'

'Mataji, my fate is such that even in my old age, I am punished like a young bride.'

'A woman, and an old one at that, is certain to turn senile. You must live as your husband keeps you, have faith in him and do not utter a word in contempt.'

'Mataji, I do not criticise him. Thakore is on his deathbed; even then he refuses to see my face. He has banished me from his life. I cannot bear this pain any longer. I know that my son Mulu is undeserving. But I was once misled by my mother's instinct. My husband is unwilling to forgive that one mistake even on his deathbed. How can I bear this? I am tired of the ways of my son. But if I am not forgiven at the moment of death, when will I be forgiven?'

'Thakurani, you have again spoken ill of Samantraj in the presence of outsiders. You do not deserve forgiveness.'

'Mataji, I have not spoken ill of him. I have come to you to seek your guidance so that I can seek his forgiveness and see him on his deathbed,' wept Samant's wife. 'Mataji, no one but you can persuade him to grant me forgiveness. A wayfarer seeks the protective shade of a banyan tree. Mataji, if the lake refuses to quench thirst, where would the thirsty go?'

'That is no longer in my sphere and authority. Now Kamala Rani, my child, has that authority. It is pointless to speak to me, disregarding her authority.'

'How can I, in my old age, plead with a child?'

'When God decides to bestow a certain authority in a child, He also grants that child light and wisdom. It is your conceit and pride which makes you say that your queen is only a child. Your son imbibed this conceit with your milk and destroyed all your husband's aspirations. Even in your old age, you are filled with this pride. Knowing this, how can I plead your case with Samantraj? There has never been and there will never be an equal to Samantraj in this state. It is your and Muluraj's duty to seek and obtain his forgiveness. What can Mena or Kamala do?'

Kamala informed Mena, 'Muluraj's brother has sent him a letter, inviting him to meet Samantraj.'

'Look at this, Thakurani! You were ashamed to ask for two drops of rain, but the rain did not wait for you to plead and showered its mercy upon you. Maniraj has already sent a letter to Muluraj; if you want to know what more he can do, you should ask him.'

Mena appeared to be deep in thought for a while. Then she addressed Kamala, 'Daughter Kamala, my pledge not to concern myself with worldly matters was broken today. I felt involved in Thakurani's problems and deviated from my religion. You must ensure that such matters do not come to me hereafter. If a platter of food is kept before one, one is likely to be tempted to have a morsel.'

Before Kamala could respond, Madhumakshika, herself an elderly woman now, came and said, 'Mataji, I met Pradhanji Vidya Chatura at the gate. I have come with a message from him and one from Maharaj Maniraj. Samantraj's body is now ready to give up life; he might slip into a coma anytime. He keeps repeating Maharaj's name and says nothing else. Maharaj Maniraj felt that his presence was required at Samantraj's bedside, and for that reason he has not been here to meet you.

'Maharaj and Pradhanji were on their way to Samantraj's house when the security officers who had gone to fetch Muluraj met them on the way. Muluraj was with them. He was captured from the ravines near the Subhadra. At the time of his capture, he had in his hand someone's decapitated head. He was charged with murder. Before the guards brought Muluraj, Pradhanji had received a message from Manchaturbhai; the message was about Kumud Sundari.'

Gunasundari and the others eagerly awaited further details. Madhumakshika continued, 'Pratapsinh, a baharvatiya from Suvarnapur, dived in after Kumud behn as she fell into the river; his intention was to abduct her. A man called Shankar was also in pursuit of Pratapsinh. Pratapsinh caught Kumud behn by her leg. Just then, Muluraj came to Kumud behn's aid—he jumped into the water and beheaded the outlaw. Muluraj came out with Pratapsinh's head and met Manchaturbhai. Maharaj has granted pardon to Muluraj. This good news will allow Samantraj's soul to leave his body without any remorse or rancour. Maharaj has taken Muluraj with him so that father and son could meet and reconcile.'

Samant's wife wept tears of joy. But this news gave no succour to Gunasundari; all her anxieties and fears remained as before. Madhumakshika continued, 'Gunasundari behn, Pradhanji said that if Muluraj had the use of both his hands, he could have saved Kumud Sundari and fought Pratapsinh at the same time, but having only one hand, he could not do so. Kumud behn was dragged by the flow of the river. Earlier, there were two things to worry about—Pratapsinh and the river; now the only concern is the river.'

Fresh tears rolled from Gunasundari's eyes. She bit her lips hard to prevent sobs from escaping her throat. Madhumakshika understood her plight and said, 'Behnji, Manchaturji and his men are now searching the river bank. Muluraj said that if Kumud behn was dragged by the river, she would eventually reach the sea. But it is now time for the high tide when the sea water enters the river; therefore, she is unlikely to be dragged into the sea.' That was some ray of hope. Madhumakshika continued, 'The place where the Subhadra meets the sea is made shallow due to sediment deposits and the water there is crystal clear; Muluraj said that it would be the best place to search for Kumud behn. Manchaturji has gone to that spot with his men.'

'God's will be done,' Gunasundari said with a forlorn sigh.

'God will be merciful,' said Mena Rani.

'Mataji, your blessings will help Kumud. But she has drowned. It is futile to hope until we get some final news,' said Gunasundari.

Madhumakshika: 'Mataji, Muluraj begs your forgiveness. He feels that he has pained you deeply.'

Mena: 'Madhumakshika, please convey to Maharaj Maniraj that before the ruler of this land and our master, the late Maharaj, became one with the immortals, he gave me a punishment. If I had felt that the punishment was undeserved, I would have been unhappy. I deserved it and did not once feel pained. Through penance, I regained the trust of the late Maharaj. Now, Maharaj Maniraj must decide what he wants to do with Muluraj.'

Samant's wife: 'Mataji, please have mercy and speak one word of forgiveness.'

Mena: 'Muluraj's crime was not against my person. His crime was against the state, the decision for which can only be taken by the Maharaj.'

Madhumakshika: 'Mataji, furthermore, Muluraj fell at the feet of the Maharaj and, with tears in his eyes, sought his forgiveness. He said that in the inebriation of youth, he had caused great misery to Maharaj Mallaraj. But his insults and crimes against you and Maharaj Maniraj were even greater, and that for this reason he was not even worthy of begging your pardon. He said that his crime was so grave that even if he were to go to all the four sacred places and do penance, his sins would not be washed away. Speaking with the Maharaj's permission, Muluraj said that earlier he held the Maharaj in low esteem, but he had now realised that the Maharaj was like a pure-blooded lion, while he was a wily, low-born fox. He praised Maharaj Maniraj's intellect, his valour, his virtues and royal power, and declared himself to be a lowly being. He further said that his pride—which held even when Maharaj Mallaraj had punished him—had melted and he fell at the Maharaj's feet, just as Vishwamitra had fallen at the feet of sage Vashishtha. He said that if the Maharaj gave him the chance to do penance, he would consider himself somewhat cleansed.

'Mataji, Muluraj further said that he was guided by his mother and failed to recognise the wisdom of his father and that instead of a sword, he chose a nail clipper. He said it was only because of the intercession of Maharaj Maniraj that his father had pardoned him and the meeting at the hour of his father's death was possible only because of the Maharaj's grace. He took a pledge in the presence of his father that just as Bharat had forsaken Kaikeyi, he, too, would forsake his mother.'

Hearing this, Samant's wife turned pale. Madhumakshika continued, 'Muluraj then turned to Pradhanji and said that the differences between them were divinely ordained. He held Jarashankar responsible for the treaty with the English, which had made the English so powerful; and he would not be able to forget that. After much debate with himself, he had realised that he had to obey Maharaj Maniraj's minister, Vidya Chatura; and as proof of that new resolve, he had slain the man who wished ill of Kumud behn, Pradhanji's daughter.

'Furthermore, Muluraj said to Pradhanji that he was a trusted friend of Pratapsinh, and that Pratapsinh had confided in him that he coveted Kumud Sundari. Muluraj did not confront him on this issue as Pratapsinh would then stop confiding in him. Muluraj was on the river bank when he saw Pratapsinh chasing Kumud. Muluraj killed him, something that Shankar had failed to do. Muluraj said, "I killed a friend—an evil one—but why? When Kumud Sundari was still a child, I had once played with her as a father would. No one knows—perhaps not even Gunasundari—that on that day I had cast an evil eye on Gunasundari, the penance for which was long due. A brahmin, whom I had met fleetingly, made me aware of the evil nature of my desire. As an act of penance and in order to reform myself, I slayed a friend who cast an evil eye on Kumud Sundari. If I am able to spend time with another brahmin, Pradhanji Vidya Chatura, I may be able to reform myself even further. I have no worldly desires left in me."'

Madhumakshika turned to Samant's wife and said, 'Thakurani, Maharaj Maniraj has said that you should proceed without delay in the company of Kamala Rani and be present by Samantraj's bedside.

Samantraj has expressed his desire to meet Kamala Rani. Maharaj has also said that Samantraj occupies the place of his father and hence, Kamala Rani should not keep purdah. He said that it is our duty to fulfill Samantraj's last wishes and seek his blessings. With Mataji's permission, Kamala Rani and Thakurani are to proceed immediately.'

Mena: 'Daughter Kamala, the king's command is a just one, and you should obey it without hesitation. Please convey this message to Samantraj: tell him that I lead a useless existence ever since Maharaj Mallaraj became one with the immortals. He had entrusted Maniraj to Samant, who was a protective shield for Maniraj. But the gods have sent for him, and His ways are not for us to fathom. Moreover, tell Samantraj that without him, Maniraj will now be left without a companion and guide; therefore, Samantraj should trust Muluraj and hand over this responsibility to him. Muluraj has learnt his lessons from life and experience; he has become a patriot and his devotion to the state and the king should not be questioned. I will join Samantraj and Maharaj Mallaraj as soon as the Creator sends for me.'

Everyone got up. Kusum walked alongside the Jain ascetic. A gosai, who was a woman ascetic from Sundargiri, and a pujaran or devotee of the Mother Goddess also walked with them. Kusum moved in-between the three of them, trying to join in their conversation. Kamala Rani, Gunasundari and Sundargauri walked ahead of everyone, but Sundargauri's attention was on Kusum's movements. She was aware of young Kusum's newfound desire to remain unmarried and perturbed by her niece's fascination with three women leading a life of devout asceticism. Sundargauri signalled to Kusum and beckoned her to join them. Kusum indicated with a movement of her head and her hands that she was not inclined to join her mother, her aunt and the queen, and she carried on her conversation with the ascetics. Finally, as they neared the gate, Kusum had to go and join her mother. She weighed in her mind all that she had heard and surmised: The Jain arja is obviously unmarried and leads a religious life. Can I, too, become an ascetic? The pujaran has a good life; she worships the Goddess, but she is married. The gosai is happy; she can choose to marry or remain unmarried and sing Mira's songs. Kusum sang to herself:

Mira has become one with Mohan
She has taken Shri Girdhari as her husband
As if the world did not matter

She repeated these lines three or four times. As she sang, Kusum intertwined her fingers with Sundargauri's and walked with a spring in her step. At the gate, the group separated. Kamala Rani and Samant's wife went away in their carriage, while Gunasundari, Sundargauri and Kusum got into the carriage waiting for them. Sundargauri promptly enquired, 'Kusum, what was it that you were discussing so intently with the arja, the pujaran and the gosai? What is so attractive about them?'

'Why? Shouldn't I be talking to them? Was I talking to some men?' Kusum responded, making a face.

'Were you plotting with the Jain arja to become like her?'

'I might have been. They are certainly happier than any married woman.'

'What is wrong with the married ones?'

'There is three-fold sorrow that befalls them—the pain of finding a husband, the pain of living with one and then the sorrow of his death. There cannot be anyone who has not experienced at least one of these.'

'Nonsense! You, a mere girl, have not experienced any of the joys of marriage and are talking of the pains of married life!'

'I may not be married, but I have seen marriages. Kumud behn found a good match, and his going away became the cause her misery. She had an unhappy married life. And look at my mother—she is happy in marriage but is in grief because of her daughter.'

Gunasundari snapped out of her pensiveness, pinched Kusum's cheek sharply and said, 'Stop! Stop, I say! You shameless girl! Speaking of your mother like this!'

Kusum turned shades of red with embarrassment and looked down. But presently, she perked up again and said, 'All right. Shouldn't one take a lesson from Samant's wife? Or from the Maharani, who exemplifies the pitiable life of a widow? What pain! I was stunned by her sorrow. Kumud behn exemplifies the agony of living with an undeserving husband. And the Maharani mourns the death of a good husband.'

'Why do you look at such examples alone? These are just your tricks to avoid marriage.'

'Do I have to go looking for examples? They are all around me, even in our own home. I am not blind that I cannot see them. Marriage means a certain fall.'

'There you go again! You keep speaking of others. You spoke about me, and now you talk about your aunt!' Gunasundari scolded her irrepressible daughter.

'All right. I will not. I spoke of her joy, not of her sorrow. Kaki, if father were to allow me to remain unmarried, I would grow into a fat cow.'

'As if your father is mad like you! Have you ever seen a spinster among our people?'

'That, too, we shall see.'

The carriage moved forward as did their conversation. Vidya Chatura had spent much time ruminating his decision to send Madhumakshika with a message for Mena Rani. Many thoughts assailed him. He thought: Ultimately, Maharaj Mallaraj has been vindicated. After all these years, Muluraj has returned to the family fold—Maharaj was right in insisting that Muluraj must not be given the death penalty. Samant and Muluraj have consistently opposed the treaty with the English. Is this because they are obstinate and unreasonable? Can one say that their opposition is not because of their devotion to Swaraj and national pride? Maharaj Mallaraj and Jarashankar Mama had assessed the political scenario and accepted this treaty. I, too, am in favour of this treaty. But can one say that there is no other aspect to it? If the natives had continued to rule India, is it not possible to imagine that like Japan, India, too, would have risen and progressed? Is it an impossible dream for a country that once had men like Madhavrao Peshwa, Madhavrao Scindia and Nana Phadnavis that it would give birth to other such jewels among men to work for the uplift of this land? Could not men of sterling qualities, like the men we have in Ratnanagari, usher the dawn of independence on this land? For kshatriyas like Samant and Muluraj, war has become a distant dream. Should it not be a cause of anger to them? A Hindu who despises them is an Anarya, not an Arya.

But Samantraj and Muluraj, that was our past. You still burn with anger towards Jarashankar. It cannot be doused. What is the reason for it? Your desires have no anchor. What if Jarashankar had reconsidered his advice and given asylum to Shubhaji Rao? I am his nephew and I can well imagine what he would have said.

Like one who doubts an elephant,
Though seeing him stride by,
And yet believes when he has seen
The footprints left; so I.[1]

Muluraj, why should you not feel aggrieved? You are a lion among men! But even Maharaj Mallaraj was a lion among men, one of the best! But unlike the lion, he was not grounded—his intellect was like an eagle, capable of soaring high and surveying a vast area, which gave his perspective both depth and breadth. He was virtuous, generous, possessed a high intellect and he nurtured virtue and righteousness in others. He surveyed the earth and gazed at the sky to ascertain his target. The treaty that Mallaraj signed with the paramount authority of the British appears to us as beneficial and necessary as the one forged by the great Akbar with his people.[2] But I am not surprised that Muluraj could not see its wisdom. How was Muluraj to fathom the great depths of Maharaj Mallaraj's heart?

[1] Arthur W. Ryder, trans. *Kalidasa: Translations of Shakuntala and Other Works* (London: J. M. Dent and Sons, 1914), 92.

[2] Author's note:

> He (Akbar) had lived long enough to convince the diverse races of Hindustan that their safety, their practical independence, their enjoyment of the religion and the customs of their forefathers depended upon their recognition of the paramount authority which could secure to them these inestimable blessings. To them he was a man above prejudices.
>
> —*Akbar*, G. B. Malleson

Vidya Chatura's mind turned to his elder daughter. Kumud! Kumud! As I contemplate your fate I am tempted like all others to believe in destiny. Happiness has never been your lot. We looked for a groom from a good family, but he proved unworthy. Wherever you went, fate snatched away sweetness from your life. You were saved from the outlaws, but the river took you away! I believe you are lost to us forever. It is futile to hope for your safe return. Your mother cries out in anguish, but I am a man; politics has made my heart stony and dried up all my tears. Perhaps what Kamakandaki said to Malati is true.

> *But how can those*
> *Feel natural affection for their offspring,*
> *Whose souls are sunken in schemes of policy?*[3]

No, that cannot be entirely true. If ... if both Pramad and Kumud are dead, it is a closed chapter. If Kumud has died, the matter is closed for me. But what if both of them are alive? How am I, the father of an ill-starred daughter, to save her from calamity? I educated her; it is up to her to navigate the worldly sea with the help of that boat. A daughter suffers the consequences of the wrong choice of husband made by her parents, and parents can do nothing but weep from afar. It is for this reason that our people do not want daughters.

Yes, so long as Buddhidhan and Saubhagya Devi are around, Kumud will be cared for. But what if the news about Pramaddhan's death is correct and Kumud is found alive? How are we to bear the pain of a widowed daughter? My Kumud, a widow! A widow, my Kumud! Oh God! Will you have no mercy upon me! Pramaddhan, you did not know how to savour the fragrance of my daughter; she withered. Vidya Chatura heaved a deep sigh.

But as a practical man, can I not see my remedy for a disease which threatens to be a fact? Other nations have it. Mine bars it. Conventional widowhood! Social terrorism! Must you stand between

[3] H. H. Wilson, trans. *Malati and Madhava or The Stolen Marriage of Bhavabhuti* (Calcutta: The Society for the Resuscitation of Indian Literature, 1901), 26.

me and my love and duty to my elder child? Here—here is a calamity; here is escape from it—and yet the poor one must suffer and not escape! And why? Because the stronger sex controls her lot. Is it proper in a father to submit to the control and see the child writhing before his eyes because he is a social-moral-coward?[4]

Kumud, Sarasvatichandra is still alive. He behaved foolishly, but his heart is still aflame for you. I have the courage to marry my daughter to him, and he has the courage to accept her in marriage. Sarasvatichandra, would you who gave up so much wealth be afraid of taking this step? Oh God! Dear Kumud, suffering and pain has robbed your father of his sanity. I do not act upon decisions taken in a state of unreason.

My father and maternal uncle are both alive. Can I act against their wishes? One does not need to consult a fortune teller to know what their verdict would be. Should I be bold and act contrary to their wishes? My old father took up the sword to protect Kumud. Is she a daughter only to me and not him?

A man who dares take such a step must in the interest of the state step down from the position of minister; my self-interest is not larger than my love for my daughter.

That is indeed true. But I do not serve Maniraj just to fill my stomach. I can put aside my self-interest. But how is one to forget his generosity? How am I to scorn his affection? Kumud, tell me which path should I take for you—this one or the other? I cannot see my way.

Vidya Chatura went blank. He lay in his carriage, feeling desolate and melancholy. Then he thought, There is no reason why one should think of the uncertain future. Who knows what news awaits me? Only, should I worry about good or bad at this point?

Meanwhile, Madhumakshika returned and informed Vidya Chatura of the events that had taken place inside the garden. By then Chandrakant, who was travelling with Vidya Chatura, had stepped outside the carriage, allowing the minister to be with his thoughts.

[4] This paragraph is in English in the original text.

Chandrakant stood on the bank of the lake, thinking about his lost friend. Sarasvatichandra, just when Vidya Chatura had promised help to look for you, we got the news about Kumud and you were forgotten. Maharaj Maniraj, too, had broached the subject, but then Samantraj took to his deathbed and you were again forgotten. I search for you, but you do not wish to be found. Even fate conspires against me. Let fate favour you, but I am not going to return without you. I receive letter after letter from home urging me to give up this futile search and return. But my foolish relatives do not know that a crown jewel has been lost. Many worthless stones like Chandrakant cannot make up for one Sarasvatichandra. As long as there is life in this body, I will not give up my search for you, Sarasvatichandra.

A mendicant was on his rounds to seek alms. He saw Chandrakant and approached him.

'Brother, you are not a resident of this city, are you?' he asked.

'No, I am from Bombay.'

'And your name?'

'Chandrakant.'

'Chandrakantji, on the other side of this lake, what appears hazy on the horizon is the beautiful mountain, Sundargiri. We live there in an ashramic community. Do visit us; it would do you good. If you visit us without such royal paraphernalia, you will see more and also receive more.'

'Alakh!' the mendicant called out and set out on his way. An ordinary English-educated person would not give a second thought to such invitations. But Chandrakant was in search of a friend. He considered: Is it not possible that Sarasvatichandra has gone there? If he has managed to escape from the outlaws, one road would lead him to Manoharpuri and the other to Sundargiri. Yesterday, I saw the map of this area with Vidya Chatura. The mountain is close to river Subhadra. Kumud drowned in that river. Destiny is strange; if Kumud has been dragged in that direction, couldn't fate have taken Sarasvatichandra there as well? Oh friend, alluring are the ways of your love!

A shadow of gloom darkened Chandrakant's face. How can Chandra and Kumud now love each other? Such love is sinful. My dear Chandra ran away from the possibility of that sin and wanders in unknown places. Yes, this is a plausible idea. Sarasvatichandra, I know you have an inclination for the life of an ascetic. I also know how you strive to attain what is dear to you. I will not impute any motives or accuse you of vile conduct.

Chandrakant gazed in the direction of Sundargiri. The play of light and shadow on the clouds took for him the shape of Kumud and Chandra. He remembered the lines of a poem that Sarasvatichandra was fond of.

The path through which that lovely twain
Have passed, by cedar, pine and yew,
And each dark tree that ever grew,
Is curtained out from Heaven's wide blue

A curtain divides us. But wherever you are, dear friend, it must be a lovely place. Like mine, there are so many minds you have captured. You shine over them like a bright star. And what does that star do?

It scatters drops of golden light,
Like lines of rain that ne'er unite;
And the gloom divine is all around;
And underneath is the mossy ground.
...
My wings are folded o'er mine ears;
My wings are crossed o'er mine eyes;
Yet through their silver shade appears,
And through their lulling plumes arise,
A Shape, a throng of sounds.
May it be no ill to thee
O thou of many wounds![5]

[5] Author's note: *Prometheus Unbound*, Percy Bysshe Shelly.

As he recited the last lines, tears welled up in his eyes; he took out his handkerchief and wiped his tears. Just then Vidya Chatura's coachman came up to him and said, 'Bhai Sahib, Pradhanji has asked for you.'

Chandrakant composed himself. Madhumakshika had left, but a policeman stood near the carriage. Vidya Chatura gave Chandrakant a ring and said, 'Chandrakant, do you recognise this ring? The rich in these parts would have such precious jewels but the shape is not familiar to these parts. I recall having seen such a ring with Sarasvatichandra.'

Chandrakant took the ring and examined it closely. There was a tiny button, which he pushed. The ring opened, and inside it was an image of Sarasvatichandra! Chandrakant enthusiastically showed it to Vidya Chatura and at the same time he asked the policeman a few questions. 'This ring and this photo are of Sarasvatichandra. Who brought it here and what is his story?'

The policeman said, 'Pradhanji, this ring was recovered from a bania called Aarthdas. He says that a man called Navinchandra gave it to him. Our people caught Aarthdas. But someone called Hiralal from Bombay claims that Aarthdas has killed the owner of this ring.'

'Who is Hiralal?'

'He is an employee of a Bombay merchant called Dhurtalal. He claims that he is here in search of Sarasvatichandra.'

'Dhurtalal's employee!' exclaimed Chandrakant, stunned. He apprised Vidya Chatura about Dhurtalal. Having heard him, Vidya Chatura said, 'Chandrakant, you go home in the police carriage and send it back immediately. Meanwhile, I will proceed to Samantraj's house. I will get to the root of this.'

Vidya Chatura, accompanied by the policeman, went to Samantraj's house. As Chandrakant got into the police carriage, his mind went into a whirl as if keeping pace with the turning wheels of the carriage. What has destiny in store for us? Evil Dhurtalal, both you and I are searching for Sarasvatichandra. I want to bring him back home and you want to keep him out. I am his friend and you, his enemy. I cannot even imagine what you are not capable of doing! Sarasvatichandra, are you alive, or have these evil ones killed you and with you, all our hopes? I can neither hope nor feel dejected.

Fate robs me of my happiness.
My heart is rent—my fibres fall apart.
The world is blank. I burn with inward fires—
My soul sinks plunged into the glooms of hell,
And dim obscurity veils every sense.
What shall I do?[6]

No, I shall not be forced into such a situation. I believe that Sarasvatichandra is alive and with us, and I will find him. Like Alexander the Great, I will always be hopeful. I will try and push these people, whether they show any enthusiasm in finding him or not. I will acquaint myself with this area. I will roam the mountains, the forest and the villages. I will call for additional men from Bombay to help me or I will employ some local men. But find you, Sarasvatichandra, I will. Aarthdas' version appears plausible. It is quite like Sarasvatichandra to give precious things away.

As the carriage moved on, Chandrakant looked intently at the distant peaks of Sundargiri and berated himself for having failed to ask the mendicant about Sarasvatichandra. As he reached home, he saw Kusum standing at the window. A new thought struck him.

Some resemblance, something of Kumud's light,
And some shadows ...
The heart pants with the effort of catching her.

Sarasvatichandra, what is this unique power of your inner world that makes others dance to your tunes and yet, their rhythms can never be in harmony with your own music?

[6] Wilson, *Malati and Madhava or The Stolen Marriage of Bhavabhuti*, 108.